MAX-PLANCK-GESELLSCHAFT

Universität Augsburg University

TECHNISCHE UNIVERSITÄT MÜNCHEN

THE GEORGE WASHINGTON UNIVERSITY

WASHINGTON, DC

MIPLC Studies

Volume 42

Jingzhou Sun

Personality Merchandising and the GDPR: An Insoluble Conflict?

Nomos

MIPLC Munich Intellectual Property Law Center
Augsburg München Washington DC

This publication was supported by the Max Planck Society.

MAX-PLANCK-GESELLSCHAFT

The Deutsche Nationalbibliothek lists this publication in the Deutsche Nationalbibliografie; detailed bibliographic data are available on the Internet at http://dnb.d-nb.de

a.t.: München, Ludwig-Maximilians-Univ., Diss., 2022

ISBN 978-3-7560-0302-0 (Print)
978-3-7489-3692-3 (ePDF)

British Library Cataloguing-in-Publication Data
A catalogue record for this book is available from the British Library.

ISBN 978-3-7560-0302-0 (Print)
978-3-7489-3692-3 (ePDF)

Library of Congress Cataloging-in-Publication Data
Sun, Jingzhou
Personality Merchandising and the GDPR: An Insoluble Conflict?
Jingzhou Sun
282 pp.
Includes bibliographic references.

ISBN 978-3-7560-0302-0 (Print)
978-3-7489-3692-3 (ePDF)

1st Edition 2022

Published by
Nomos Verlagsgesellschaft mbH & Co. KG
Waldseestraße 3–5 | 76530 Baden-Baden
www.nomos.de

Production of the printed version:
Nomos Verlagsgesellschaft mbH & Co. KG
Waldseestraße 3–5 | 76530 Baden-Baden

ISBN 978-3-7560-0302-0 (Print)
ISBN 978-3-7489-3692-3 (ePDF)
DOI https://doi.org/10.5771/9783748936923

Onlineversion
Nomos eLibrary

Acknowledgments

This work was accepted as a doctoral thesis by the Law Faculty at the Ludwig-Maximilians-Universität München in the summer semester of 2022. Therefore, I could take more recent developments into account until June 2022.

My thanks go first and foremost to my revered Ph.D. supervisor (Doktorvater), Prof. Dr. Ansgar Ohly. He has not only led me to this fascinating topic through his informative and exciting courses but also supervised the work with critical and sympathetic suggestions. I would also like to thank Prof. Dr. Matthias Leistner, the second evaluator of my dissertation, for introducing me to the Munich Intellectual Property Law Center (MIPLC) and the Max Planck Society. The MIPLC was like a family to me, whereas the Max Planck Society provided me with an academic ecosystem and generous funding. Without any one of them, I could not have completed my dissertation within three years. Finally, I am indebted to the MIPLC board and the Nomos Verlag for including my dissertation in the series of "MIPLC Studies".

I will always treasure the years I spent in Munich, working and learning with colleagues from all over the world in the beautiful Hofgarten. Covid-19 may impede human contact, but not the exchange of ideas and knowledge.

Dr.-Ing. Xu Xiang has not only endured my unending lecturing about personal data protection but also provided professional explanations on technical issues regarding data processing. My parents, Sun Hong and Guo Yanhong, have given me tremendous support and encouragement throughout my doctoral studies. To them, I dedicate this book with gratefulness.

Table of Contents

List of abbreviations

AcP	Archiv civilistischer Praxis
AG	Local Court (Amtsgericht)
AfP	Zeitschrift für das gesamte Medienrecht aktuell und kompetent über Veränderungen im Medienrecht.
Anm.	explanatory note (Anmerkung)
ArbG	Arbeitsgericht (Labour Court)
Art.	Article
B2B	business-to-business
B2C	business-to-consumer
BAG	Bundesarbeitsgericht (Federal Labour Court)
BB	Betriebsberater
BDSG	Federal Data Protection Act (Bundesdatenschutzgesetz)
BGB	German Civil Code (Bürgerliches Gesetzbuch)
BGH	German Federal Court of Justice (Bundesgerichtshof)
BT-Drs.	Official Document of the Federal Parliament (Bundestagsdrucksache)
BVerfG	Federal Constitutional Court (Bundesverfassungsgericht)
BVerfGE	Decision of the Federal Constitutional Court (Entscheidung des BVerfG)
BVerwG	Federal Administrative Court (Bundesverwaltungsgericht)
Charter	Charter of Fundamental Rights of the European Union (2009)
CJEU	Court of Justice of the European Union
COM	Publications of the Commission of the EU
CR	Computer und Recht
DuD	Datenschutz und Datensicherheit
DVBL	Deutsches Verwaltungsblatt
ECHR	European Convention on Human Rights
ECJ	European Court of Justice
ECtHR	European Court of Human Rights
EDPB	European Data Protection Board
ed/eds	editor/editors
EDPS	European Data Protection Supervisor

e.g.	exempli gratia
EU	European Union
EuZW	Europäische Zeitschrift für Wirtschaftsrecht
ff.	folgend (and following)
GDPR	General Data Protection Regulation
GG	Basic Law (Grundgesetz)
GRUR	Zeitschrift zum Gewerblichen Rechtschutz und Urheberrecht
GRUR Int	Gewerblicher Rechtsschutz und Urheberrecht, Internationaler Teil
GRUR-Prax	Gewerblicher Rechtsschutz und Urheberrecht, Praxis im Immaterialgüter und Wettbewerbsrech
i.e.	id est
IIC	The International Review of Intellectual Property and Competition Law
IPRB	Der IP-Rechtsberater
JA	Juristische Arbeitsblätter
JuS	Juristische Schulung
JZ	Juristenzeitung
K&R	Kommunikation und Recht
KUG	Act on the Protection of Copyright in Works of Art and Photographs (Kunsturhebergesetz)
LAG	Landesarbeitsgericht (Regional Labour Court)
LG	Landgericht (Regional Court)
MarkenG	Trademark Act (Markengesetz)
MDR	Monatsschrift für deutsches Recht
MMR	Multimedia und Recht
NJW	Neue Juristische Wochenschrift
NJW-RR	Neue Juristische Wochenschrift-Rechtsprechungsreport
NZA	Neue Zeitschrift für Arbeitsrecht
NZFam	Neue Zeitschrift für Familienrecht
OECD	Organisation for Economic Co-operation and Development
OGH	Obersten Gerichtshof (Austrian Supreme Court of Justice)
OLG	Oberlandesgericht (Higher Regional Court)
para/paras	paragraph/paragraphs
PatG	Patent Act (Patentgesetz)
PinG	Privacy in Germany
r+s	recht und schaden

RdA	Recht der Arbeit
RDV	Recht der Datenverarbeitung
RG	Reichsgericht (Imperial Court 1879–1945)
RGZ	Sammlung der Entscheidungen des Reichsgerichts in Zivilsachen (Collated Decisions of the Imperial Court in Civil Cases)
TFEU	Treaty on the Functioning of the European Union
UK	United Kingdom
US	United States
UrhG	Copyright Act (Urheberrechtsgesetz)
VG	Administrative Court (Verwaltungsgericht)
vol/vols	volume/volumes
WIPO	World Intellectual Property Organization
WP29	Article 29 Data Protection Working Party
WRP	Wettbewerb in Recht und Praxis
ZD	Zeitschrift für datenschutz
ZEuP	Zeitschrift für Europäisches Privatrecht
ZfPW	Zeitschrift für die gesamte Privatrechtswissenschaft
ZPO	Code of Civil Procedure (Zivilprozessordnung)
ZUM	Zeitschrift für Urheber- und Medienrecht

Zusammenfassung

Der breite Anwendungsbereich der Datenschutz-Grundverordnung (DSGVO) und ihr Vorrang vor nationalem Recht stellen einige Herausforderungen für die Vereinbarkeit mit etablierten nationalen Gesetzen in Bezug auf die kommerzielle Verwertung von Personenbildern zu Werbezwecken dar. Es gibt ein Rechtsgebiet, das als Modell zur Veranschaulichung dieses Diskurses dienen könnte, nämlich Deutschland.

Die DSGVO soll die Kontrolle über personenbezogene Daten verbessern, indem sie die persönliche Autonomie im Privatrecht einschränkt, da die Einwilligung zunehmend als Instrument genutzt wird, um personenbezogene Daten unter dem Deckmantel der persönlichen Autonomie zu verwerten. Im Gegensatz dazu erkennt das deutsche Rechtssystem ausdrücklich die vermögensrechtliche Komponente des Rechts am eigenen Bild an und bestätigt de facto die Lizenzierbarkeit des Rechts am eigenen Bild, um dem unvermeidlichen und weit verbreiteten Markt der Kommerzialisierung von persönlichen Porträts zu begegnen. Daher wartet ein interessanter Kontrast auf seine Erkundung. Sowohl das deutsche Rechtssystem als auch die DSGVO verfolgen (teilweise) dasselbe Ziel, nämlich die Stärkung der informationellen Selbstbestimmung, und beide sollen die weit verbreitete Kommerzialisierung der Persönlichkeit bis zu einem gewissen Grad bekämpfen. Sie nutzen jedoch unterschiedliche rechtliche Instrumente.

Bei nahezu identischen Anwendungsvoraussetzungen soll die DSGVO dem deutschen Rechtsregime für die kommerzielle Verwertung von Personenbildern zu Werbezwecken vorgehen, wenn der Spielraum der DSGVO (Art. 85 DSGVO) in diesem Szenario nicht anwendbar ist. Dies wirft die folgenden Forschungsfragen auf: Wie würde die DSGVO die kommerzielle Verwertung personenbezogener Bilder zu Werbezwecken regeln? Sind die Konsequenzen praktisch angemessen und theoretisch gerechtfertigt? Schließlich scheint die Erzwingung instabiler Rechtsbeziehungen zwischen betroffenen Personen und für die Verarbeitung Verantwortlichen nicht den Bedürfnissen von Prominenten und Unternehmen nach Zusammenarbeit zu entsprechen. Sollte die Regelung der DSGVO in dieser Hinsicht nicht angemessen oder vernünftig sein, könnte ein Nebeneffekt sein, dass die deutschen Erfahrungen im Umgang mit der Monetarisierung von personenbezogenen Daten für die DSGVO wertvoll sind, um einen fairen Ausgleich zwischen den Interessen der Datenwirtschaft durch die Verwertung personenbezogener Daten und dem Schutz natürlicher Personen vor negativen Folgen der Verwertung zu finden. Insgesamt stützt sich der risikobasierte Ansatz der DSGVO auf die Klärung und Bewertung von Risiken in spezifischen Sektoren, und in dieser Hinsicht bietet das KUG mehr als 100 Jahre Erfahrung auf dem reifen Markt der kommerziellen Verwertung von Personenbildern zu Werbezwecken.

Teil I schafft einen Rahmen, der erklärt, wie das deutsche Rechtssystem das Merchandising mit einer Aufteilung zwischen Vertrags- und Deliktsrecht geregelt hat. Teil II untersucht die Anwendung der DSGVO auf unerlaubtes Merchandising und Merchandising mit Einwilligung. Die regulatorischen Unterschiede zwischen dem deutschen Ansatz und dem Schutz, den die DSGVO bietet, werden in Teil III dargestellt. Vor diesem Hintergrund bietet Teil IV Lösungen in Form von de lege lata und de lege ferenda für die festgestellten Unstimmigkeiten. Teil V schließlich schließt die Dissertation in 25 Thesen ab.

Da diese Dissertation darauf abzielt, konkrete Lösungen für ein sehr praktisches Problem vorzuschlagen, sind Fallstudien unerlässlich. Daher werden zu Beginn von Teil I mehrere deutsche Merchandising-Fälle aufgeführt und im Laufe der Arbeit untersucht, da sie einen guten Ausgangspunkt für den Vergleich verschiedener Rechtssysteme bieten. Einerseits werden durch die Wiederholung derselben Fälle, die von deutschen Gerichten im Rahmen der DSGVO entschieden wurden, Probleme im Zusammenhang mit der Regulierung der DSGVO im Bereich des Merchandising anschaulich dargestellt. So sind die Erkenntnisse über die Unvereinbarkeit zuverlässig und überzeugend. Andererseits können die in Teil IV vorgeschlagenen Lösungen in realen Fällen daraufhin überprüft werden, welche davon robust genug sind, um ein Regelungsergebnis zu erzielen, das dem des deutschen Rechtssystems nicht nachsteht.

Um sicherzustellen, dass das Gesamtbild der deutschen Rechtsordnung und der DSGVO nicht durch die ausführliche Schilderung von Fällen beeinträchtigt wird, wird in den ersten Kapiteln von Teil I und Teil II stets eine historische und ausführliche Betrachtung der Rechtsprechung und Literatur zu beiden Rechtsordnungen vorgenommen. Schließlich ist die Fallstudie nur ein Hilfsmittel, um die Regelungsunterschiede herauszuarbeiten. Die Lösungsvorschläge beruhen jedoch auf einem umfassenden und vertieften Verständnis der Grundsätze und Ziele der DSGVO und des deutschen Rechts bei der Regulierung der Verarbeitung personenbezogener Daten für Merchandisingzwecke.

Introduction

1. *The research questions*

The GDPR's broad scope of application and its supremacy over national law present some challenges for the reconciliation with established national laws regarding the commercial exploitation of personal likenesses for advertising purposes. There is one legal territory that could serve as a model to illustrate this discourse, namely Germany.

The GDPR is devised to enhance one's control over personal data by limiting personal autonomy in private law as consent is increasingly used as a tool to exploit personal data under the cloak of personal autonomy. On the contrary, the German legal regime explicitly recognizes the pecuniary components in the right to one's image and *de facto* confirms the licensability of the right to one's image to cope with the inevitable and widespread market in the commercialization of personal portraits. Therefore, an interesting contrast awaits exploration. Both the German legal regime and the GDPR (partly) are pursuing the same objective of enhancing informational self-determination and they are both purported to tackle the widespread commercialization of personality to some extent. However, they take different legal instruments.

Upon almost identical conditions of application, the GDPR shall take precedence over the German legal regime for the commercial exploitation of personal images for advertising purposes if the leeway provided by the GDPR (Art. 85 GDPR) is inapplicable in this scenario. It raises the following research questions: How would the GDPR regulate the commercial exploitation of personal images for advertising purposes? Are the consequences practically appropriate and theoretically justified? After all, forcing legal relationships between data subjects and controllers to become extremely unstable does not seem to meet the needs of celebrities and businesses to work together. If the GDPR's regulation in this respect is not appropriate or reasonable, a spin-off result could be that the German experience in coping with the monetization of personal indicia is valuable for the GDPR in striking a fair balance between the interests of the data economy by exploiting personal data and the protection of natural persons from negative consequences of the exploitation. All in all, the risk-based approach adopted by the GDPR relies on the clarification and evaluation of risks in specific sectors, and in this respect, the KUG offers over 100 years of experience in the mature market of the commercial exploitation of personal likenesses for advertising purposes.

2. *Limiting the subject of the research and the terminology*

To present a comprehensive yet focused picture of the discrepancy between the German legal regime and the GDPR in regulating the commercial exploitation of personal images, the present research concerns itself exclusively with the exploitation of the images of models and celebrities for advertising purposes in Germany. This limitation would not weaken the applicability of the argumentation because the German legal regime in regulating the commercial exploitation of personal indicia is pioneered by the regulation of the commercialization of personal images.[1]

It is well known that some German academic literature has used varied terms to describe the commercialization of personal indicia for doctrinal reasons.[2] However, more and more scholarship in Germany denotes an appreciation of the term "merchandising" in order to be in line with the rest of the world.[3] Merchandising, albeit not legally defined, is the most popular and common term to describe the commercial exploitation of one's identity for advertising purposes around the globe. The most authoritative German commentary on personality rights refers to merchandising in the widest meaning as "commercial exploitation of images, characters, names and motifs from audiovisual works."[4]

Despite some disagreements, this concept can be loosely summarized as a collective term for a business practice that signifies commercial exploitation of personal indicia and fictitious characters in functional rela-

---

1 *Lausen*, ZUM, 1997, 86 (90); *v. Gamm*, Wettbewerbsrecht, Kapital 24 Rn. 17.

2 For instance, *Beuthien and Schmölz*, Persönlichkeitsschutz durch Persönlichkeitsgüterrechte, S. 11, 27; *Götting*, Persönlichkeitsrechte als Vermögensrechte, S. 266 - 267; *Vacca*, Das vermögenswerte Persönlichkeitsbild, S. 165ff.; *Loef*, Medien und Prominenz, S. 242ff.

3 Examples in Büchner, in *Pfaff/Osterrieth*, Lizenzverträge: Formularkommentar, B. VI. Merchandising License Agreement, 407 ff.; Schertz, in *Loewenheim*, Handbuch des Urheberrechts, Merchandising Verträge, § 79 para.6; *McCarthy and Schechter*, The rights of publicity and privacy, § 10:50.

4 *Castendyk*, in *Götting/Schertz/Seitz*, Handbuch Persönlichkeitsrecht, § 35 para. 36.

tion to promoting sales regarding commodities/services.[5] While character merchandising that solely concerns fictitious characters in fairytales and cartoons is no less significant than personality merchandising that exploits personal identities, such as one's images, names, voices, and slogan,[6] this research devotes exclusive attention to personality merchandising spurred by the presumption that the GDPR provides sweeping and much stronger protection for personal data than the German legal *status quo*.

The present research chooses the term "merchandising" not only because it vividly describes the process of turning personal indicia into various merchandise, but also because of its simplicity and lucidness. In this wise, the research can present a candid and internationally unambiguous discourse on the substantive rules and gap(s) between the German legal regime and the GDPR in respect of personality merchandising. Moreover, as mentioned above, the present work does not intend to offer an overall discussion about personality merchandising but only focuses on the right to one's image. Therefore, the term merchandising is defined in a much narrower sense to indicate the secondary exploitation solely of personal images.

It is necessary to delineate the right to one's image in Germany – the legal basis of merchandising defined in this work – from the right to publicity in the US. The latter seems, at first sight, quite similar to the German legal position since they both contain commercial value and are exclusive rights as well as licensable. However, the right to publicity is a property right and covers all merchandising objects in various forms,[7]

---

5 *Schertz*, Merchandising, para. 1; *Schertz and Bergmann*, in: *Ruijsenaars, Character Merchandising in Europe*, 127; Büchner, in *Pfaff/Osterrieth*, Lizenzverträge: Formularkommentar, Rn. 1151 and 1139; The Cambridge Dictionary explains merchandising as "products connected with a popular film, singer, event, etc., or the selling of these products", <https://dictionary.cambridge.org/dictionary/english/merchandising>; WIPO defines merchandising of character as "the adaptation or secondary exploitation, ..., of the essential personality features (such as the name, image or appearance) of a character in relation to various goods and/or services with a view to creating in prospective customers a desire to acquire those goods and/or to use those services because of the customers' affinity with that character". Bureau, Character Merchandising, 1994, at 6.

6 *Ruijsenaars*, Character Merchandising, S. 12f.; The Walt Disney Company as the pioneer in character merchandising business has a turnover of about 57 billion US dollars in 2016, see Brandt, Merchandising ist ein Milliardengeschäft, at https://de.statista.com/infografik/11520/die-zehn-groessten-merchandising-lizenzgeber/.

7 Haelan Labs., Inc. v. Topps Chewing Gum, Inc. 202 F.2d 866 (2d Cir. 1953), 868; Melville, 19 Law and contemporary problems 203 (1954).

while different personality rights regulate different merchandising objects according to corresponding legal statutes in Germany.[8]

There are three typical forms of merchandising.[9] One is to use merchandising objects – personal pictures – as commodities *per se* to allure fans to demonstrate their affection and support for their beloved celebrities. The memorabilia are normally highly substitutable products such as posters, mugs, T-shirts, etc., and their substantial value stems from celebrities' images. In doing this, manufacturers, celebrities, and fans get a triple-win situation by achieving their objectives (i.e., promoting sales, increasing publicity, and expressing self-emotions and identity). This is merchandising in a narrow sense in the US.[10] Another form of merchandising is to register or use one's images as trademarks or trade names. This situation, albeit not uncommon, is generally excluded from this research because it is more entangled with the trademark law than personality rights.[11] The last genre of merchandising is to use personal icons for advertising. Characterized by image-transfer, merchandising objects are used as role models or endorsements to create a persuasive effect on influencing consumer decisions. Nowadays, thanks to the advancement of the attention economy,[12] more and more merchandising objects are simply used as attention-grabbing devices (*Blickfang*) without an effort for persuasion.[13] All in all, both approaches lead to an incentive to consumption.

---

8 § 12 BGB stipulates the right to one's name, while §§ 22-24 KUG explicitly provides the scope, conditions, and limitations of the right to one's image. The merchandising objects of personal indicia besides their names and images have to resort to the general personality right (*das allgemeine Persönlichkeitsrecht*) based on Section 823 I BGB and art. 1 and 2 GG. The general personality right is developed by the judiciary after the World War II, and stems from the fundamental principles of the untouchable human dignity in art. 1 GG and the free development of personality in art. 2 GG.

9 *Schertz and Bergmann*, in: *Ruijsenaars, Character Merchandising*, 127 (128f.).

10 See ETW Corp. v. Jireh Publ'g, Inc. 332 F.3d 915, 922 (6th Cir. 2003); See Dougherty, 27 Colum. J.L. & Arts 1 (2003), at 62; Dogan and Lemley, 58 Stanford Law Review 1161 (2006), 1176 et seq.

11 In early days, the right of trade names was regarded as a personality right but nowadays it is regulated entirely in the German Trademark Law (*Markengesetz*) in §§ 7, 27 I MarkenG. See RGZ 9, 104 - Befugnis des Konkursverwalters zur Veräußerung der Firma des Gemeinschuldners, 105 f.; RGZ 69, 401 - Nietzsche-Briefe, 403.

12 See *Franck*, Ökonomie der Aufmerksamkeit, S. 115ff.; *Loef*, Medien und Prominenz, S. 88f.

13 OLG München, 25.6.2020 – 29 U 2333/19 - Blauer Plüschelefant; BGH, GRUR 2013, 196 - Playboy am Sonntag.

Given the prevalence of social networks nowadays, one does not have to be a person *par excellence*[14] to make his or her identity valuable for advertising agencies. As the vision of "making your customers your marketers" has turned into the golden rule of the new Internet business,[15] the use of one's likeness in advertising is no longer the preserve of celebrities.[16] While this user's merchandising scenario is intriguing and is increasingly thriving, it differs from the merchandising defined above in many ways (Part I Section 2.1.3). Therefore, users' merchandising is excluded from this dissertation. It may be employed now and then to address the difference between the self-sufficient models and average internet users who are suffering from information and power asymmetry against online platforms.

3. *The current state of research regarding the regulation of the GDPR in merchandising*

There are three monographic works that offer excellent results for some parts of the present research: the works of *Barath*, *Bienemann*, and *Voigt*. Based on a critical appraisal, the present research provides a reflection on their findings to some extent.

Barath develops a general dogmatic framework on the contractual disposition of personality rights to respond to real-world needs – in particular regarding the commercialization of sportsmen and sportswomen.[17] By analogy with the transfer of rights of use in copyright law, the legal

---

14 There is a list of occupations that are candidates for persons *par excellenc*, such as religious figures, politicians, athletes, artists, musicians, and business executives, summarized by German scholars, see Strobl-Albeg, in: *Wenzel, Burkhardt, Gamer, Peifer and Strobl-Albeg*, Das Recht der Wort- und Bildberichterstattung, § 8 Rn. 11.

15 Quoting from Facebook COO Sheryl Sandberg, see Fraley v. Facebook, Inc. 830 F. Supp. 2d 785, 808 (N.D. Cal. 2011), para. 792.

16 More and more ordinary people's likenesses are involved in advertisements recently. In Germany, an employee asked his former employer to stop showing the promotional video of the company that includes him on the company website. See BAG, GRUR 2015, 922 - Veröffentlichung von Arbeitnehmer-Bildnissen zu Werbezwecken; A hair salon published an advertising video clip on its Facebook fan page staring by a customer who was neither a professional model nor someone famous. See LG Frankfurt am Main, 3.09.2018 - 2-03 O 283/18 - Friseursalon. In the US, similar lawsuits brought up by ordinary people are common. See Fraley v. Facebook, Inc. 830 F. Supp. 2d 785, 808 (N.D. Cal. 2011); Perkins v. LinkedIn Corp. 53 F. Supp. 3d 1190 (2014).

17 *Barath*, Kommerzialisierung der Sportlerpersönlichkeit, S. 25ff.

concept of the "license of personality" is developed and embedded in the general dogmatics of civil law.[18] This study's empirical analysis of various types of commercial contracts (advertising, sponsorship, sales of fan products, and agency-agreements) within the sports sector provides meaningful research material for the present study. It helps to analyze the specific rights and obligations of contracting parties (the marketer on the one hand and the holder of the rights of personality on the other hand) in comparison with the rights and obligations under the GDPR.

Bienemann examines whether digitalization has triggered a need for a reform of the KUG on the premise of the unrestricted applicability of the KUG alongside the GDPR due to the optional general opening clause (*fakultative allgemeine Öffnungsklausel*) of Art. 85 (1) GDPR.[19] In this respect it relates to the current study. *Bienemann's* conclusion that the GDPR itself and its legislative history are inconclusive and intentionally ambiguous as to the nature of Article 85 (1) GDPR is largely agreed upon by the present research.[20] However, in the absence of an explicit notification by the Member State (art. 85 (3) GDPR), this paper argues for a more cautious approach that excludes the purely commercial exploitation of personal portraits (advertising, sales of fan products, etc.) – merchandising – from the scope of Art. 85 GDPR.[21]

The work of *Voigt*, unlike the above-mentioned two studies, researches a sheer question of the GDPR, namely the extent to which consent in the data protection law achieves the goals it sets out.[22] While her answer and suggestions largely focus on how to improve the informational self-determination envisioned by the GDPR – facilitating fully informed and truly free consent, her discourse on the digital economy and the need to dispose of economic elements embedded in personal data provides inputs for the present study.[23] Given that the present thesis maps out the challenges (and impediments) that the GDPR's consent model poses to the established commercial practice of personality merchandising, it searches for a solution of the possible incompatibility between the GDPR and the practice instead of improvements of the GDPR's efficiency.

---

18 *Ibid.*, S. 27.

19 *Bienemann, Reformbedarf des Kunsturhebergesetzes im digitalen Zeitalter,* S. 17ff.

20 *Ibid.*, S. 71.

21 Instead, Bienemann argues for a continued application of the KUG (*lex specialis*) under the GDPR provided on an extensive reform of the KUG. *Ibid.*, S. 242ff.

22 *Voigt,* Die datenschutzrechtliche Einwilligung, S. 38.

23 *Ibid.*, S. 489ff.

4. Methodology and structure of the dissertation

Part I builds a framework that explains how the German legal regime has regulated merchandising with a division between contract and tort law. Part II explores the application of the GDPR to unauthorized merchandising and authorized merchandising. The regulatory differences between the German approach and the protection provided by the GDPR are reflected in Part III. Against this backdrop, Part IV offers solutions in manners of *de lege lata* and *de lege ferenda* to the identified inconsistencies. Part V, finally, concludes the dissertation in 25 theses.

Given that this dissertation aims to propose concrete solutions to a very practical problem, case studies are essential. Therefore, several German merchandising cases are listed at the beginning of Part I and studied throughout the thesis because they serve as a good standpoint for comparing different legal regimes. On the one hand, by revisiting the same cases decided by German courts under the GDPR, problems revolving around the regulation of the GDPR on merchandising present themselves vividly. In this wise, insights into the incompatibility are reliable and convincing. On the other hand, the solutions proposed in Part IV can be tested in real cases to see which one is robust enough to provide a regulatory result that is not inferior to that of the German legal regime.

To ensure that the whole picture of the German legal regime and the GDPR is not compromised by the recount of cases in great detail, a historic and extensive reflection on the case law and literature regarding both legal regimes is always presented in the first chapters of Part I and Part II. After all, the case study is merely a tool for pinpointing the regulatory differences. The proposal for solutions, nevertheless, relies on a comprehensive and in-depth understanding of the principles and objectives of the GDPR and German law in regulating personal data processing for merchandising purposes.

Part I Substantive legal protection for merchandising in Germany

1. *Introduction*

Part I builds a framework that explains how the German legal regime has regulated merchandising with a division between unauthorized merchandising under tort law and authorized merchandising under contract law. While advertising using celebrities' names and likenesses seemed hackneyed, its legal regulation in Germany underwent some critical changes. The legal recognition of authorized merchandising, in particular, has not yet been explicitly recognized by the German Supreme Court even now. Therefore, a chronological description of the case law is necessary to pave the way for articulating the judgments of the selected cases that serve as the connection point for comparing the German legal regime and the GDPR.

Chapter 2 recounts the German legal protection of the right to one's image against unauthorized merchandising and the implementation of remedies for such tortious infringements in light of the case law and literature. Subsequently, the *clickbait* case illustrates how the guidelines distilled by German courts were upheld in the network environment. Admittedly, the *clickbait* case is not as classic as the *Paul Dahlke* case. However, as it reflected a new application of merchandising that may become increasingly common, an in-depth study of this case under the GDPR is more informative in the long-term perspective.

The *clickbait* case[24]

The defendant owns a TV magazine and operates a related website. To boost the number of hits, the defendant published portraits of four well-known TV moderators and titled the pop-up window "One of these presenters has to retire from the public due to cancer." Therefore, internet users are intrigued to click the link/portraits to find out which of the four moderators was meant by the title. The plaintiff was one of the other three who were not suffering from cancer and required the defendant to stop showing his likeness in the advertisement and damages.

24 BGH, GRUR 2021, 636 - Clickbaiting.

Chapter 3 completes the framework by discussing merchandising under contract law. Since it is not the objective of this research to discuss the permissibility of merchandising from legal philosophy and policy perspectives, it merely examines the legal recognition of merchandising agreements in light of judiciary decisions with a necessary reflection on scholarly literature. Two cases are significant in providing a standpoint for the subsequent contrast with the GDPR: the *landlady* case and the *company-advertising* case.

The *landlady* case[25]

> *The plaintiff, a well-known model/actress, had a series of nude photos taken by one of the defendants, the photographer. Although the plaintiff admitted in the court that she authorized the photographer to permit magazines operated by the other defendants to publish the series of photos without an explicit limitation on duration, she would like to revoke the consent and require the defendants to cease publication.*

The *company-advertising* case[26]

> *The defendant operated an air conditioning company and wanted to make a promotional film for his company. By signing his name on a list, the plaintiff agreed that film recordings by him "may be used and broadcast" for free as part of the defendant's public relations work. In the company-advertising film available on the company's internet homepage, the plaintiff was shown for several seconds. After the business relationship ended, the plaintiff sent a lawyer letter to revoke his "possibly" granted consent to use his images and request the defendant remove the video from the company's homepage.*

Practical issues about merchandising agreements are also articulated in detail including the taxonomy of merchandising contracts, the advantages of varied contracts, and the contractual rights and privileges for the person depicted.

At last, Chapter 4 presents the findings in previous Chapters awaiting the comparison with the regulation offered by the GDPR.

25 OLG München, NJW-RR 1990, 999 - Wirtin.

26 BAG, GRUR 2015, 922 - Veröffentlichung von Arbeitnehmer-Bildnissen zu Werbezwecken, Rn. 1-3.

2. Merchandising under tort law

2.1 The law against unauthorized merchandising

2.1.1 The right to one's image in German law

As a specific personality right codified in 1907, the right to one's image was purported to close a regulatory loophole without delaying the historical birth of the BGB.[27] Even though most of the KUG was abolished afterwards, provisions for the right to one's image have remained effective for over 100 years. § 22 KUG protects every natural person against disseminating or exhibiting his or her portraits without consent. § 23 KUG limits this extensive ambit to a justified scope. §§ 37 KUG et seq., additionally, grant specific remedies for the depicted person to destroy the illegal depictions as well as the device for such production upon conditions.[28]

With the assistance of abundant cases, the right to one's image has kept pace with technological advancements. Firstly, German courts confirm that personal portraits in § 22 KUG cover every type of image if the reproduction of the external appearance of a natural person is recognizable by friends and relatives.[29] Besides, Germany promotes an extensive interpretation of public presentation (*öffentliche Zurschaustellung*) and dissemination

---

27 Vgl. *Helle,* Besondere Persönlichkeitsrechte im Privatrecht, S. 45; In the BGB, there are statutory provisions to protect one's life, body, health, freedom of movement, and name against violations. This limited protection of personality soon presented a deficiency in protecting one's likenesses even before the BGB came into force shown in the case of *Bismarck auf dem Totenbett* in 1899. Two journalists sneaked into Bismarck's ward and photographed his appearance after death. The image of the thin and weak man formed a strong visual contrast with the glory of the "Iron Chancellor". Every German was shocked. The court felt compulsory to condemn this highly offensive act but lacked the necessary basis in positive law to prohibit the publication and dissemination of the photos as the journalists were the copyright holders. See RGZ 45, 170 - Bismarck auf dem Totenbett.

28 There are other effective provisions in the KUG. For instance, § 24 KUG grants exceptions to the right of images mainly for public authorities, §§ 42-44, 48 and 50 KUG offer a more detailed description of the remedies associated with this right.

29 BGH, GRUR 1958, 408 - Herrenreiter, 409; BGH, GRUR 1962, 211 - Hochzeitsbild, the first Guideline; BGH, GRUR 1979, 732 - Fußballtor, 734; BGH, GRUR 2000, 715 - Der blaue Engel, 717-718; *Dreier and Spiecker Döhmann,* Die systematische Aufnahme des Straßenbildes, S. 39 f.

(*Verbreitung*).[30] Dissemination extends from physical transfer to a digital change of control.[31] In this wise, online sales of fan products, using personal photos as a clickbait, and uploading advertising into fan pages in social platforms are falling under the scope of the prohibited acts in § 22 KUG when they are committed without consent.[32]

While the statute of the right to one's image provides clear constitutive elements of an infringement and thus certainty in judiciary decisions, intrusive behaviors such as (re)producing, storing, and uploading personal photos into the Cloud without public display are not covered by § 22 KUG.[33] It is also controversial whether this right is applicable when the identifier is not one's appearance.[34] Against this backdrop, the general personality right (*das allgemeine Persönlichkeitsrecht*), born in the judiciary,[35] has a shining résumé in closing statutory loopholes and completes all-embracing protection of personality.[36] Although the general personality right is not codified in the BGB due to valid legal and practical reasons,[37] it,

---

30 LG Oldenburg, NJW 1988, 405 - Grillfest, the second Guideline; OLG Düsseldorf, 23.07.2013 - I-20 U 190/12 - Veröffentlichung von Fotos im Pop-Art-Stil, Rn. 18; OLG Hamburg, ZUM 2017, 517 - Haftung eines Onlineshop-Betreibers, para. 42.

31 Specht in *Dreier/Schulze,* Urheberrechtsgesetz, § 22 KUG Rn. 9.

32 *Einwilligung* is the term used in § 22 KUG, and it is dictionary translation is consent. It, in its broadest meaning, can cover varied labels in different scenarios such as license in copyright law, free revocable consent in medicine law, authorization in a contractual relationship, and simple permission in daily life. The maxim *volenti non fit iniuria* in civil law underlining these various labels suggests the fundamental legal principle that a natural person is allowed to dispose of his or her interests and rights. See, *Ohly,* "Volenti non fit iniuria": die Einwilligung im Privatrecht, S. 63, 54-58; Ingman, 26 Jurid. Rev. 1 (1981), at 2.

33 LG Heidelberg, MMR 2016, 481 - Zulässiges Hochladen von Fotos in eine Cloud, para. 30f.

34 OLG Köln, GRUR 2015, 713 - Doppelgängerwerbung, the Guideline.

35 See BGH, GRUR 1955, 197 - Leserbrief, the Guideline; BGH, NJW 1965, 685 - Soraya, 687. An articulation of developments of the general personality right, see *Ehmann,* in: *Stathopulos, Festschrift für Apostolos Georgiades zum 70. Geburtstag,* S. 113ff.

36 BGH, GRUR 2009, 150 - Karsten Speck, Rn. 43 und 26f.; BGH, GRUR 1957, 494 - Spätheimkehrer, the 3. Guideline; BGH, GRUR 2016, 315 - Sexfotos vom Ex-Partner, Rn. 40; *Lettmaier,* JA, 2008, 566.

37 A detailed introduction of the dispute about the incorporation of the general personality right into the BGB, see in *Forkel,* Das allgemeine Persönlichkeitsrecht – Betrachtung einer fünfzigjährigen Entwicklung der Persönlichkeitsrechte im deutschen Privatrecht, S. 9ff.; On the topic about the reasons against the incorporation of the general personality right into the BGB, and the strong resistance by

as a frame right (*Rahmenrecht*), is complementary for statutory personality rights, such as the right to one's image.

The ambit of § 22 KUG is extensive as it seems to grant individuals absolute control over their likenesses. § 23 (1) KUG, at this point, provides four exceptions to § 22 KUG. However, since the exceptions are also broad and abstract to some extent, § 23 (2) KUG requires a balancing of interests when an exception is available in the case. Therefore, courts must weigh the legitimate interests of the person depicted against the counter values gained by such interference concretely. Thus, the unwitting exploitation of the image, albeit meeting the exception in § 23 (1) KUG, is proportionate. The purpose of the balancing test is to ensure that the exercise of freedom of expression, art, and information does not come at the expense of the core interests of the right holder.

In summary, the clear boundary of the right to one's image enables the codification, while sometimes the general personality right with the flexible characteristic is necessary for the protection of personality. The judiciary and scholars work in tandem on interpreting and developing the statutory provisions in §§ 22 and 23 KUG so that they still provide *vires* for personality protection against technological and societal changes after more than one century.

2.1.2 The case law of unauthorized merchandising

The *Paul Dahlke* case is the trend-setting case in Germany regarding unauthorized merchandising. Before it, two major decisions delivered by the highest court in Germany both suggested a narrow understanding of the protective interest of the right to one's image, namely the moral interests.[38] Thus, celebrities, the people from the sphere of contemporary history, were virtually deprived of protection for using their likenesses in public.

In the *Graf Zeppelin* case in 1910, which is a typical merchandising case in today's perspective, the court considered that any "sensitive person" (*ein feinfühliger Menschen*) would feel morally damaged (*moralisch geschädigt*) by

---

the media and press against the legislative bill of the Federal Government in 1957 for another attempt to incorporate the general personality right into the BGB. See *Ehmann*, in: *Canaris, Festgabe 50 Jahre Bundesgerichtshof*, 613 (614 und 615f.).

38 The results for unauthorized merchandising were inconsistent. See Götting, in *Götting/Schertz/Seitz*, Handbuch Persönlichkeitsrecht, § 2 Rn. 25.

commercial exploitation of his name and portraits with certain goods.[39] This consideration contradicted to the fact because Zeppelin himself was not feeling mentally aggrieved at all and eager to merchandise.[40] Perhaps being aware of the huge discrepancy between vision and reality, the RG recognized that there was no moral damage for the person depicted and thus denied protection for a famous football player in the *Tull Harder* case.[41] Not only did this thesis resemble closely the right of privacy in the US the only protects a natural person against moral damages, but also rendered almost all merchandising involving celebrities lawful because celebrities usually make a living through publicity: They do not object to merchandising itself, but only to the fact that they cannot get paid accordingly.

In the 1950s, the BGH faced an unauthorized merchandising case again. In the *Paul Dahlke* case, in which the photos of a famous German actor had been used in advertisements for a motorcycle. The BGH concluded that such merchandising practice, which was motivated by purely commercial interests and pursued sales increase, was excluded from the exception in § 23 KUG.[42] According to the systematic reading of § 23 (1) (a) and (2) KUG, the freedom of personal depiction belonging to contemporary history should have an inherent limitation, namely the depiction must present public interests in accessing that information. The BGH argued, on the one hand, it must be left to the individual to decide freely whether he or she wished to use images as an inducement to purchase goods based on the *Graf Zeppelin* case. On the other hand, this "natural consequence of his personality right" must be balanced with the general public's need for information.[43] The BGH concluded that the advertising in the *Paul Dahlke* case lacked the information value compared with the *Tull Harder* case since the picture of Paul Dahlke had been exclusively used as an incentive for consumers to buy the goods through "image transfer".[44] Thus, unauthorized merchandising violated the free decision of the individual

---

39 See RGZ 74, 308 - Graf Zeppelin.

40 The plaintiff had authorized another tobacco company to register his name and portraits as its trademarks against a license fee. See Götting in *Götting/Schertz/Seitz*, Handbuch Persönlichkeitsrecht, § 2 Rn. 23.

41 See RGZ 125, 80 - Tull Harder, 82f.

42 BGH, GRUR 1956, 427 - Paul Dahlke.

43 *Ibid.*

44 *Ibid.*, 430.

about whether to make his image an inducement for purchasing goods without a justified reason.[45]

On the surface, the BGH reached a convincing verdict in the *Paul Dahlke* case without dismissing the previous case law. In essence, it indicated a changed mindset that the right to one's image also protects economic interests besides the moral ones.[46] By viewing the *quid pro quo* relationship between the exploitation of celebrities' indicia and consideration as a norm, the BGH asserted that unauthorized merchandising was "an inadmissible encroachment on the depicted person's economic exclusive right" in the *Paul Dahlke* case.[47] Thus, unauthorized merchandising also impinged the free decision of the individual as to whether and in what way he or she wished to make images serviceable for the business interests of third parties.

Ever since the *Paul Dahlke* case, German courts have ruled unauthorized merchandising cases by the same token. Solely commercial interests of the third party, as in general merchandising scenarios, are subordinated to the personality interest protected by the right to one's image because the person depicted has the right to self-determination about whether, when, and how his or her persona is exploited as incentives for consumers to purchase goods/services.[48]

The underlined rationale of this guideline forecasted the stance taken by the ECtHR in the case of *von Hannover v Germany*.[49] In fact, it is a valid opinion that the proposition of the ECtHR simply brought the implicit protective purpose purported in § 23 (1) (a) and (2) KUG to the

---

45 *Ibid.*

46 *Götting,* Persönlichkeitsrechte als Vermögensrechte, S. 49f.; Specht in *Dreier/ Schulze,* Urheberrechtsgesetz, Vorbemerkung § 22 Rn. 1; BGH, GRUR 1968, 552 - Mephisto, 555; BGH, GRUR 2000, 709 - Marlene Dietrich, Rn. 27; The previous understanding that this right protected the right to honor, or privacy is overturned by valid arguments. See *Dasch,* Die Einwilligung zum Eingriff in das Recht am eigenen Bild, S. 10ff.

47 BGH, GRUR 1956, 427 - Paul Dahlke, 430.

48 For instance, see BGH, GRUR 1979, 732 - Fußballtor; BGH GRUR 1992, 557 - Talkmaster; BGH GRUR 2000, 715BGH, GRUR 2000, 715 - Der blaue Engel; OLG Hamburg, ZUM 2004, 309 - Oliver Kahn; BVerfG, GRUR-RR 2009, 375 - Sarah Wiener; OLG Köln, MDR 2020, 112 - das Traumschiff, confirmed by the Supreme Court in BGH, GRUR 2021, 643 - Urlaubslotto.

49 ECtHR, von Hannover v Germany (no 2), Application No. 40660/08 and 60641/08, § 102.

forefront,[50] since the public role played by the person depicted is not and never was a determinant but merely a factor in an overall assessment. Therefore, the guideline distilled in the *Paul Dahlke* case remains effective after the case of *von Hannover v Germany*.[51]

2.1.3 Cases at the margins

Merchandising, seemingly hackneyed, is full of surprise. Some merchandising might contribute to a debate of public interest in society as it fulfills the public's need for information (*Informationsbedürfnis*),[52] or revolves around self-promotion of the press;[53] Some may infringe moral interests of the person depicted more prominently.[54] While the lawfulness of the first category must be assessed in a concrete manner due to the public interest

---

50 Vgl. *Ohly*, GRUR Int, 2004, 902 (905). It argues that there were some apparent misunderstandings by oversimplifying the German legal protection for the right to one's image from the ECtHR's perspective.

51 The new approach adopted by German jurisprudence, the graduated protection (*abgestuftes Schutzkonzept*), essentially integrates the last two steps - the rebuttable exception and a subsequent balancing test - into one overall assessment rather than replacing them. Instead to cite many, see BGH, GRUR 2007, 523 - Abgestuftes Schutzkonzept I.

52 Cf. *Zagouras*, IIC, 2011, 74; *Götting*, GRUR Int, 2015, 657; *Andersen*, Gesellschaftspolitische Meinungsäußerungen in der Werbung, S. 166 ff.; See BGH, GRUR 2007, 139 - Rücktritt des Finanzministers, para. 20. The court found that the satiric statements involving celebrities did not allude misleading or wrongful indication of an image transfer or endorsement, but since the advertisement depicted a recent public event in "a satirical and mocking manner" (*in satirisch-spöttischer Form*), it served public's need for information intentionally; similar cases see BGH, GRUR 2008, 1124 - Zerknitterte Zigarettenschachtel; BGH, WRP 2008, 1527 - Dieter Bohlen.

53 Despite the commercial nature of such an advertising campaign, the press privilege it enjoys and the public interest in promoting and boosting newspaper sales *per se* cannot be generally ruled out. So, courts tend to assess details in contexts and exercise a balancing test between the public interest in having the information against the concerned personality interests. See OLG Köln, AfP 1993, 751 - Kundenzeitschrift, Rn. 25; BGH, NJW-RR 1995, 789 - Chris Revue. 790-791; BGH, GRUR 2009, 1085 - Wer wird Millionär, para.27; *Lettmaier*, WRP, 2010, 695 (701); *Ladeur*, ZUM, 2007, 111.

54 See BGH, GRUR 1958, 408 - Herrenreiter; BGH, GRUR 1959, 430 - Caterina Valente; BGH, GRUR 1962, 105 - Ginsengwurzel; BGH, GRUR 2007, 139 - Rücktritt des Finanzministers.

conveyed by the merchandising,[55] the latter merely proves, from the other direction, that the right to one's image contains moral and property interests simultaneously (more details in Section 2.2.1). Moreover, they do not prejudice the distilled guideline for unauthorized merchandising: in the absence of information interest, one has the sole right to decide whether to make own images as an incentive for merchandise, regardless of his or her social role. As they are rather exceptional cases in merchandising, an overemphasis on these cases would lead to a weakening of the topic of this research. It is necessary to forgo the complex between freedom of expression and the right to one's image and data protection to avoid unwarranted discussion about applicability issues arising from Art. 85 GDPR. Thus, merchandising of the focus of this research is the one-sidedness of economic exploitation of the personality.

Another questionable scenario is users' merchandising. It depicts the trend that more and more ordinary people participate in promoting the platforms' own business or third parties' services/goods via functions like fan pages and the "Like-button" on social platforms such as Facebook, Instagram, and Tiktok.[56] Enlightened by "making your customers your marketers", the strategy of inviting ordinary people to advertise is promised with success because it highlights a new kind of influence, namely credibility, affinity, and closeness to life. A leveling-down in merchandising seems to be ongoing and calling for attention.[57]

On the one hand, the right to one's image in Germany protects everyone. As users' merchandising is by no means a bad business given the fact that users usually get consideration against such commercial exploration such as coupons, free WLAN services, or generally "free" services provided by the platform,[58] the commercial exploitation of portraits of ordinary people implies that their portraits contain some economic value that has been attributed to the person depicted by law. In this wise, the jurisprudence regarding celebrity's merchandising, on which this dissertation focuses, appears to be applicable here. The economic value of one's likeness is to be calculated based on the market mechanism, i.e., supply and de-

55 Vgl. *Götting*, GRUR Int, 2015, 657 (663).

56 LG Frankfurt am Main, 3.09.2018 - 2-03 O 283/18 - Friseursalon; VG Hannover, 27.11.2019 - 10 A 820/19 - Fanpage einer Partei bei Facebook; Cf. 830 Fraley v. Facebook, Inc. 830 F. Supp. 2d 785, 808 (N.D. Cal. 2011).

57 *Peifer*, JZ, 2013, 853 (854).

58 See Dancel v. Groupon, Inc. 940 F.3d 381, 383 (7th Cir. 2019).

mand, instead of law.[59] On the other hand, most merchandising cases concern famous people. The more prominent the person is, the more likely his or her image is used in connection with goods and/or services as an attention-grabbing or image-transfer device for advertising purposes. Moreover, users' merchandising differentiates from merchandising of celebrities in respect of means, context, purpose, effects, and the dynamic between the participants.[60] Firstly, internet users, unlike celebrities, are in a significantly weaker position relative to the platform. For one, they usually do not understand the business logic of merchandising, nor are they aware of the commercial value of their images. Thus, internet users usually allow the platform to use their images to promote products/services for free unconsciously. Second, neither the platform nor the user expects or needs a stable partnership. The promotion/invitation sent by the user to his or her friends is often instantaneous, and the friends do not bind the user to the product/service in a way that is similar to the strong connection between a celebrity and the endorsed product. Thirdly, users' merchandising allows the platform to access users' social relationships and thus establish social graphs of them. It means significantly more personal data than images are open to platforms, which needs to be scrutinized according to the content and nature of the personal data. Fourth and most importantly, users have different purposes than celebrities in merchandising. In social networks, the impulse and expectation of ordinary users to share information may include commercial interests, but they are generally not the main purpose. Social needs and personality expression are the mainstream.

A direct application of the jurisprudence regarding merchandising defined in this dissertation in users' merchandising is likely to ignore these differences. In terms of unauthorized merchandising, as noted in the third point above, this approach can leave out the additional damages for, say, intrusion to privacy.[61] In the case of authorized merchandising, more incompatibilities are evident in light of all points argued above. Therefore,

---

59 The statement of *Nimmer* also indicates the same rationale that damages should be dependent upon the "value of the publicity appropriated". See Melville, 19 Law and contemporary problems 203 (1954), at 217.

60 Different opinion, See Bruni, 41 CARDOZO LAW REVIEW 2203 (2020).

61 There is an interesting case in China in 2019. The user claimed that Tiktok had illegally pushed marketing information to his friends in his contacts book, causing privacy violations, especially Tiktok had pushed information to his ex-girlfriend, causing him serious mental distress. See "凌某某诉北京微播视界科技有限公司隐私权、个人信息权益网络侵权责任纠纷案", (2019) 京 0491 民初 6694 号(Mr. Ling v. Beijing Microvision Technology Co., Ltd. regarding tort

given these significant differences between the contexts of celebrity and users' merchandising, an undifferentiated discussion would easily lead to a disguise of the real needs of data subjects and, eventually, misplaced protection for them. Users' merchandising is, hence, excluded from the scope of this research.

On the contrary, sales of fan products printed or painted with celebrities' indicia are merchandising cases included in the scope of this research. Some American scholars argue that sales of fan products may constitute a quasi-fair use if it involves a transformative use, i.e., the deployment of one's persona is mainly for expressing opinions or emotions rather than for commercial purposes.[62] In the view of German courts, commercial interests pursued by the merchandiser in sales of fan products typically outweigh the information value. There was a tendency in German jurisprudence to draw a clear line between unlawful advertising and lawful sales of fan products because a legitimate interest of the public in the dissemination of the photos might surface in the latter scenario. For instance, the BGH ruled in the *Ligaspieler* case that the sale of card packs bearing famous football players violated the commercial interests of their right to one's image. In contrast, after about ten years, it reached the opposite decision that the sale of calendars with photos of (football) matches was legal because of the public interest in disseminating and receiving information conveyed by celebrities' images.[63] This argument might seem plausible at first glance. Celebrities' images might constitute social icons and thus be essential to foster cultural diversity,[64] and the dissemination thus might convey particular informational and aesthetic value.[65] However, as individuals may invoke the freedom to express self-identity, affections, aesthetic, or political views by showing the cards and calendars bearing their beloved celebrities, merchandisers who exploit consumers' desire for expression by

---

against privacy and personal Information rights, (2019) Peking 0491 Civil First Instance No. 6694).

62 See *McCarthy and Schechter,* The rights of publicity and privacy, § 8:72.

63 BGH, GRUR 1968, 652 - Ligaspieler. "Es ist nicht einzusehen, daß die Kl. einseitig den Ruhm der Spieler in Geld ummünzen darf", 654; BGH, NJW 1979, 2203 - Fußballkalender, 427.

64 *Biene*, IIC, 2005, 505 (523); Dogan and Lemley, 58 Stanford Law Review 1161 (2006), at 1176.

65 BGH, GRUR 1968, 652 - Ligaspieler; BGH, NJW 1979, 2203 - Fußballkalender, 2204; OLG München, NJW-RR 1990, 1327 - Werbung für eine Gedenkmedaille; *Schertz,* Merchandising, Rn. 341; *Thalmann,* Nutzung der Abbilder von Personen des öffentlichen Interesses zu Werbezwecken, S. 155f.

selling fan products in pursuit of profit can hardly be justified by the defense of public interests. It is not saying that German courts do not attach great attention to the information value that merchandising may contain as American courts do. As pinpointed above, many satire-advertising and self-promotion of newspapers are justified by their contributions to the public debate.

As *Götting* and *Schertz* aptly pointed out, the clash between the public interest in information and the commercial interests of celebrities in their images remains probably in every unauthorized exploitation. It is thus critical to examine which motive of the merchandiser is in the superior position.[66] Thus, in the landmark *Nena* case, the BGH recognized fan products sales (named merchandising in the case) as a form of commercial exploitation of personal indicia the same as advertising. It made more apparent in the *Abschiedsmedaille* case that fan products sales presented an outright purpose of making a profit.[67] As a consequence, the judiciary guideline for advertising cases is also applicable for fan products sales.[68]

2.2 Remedies for tortious unauthorized merchandising

2.2.1 Monetary remedies

The claim to monetary remedies in merchandising cases is usually based on delictual liability pursuant to § 823 BGB or restitution for the unjust enrichment according to §§ 812 and 818 II BGB.[69] While the amount of compensation flowing from these two legal bases is equivalent to the license fee that the person depicted could have demanded in a similar

66 *Götting*, Persönlichkeitsrechte als Vermögensrechte, S. 60; *Schertz*, Merchandising, Rn. 341.
67 BGH, AfP 1996, 66 - Abschiedsmedaille, 68; Vgl. *Lauber-Rönsberg*, GRUR-Prax, 2015, 495 (497).
68 See *Schertz*, Merchandising, Rn. 342.
69 BGHZ 169, 340 - Rücktritt des Finanzministers, para. 12; BGH, GRUR 2009, 1085 - Wer wird Millionär, para. 38.

situation according to the licensing analogy (*Lizenzanalogie*),[70] the logic and constitutive elements for the claims are fundamentally different.[71]

§ 823 BGB is the common monetary remedy in German law if the damaged interests of the victim are economical. It reads,

> *A person who, intentionally or negligently, unlawfully injures the life, body, health, freedom, property, or any other rights of another person is liable to make compensation to the other party for the damage arising from this.*

Since the right to one's image as a specific personality right in written law belongs to "*other rights*" in this paragraph,[72] and its economic attributes are exploited by the infringer in unauthorized merchandising, the victim is entitled to claim damages if she or he can further prove the fault of the infringer and the causality between the infringement and damages. According to § 249 I BGB, the damage suffered by the victim is calculated based on a hypothetical comparison between the reality and the situation where the victim would have been had the violation not occurred. In this wise, the licensing analogy is generally regarded as an abstract rather than a concrete comparison that § 249 I BGB requires.[73] The liability is usually established in unauthorized merchandising cases when the merchandiser fails to prove due diligence in examining the authorization certificate of the person depicted provided by the third party.[74] Therefore, it is recommendable for agencies, photographers, and enterprises who commence with merchandising to prepare complete documentation.[75]

The claim for delictual damages faces problems when the damages flowing from merchandising are not substantial but immaterial. First of all, the claim basis is slightly different. The BGH abandoned the legal basis for a solatium according to § 253 BGB because the right to one's images is not stipulated in § 253 II, and § 253 I BGB prohibits a broad reading of this claim. The current legal basis is § 823 I BGB in combination with Art. 1 I,

---

70 See *Beverley-Smith, Ohly and Lucas-Schloetter,* Privacy, Property and Personality, 140 et seq.; *Götting,* Persönlichkeitsrechte als Vermögensrechte, S. 54f.

71 *Kraßer*, GRUR Int, 1980, 259; *Sack,* in: *Forkel and Kraft, Beiträge zum Schutz der Persönlichkeit und ihrer schöpferischen Leistungen: Festschrift für Heinrich Hubmann zum 70. Geburtstag*, 373f.

72 See Schertz in *Götting/Schertz/Seitz,* Handbuch Persönlichkeitsrecht, § 12 para.1.

73 *Beverley-Smith, et al., Privacy, Property and Personality,* 142 et seq.

74 BGH, GRUR 1965, 495 - Wie uns die anderen sehen, 497; OLG Hamm, NJW-RR 1997, 1044 - Nacktfoto, 1045; *Schippan*, ZUM, 2011, 795 (799f.); *Lettl*, WRP, 2005, 1045 (1082).

75 Specht, in *Dreier/Schulze,* Urheberrechtsgesetz, § 22 KUG Rn. 39.

2 I GG.[76] Secondly, the licensing analogy would not be reconciled to the claim for delictual damages in this scenario. The person depicted would not have received the remuneration if the violation had not occurred because he would never grant such humiliating exploitation. In this sense, the method of calculating compensation would no longer be the fictive license fee but actual moral damages. While some exceptions about sky-high immaterial damages exist,[77] immaterial damages are generally significantly lower than fictive license fees.[78] This thus led to a "cynical result" in practice that people who suffered from grave mental damages would have to claim the fictive license fee to get more compensation, which, however, implied that he or she would like to authorize such exploitation given an opportunity in light of § 823 I BGB.[79]

In this respect, the law of unjust enrichment suits better. It differs from the logic of delictual damages in focusing on the increase in the assets of the infringer instead of the reduction in the assets of the right holder.[80] As the observation from the perspective of the infringer orders: The merchandiser cannot on the one hand benefits financially by illegally exploiting the rights of others, and on the other hand deny restitution of the benefits he has received by claiming that the rights are non-substantial.[81] Therefore, the claim for restitution based on the law of unjust enrichment enables the licensing analogy as a "hypothetical device" to quantify the compensation.[82]

---

76 BGH, GRUR 1995, 224 - Caroline von Monaco I, 230; BGH, NJW-RR 2016, 1136 - Kein "Schmerzensgeld" wegen Beleidigung per SMS, Rn. 3;

77 See OLG Hamburg, NJW 1996, 2870 - Caroline von Monaco, 2871. The amount of the monetary compensation was DM 180,000 in total; LG Köln, - Eine Million Euro Schadensersatz für Altkanzler Kohl.

78 In practice, the amount of solatium for infringements to personality rights would range from 1,000 to 7,000 EUR. See *Wybitul, Neu and Strauch*, ZD, 2018, 202 (206); Vgl. *Pietzko*, AfP, 1988, 209 (220). That is probably why the claimant in the famous *Herrenreiter* case asked for a fictive license fee instead of a solatium despite a clear insult suffered by the advertising. BGH, GRUR 1958, 408 - Herrenreiter.

79 *Beverley-Smith, et al.*, Privacy, Property and Personality, 141; *Götting*, GRUR, 2004, 801; *Beuthien and Schmölz*, Persönlichkeitsschutz durch Persönlichkeitsgüterrechte, S. 44.

80 *Ettig*, Bereicherungsausgleich und Lizenzanalogie bei Persönlichkeitsrechtsverletzung, S. 99f.; *Beverley-Smith, et al.*, Privacy, Property and Personality, 143.

81 *Götting*, Persönlichkeitsrechte als Vermögensrechte, S. 53.

82 BGH, GRUR 1958, 408 - Herrenreiter, 409; *Götting*, Persönlichkeitsrechte als Vermögensrechte, S. 54f.; See *Beverley-Smith, et al.*, Privacy, Property and Personality, 141.

The German legal academia developed various types of unjust enrichment upon the law of unjust enrichment in § 812 BGB. The relevant one in merchandising is the encroachment on a legal position that assigns certain commercial benefits to its holder (*Eingriff in eine Rechtsposition mit Zuweisungsgehalt - Eingriffskondiktion*).[83] This method spread out in unauthorized merchandising cases ever since the BGH recognized the commercial interests of the right to one's image in the *Paul Dahlke* case and upheld that infringer was obliged to restore what he had gratuitously gained (*Erlangten*) at the expense of the person infringed.[84] To clarify, what the merchandiser has gained without a legitimate reason is the unauthorized exploitation of the pictures of the person depicted, which cannot be surrendered by nature. Hence, the merchandiser should compensate the license fee that the person depicted could have demanded in a similar situation according to § 818 II BGB.[85] The calculation is critical to ensure that the fictive license fee is equivalent to the value of the exact unauthorized exploitation. As the German judiciary continues to specify the relevant indicators and exclude the irrelevant ones over time, some rules can be distilled.[86] The market value of the personal image, the content, means, and circulation of the advertising campaign are indispensable indicators,[87] while how much the merchandiser has factually obtained as a result of the commercial use of the celebrity's persona,[88] and the willingness of the person depicted for merchandising[89] should be excluded from consideration.

83 *Beverley-Smith, et al.*, Privacy, Property and Personality, 140.

84 BGH, GRUR 1956, 427 - Paul Dahlke, 430; BGH, GRUR 1979, 732 - Fußballtor, 734; BGH GRUR 1987, 128 - Nena, 129; *Götting*, Persönlichkeitsrechte als Vermögensrechte, S. 50; See *Beverley-Smith, et al.*, Privacy, Property and Personality, 140.

85 *Kleinheyer*, JZ, 1970, 471 (473-474); Seitz, in *Götting/Schertz/Seitz*, Handbuch Persönlichkeitsrecht, § 47 Rn. 34;

86 BGH, GRUR 2000, 715 - Der blaue Engel716; BGH, GRUR 2007, 139 - Rücktritt des Finanzministers, para. 12; BGH, GRUR 2009, 1085 - Wer wird Millionär, para. 34.

87 An overview of the relevant criteria, see *Ettig*, Bereicherungsausgleich und Lizenzanalogie bei Persönlichkeitsrechtsverletzung, , S. 181f.

88 Vgl. BGH, GRUR 1961, 138 - Familie Schölermann, 141.

89 Vgl. *Götting and Lauber-Rönsberg*, Aktuelle Entwicklungen im Persönlichkeitsrecht, S. 30. Once upon a time, the BGH has created an additional *proviso* to enable restitution in the amount of a fictive license fee that the man depicted needed to be willing to authorize such commercial exploitation in the first place (*die Lizenzbereitschaft*), and thus denied the approach of fictive license fees in untypical merchandising cases where the advertising was humiliating and ridiculous for the person depicted. See BGH, GRUR 1958, 408 - Herrenreiter, the 2. Guideline;

Note that even being called the fictive license fee, the restitution is not an *ex post* consent to the merchandising. After all, instead of filling the victim's loss from his point of view, the law of unjust enrichment is aimed to force the infringer to surrender his gratuitous gain so that "no one should be placed in a better position" because of his or her violation against the law than observance.[90] In addition, according to § 687 II BGB, the victim can ask for the profits flowing from the violation if the infringer violates the law intentionally. Since it is unlikely that all the profits acquired by the merchandiser are attributed to the related advertising campaign,[91] the claim based on § 687 II BGB is seldom in merchandising cases.

The practical differences between claims based on § 823 BGB and §§ 812 and 818 II BGB are not evident in the absence of grave mental damages since they both rely on the licensing analogy. Moreover, as damages for unauthorized merchandising were developed based on the analogy with the ones available to IP rights in the *Paul Dahlke* case,[92] the remedies against infringements to IP rights are also gradually introduced and applied in unauthorized merchandising cases. Consequently, the person depicted may choose from three alternatives to calculate the compensation, namely the actual loss, the fictive license fee, and the lost profits.[93] Among them, the fictive license fee that has "the status of customary law" in the IP field is the most common remedy in unauthorized merchandising cases.

BGH, GRUR 1959, 430 - Caterina Valente, 434; BGH, GRUR 1962, 105 – Ginsengwurzel, 107. After receiving compelling criticism from the literature, German courts have abandoned this artificial *proviso* since the *Lafontaine* case (BGH, GRUR 2007, 139 - Rücktritt des Finanzministers). The criticism see *Götting*, Persönlichkeitsrechte als Vermögensrechte, S. 53f.; *Beuthien and Schmölz*, Persönlichkeitsschutz durch Persönlichkeitsgüterrechte, S. 44; *Schlechtriem*, in: *Fischer, et al., Strukturen und Entwicklungen im Handels-, Gesellschafts- und Wirtschaftsrecht: Festschrift für Wolfgang Hefermehl zum 70. Geburtstag am 18. September 1976*, 445 (456f.).

90 BGH, GRUR 1956, 427 - Paul Dahlke, 430

91 Vgl. *Hubmann*, in: *Roeber, Der Urheber und seine Rechte: Ehrengabe für Eugen Ulmer*, 108 (121).

92 The BGH made an analogy between the inadmissible encroachment on the right to one's image and the infringement of IP rights, the methods for assessing monetary remedies for IP rights, especially §§ 97ff. UrhG. BGH, GRUR 1956, 427 - Paul Dahlke, 430. See *Beverley-Smith, et al.*, Privacy, Property and Personality, 144; §§ 11, 29 I and 31 UrhG clarify that German copyright contains both economic and moral interests of the author, thus it cannot be assigned entirely *inter vivos* but licensable.

93 Schertz, in *Götting/Schertz/Seitz*, Handbuch Persönlichkeitsrecht, § 12 para.197; Specified in BGH, GRUR 2000, 709 - Marlene Dietrich, para. 53.

2.2.2 Non-monetary remedies

Injunction and the auxiliary claim for access to information and accounting are widely used in unlawful merchandising cases, whereas claims for destruction, rectification, and publication of a counterstatement are, albeit legally available, not very common in practice.

The basis of an injunction lies in the 2. sentence of § 1004 I BGB.[94] It has two requirements, namely an unlawful interference and danger of further interferences simultaneously, which are often met in unauthorized merchandising cases.[95] Upon an injunctive relief, the infringer must stop (online) exhibition or distribution of the merchandising objects.[96] Thus, injunctive reliefs are of great importance in unauthorized merchandising cases because they provide the person depicted a negotiating edge by immediately stopping all promotional activities conducted by the merchandiser. Moreover, when taking interlocutory injunction (*einstweilige Verfügung*) into account, which is devised to maintain a specific condition until the final settlement of a dispute,[97] the swiftness and convenience of this relief make it the most popular relief in practice even compared to monetary remedies.

---

94 The legal text of § 1004 BGB only grants injunction to owners of (material) property against (potential) interferences, whereas such protection for owners of immaterial rights such as IP rights and the right to name in § 12 BGB is provided in respective specifical laws. However, this "intentional" loophole has been closed in case law. See *Beverley-Smith, et al.*, Privacy, Property and Personality, 138.

95 BGH, GRUR 1997, 379 - Wegfall der Wiederholungsgefahr II, 380; *Henry*, International Privacy, Publicity and Personality Laws, para. 12.88 et seq.; *von* Hutten, in *Götting/Schertz/Seitz*, Handbuch Persönlichkeitsrecht, § 42 Rn. 4f.

96 LG Frankfurt am Main, 3.09.2018 - 2-03 O 283/18 - Friseursalon, para. 60.

97 The German legal basis for this claim rests on §§ 935, 940 ZPO. For a brief introduction to its conditions and consequences, see *Beverley-Smith, et al.*, Privacy, Property and Personality, 139. It is noteworthy that the granting of an interlocutory injunction requires a balancing of interests of both parties.

A claim for elimination of interference (*Beseitigung der Beeinträchtigung*) is provided by § 37 KUG[98] and the first sentence of § 1004 I BGB.[99] In scenarios of personality infringements revolving around false reports about facts, the claim for rectification (*Berichtigungsanspruch*) stemming from § 1004 I BGB is also very important.[100] This claim might be applied in false endorsement cases where the merchandiser claims that a celebrity favors something, but he or she does not. Along the same line, the claim to publish a counterstatement stated by the victim is also available in German law (mostly state laws) for cases involving infringements of reputation.[101]

Noteworthy, claims for destruction, rectification, and publication of a counterstatement are not very common in unauthorized merchandising cases. It is not surprising because most of these claims focus on moral interests that are not at issue in unauthorized merchandising cases. Moreover, if the celebrity frowns on the low-grade advertising, as in the situation in the *Herrenreiter* case, the last thing he or she wants to do is to increase its exposure by issuing a condemnation statement or recycling all advertising brochures with great fanfare. It is also the reason why many state laws in Germany exclude the applicability of the claim for publication of a counterstatement in merchandising that only impinges on economic interests.[102] Plaintiffs in unlawful merchandising cases also seldom deploy the claim for destruction even though they would destroy all illegal merchandising objects, such as printed advertising brochures.[103] Reasons are two-folded. The claim cannot provide more advantages than

---

98 § 37 KUG prescribes a claim for destruction when portrait copies are unlawfully produced, distributed, performed, or publicly displayed without the risk of repetition. In addition, the ambit of § 37 KUG extends to the devices exclusively for manufacturing unlawful exemplars of personal portraits. It resembles the claim for the destruction of devices that are exclusively for producing IP rights-infringing products.See § 98 UrhG; BGH, GRUR 1960, 443 - Orientteppich, para. 37; *von* Strobl-Albeg, in *Wenzel, et al.*, Das Recht der Wort- und Bildberichterstattung, § 9, Rn. 11. § 38 KUG provides a claim for delivery-up of the unlawful copies.

99 See *Beverley-Smith, et al.*, Privacy, Property and Personality, 139; *Golla and Herbort*, GRUR, 2015, 648.

100 See Gamer/Peifer, in *Wenzel, et al.*, Das Recht der Wort- und Bildberichterstattung, § 13 para. 7.

101 *Seitz and Schmidt*, Der Gegendarstellungsanspruch, § 1 para. 27.

102 Ibid.§ 5 para. 230. However, some scholars see this exclusion being unconstitutional. See Burkhardt, in *Wenzel, et al.*, Das Recht der Wort- und Bildberichterstattung, § 11 Rn. 47 and 48.

103 BGH, GRUR 1961, 138 - Familie Schölermann, para. 26. It might be the only one in which the claim for destruction has been applied.

injunctive relief. More importantly, as persons depicted in merchandising cases, often celebrities, also pursue commercial benefits and live partially or even mainly on merchandising,[104] they do not want to get into such a complete standoff with potential business partners. Therefore, claims for destruction, rectification, and publication of a counterstatement are, albeit available legally, withdrawing from the stage of merchandising.

The claim for access to information and accounting is an auxiliary claim that presupposes a valid principal claim such as an injunction, restitution, damages, etc. Its legal basis rests on the principle of good faith in § 242 BGB.[105] In this sense, the plaintiff must, on the one hand, demonstrate that the access to information and accounting is necessary to compute the amount of fictive licenses fee and stop the circulation, and, on the other, exercise this claim in good faith to ascertain that the execution does not impose an excessive, unreasonable, or disproportionate difficulty on the infringing party.[106] This claim must be distinguished with the right to inspection of accounts (*Bucheinsichtsrecht*) that appears in almost every merchandising contract (see below). Even though they are both useful tools for quantifying and verifying royalties, the claim for access to information and accounting is a remedy upon a violation of the right to one's image, while the other is a contractual right.

2.3 The judgment in the *clickbait* case

After a chronological review of the German legal regime regarding unauthorized merchandising, it is time to explore how the judgment in the *clickbait* case followed the guidelines distilled from the jurisprudence despite new characteristics emerging in the online environment.

---

104 Based on the anatomy of the music industry, singers make most of their income not from records but concerts and merchandising in the broad meaning, including endorsements, commercials, etc. See *Passman,* All You Need to Know About the Music Business, 94 et seq., and 424 et seq.; *Fisher,* Promises to Keep: Technology, Law, and the Future of Entertainment, 54 et seq., and Appendix I. By presenting tables showing "where did the money go" in the record business in Appendix I, the author argues that the amount of money a singer can get from an album is grossly exaggerated. Some singers never even receive a bill that they do not owe the record company money (at 35, quoting from Janis Ian, "The Internet Debacle – An Alternative View").

105 Burkhardt, in *Wenzel, et al.,* Das Recht der Wort- und Bildberichterstattung, § 15 Rn. 4.

106 Freund, in *Götting/Schertz/Seitz,* Handbuch Persönlichkeitsrecht, § 48 para.14.

The *clickbait* case was at first labeled as "atypical" merchandising for two reasons: The merchandiser used the celebrities' icons in the opening credits (*Vorspann*) to attract internet users' attention, and advertising revenues for the website flowed in directly from the internet traffic at the time curious internet users click.[107] In this wise, the *clickbait* case differed from the classic mechanism of "image-transfer" in typical merchandising cases and the traditional device of "attention-grabbing" reflected in the case of *Wer wird Millionär*.[108] However, by revealing the thin veil covering the same commercial logic deployed by the device of "attention-grabbing", it was rightfully contended by German courts that clickbait was rather an adapted form of merchandising in the online environment.[109] Moreover, clickbait online was not necessarily as frightening as the one in the present case ("cancer", "to retire from the public"). The clickbait here was on the borderline of fake news.[110]

Against this backdrop, the German courts followed the guidelines for unauthorized merchandising that the person depicted has the sole right to decide the exploitation of his or her images in the absence of informative value. The article discussing the retirement of a public person due to a severe disease might present a legitimate interest of the public in knowing such information, but the merchandiser obviously downplayed this information by using pictures of irrelevant but famous persons, especially the plaintiff who was more popular than others, to create a riddle alluring internet users to click and open his website.[111] In this wise, even though the article and the depiction of the moderator planning to retire from the public might be legal due to public interests, the commercial interests pursued by the merchandiser in using the plaintiff's picture were in the foreground. It thus rendered the exploitation without the plaintiff's authorization unlawful.

Regarding remedies, the claim for destruction would be meaningless, while the injunction is critical in the digital age since advertising increasingly takes place online.[112] In computing the fictive license fee, the BGH rightfully rejected the argument advanced by the merchandiser. He man-

107 BGH, GRUR 2021, 636 - Clickbaiting, para. 28 and 30.
108 *Ibid*., para. 68. In the *Wer wird Millionär* case, the picture of the moderator took up almost 1/3 of the magazine cover.
109 *Ibid*., para. 30.
110 *Ibid*., para. 48.
111 *Ibid*., para. 56.
112 In the *clickbait* case, the merchandiser deleted this post within 3 hours after pushing this message.

aged to avoid the restitution of a fictive license fee by deliberately mixing up the revenue earned from the unlawful advertising and the unjust enrichment – the unauthorized exploitation of personal images.[113] One cannot be exempt from paying the license fee that he should have paid just because the unlawful merchandising was a failure, and one certainly cannot avoid the payment for license by paying (small) proceeds. The victim cannot shoulder all in all, the business risk in merchandising. The plaintiff could also claim the advertising revenue mentioned by the merchandiser based on § 687 II BGB in addition to the fictive license fee according to § 812 and 818 II BGB. Now, based on the commonly used model of "pay-per-click" (PPC) for calculating the advertising revenues, it is possible that the person depicted can claim the restitution for the fictive licensee fee plus the gaining by internet trafficking. The technical advancement in calculating specific advertising revenues helps facilitat the application of § 687 II BGB.

It is arguable whether the court's quantification of the fictive license fee is convincing. As mentioned above, the compensation should be equivalent to the license fee that the plaintiff could have demanded for exploitation under similar conditions, such as the size of the image, the manner, extent, and time of distribution, etc. Therefore, the merchandiser challenged the analogy drawn by the court to the *Wer wird Millionär* case because the size of images, the means and scope of distribution in that case were markedly different from his merchandising; Thus, he argued that the calculation of the fictive license fee was unfair.[114] The BGH did not respond to this accusation but stated that the amount was reasonable given the shocking and quasi-fake content of the advertising in the *clickbait* case.[115] It seemed that the court held the opinion that though the scope of distribution of the advertisement was relatively limited, the ample license fee was justified because of its serious impact on the plaintiff's moral interests. Apparently, the court's reasoning deviated from the law of unjust enrichment – to even out the increase including saving in the assets of the

113 BGH, GRUR 2021, 636 - Clickbaiting, para. 60. The merchandiser advanced that the amount it ought to restore should be the advertising revenue earned from the unlawful use of the plaintiff's likeness. Since the revenue was max. 300 euros the compensation ordered by the first two instances quantified as 20,000 euros was too high.

114 *Ibid.*, para. 68. In the *Wer wird Millionär* case, the picture of the moderator took up almost 1/3 of the magazine cover, and its distribution was significantly extensive than the *clickbait* case.

115 *Ibid.*, para. 69.

infringer.[116] Rather, it was to compensate the moral damages of the plaintiff. As *Ettig* argues, it presents, in essence, a confusion between solatium and unjust enrichment.[117]

All in all, while some improvements in calculating the compensation are conceivable, main guidelines regarding the unlawfulness of unauthorized merchandising and remedies are still followed in merchandising cases occurring online.[118]

2.4 Preliminary summary

The legal developments in unauthorized merchandising cases build on the recognition of economic components in the right to one's image. From one side, it enables protection for celebrities who were *de facto* deprived of any rights against commercial exploitation by advertisers. On the other side, it triggers material claims for fair compensation that significantly enhances the level of protection.[119]

In this wise, *Ulmer*'s famous metaphor for copyright is noteworthy and analogous here: the right to one's image is like the trunk of a tree.[120] Its moral and economic interests are the roots of the tree growing underground, and the commercial exploitation of the portrait is one of the branches. It reflects both moral and pecuniary interests, and the infringement of it – the free decision of the individual about whether to make his or her image an inducement for purchasing goods – harms the two types of interests simultaneously.[121] While it should accord to the perspective of the person depicted about the nature of the impinged interest standing in the foreground, the application of the claim based on unjust enrichment is not undermined as this claim is assessed from the infringer's perspective.

---

116 *Götting*, Persönlichkeitsrechte als Vermögensrechte, S. 53; *Ettig*, Bereicherungsausgleich und Lizenzanalogie bei Persönlichkeitsrechtsverletzung, S. 99f.

117 *Ettig*, NJW, 2021, 1274 (1277).

118 More examples, see BGH, GRUR 2021, 643 - Urlaubslotto.

119 It is especially beneficial regarding the personality rights of the deceased. Whereas the moral components of the right to one's image are not descendible, the economic interests are inheritable, and thus, the successor is legitimate for claiming compensation or restitution for unauthorized merchandising of the ancestor. See BGH, GRUR 2000, 709 - Marlene Dietrich, para. 37.

120 *Rehbinder and Peukert*, Urheberrecht: ein Studienbuch, S. 170, Rn. 543.

121 *Schlechtriem*, in: *Fischer and Ulmer, Strukturen und Entwicklungen im Handels-, Gesellschafts- und Wirtschaftsrecht*, 455 (465); *Götting*, Persönlichkeitsrechte als Vermögensrechte, S. 266.

This consideration complies with the ideological and constitutional basis of personality rights. The rights root in the autonomy to free develop one's personality and unfold one's value.[122] Also, it leads to several effects. First, it sets Germany on a completely different path than America, where a new property right emerged.[123] On the one hand, the persistent controversy among American scholars about the justification of the right to publicity thus never took place in Germany.[124] The German legal protection for the economic interests residing in the right to one's image is the natural result of the self-determination guaranteed by personality rights and a gift from advancements of technologies and markets. The right to one's image hence cannot be alienated from the natural person unlike the right to publicity in the US (discussed below).[125] However, on the other hand, as merchandising becomes more popular and independent from other practices, such as journalistic reports, Germany borrows the term "merchandising" directly from the English vocabulary and devotes to integrating merchandising into the legal regime of personality rights.[126] Secondly, unlike the right of publicity, different merchandising objects have to obey peculiar legal statutes as well as case law for respective personality rights, such as the right to name, the right to one's image as well as the general personality right. Last but not least, it must be conceded that the German statutory law has been left largely behind in this regard. Instead, one has to look into a body of case law to draw a counter to merchandising licensing in Germany.

---

122 See *Hubmann,* Das Persönlichkeitsrecht, S. 82.

123 Haelan Labs., Inc. v. Topps Chewing Gum, Inc. 202 F.2d 866 (2d Cir. 1953); Melville, 19 Law and contemporary problems 203 (1954); William, 48 California law review 383 (1960); Gordon, 55 Northwestern University law review 553 (1960); Zacchini v. Scripps-Howard Broad. Co. 433 U.S. 562 (1977).

124 Since the right of publicity is an intangible and exclusive right with only economic value, its justification must demonstrate incentives for creating the intangible goods or a market deficiency in lacking the exclusive right. On the contrary, the right of publicity fails to provide both. However, it is doubtful that people would not want to be celebrities if the right of publicity did not exist.

125 Bergmann, 19 Entertainment law journal 479 (1999) (480-482); *Götting,* in: *Götting and Schlüter, Nourriture de l'esprit: Festschrift für Dieter Stauder zum 70. Geburtstag,* S. 69 (73-74).

126 See BGH GRUR 1987, 128 - Nena; OLG Köln, GRUR-Prax 2021, 114 - Tina Turner, para. 20, 38; *Magold,* Personenmerchandising, S. 1; *Ruijsenaars,* Character Merchandising, S. 1; *Schertz,* Merchandising, para.1

3. Merchandising in contract practice

3.1 Consent in merchandising agreements

3.1.1 The legal nature of consent

(1) Consent as a legal act and *the ladder of permissions*

The second sentence in § 22 KUG has long recognized the exchange relationship between money and consent by stating (in case of doubt), "the consent shall be deemed to have been granted if the person shown received a consideration to produce the image". However, the lack of a definition of consent raises disputation about the legal nature of consent.[127] From a historical perspective, the tradability of the right to one's image was inherently contradictory to its nature as a personality right because it would seem to equal natural persons with objects. However, as *Hubmann* wrote poetically, life consists not of sharp boundaries but transitions; while there are some untransferable and indispensable interests underlining one's personality, some interests of the person pass slowly into the distance.[128] The *Paul Dahlke* case let German courts admit that merchandising has long been common practice in the advertising industry. Turning a blind eye to the fact that many people are willing to exploit their identities for publicity, fame, and money cannot make this phenomenon disappear. Rather, it would create confusion and increase transaction costs.[129] Moreover, an outright exclusion of the tradability of the right to one's image could not withstand the question: since merchandising is not illegal, why the right holder only has the right to claim compensation in the face of unauthorized merchandising by others, but not the freedom to enter into merchandising contracts on own initiative.[130]

---

127 A review of conflicting opinions, see *Dasch,* Die Einwilligung zum Eingriff in das Recht am eigenen Bild, S. 82 ff.

128 *Hubmann,* Das Persönlichkeitsrecht, S. 133.

129 For instance, lawsuits in the UK about the triangular relationship among Mr. and Ms. Douglas, the magazines OK!, and Hello! illustrates not only that a denial of legal protection for one's images cannot eliminate the trade of them but also how complicated the construction of such contracts and the disputes afterwards (the transaction cost) can be. See Douglas v Hello! Ltd [2007] 2 WLR 920.

130 Vgl. *Götting,* Persönlichkeitsrechte als Vermögensrechte, S. 66.

Against this backdrop, consent in § 22 KUG must be interpreted in a way that can not only enable the right holder to dispose the right to some extent for remuneration but also provide a fair balance between the personality interests (including the ideal ones that appear to be withdrawn in merchandising cases) of the right holder and reliance interests of the merchandiser who must invest money, time, and resources in a not insignificant manner. Noteworthy, a protection model that is overly biased in favor of the person depicted may lead to a lose-lose situation as he or she will never find a partner to work with.[131] In the literature, while a few authors generally object to the idea of commercial exploitation of personal indicia including images,[132] scholars who accept merchandising business also recognize the validity of merchandising agreements and thus view consent in this scenario as a legal act or at least a quasi-legal act.[133]

The licensing of the right to one's image was admitted as "controversial" (*umstritten*) in the BGH in the *Nena* case in 1986.[134] Subsequently, the BGH actively discussed the tradability of personality rights in the trend-setting decision in the *Marlene Dietrich* case. It argued that the law, instead of being a set-in-stone mechanism, needs to adjust to the changing reality regarding the tradability of objects that are protected by subjective rights.[135] Taking the occurred legal shifts as examples,[136] an incontestable task of civil law faced with an innovative marketing model is to provide a regulatory framework that adheres to the principle of private autonomy

---

131 Vgl. *Ohly*, "Volenti non fit iniuria": die Einwilligung im Privatrecht, S. 160.

132 See Schack, AcP, 1995, 594 (599, 600); Schack, Urheber- und Urhebervertragsrecht, Rn. 51; Peifer, Individualität im Zivilrecht, S. 315f., 325f.

133 *Klippel*, Der zivilrechtliche Schutz des Namens, S. 523 ff.; *Forkel*, GRUR, 1988, 491; *Helle*, Besondere Persönlichkeitsrechte im Privatrecht, S. 117; *Freitag*, Die Kommerzialisierung von Darbietung und Persönlichkeit des ausübenden Künstlers, S. 165 ff.; *Ruijsenaars*, Character Merchandising, S. 497, 506; *Schertz*, Merchandising, Rn. 380 und 388; *Hahn*, NJW, 1997, 1348 (1350); *Lausen*, ZUM, 1997, 86 (92); *Götting*, Persönlichkeitsrechte als Vermögensrechte, S. 149ff.; *Ernst-Moll*, GRUR, 1996, 558 (562); *Ullmann*, AfP, 1999, 209 (210 ff.); *Beuthien and Schmölz*, Persönlichkeitsschutz durch Persönlichkeitsgüterrechte, S. 32 ff. u. 62 f.; *Dasch*, Die Einwilligung zum Eingriff in das Recht am eigenen Bild, S. 85ff.; von Strobl-Albeg, in *Wenzel, et al.*, Das Recht der Wort- und Bildberichterstattung, § 7 Rn. 204; *Damm, Rehbock and Smid*, Widerruf, Unterlassung und Schadensersatz in den Medien, Rn. 169; *Hermann*, Der Werbewert der Prominenz, S. 45.

134 BGH GRUR 1987, 128 - Nena, the Guideline.

135 BGH, GRUR 2000, 709 - Marlene Dietrich, para. 38.

136 The judgment took the change of whether a trade name separately (from the business) was transferable as an example, see *ibid.*, para. 32f.

within the confines set by higher-ranking legal or ethical principles.[137] Upon the distinction between moral and economic interests in the right to one's image, the BGH conceded that the pecuniary components of personality rights are not indissolubly linked to the person in the same way as the ideal ones.[138] While a definitive legal recognition of the nature of consent in merchandising agreements is stalled till today in the BGH, judgments handed out by regional courts have admitted that consent of the person depicted is a legal act (*Rechtsgeschäft*) or at least a quasi-legal act (*rechtsgeschäftsähnliche Erklärung*).[139]

For instance, in the *landlady* case mentioned in the Introduction, the court at the outset underlined that the consent in this scenario was a legal act that included the declaration of will (*Willenserklärung*) of the person depicted because she intended to achieve a legal result by granting the receiver a protectable legal position.[140] Thus, when the offer proposed by the model that she was willing to license any subsequent publications of her photos for no less than 30% of the revenues had been accepted by the photographer on the telephone, the contract between them concluded in any case ("*ohnehin*"), and the consent for publishing photos was not freely revocable.[141] Moreover, since this contract was open-ended due to the lack of a time limit clause, the withdrawal of consent was only permissible provided on significant reasons or the principle of change of circumstances. In the *company-advertising* case, although no remuneration was granted against the commercial exploitation of the plaintiff's images (see Introduction), the BAG denied consent as a real act (*Realakt*) commonly seen in medicine law but viewed consent as a legal act or a quasi-legal act by. The court addressed that the consent should be applied and interpreted in accordance with the provisions about the declaration of will in the BGB in any case.[142]

---

137 *Ibid.*, para. 38, with further references.

138 *Ibid.*, para. 31.

139 OLG München, NJW-RR 1990, 999 - Wirtin, 1000; LG Köln, AfP 1996, 186 - Model in Playboy, 188; OLG Frankfurt, ZUM-RD 2011, 408 - Einwilligung zur Bildveröffentlichung kann nicht ohne Weiteres widerrufen werden, Rn. 37; OLG Düsseldorf, I-20 U 39/11 - Widerruf einer Einwilligung nach § 22 KUG, Rn. 8; BAG, GRUR 2015, 922 - Veröffentlichung von Arbeitnehmer-Bildnissen zu Werbezwecken, Rn. 37f.

140 OLG München, NJW-RR 1990, 999 - Wirtin, 1000

141 Ibid..

142 BAG, GRUR 2015, 922 - Veröffentlichung von Arbeitnehmer-Bildnissen zu Werbezwecken, Rn. 23.

In light of the practical need and the judiciary controversy for consent in the KUG, scholars kept finding doctrinal solutions for interpreting consent and incorporating it into legal doctrines in civil law. Enlighted by *the ladder of permissions* (*die Stufenleiter der Gestattungen*) developed by *Ohly*, the legal term of consent stipulated in § 22 KUG provides an all-embracing normative starting point.[143]

According to *the ladder of permissions,* the term consent, in its broadest meaning, is a sophisticated concept that covers almost all patterns of exercising rights underlying the maxim of *volenti non fit iniuria* – loosely translated, one who consents cannot complain[144]. According to the theory, consent may indicate an assignment of right (*translative Rechtsübertragung*), a constitutive transfer (*konsitutive Rechtsübertragung*) that facilitates a third party's use by creating a right of use on the object, such as an exclusive license, contractual permission (*schuldvertragliche Gestattung*), and a bare and freely revocable consent like provisional parking permission.[145] The abovementioned varied patterns to exercise rights show a decreasing intensity of restraint on the subject. however, not all "steps" of the ladder need to be available to dispose of a right or interest attributed by law. Rather, the pattern(s) of exercising the right is (are) prescribed by the nature of the right, the higher-ranking law, ethical principles, and probably the need for legal paternalism.[146] Accordingly, the exclusion of a pattern can only lead to the exclusion of the pattern(s) above it residing on *the ladder of permissions*, but not lead to the exclusion of the pattern(s) below it. For instance, the inalienability of the right to one's image from the person depicted shall exclude an assignment of right because one cannot demonstrate the right of self-determination by giving it up entirely. After all, it would lead to an ultimate loss of autonomy. However, since the person depicted does not lose the specific personality right if he or she licenses a right to use images to others while holding the ultimate control over the right to one's image, they should not be deprived of other possibilities for disposition, such as through a revocable consent, contracts, and (in)exclusive licensing.[147] In other words, scholars who are adherents to excluding other steps of *the ladder of permissions* except for an anytime revocable consent must

---

143 See *Ohly*, "Volenti non fit iniuria": die Einwilligung im Privatrecht, S. 147.

144 See Bachmann, 4 German Law Jounral 1033 (2003).

145 See *Ohly*, "Volenti non fit iniuria": die Einwilligung im Privatrecht, S. 147.

146 *Ohly*, "Volenti non fit iniuria": die Einwilligung im Privatrecht, S. 97ff.

147 *Götting*, Persönlichkeitsrechte als Vermögensrechte, S. 279; *Forkel*, GRUR, 1988, 491; *Peukert*, ZUM, 2000, 710 (719ff).

demonstrate other reasons than the inalienability of personality rights.[148] Otherwise, it would present an unjustified legal paternalism restricting private autonomy unduly.

From another angle, the varied connotations of consent make its interpretation critical especially when both parties do not explicitly clarify its nature. Nevertheless, consent is more likely to be binding rather than readily revocable in merchandising scenarios. The parties conclude a *quid pro quo* contract to establish a relatively long cooperative relationship. Furthermore, celebrities sometimes want to be free from the day-to-day management of their merchandising business by entrusting some professionals to help them negotiate licensing fees and develop their careers. In this situation, the soft-licensing model (*gebundene Rechtsübertragung*) based on the analogy with the German Copyright Law in light of the monistic theory is the most suitable solution to cater to this need: The person depicted transfers the right of use of the commercial interests in the right to one's image that derives from the right of personality, and thus establishes the right of action of the licensee against third parties, which ensures him a secure legal position; The advantages of the soft-licensing model are, for one, that the right to use is limited in content, time and space, and serves the specific contractual purpose, and for another that the licensor can release the authorized right at any time for justified reasons because of the inseparability of the personality right from him or her and the close link between moral and commercial interests.[149] In short, the right to one's image is transferable as a right of exploitation.[150] Without surprise, the soft-licensing model is preferred by agencies.

The principle of *pacta sunt servanda* is respected in merchandising agreements in German courts, and the *ladder of permissions* paved the way for the judicial interpretation of consent in § 22 KUG by providing a proper doctrinal foundation.

---

148 See *Ohly*, "Volenti non fit iniuria": die Einwilligung im Privatrecht, S. 162.

149 *Ibid*., S. 160 et seq.; *Forkel*, GRUR, 1988, 491; *Forkel*, Gebundene Rechtsübertragungen: ein Beitrag zu den Verfügungsgeschäften über Patent-, Muster-, Urheber- und Persönlichkeitsrechte, § 6 VII, S. 44ff.; Specht, in *Dreier/Schulze*, Urheberrechtsgesetz, § 22 Rn. 36; *Specht-Riemenschneider*, Konsequenzen der Ökonomisierung informationeller Selbstbestimmung, S. 78f.; *Wandtke*, GRUR, 2000, 942 (949); *Ullmann*, AfP, 1999, 209; *Ernst-Moll*, GRUR, 1996, 558 (562); *Götting*, Persönlichkeitsrechte als Vermögensrechte, S. 66f.; *Hubmann*, Das Persönlichkeitsrecht, S. 132f.

150 A paraphrase for the statement of „das Urheberrehct ist als Nutzungsrecht übertragbar“, see *Rehbinder*, Schweizerisches Urheberrecht, Rn. 155.

(2) The revocability of consent for merchandising

The revocability of consent is sensitive. For one thing, consent in merchandising scenarios is not like consent in medicine law as a real act that is freely revocable. Rather, it is a legal or quasi-legal act, containing a declaration of will. For another, the revocability of consent in merchandising cannot be excluded because the exploitation of personal photos simultaneously involves both ideal and commercial interests, according to the monistic theory. The difference is that commercial interests stand in front of the stage in the eyes of the person depicted.[151] Thus, scholarly literature and German courts advocate an analogy with § 42 UrhG because the monistic theory also undergirds the ideal-interest-friendly construction for authors.[152] In this wise, courts allow the withdrawal of consent for merchandising but only provided on the due cause.[153] In other words, the person depicted must demonstrate a change of belief to persuade the court that the contract must be terminated now otherwise the integrity of her personality would be inevitably compromised. In addition, a balancing of interests between the two parties may also take place to assess the personality interests of the person depicted against the reliance interests that trigger substantial investments of the merchandiser.

This approach was reflected in the *landlady* case, which became the seemingly model case for jurisprudence. Although *OLG München* acknowledged the sensitivity of the publications of nude photos in the case as they normally involve the core interests of one's personality,[154] it denied the model's claim to withdraw her consent because she did not present a change of her belief or attitude towards nudity.[155] In a similar case in *LG*

---

151 Götting, in *Götting/Schertz/Seitz,* Handbuch Persönlichkeitsrecht, § 10 Rn. 15; *Götting,* Persönlichkeitsrechte als Vermögensrechte, S. 52; *Büchler*, AcP, 2006, 300 (324).

152 Vgl. *Frömming and Peters*, NJW, 1996, 958 (960).

153 OLG München, NJW-RR 1990, 999 - Wirtin, 1000; LG Köln, AfP 1996, 186 - Model in Playboy, 188; OLG Frankfurt, ZUM-RD 2011, 408 - Einwilligung zur Bildveröffentlichung kann nicht ohne Weiteres widerrufen werden, Rn. 37; OLG Düsseldorf, I-20 U 39/11 - Widerruf einer Einwilligung nach § 22 KUG, Rn. 8; BAG, GRUR 2015, 922 - Veröffentlichung von Arbeitnehmer-Bildnissen zu Werbezwecken, Rn. 37f.

154 Specht, in *Dreier/Schulze,* Urheberrechtsgesetz, § 22 Rn. 6; BGH, GRUR 2016, 315 - Sexfotos vom Ex-Partner, the guideline. The BGH considered that the consent to possessing nude photographs was limited to the duration of the romantic relationship.

155 OLG München, NJW-RR 1990, 999 - Wirtin, 1000.

Köln in 1995, the court not only followed the guideline outlined in the *landlady* case, but also explained how to understand the change in one's attitude in scenarios of merchandising.[156] The BAG in the *company-advertising* case also adopted this approach and denied the withdrawal as well because the plaintiff did not present convincing reasons why he needed to exercise the right to informational self-determination in the exact opposite way of his previous behavior.[157]

Noteworthy, a balance of interests was exercised in all abovementioned cases. If the person depicted wants to deprive the legally protected interests of the merchandiser by withdrawing the consent, he has to convincingly demonstrate that the need for personality protection trumped those interests. In the *landlady* case and the similar case in Cologne, it was submitted that the personality interests, especially the ideal ones, were prone to inferences, and the damages were likely irreversible. However, the persons depicted, professional models, knew exactly the lifestyle they opted into and were willing to allow the third party's commercial use in return for money. The reliance interests of merchandisers in trusting this thoughtful decision warranted protection. In the *company-advertising* case, the BAG also spent a lot of ink on the balance of interests. As the merchandiser exploited the images for free, it might seem fair that the person depicted could withdraw his consent under less restrictive conditions. However, the court emphasized the fact that the employee – the person depicted was aware of and agreed on the binding nature of the consent by singing the unlimited timewise statement.[158] His voluntariness to give consent could be challenged due to the context of an employment relationship, it was

156 The court has listed plenty of interviews with the plaintiff to demonstrate that she has never changed her positive attitude towards nude portraits, and there was also no guarantee that she would not present similar portraits as well. Furthermore, the model's argument that "the old nude portraits … belong to a closed capital, from which she has long since turned away as an actress" cannot justify an exceptional termination of a long-term and synallagmatic contract because it is, in essence, a wish to conceal her past to avoid negative and judgmental opinions instead of an indication of a change of beliefs. LG Köln, AfP 1996, 186 - Model in Playboy, 187f.

157 See BAG, GRUR 2015, 922 - Veröffentlichung von Arbeitnehmer-Bildnissen zu Werbezwecken, Rn. 38.

158 On the one hand, there was no time limit on the statement's content. On the other hand, the portrayal of the plaintiff in the advertisement did not highlight his personality but rather as a "typical" employee of the company. See ibid., Rn. 34-36.

neither brought up by him nor proved on the court's initiative.[159] Moreover, the content of the advertising film suggested that the employee's personality interests were not prominent considering that his appearance was extremely short and mostly in a group.[160] The time point of the withdrawal further supported the view that the affected personality interests, if any, were not significant for the employee himself because he had waited too long (10 months) before he raised the claim.[161]

In light of the judiciary advancements especially developed by lower instances in Germany, it is discernable that consent in merchandising is a (quasi-)legal act and neither irrevocable nor freely revocable. The close cooperation between the academic and practical communities is significant and conducive. It must be borne in mind that the special protection of personality rights by law and the freedom of contract based on individual autonomy are in strong tension. The guideline in the revocability of consent, qualified as "good law", is a reasonable solution to alleviate this tension as it guarantees the private autonomy without dismissing human dignity and personality.[162]

3.1.2 The construction of consent in merchandising agreements

Even in merchandising scenarios where participants are generally professional models and actors who understand the business model very well and benefit significantly from it, their consent also needs interpretation now and then. A possible reason could be that since their photos are valuable, merchandisers often attempt to maximize their interests by interpreting the scope of authorization as widely as possible. Unfortunately, in doing so, it is likely to exceed the scope of the authorization that the person depicted envisioned when he concluded the contract, thus creating a dispute.

Once again, scholarly literature and courts resort to the German Copyright Law in interpreting the consent for disposing of one's likeness.[163]

---

159 *Ibid.*, Rn. 31-33. Thus, the court has ruled out a challenge based on the unlawful threat (§ 123 (1) BGB), even though the plaintiff has not raised the claim.

160 *Ibid.* Rn. 39.

161 *Ibid.* Rn. 40.

162 *Sattler*, in: *Lohsse/Schulze/Staudenmayer, Data as Counter-Performance – Contract Law 2.0?*, 225 (235).

163 Castendyk, in *Wenzel, et al.*, Das Recht der Wort- und Bildberichterstattung, § 35 Rn. 15; Götting, in *Schricker/Loewenheim*, Urheberrecht, § 22 Rn. 16; *Schertz*,

Stemming from the principle of purpose limitation (*Zweckbindung*),[164] § 31 (5) UrhG undergirded by the theory of purpose transfer requires that, in case of doubt, the ambit of the grant of the right of use must be interpreted to the extent that is necessary to achieve the purpose of the contract. Thereby, authors can participate in the profits that the work yields in an appropriate manner.[165] Against the background of merchandising, the analogy means that, in constructing the ambit of consent in case of doubt, one should inquire into the purpose of the contract concluded by the parties, while a blanket authorization must be carefully assessed against the contractual purpose agreed by both parties. If the contractual purpose is not prescribed in the contract, other factors including preliminary negotiations, customary practices, business style, and the usual course of business can be deployed to determine the purpose.[166] It is discernible that the theory of purpose transfer does not require an interpretation following the preference of the right holder of personality rights.[167] The contractual purpose stated in or implied from the contract is foremost decisive.

According to the guidelines, consent from professional models and actors/actresses without a clear intention or remuneration generally does not legitimize merchandising.[168] As merchandising provides substantial incomes for celebrities, it is uncommon for them to grant merchandising without consideration. In addition, the theory of purpose transfer helps in developing the restrictive permission for interferences with ideal interests underlying one's images caused by the commercial exploitation.[169] Since merchandising is mainly involved with the allocation of economic interests, consent also extends to standard forms of presentation in light of the commercial practice, which should be anticipated by the person

---

Merchandising, Rn. 382; OLG Köln, ZUM 2014, 416 - Werbekatalog, Rn. 50; BGH GRUR 1992, 557 - Talkmaster, 558.

164 *Burda,* Die Zweckbindung im Urhebervertragsrecht, S. 9.

165 Ohly, in *Schricker/Loewenheim,* Urheberrecht, § 31 Rn. 52, with further references.

166 Ohly, in ibid.§ 31 Rn. 65; *Burda,* Die Zweckbindung im Urhebervertragsrecht, S. 112f.

167 *Schricker/Loewenheim,* Urheberrecht, , § 31 Rn. 64.

168 For instance, consent of celebrities to shoot pictures for interviews, restore memories, or during public events, does not constitute a free pass for commercial exploitation. See BGH, GRUR 1956, 427 - Paul Dahlke; OLG Frankfurt, GRUR 1986, 614 - Ferienprospekt; BGH GRUR 1992, 557 - Talkmaster, 558.

169 Castendyk, in *Wenzel, et al.,* Das Recht der Wort- und Bildberichterstattung, § 35 Rn. 15-17.

depicted.[170] Instead, a severe interference with ideal interests must be legitimatized by informed and explicit consent. For instance, the *LG Frankfurt am Main* found it inexcusable when the merchandiser posted a nude photo online with stink fingers pasted on the breasts even when the plaintiff granted a blanket authorization regarding the nude photos because this presentation was "distasteful" (*geschmackslos*) and constituted an affront to the model undermining her personality.[171] A blanket authorization cannot legitimatize it.

In addition to these two general rules in constructing consent in merchandising, the theory of purpose transfer can also work on a small granularity. An illustrative example presents the *landlady* case. As the duration of consent was not clear in that case, it should be constructed in the way necessary to fulfill the purpose agreed upon by both parties, i.e., the remuneration for publication should be no less than 30%. Accordingly, the business practice in the publishing industry for pornographic pictures should be considered: if high payouts are only possible in the first five years of the publication, then the permissible duration of consent should be limited by this range.

A more meaningful embodiment of the theory of purpose transfer is in the *"stink fingers"* case. Both parties agreed on a time-for-print contract, according to which models do not have to pay photographers for shooting pictures. In contrast, photographers can keep the negative films of the images produced as remuneration.[172] This type of contract is very popular in the modeling community.[173] Given the intensive competition in this business, such an allocation of interests and rights is meaningful for young models to start their careers as they usually cannot afford the photography provided by professional photographers. Against this backdrop, the German court keenly observed that the time-for-print contract

170 Some scholars argue that the combination of the core theory and the theory of foreseeability suggested by the theory of purpose transfer is warranted here. See ibid., § 35 Rn. 19.

171 LG Frankfurt/Main, 30.05.2017 - 2-03 O 134/16 - Stinkefingers, para. 53 and 54.

172 Ibid. para. 68 and 70 with further references.

173 Time-for-print contracts are also popular in China. There are Chinese cases concerning similar questions including the ambit of the legitimate use of nude photos by the photographer. However, the Chinese court did not consider the photographer's use of self-marketing legitimate. See 壹飞视觉摄影（广州）有限公司、白利益等一般人格权纠纷民事二审，（2021）粤 01 民终 16859 号 (the Second Civil Judgment on the Dispute over the General Personality Rights of Bai Liyi, etc., and Yifei Photography (Guangzhou) Co., (2021) Guangzhou 01 civil final no. 16859).

reflected a reciprocal relationship between photographers and models. If consent in this scenario was not allowed because young models seem to be caught in unfair exploitation,[174] photographers, especially professional ones, would be reluctant to devote time, money, and professional sets to young models entering the industry. It would ultimately deny their career possibilities. Therefore, the court argued that the possibility of both parties making some commercial use of the photographs is the basis for such a contract. Otherwise, neither models nor photographers would like to conclude these agreements. Accordingly, this purpose should be anticipated and agreed upon by the model who wishes to develop her modeling career with minimal cost. Conceivable objections would be that the authorization exceeds the necessary extent to obtain the free service, or the model does not understand the scope of her authorization due to lack of experience.[175] These were, however, not visible in the case.

While the theory of purpose transfer can regulate merchandising at a suitable granularity to reach an accurate result, it is an *ex post* measure to construct consent, which can be accused of undermining legal certainty.[176] Maintaining consent is difficult, a written contract is thus always recommended with proper documentation about the purposes, means, rights, and obligations of merchandising.

3.2 Merchandising agreements

3.2.1 Types of merchandising agreements

There are different types of merchandising agreements to cater to the different needs of the merchandisers and the owner of the right to one's

174 *Vogler*, AfP, 2011, 139 (141).

175 LG Frankfurt/Main, 30.05.2017 - 2-03 O 134/16 - Stinkefingers, para. 70 with further references.

176 For example, *LG Düsseldorf* ruled that a model's performance in a public fashion show does not include authorization for advertising purposes of that show. See LG Düsseldorf, AfP 2003, 469 - Veröffentlichung von Fotografien einer Modenschau, para. 23 und 24; In contrast, the BGH constructed an actor's smile at cameras wearing a fashion house's glasses at its opening ceremony as consent to advertising this very fashion house using that image. However, it did not extend to other chain stores of that fashion house. BGH GRUR 1992, 557 - Talkmaster.

image. Nevertheless, the core of a merchandising agreement is to specify which portraits are to be used, how, and for what consideration.

The time-for-print agreement in the *"stink fingers"* case is a variant of the standard merchandising agreement (*Standardlizenzvertrag*). Under the standard merchandising agreement, the merchandiser is allowed to commercially use one's likenesses in a fixed manner, be it in the form of posters, advertisements, or fan products.[177] On the contrary, the so-called agency-merchandising agreement (*Agenturvertrag*) is more common for professional models and actors/actresses by facilitating a blanket authorization for commercial exploitation of one's images for merchandising purposes.[178] As the name indicated, this type of agreement is generally concluded with an agency, a professional organization specializing in managing and operating merchandising for models and actors/actresses. In this case, the agency-merchandising agreement provides convenience by taking care of operations for merchandising and profound and professional business planning for models and actors/actresses.

Taking the "Merchandising-Sponsor-Promotion-Contract" in the *Nena* case as an example, the famous singer who performs under the stage name NENA has transferred all her commercially exploitable rights, especially her right to images, to the plaintiff, the agency. Coupled with the template for an agency-merchandising agreement provided in literature by professional lawyers in the industry,[179] the main content in a typical agency-merchandising agreement is:

> *The agency is authorized worldwide and exclusively to operate merchandising for XX (the licensor – the person depicted) as well as to conclude sponsorship and promotion contracts....*
> *XX hereby assigns all rights necessary for the commercial use of the acoustic and visual environment of XX to the agency, in particular the right to the own picture, the right to the name XX, the right to the logo (Trademark)...*
> *This contract is concluded for ... years. During this period, it can only be terminated for good cause. It shall be extended by 2 years at a time if it is not terminated with one year's notice....*

177 Büchner, in *Pfaff/Osterrieth*, Lizenzverträge: Formularkommentar, B. VI, Rn. 614 ff.

178 *Schertz*, Merchandising, Rn. 393.

179 Büchner, in *Pfaff/Osterrieth*, Lizenzverträge: Formularkommentar, B. VI. Rn. 635.

Therefore, the agency is not only authorized to conclude standard merchandising agreements with others but also allowed to press charges against infringers in its name instead of the licensor. The agency's multiple roles, including bargaining, quality certification, supervision, and business strategizing, render agency-merchandising agreements doubtless the most popular type of merchandising agreements for professionals. Noteworthy, given the restrain of the person depicted from an exclusive licensing, the duration is usually shorter than standard merchandising agreements.

3.2.2 Typical contractual rights for the person depicted in merchandising agreements

To achieve the primary purpose of a merchandising contract, i.e., that the licensor transfers the right of commercial exploitation of images, and the licensee pays consideration, there are some ancillary rights and obligations for both parties. For instance, given the ambiguous legal recognition about the licensability of the right to one's image, the licensee is usually obliged not to challenge the licensor's legal status.[180] Moreover, the licensor must provide necessary assistance to the exclusive licensee against infringements by third parties.[181]

Several contractual rights from the licensor's perspective are highlighted below. Besides being common and essential in practices, they share similarities with some of the rights granted to data subjects by the GDPR. It thus provides an exciting perspective for making comparisons.

(1) The right to access information and accounting

Qualified as rights to inspect accounting (*Bucheinsichtsrechte*), some view this contractual right as essential to securing the licensor's financial interest because the calculation model for license fees often relies on the dealer's selling price or revenues.[182] In this spirit, the merchandiser must

---

180 The contract usually states that the agency acknowledges the XX's ownership of the rights.

181 Büchner, in *Pfaff/Osterrieth*, Lizenzverträge: Formularkommentar, B. VI, § 7 Books of Account and Audits in a merchandising license agreement template, Rn. 648.

182 Vgl. *Schertz*, Merchandising: Rechtsgrundlagen und Rechtspraxis, Rn. 405; With the rise of E-commerce live streaming in China, the commercial value of each

maintain not only complete and accurate books of account concerning all transactions regarding the merchandising objects but also aid with the licensor's audit.[183] Nonetheless, it is supported here to consider the right to access information and accounting an enabling right. After all, the portrait owner's control depends on the mastery of the circumstances of the authorization, including merchandising marketing timetable, status quo of the sales as well as projections, and so on.[184] Thus, the licensor must have a holistic yet detailed understanding of the market plan to exercise the right to self-determination and fully realize his or her personality.

(2) The right for reservation for approval

The right for reservation for approval (*Genehmigungsvorbehalt*) stems from the inseparable personality interests underlying the right to one's images. Upon this, licensors reserve the right to veto the specific form of merchandising, namely the presentation of their images in the advertising or fan products.

The right usually supports the right to reservation for approval for quality control (*Qualitätskontrolle*), which contains both aesthetic control and quality control over the goods. To prevent the personal image from distortion[185] and the reputation from being devalued by negative news about the goods,[186] this right with associated controls is beneficial for licensors in the long run. Consequently, celebrities who care about their reputation and the commercial value of their images are advised to have the right to quality supervision regulated in the contract.

In summary, the right for reservation for approval, together with the right for quality control, are, in essence, a right to object when the core interests protected by the right to one's image are harmed or the image

---

celebrity can be quantified by the amount and value of goods he or she sells live. For instance, an internet influencer could sell 15,000 lipsticks in 5 minutes and become one of the most valuable celebrities in China.

183 Schertz, in *Götting/Schertz/Seitz*, Handbuch Persönlichkeitsrecht, § 38 Rn. 50.

184 Büchner, in *Pfaff/Osterrieth*, Lizenzverträge: Formularkommentar, B. VI, § 8 (1) Marketing Plan, Rn. 651.

185 Bureau, Character Merchandising, 1994, WO/INF/108, 1994, 21.

186 *Ruijsenaars*, GRUR Int, 1994, 309 (311); In merchandising agreements in the US, the right for quality control in a technical manner is of great importance. See Büchner, in *Pfaff/Osterrieth*, Lizenzverträge: Formularkommentar, B. VI, Rn. 652.

of the licensor may thus face distortion and devaluation. If the dispute raised by the right to objection cannot be reasonably solved, a claim for an extraordinary opt-out right is conceivable.

(3) An extraordinary opt-out right

As stated in the "Merchandising-Sponsor-Promotion-Contract" in the *Nena* case, a contractual clause for an extraordinary opt-out right is common in merchandising contracts irrespective of the length of the contract. Therefore, it leads to the termination of that contract.

It could be argued that this clause might be superfluous from the perspective of the person depicted because the consistent German case law recognizes the revocability of consent upon the due cause. However, the extraordinary exit clause serves both licensor and licensee because the licensor's malfeasance could undermine the licensee's products' value.[187] In a sense, a merchandising contract binds the image of the product/company to the image of the star. An endorsement contract creates a closer relationship, whereas a merchandising contract regarding fan products may have a far more significant impact on the star than the manufacturer. The celebrity's image can either reinforce or undermine the goodwill of the agency, company, or manufacturer, and *vice versa*.

In essence, while the most involved interests in merchandising are economical, the ideal interests of both sides also need protection, which gives *vires* for the claim for opt-out of the contract following the similar rationale underlined the revocability of the consent given by the licensor.

(4) Disposable contractual rights

Considering that most of them benefit only the licensor and restrict the licensee's freedom, it is conceivable that the licensee, if it has greater power or financial resources, would be willing to omit these rights or at least

187 Vgl. Schertz, in *Götting/Schertz/Seitz*, Handbuch Persönlichkeitsrecht, § 39 Rn. 25-26; The District Court Munich (*LG München*) has given a strict interpretation of the licensor's "duty of good performance" (*Wohlverhaltenspflichte*) in the contract to protect the rights of the portrait owner by reasonably limiting the merchandiser's extraordinary opt-out right. See LG München II, ZUM-RD 2007, 542 - Wohlverhaltenspflichten eines Testimonials, the Guideline.

make some derogation in exercising the rights. Against the backdrop that these rights mainly stem from the personality interests, especially the ideal ones protected by the right to one's image, it is arguable whether these contractual rights should be regulated as mandatory.

Arguments for this legal innovation would be two-folded. For one, these rights are indispensable to protect the personality interests of the person depicted. As argued above, the right to access information and accounting is the enabler for controlling the merchandising for the person depicted. Consent without necessary information cannot sustain an effective execution of the right to self-determination. The right for reservation for approval coupled with the right for quality control is devised to prevent one's personality from distortion and devaluation. The extraordinary opt-out right is the final guarantee for the portrait owner to protect their personality. For another, the unique investment model in merchandising business indicates mandatory rights of the person depicted to develop a fair and reasonable contractual relationship. The person depicted, especially a celebrity, needs uneven protection provided by the contract because his or her losses are often irreparable and catastrophic. In practice, the licensee – be it an agency, a manufacturer, or a company – invests in phases, and each investment is negligible. In contrast, once the celebrity consents to the merchandising, his or her image is tied with the licensee. Thus, the investment pattern of the person depicted is to place all his or her "bets" at once. If something goes wrong, the agency and manufacturer can stop their investment in time, but the popularity and reputation embodied in the celebrity's image, which builds on years, even decades of dedicated work, can disappear entirely and quickly.

However, the principle of freedom of contract coupled with the uneven protection of personality interests incites confrontations. Counterarguments to regard these rights as indisposable are also evident and cogent. First, the absence of these rights does not indicate a severe infringement of personality interests. For instance, in a time-for-print contract like the one in the *"stink fingers"* case, the contractual rights such as the right to access information and accounting, the right for reservation for approval, and the extraordinary opt-out right are hardly necessary because the relationship is provisional, the form of merchandising is straightforward, and the impact on the person depicted is determined and insignificant. In other words, given the simplicity of this merchandising relationship, the person depicted does not need these rights to assist him in exercising individual self-determination free from compromise. Legal intervention is thus unwarranted and ineffective and a burden to both parties.

Secondly, contrary to a standard merchandising agreement, the agency-merchandising agreement is relatively long and extensive so that it can impact and restrict the free development of personality in a more significant deal. Thus, these rights are likely indispensable in striking a fair balance between the freedom of contracts and protection for personality interests in an agency-merchandising agreement. However, in this case, the person depicted, especially a celebrity, would have a strong incentive to take these rights seriously. As admitted by lawyers in this business, celebrities are usually assertive in fixing these rights down. Thus, the more significant the possible impact of the merchandising contract on the personality interests of the person depicted, the more incentive there is to encourage the inclusion of these rights in that contract. Lastly, there is a lack of clear statutory and jurisprudence on the mandatory nature of these contractual rights.

Nevertheless, it can be argued that the absence of these rights could be seen as a benchmark for measuring the fairness of standard contracts that have been drafted by one party, say, the agency and the counterparty can only take it or leave it (§§ 305 and 307 BGB). For instance, contracts signed between young people and large agencies in Korea's developed "idol trainee" industry are labeled as "slave contracts". They usually last for more than ten years and prescribe no rights for the trainees. Still, large amounts of money for breach of contract.[188] However, this case is rather extreme and concerns performance management contracts that include agency contracts, service (provision of training), and merchandising contracts. Albeit interesting, it is not the subject of this thesis.

All in all, these contractual rights are disposable in merchandising, albeit essential and meaningful. At most, the absence of these rights could play a role in measuring the fairness of standard contracts according to §§ 305 and 307 BGB.

---

188 Williamson, Lucy, The dark side of South Korean pop music, BBC News, 06-15-2011, at https://www.bbc.com/news/world-asia-pacific-13760064; John Seabrook, Factory Girls: Cultural technology and the making of K-pop, The New Yorker, 10-01-2021, at https://www.newyorker.com/magazine/2012/10/08/factory-girls-2. "Idol trainees" are refereed to young people, normally teenagers who wish to be idols or celebrities in the field of K-pop in fandom culture and thus sign contracts with agencies which provide them with necessary training and competition opportunities. After the training, the winners normally form a team or band and make their official debut. At this point, they may sign with another company and use the signing fee to pay their previous agency a significant amount to end that contract. As one can imagine, their chances of success are not very good. That is why the agency's contract with them usually includes very strict revenue sharing rules.

3.3 Preliminary summary

Stemming from the monistic theory, several analogies to the German copyright have been drawn to protect personality interests, especially the ideal ones of the person depicted. For instance, consent in merchandising, albeit legal, is subject to revocability with due cause. The theory of purpose transfer also helps construct the authorization in case of doubt so that interferences to the self-determination regarding one's images would be limited to the necessary performance of the contract. Thus, written and specialized counsel-drafted merchandising agreements are essential for a complex and continuous cooperative relationship.

According to the prevailing classification, standard merchandising agreements and agency-merchandising agreements for merchandising are common and cater to different situations. A blanket license is popular among professional models and actors/actresses because of the triple functions provided by agencies, namely negotiation power, management via sub-licensing, and career planning. Despite different taxonomy, the objective is to specify which portraits will be used, how, and for what consideration. In doing so, some synallagmatic clauses have evolved in practice and become the principal contents in merchandising agreements, including the exchange of licenses and fees, recognition of the licensor's rights by the licensee, and the provision of judicial assistance by the licensor, etc.

Highlighted are the contractual rights in favor of the person depicted. The right to access information and accounting, the right to reservation for approval including the right to quality control, and the extraordinary opt-out right are the common rights for a licensor in a merchandising agreement. Although these contractual rights are important and meaningful as they derive from and serve the personality interests protected by the right to one's image, they are optional in merchandising because of the principle of freedom of contract. However, the greater the possible impact of the merchandising contract on the personality interests of the person depicted, the more reasons there are to encourage the inclusion of these rights in that contract.

4. Conclusions

Upon the legal recognition that the right to one's image contains economic and moral components, the uniform legal regime of the right to one's image provides an all-embracing right to self-determination regarding personal pictures.

From a defensive perspective, models who do not suffer from moral damages by unauthorized merchandising are protected against commercial exploitation as the economic and moral interests are working in tandem. Irrespective of the nature of the damages, one always has the right to claim restitution computed on the fictive license fee based on the law of unjust enrichment because the commercial interests have been attributed to the person depicted. In practice, claims for fictive license fee, injunctive relief, and the auxiliary claim for access to information and accounting are virtually the customary reliefs in unauthorized merchandising cases. On the other hand, claims for destruction, correction, and publication of a counterstatement, albeit legally available, are hardly visible because they do not fulfill the needs of the exploited person.

From an active perspective, the dual interests of the right to one's image pave the way for legitimizing the *de facto* authorized merchandising. Merchandising has long been a reality, and no higher-ranking law or moral values prohibit it in general, especially regarding the transferability of the commercial interests protected by the specific personality right. The soft-licensing model developed in the German Copyright Law in light of the monistic theory is prevailing in merchandising business because it enables a stable cooperative relationship between models and merchandisers in commercially exploiting images while preserving the control of the person depicted over the images to some extent.

Therefore, the lack of an independent legal basis to govern commercial exploitation of personal indicia – like the right of publicity in the US – does not hinder the widespread merchandising in Germany and insulates German scholars from endless debates about the legitimacy of legal protection for merchandising. In this scenario, merchandising constitutes a right of use in respect of the right to one's image.

To strike a fair balance between private autonomy and special protection for personality interests, "the action is in the details".[189] Consent given by the person depicted is a legal act revocable with due cause. The analogy with the theory of purpose transfer rooted in the German Copyright Law mandates that consent, in case of doubt, should be limited to the necessary extent of the contractual purpose. While there are different merchandising agreements, agency-merchandising agreements are welcomed among professionals due to the triple functions provided by agencies, namely man-

189 *Williamson,* The mechanisms of governance, 6.

agement, sub-licensing, and career planning. Moreover, several rights and privileges for the person depicted deriving from and serving personality interests are common in these merchandising agreements, such as the right to access information and accounting, the right to reservation for approval, including the right to quality control, and the extraordinary opt-out right, to protect personality interests of licensors.

From the developments described above, both the defensive and active perspectives are indispensable to guarantee the legal rule in merchandising, namely, the person depicted has the sole right to decide whether to make his or her image available as an incentive for the sale of goods regardless of the social role if the exploitation serves the commercial interests of the merchandiser exclusively. In this wise, the legal recognition of the licensability of personal images is not surrendered to the market but instead granted a doctrinal success in facilitating more private autonomy. As technology and social advancements reduce the controversy over the separability of personal photographs and their depicted persons, legal paternalism in prohibiting any forms of disposing of the right to one's image appears increasingly groundless. After all, a market based on private property and voluntary exchange – restricted in the right to one's images – is also indispensable and significant for the thriving and sound progress of art and culture.[190]

190 *Cowen*, In praise of commercial culture, 2, 15-43 discussing the reasons, and 83-128 illustrating this argument by history.

Part II Merchandising under the GDPR

1. *Introduction*

After the EU data protection law emerged, a few German scholars have observed that its extensive applicability would impact merchandising.[191] This concern became evident and inevitable after the GDPR became effective. Therefore, it is time for a comprehensive discussion of how the GDPR regulates merchandising.

After a brief introduction to the GDPR and, in particular, its new features compared to previous EU data protection laws, Chapter 2 proves that the GDPR applies to merchandising cases. This may seem self-explanatory. However, as this Chapter unfolds, we can see that the GDPR's broad material and territorial scope of application also leaves some small spots. Chapters 3 and 4 discuss the application of the GDPR to unauthorized merchandising and authorized merchandising, respectively. It is to echo the structure of Part I for a more apparent contrast. More importantly, the two different forms of merchandising represent heteronomy and autonomy, respectively. A separate review of how the GDPR regulates these two modes of commercial exploitation of personal information allows a better examination of whether it achieves its dual objectives – data protection for data subjects and free flow of data (Art. 1 (2) and (3) GDPR).

Chapter 3 validates the unlawfulness of unauthorized merchandising under the GDPR and examines the possible remedies provided in the GDPR. Section 3.1 applies Art. 6 (1)(f) GDPR in unauthorized merchandising cases after a substantive interpretation of this provision using the GDPR's narrative. It accompanies an evaluation of the current approach adopted by German courts in dealing with merchandising cases.[192] Sec-

---

191 *Sattler, in: Lohsse/Schulze/Staudenmayer, Data as Counter-Performance – Contract Law 2.0?*, 225 (243 et seq.); *Schnabel*, ZUM, 2008, 657 (661).

192 This approach in merchandising cases has to be distinguished from the courts' argument in news coverage cases. In the latter context, German courts usually make it clear at the outset that because images were used for journalistic or artistic purposes, the KUG can be considered appropriate national law under Art. 85 (2) GDPR, which reconciles the freedom of expression and personal data protection because it meets the ECtHR's interpretation. See BGH, NJW 2022, 1676 - Tina Turner, Rn. 27-36; BGH, MMR 2021, 150 - Zulässigkeit einer iden-

tion 3.2 explores how the data subjects unauthorized merchandising cases would be compensated according to Art. 82 GDPR. Not only are damages caused by unlawful data processing discussed, but whether and how the data subject's rights can be used to claim damages is also analyzed. Some case studies regarding the cases mentioned in the Introduction of Part I present themselves to highlight the contrast without compromising the generalizability of the analysis.

Chapter 4 regarding authorized merchandising seeks the legal basis of merchandising contracts under the GDPR and reckons the applicability of the data subject's rights in merchandising cases. Before diving into the scrutiny of the lawful grounds in Art. 6 (1) GDPR, Section 4.1 addresses the question of whether the processing of personal images for merchandising falls under Art. 9 (1) as sensitive data. After excluding the application of Art. 9 GDPR in general, Sections 4.2 and 4.3 examine respectively the applicability and consequences of consent in Art. 6 (1) (a) and contracts in Art. 6 (1) (b) GDPR in authorized merchandising. As case law in the CEJU is not very rich, especially regarding Art. 6 (1) (b) GDPR, the analysis here is largely supported by the official documents issued by the WP29, the EDPB, and the EDPS as well as scholarly literature.

After concluding the findings in Section 4.4, the rights of data subjects in merchandising scenarios according to the GDPR are enumerated and examined for their feasibility and effectiveness in Section 4.5. Case studies are conducted alongside the discussion for clarification so that the comparison between the GDPR and German law in regulating merchandising is concrete and not devoid of content. Chapter 5 finally concludes this Part.

2. *The applicability of the GDPR in merchandising*

2.1 A brief introduction to the GDPR

Before diving into the overlap in the scope of application of the GDPR and the KUG in merchandising, it is necessary to review the advancements in data protection in the EU and Europe to better comprehend the substantial protection and objectives pursued by the GDPR. After all, history is a

tifizierenden Bildberichterstattung auf Internetseite einer Tageszeitung, Rn. 23; OLG Köln, ZUM-RD 2018, 549 - Anwendbarkeit des KUG neben der DSGVO, Rn. 9. Thus, it differs from merchandising cases defined in this dissertation, which are unrelated to news coverage or art at all.

continuous process, and by focusing on how things were formed, we can gain clarity on the things we face now.

Perceiving the threats that digitalization might pose to individual freedoms and rights, the German Federal State of Hesse issued the first personal data protection law in 1970,[193] and this wave of legal protection soon swept through Sweden, the Federal Republic of Germany, Austria, and the rest of the European Union. The Council of Europe has formulated the "Convention for the Protection of Individuals with regard to Automatic Processing of Personal Data" (afterward the 108 Convention) in tandem with the OECD around 1980 to provide new *vires* to the ECHR drafted in the 1950s.[194] Although the 108 Convention is a non "self-executing" treaty,[195] its core notions including that individuals are the protected subjects of data protection law in respect of fundamental rights and freedoms, the omnibus approach to governing both public and private sectors alike,[196] as well as some key terms' definitions have profoundly influenced the subsequent legislation of the EU.[197]

By using its competence in governing the internal market,[198] the EU, in the 1990s, became the chief actor in data protection. The acute consciousness of "free flow" of personal data (within the EU) rendered the Directive 95/46 beyond a faithful transform of the 108 Convention as well as the ECHR. Consequently, this unique character, coupled with protection for fundamental rights and freedoms of natural persons, lays down the EU's dual-objectives structure for the data protection law (Art. 1 (1) and (2) of

193 Datenschutzgesetz, Hessisches Datenschutzgesetz, 1970.

194 OECD, Guidelines on the Protection of Privacy and Transborder Flows of Personal Data, at http://www.oecd.org/digital/ieconomy/oecdguidelinesontheprotectionofprivacyandtransborderflowsofpersonaldata.htm; Council of Europe, Convention for the Protection of Individuals with regard to Automatic Processing of Personal Data, European Treaty Series (ETS) No. 108, Nr. 14.

195 Council of Europe, Explanatory Report to the Convention for the Protection of individuals with regard to automatic processing of personal Data, Nr. 38.

196 Simitis/Hornung/Spiecker gen. Döhmann in, *Simitis, Hornung and Döhmann*, Datenschutzrecht, Einleitung Rn. 116.

197 Art. 1 both in the 108 Convention and the Directive 95/46 state that (one of) their main purposes are to protect natural persons and respect human rights and fundamental freedoms. Art. 3 in the Directive 95/46 very much resembled Art. 3 in the 108 Convention regarding the applicable scope, the definitions as regard "personal data", "(automatic) processing, "special categories of data", etc.

198 Art. 95 EEC, now Art. 114 TFEU; The first sentence of the Preamble of the Directive 95/46; Art. 1 (2) of the Directive 95/46.

the Directive 95/46).[199] The 21st century ushered in a new phase of the EU data protection law. The right to the protection of personal data has been enshrined as a fundamental human right in Art. 8 of the Charter and granted with primary law status in the Treaty of Lisbon in 2009.[200] Using these new *vires* and under the impression of the Edward Snowden revelations, a directly applicable EU regulation,[201] namely the GDPR, replaces the Directive 95/46 aiming at full harmonization within the EU.[202]

Against this backdrop, the GDPR does not emerge *ex nihilo*.[203] Given the shortcomings of the Directive 95/46 and the existing legal fragmentation across the Member States, the GDPR, equipped with "real teeth", introduces a multitude of adjustments to expand and strengthen the EU data law substantially, especially in terms of legal provisions and execution.[204] Although there is some room to maneuver to the Member States prescribed intentionally by the GDPR,[205] they are mostly only allowed to concretize the provisions. After all, provisions and legal concepts of the GDPR are subject to autonomous interpretation by the EU. In this wise, the preliminary rulings carried out by the CJEU, as well as the Guidelines, Opinions, Recommendations, and Best Practices offered by the EDPB (previously the WP29) are of great importance in understanding the GDPR. Moreover, two chapters of the GDPR dedicate to the regulations on supervisory authorities for data protection EU-wide regarding their operating mechanism and, foremost important, consistency.[206]

The realized significant threats resulting from data technologies and ubiquitous data-harvesting practices lead to the new strategies codified in the GDPR. In addition to the expanded territorial scope,[207] strengthened

---

199 Subsequently, the dual-objectives structure has been almost literarily transformed in the GDPR (Art. 1(2) and (3) GDPR).

200 Art. 16 TFEU.

201 CJEU, Flaminio Costa v E.N.E.L, C-6/64; Art. 288 TFEU.

202 Rec. 3, 6, 7, 9 and 10 GDPR; Art. 99 (2) GDPR; *Schantz*, NJW, 2016, 1841.

203 *Fuster,* The Emergence of Personal Data Protection as a Fundamental Right of the EU, 3.

204 Recital 9 of the GDPR.

205 While there are more than 69 opening clauses, their scope of application is narrower, and their interpretation should be stricter and subject to final determination by the EU. Cf. *Miscenic and Hoffmann*, EU and comparative law issues and challenges series (ECLIC), 2020, 44 (50).

206 Chapter 6 "Independent supervisory authorities" and Chapter 7 "Cooperation and consistency".

207 Art. 3 GDPR

governance of data transfers,[208] new types of sensitive data,[209] and broadened data subject's rights,[210] the materialized principle of accountability and the adopted risk-based approach are highlighted advancements of the GDPR.[211] On the one hand, the principle of accountability is inevitable because it flows from the inherent task of the GDPR to cope with uncertainties,[212] such as developments of technologies, transnational and global collaboration in data processing and protection, and the vagueness between violations of data protection rules and damages to data subjects. Thus, omissions of these obligations, even without damages, could lead to exorbitant administrative fines.[213] On the other hand, the risk-based approach mitigates the disproportionate burden of accountability resulting from the broad application of conditions and strict obligations to some extent.[214] It has not just been regulated in the text of the GDPR,[215] but also applied in interpreting some terms and concepts of the GDPR, for instance, the fulfillment of the burden of proof stemming from the principle of accountability, the ambit of sensitive data, the balancing of competing interests between the data subject and controller and/or third parties in Art .6 (1) (f) GDPR.[216] Thus, large and influential data controllers are generally more obliged to adhere to the detailed and elaborate compliance rules than small and more conventional controllers whose processing is unlikely to result in a risk to the rights and freedoms of data subjects, or

208 Art. 44-49 GDPR.

209 The GDPR includes genetic data and biometric data for the purpose of uniquely identifying a natural person. See Art. 9 (1) in connection with Art. 4 (13) and (14) GDPR.

210 I.e., the GDPR has codified the right to erasure following the *Google Spain* case, now known as the "right to be forgotten" (Art. 17 GDPR), with more grounds for data subjects and an obligation for data controllers to notify every recipient. The GDPR has facilitated data subjects the right to portability (Art. 20 GDPR), the right not to be subject to a decision based solely on automated processing (Art. 22 GDPR), and the right to withdraw their consent at any time (Art. 7 (3) GDPR).

211 *Schröder*, ZD, 2019, 503; *Veil*, ZD, 2015, 347.

212 Hornung/Spiecker gen. Döhmann, in *Simitis, et al.*, Datenschutzrecht, Art. 1 Rn. 2.

213 Art. 83-84 GDPR.

214 Recital 15; *Renz and Frankenberger*, ZD, 2015, 158; *Veil*, ZD, 2015, 347.

215 For instance, Art. 24(1), 25(1), 27 (2) (a), 30 (5), 32 (1), and 35 GDPR.

216 Vgl. *Schröder*, ZD, 2019, 503 (504, 506); Vgl. Schantz, in *Brink/Wolff*, BeckOK Datenschutzrecht, Art. 5 Rn. 38.

is occasional.[217] However, the risk-based rules do not lend themselves to easy execution but require thorough guidelines.[218] In addition, the final decision for their interpretation lies in the hand of the CJEU, which leaves room for uncertainty in national courts and to legislators.

All in all, as a pivotal plank of the European Commission's Digital Single Market strategy,[219] the ambitious purpose of the GDPR coupled with its supremacy and the "one size fits all" solution might lead to a sweeping effect on national legal regimes that do not endeavor to protect personal data but are entangled with personal data, such as administrative rules about foreigners,[220] transparency of government subsidy policy,[221] schooling,[222] and, of course, merchandising. This concern and probably factual consequence give importance to this dissertation's research question: If the

---

217 Art. 30 (5) GDPR. The compliance rules include, for instance, incorporating date protection measures by design and default (Art. 24-25), keeping records of processing activities (Art. 30), conducting data protection impact assessment" (Art. 32-36), and pointing data protection officer (Art. 37-39).

218 The WP29 as well as its succeeding body, the EDPB, have issued plenty of guidelines and opinions to shed light on the operation of the principle-alike rules in the GDPR. For example, WP29, Opinion 06/2014 on the notion of legitimate interests of the data controller under Article 7 of Directive 95/46/EC, WP 217, 844/14/EN; EDPB, Guidelines 4/2019 on Article 25 Data Protection by Design and by Default, 14 et seq.; EDPB, Guidelines 3/2018 on the territorial scope of the GDPR (Article 3), 5 et seq.

219 European Commission, Communication from the Commission to the European Parliament, the Council, the European Economic and Social Committee and the Committee of the Regions, A Digital Single Market Strategy for Europe, COM(2015) 192 final, at http://ec.europa.eu/priorities/digital-single-market/docs/dsm-communication_en.pdf.

220 See CJEU, Minster voor immigratie v. M., Joined Cases C-141/12 and C-372/12, para. 48. In this case, the court considered data contained in an application for a residence permit as well as in the legal analysis of this application personal data so that it should be subjected to the EU data protection law.

221 CJEU, Volker und Markus Schecke, Joined Cases C-92/09 and C-93/09, para. 80ff. The court has invalided the respective regulations because they did not strike a fair balance between the necessity to enhance the transparency of public policy and the right to the protection of personal data and the right to privacy.

222 See CJEU, Peter Nowak, C-434/16, para. 49. In the *Nowak* case, the court found out that written answers of a candidate at an examination and any related comments made by an examiner are personal data that should be protected under the EU data protection law. It might impose schools as well as teachers with onerous compliance obligations prescribed by the GDPR and astronomical penalties. For example, the Swedish DPA has fined a municipality almost 20000 euros because it used facial recognition technology to monitor the attendance of students in school. See Facial recognition in school renders Sweden's first

GDPR is applicable in merchandising where the commercial value of personal data prevails, and private autonomy without too much paternalistic protection is acclaimed, would its regulation be appropriate and proper?

2.2 The material and territorial scope of the GDPR

Art. 4 GDPR provides 26 essential definitions for the terms including the ones that are decisive for the material applicable scope of the GDPR, namely "personal data" in Art. 4 (1) and "processing" in Art. 4 (2). One characteristic of the EU data protection law is that it chooses the term "data" commonly used in digitalization instead of "information". Contrarily, the latter is the legal term used in China and the US for their modern acts of privacy protection.[223] Data under the GDPR is understood broadly with regards to its physical form, content, properties, dimensions, and conceptual levels so that both raw and unorganized data meaning nothing to human beings as well as semantic data as in personal images taken by cameras are (personal) data in the meaning of the GDPR.[224] Nevertheless, the emphasis on digitalization should not be exaggerated since "data" and "information" have been consistently used interchangeably in the GDPR and the EU official documents.[225]

GDPR fine, EDPB, at https://edpb.europa.eu/news/national-news/2019/facial-recognition-school-renders-swedens-first-gdpr-fine_sv.

223 In China, the newly issued "Personal Information Protection Law of the People's Republic of China" (effected on 11-01-2021) chooses to use the term information, while the bill has obvious similarities to the GDPR. For instance, the definition of personal information in the Chinese law states (Art. 4 (1)), "Personal information means all kinds of information related to identified or identifiable natural persons that are electronically or otherwise recorded, excluding information that has been anonymized." In the US, the segmented privacy protection laws do not affect their unanimous choice for the term information. See for instance 114th Congress, Administration Discussion Draft: Consumer Privacy Bill of Rights Act of 2015; See California Consumer Privacy Act of 2018; Ohm, 88 Southern California law review 1125 (2015) (1130 et seq.).

224 See CJEU, Rynes, C-212/13, para. 22; Karg, in *Simitis, et al.*, Datenschutzrecht, Art. 4 Rn. 26.

225 See Art. 4 (1), (13) and (15) GDPR, and Recitals 6, 26, 29, 30 and 50; WP29, Opinion 4/2007 on the concept of personal data, WP136, pp.6-8; European Commission, Commission staff working document on the free flow of data and emerging issues of the European data economy Accompanying the document Communication Building a European data economy, SWD(2017) 2 final.

The GDPR essentially mirrors the definition of "personal data" in Art. 2 (a) of the Directive 95/46/EC about "any information relating to an identified or identifiable natural person". The typical risk-based definition – the simpler it is for the data controller and any others to single the person out in terms of cost, time, and technology, the more the GDPR tends to qualify the data as personal data – conspicuously expands the scope of personal data.[226] This relatively objective assessment,[227] coupled with the principle of accountability, obliges data controllers to prove that the data cannot be attributed to a natural person, for instance, by using anonymization as a default rule.

The last key factor in specifying the applicable material of the GDPR is the term "processing" pursuant to Art. 2 (1) with the definition under Art. 4 (2) GDPR. It covers all automated operations along the value chain of data processing, from collecting, storing, and using to erasing and deleting. More importantly, the term "processing" also extends to unautomated means. Art. 2 (1) GDPR excludes wholly unautomated means from the applicability of the GDPR, for example, noting down someone's phone number on a piece of paper. This exception is overruled if this note forms part of a directory organized alphabetically. In fact, given the widespread of digital products, the CJEU has concluded that photography and surveillance of people are processing personal data.[228]

As a pioneer in protecting personal data at a high level, the EU addresses a wide territorial applicable scope in respect of international trade and borderless communication to prevent forum shopping. Highlighted in the *Google Spain* case, the general rule of the establishment principle – the choice of law depends on where an entity is established – has been expanded by interpreting "establishment" and "in the context of the activities" flexibly.[229] It is no longer contingent on whether the establishment within the EU has carried out the data processing *per se*, economical support sustains the application of the EU data protection law.[230]

Nevertheless, against the E-commerce backdrop, which enables providers without residing in any Member States to provide services for data subjects within the EU, the establishment principle cannot tackle this

226 Recital 26 of the GDPR; CJEU, Patrick Breyer v Bundesrepublik Deutschland, C-582/14, para. 44 et seq.

227 *Brink and Eckhardt*, ZD, 2015, 1.

228 CJEU, Rynes, C-212/13, para. 22-25; CJEU, Sergejs Buivids, C-345/17, para. 31-36.

229 See CJEU, Google Spain, C-131/12, para. 52, 53 and 55.

230 *Spindler*, DB, 2016, 937 (938); *Albrecht*, CR, 2016, 88 (90).

problem, no matter how far stretched. The GDPR introduces the *Marktortprinzip* (principle of the market) in Art. 3 (2) GDPR to regulate data controllers outside the EU provided on either an economic connection or influence in people inside the EU by data processing.[231] Thus, if the entities without an establishment in the EU offer goods or services to data subjects in the EU or aim to monitor EU customers' behavior in any form of web tracking, they shall obey the rules established in the GDPR and likely have to appoint a representative as a contact point for data subjects and supervisory authorities within the EU.[232] It is also noteworthy that the location of data subjects instead of their nationality is decisive for applying the GDPR. All in all, one could argue that, broadly speaking, the location of data subjects instead of the controllers is decisive for applying the GDPR.

However, the GDPR also lists four exceptions for its material applicable scope in Art. 2 (2) GDPR and mandates the Member States to make some derogations and exemptions to specific parts of the GDPR according to Art. 85 GDPR. Compared to Directive 95/46/EC, the GDPR does not grant the Member States much discretion regarding its material scope and substantive protection. On the one hand, the exceptions are constructed restrictively. For instance, while the GDPR excludes its application in data processing "by a natural person in the course of a purely personal or household activity" in Art. 2 (2) (c) GDPR, it does not affect its governance over "controllers or processors which provide the means for such personal or household activities".[233] This exception to exception puts Apps for communication and social platforms under a magnifying glass, even though they focus only on providing instant messaging dominated by data subjects, or social networking existing between "real" friends. On the other hand, the authority for interpreting the general opening clause of Art. 85 GDPR is reserved by the CJEU. Without a clear and determined answer from the CJEU, the ambit of Art. 85 GDPR is still undecided (detailed discussion see below).

231 Recital 24 GDPR; *Schantz*, NJW, 2016, 1841 (1842); *Hornung*, ZD, 2012, 99 (102).

232 Art. 27 in combination with 4 (17) GDPR.

233 Art. 2 (2) (c) GDPR in connection with Recital 18.

2.3 Questions regarding the applicability of the GDPR in merchandising

At first glance, the GDPR applies to merchandising smoothly. First, being identified is the foremost important condition for merchandising because the person depicted, usually, a celebrity, must be identified to attract consumers' attention or trigger an image transfer. Second, in the digital age, almost every link in the production chain for merchandising, ranging from taking photos, over uploading data into computers for editing, storing, printing, to manufacturing the exemplars, has been "datafied.[234] Thirdly, the exceptions provided in Art. 2 (2) GDPR are generally not applicable. There is no need to elaborate that the public nature inherent in merchandising renders the exception for personal and household activities inapplicable. Moreover, the exception for deceased people's data in recital 27 of the GDPR is not problematic for merchandising because not only must the purposes of the processing but also its contents, means, and consequences be taken into consideration to determine whether this exception is applicable; Thus, data concerning deceased persons might be relevant for their relatives.[235] Since post-mortem personality protection in Germany rooted in human dignity anchored in Art. 1 GG is maintained by one's relatives as fiduciaries,[236] and merchandising of a deceased celebrity could result in wealthy increase or lawsuits of his or her successors, living relatives of the deceased celebrity may be at least indirectly affected by the processing from the GDPR's perspective.[237] It is hence suggested for data

234 This word is *borrowed* from Lupton and Williamson, 19 New Media & Society 780 (2017). However, sometimes purely handmade fan products exist, such as portraits of celebrities painted by street artists, etc. The GDPR is impossible to apply here because there is no data processing in the sense of GDPR. Nonetheless, this is exceptional given its negligible proportion of revenue and possible defenses for freedom of speech and art. However, as the whole production chain of fan products consists of various operations, and most of them are "datafied", the GDPR at least is partially applicable. Moreover, against the backdrop that merchandising occurs increasingly frequently and preferably on the internet, it is increasingly unproductive to focus on the exceptions.

235 *Paal and Pauly,* DS-GVO BDSG, Art. 4, Rn. 6; *Brink/Wolff,* BeckOK Datenschutzrecht, Art. 4, Rn. 5; *Voigt and Bussche,* The EU General Data Protection Regulation (GDPR): A Practical Guide, 11.

236 *Fischer,* Die Entwicklung des postmortalen Persönlichkeitsschutzes: von Bismarck bis Marlene Dietrich, 129ff.; *Gregoritza,* Die Kommerzialisierung von Persönlichkeitsrechten Verstorbener, 51ff.

237 CJEU, Volker und Markus Schecke, Joined Cases C-92/09 and C-93/09, para. 53; Karg in, *Simitis, et al.,* Datenschutzrecht, Art. 4 (1) Rn. 4; For instance, the WP 29's opinion has further argued that deaths caused by the genetic deficiency

controllers to obey the rules in the EU data protection law even when they process data about deceased people.[238]

Nevertheless, two questions remain about the applicability of the GDPR in merchandising.

2.3.1 Exceptions for the territorial applicability

Given the flourishing cultural and entertainment industry in Europe, it is common that European celebrities are invited by foreign brands to shoot advertisements either abroad or aiming at foreign markets, say, the Chinese market. It is questionable whether it falls under the scope of Art. 3 GDPR. Imagine three scenarios. One is that Thomas Müller, the famous German football player, travels to China to shoot an advertisement for a Chinese company producing running shoes. In the second scenario, Müller handles the merchandising business by himself (this is more likely for models who have just begun their careers). Instead of taking a long journey, he shoots a video and sends it to the Chinese company abroad. The last scenario is perhaps more common. Müller has authorized his merchandising rights in gross to an agency in Germany (like Nena did in the *Nena* case), which makes the commercial in tandem with the Chinese company and transfers the data to China. The advertisements in all scenarios are shown with Chinese subtitles and only broadcasted within China.

The first constellation is without a doubt ungoverned by the GDPR according to Art. 3 GDPR since the Chinese company neither has an establishment within the EU nor offers service/goods to data subjects in the Union. Even though the nationality of the data subject – Thomas Müller – is German, processing of his data taking place in a third country does not trigger the application of the GDPR because the term "data subjects who are in the Union" in Art. 3 (2) GDPR refers to the location of the data subject at the time when data processing takes place instead of the nationality or residence.[239]

---

may be considered as personal (sensitive) data about the deceased's children since such deficiencies are heritable. See WP29, Opinion 4/2007 on the concept of personal data, WP136, 22.

238 Ibid. 24.

239 See EDPB, Guidelines 3/2018 on the territorial scope of the GDPR (Article 3), 14-15.

On the contrary, the third scenario is undoubtedly regulated by the GDPR and even triggers an additional legal regime prescribed by the GDPR for data transfers. The agency in Germany and the Chinese shoemaking company are co-controllers in the sense of the GDPR since they decide together about the purpose and means of the processing of personal data. In this sense, the German agency must meet the two-tier requirement pursuant to Art. 44 GDPR. More specifically, it must at first comply with the general provisions in the GDPR as regards the general principles of processing, especially the lawfulness, rights of data subjects, etc. and the special rules for data transfers in Art. 46-50 GDPR as the designated country, China, is not "safe" according to the decision of the EU Commission to ensure an adequate level of data protection when personal data have been transferred to any country other than the EU Member States.[240]

The second scenario, however, illustrates the implementation issues resulting from the *Marktortprinzip*. Although the Chinese company does process personal data of a data subject located in the EU and arguably makes an offer for (merchandising) service to that data subject (Art. 3 (2) (a) GDPR),[241] the EU lacks the necessary grip to manage the data controller.

If the merchandising contract is not regarded as a provision of services to data subjects within the EU, it poses a risk of legal circumvention when controllers conclude contracts with data subjects separately. For instance, a US-based genetic testing company offers its services in a direct-to-consumer manner online and concludes hundreds and thousands of contracts with data subjects in the EU individually.[242] In this case, if the GDPR does not apply, the objective of the newly added *Marktortprinzip* – to prevent data controllers from circumventing the GDPR by establishing outside the EU – would be rendered futile.[243] However, if any contractual relationship leads to an application of the GDPR when one party or even a third party benefited from the contract is in the EU, even though the controller does not have the ambition to set foot in the EU market, the rigorous and extensive compliance rules outlined in the GDPR would constitute a great burden on the controller. Predictably, this will significantly increase the cost for foreigners to cooperate with EU data subjects, and ultimately dis-

240 Recital 6, 23, and 101 of the GDPR.

241 Plath, in *Plath,* DSGVO/BDSG, Art. 3 Rn. 20.

242 Mahmoud-Davis, 19 Wash. U. GLOBAL Stud. L. REV. 1 (2020) (8).

243 Schantz, in *Simitis, et al.,* Datenschutzrecht, Art. 44 Rn. 13 - 15.

courage the international corporation between EU and foreign companies, under which the EU market is not the target.

More importantly, insurmountable obstacles at the implementation level would emerge if the GDPR applied. For instance, when data transfers are involved, the controller must, besides fulfilling the general requirements in the GDPR, facilitate the EU Standard Contractual Clauses (SCC) pursuant to Art. 46 (2) (c) and (d),[244] or demonstrate conditions prescribed in Art. 49 (1) GDPR.[245] However, the functioning of these regulations is premised on that there is a data controller or a processor inside the EU. When the partner of the controller abroad is the data subject himself,[246] like in the hypothetical scenario, it lacks a grip for the GDPR to oblige the Chinese company to apply the GDPR. Consequently, the whole system runs into difficulties. After all, it is impossible to implement the GDPR abroad since the authority and investigative powers of DPAs are significantly limited.[247] Eventually, the lack of legal enforcement would lead to disregard and unawareness of the law.[248] Perceiving the dilemma, the GDPR requires companies abroad to maintain a representative in the EU (Art. 27 (1) GDPR). It could alleviate tensions between "reality" and "illusion" in enforcing rules about data protection and transfers,[249] but would eventually discourage the international corporation, in which the EU market is not the target. After all, the effectiveness of the *Marktortprinzip* relies on the absolute attractiveness of the EU market. It is questionable whether

244 Because it comes from a country that is not "safe" according to the decision of the EU Commission. Insofar, the European Commission has only considered the following countries providing an adequate level of protection as the EU, Andorra, Argentina, Canada (commercial organizations), Faroe Islands, Guernsey, Israel, Isle of Man, Japan, Jersey, New Zealand, Switzerland and Uruguay. See Adequacy decisions, EU Commission, at https://ec.europa.eu/info/law/law-topic/data-protection/international-dimension-data-protection/adequacy-decisions_en.

245 For instance, explicit consent of the concerned data subject (Art. 49 (1) (a)), or a necessity of performing contracts (Art. 49 (1) (b)).

246 The GDPR, albeit implicitly, assumes that data subjects should not be considered controllers even though they decide the purpose and means of the processing of their data. Cf. Edwards, Finck, Veale and Zingales, Data subjects as data controllers: a Fashion(able) concept?, Internet Policy Review, at https://policyreview.info/articles/news/data-subjects-data-controllers-fashionable-concept/1400.

247 CJEU, Maximillian Schrems v Data Protection Commissioner, C-362/14, para. 43; Vgl. Schantz, in *Simitis, et al.*, Datenschutzrecht, Art. 44 Rn. 13 - 14.

248 *Veil*, Neue Zeitschrift für Verwaltungsrecht, 2018, 686 (696).

249 Cf. Kuner, 18 German Law Journal 881 (2017).

entering the EU market is still attractive to small companies after weighing the benefits and costs, especially compliance costs.

Against this backdrop, *Hornung* argues for the exclusion of the GDPR in its entirety for a one-time contract between one person inside the EU and a data controller outside the EU due to the absence of the need for protection (*Schutzbedürftigkeit*).[250] This teleological reduction in interpreting Art. 3 (2) (a) GDPR has merit because it avoids the dilemma described above. A one-time contract concerning one person inside the EU illustrates a fundamentally different picture than the one Art. 3 (2) GDPR envisaged on the internet environment where data-harvesting practices, automated profiling, and targeting advertisements overrun.[251] It is also significantly different from the genetic testing company mentioned above, which systematically and continuously processes data on many EU data subjects. Moreover, this finding is supported by the underlined rationale of Art. 27 (2) GDPR, which agrees to waive the requirement to maintain a representative in the EU, if the processing "is occasional" and "does not include, on a large scale, special categories of data", and "is unlikely to result in a risk to the rights and freedoms of natural persons".

Thus, one would argue that the GDPR does not apply to the Chinese company in the second hypothetical scenario because the personal data that the Chinese company processes are exclusively Müller's, the processing is on a small scale and occasional. Moreover, the conventional processing methods without profiling or behavioral analysis hardly present a risk to the rights and freedoms of the data subject.

2.3.2 The leeway for national laws offered by Art. 85 GDPR

The second issue is more important because its answer may lead to outright exclusion of merchandising from the scope of the GDPR, namely the leeway for national laws offered by Art. 85 GDPR. Its first paragraph states its objective and reads:

> *Member States shall by law reconcile the right to the protection of personal data pursuant to this Regulation with the right to freedom of expression and information, including processing for journalistic purposes and the purposes of academic, artistic or literary expression.*

250 Hornung, in *Simitis, et al.*, Datenschutzrecht, Art. 3 Rn. 52.
251 Recital 23 of the GDPR.

There are other provisions in the GDPR that also give judges some discretion to achieve the same objective, such as Art. 6 (1) (f), Art. 9 (2) (g), Art. 17 (3) (a), etc. However, they are much more restrictive and focused than Art. 85 GDPR. Art. 85 (2) GDPR sets out two conditions for the Member States to derogate or exempt from the application of the GDPR and specifies the provisions from which derogations or exemptions can be made. For one, derogations or exemptions must be made only for data processing for journalistic purposes or purposes of academic, artistic, or literary expression. For another, it must be "necessary to reconcile the right to the protection of personal data with the freedom of expression and information." Art. 85 (3) GDPR at last orders the Member States to notify the Commission of their derogations or exemptions without delay.

Thus, reviewing whether merchandising has journalistic purposes or purposes of academic, artistic, or literary expression is the key to determining whether Art. 85(2) GDPR is applicable. Admittedly, journalistic purposes should have a wide and contemporary meaning under the active influence of the CJEU and ECtHR as the term "citizen journalism" (*Bürgerjournalismus*) implies.[252] The critical factor is thus not the "means of transmission" but whether the statement's "purpose is to disseminate information, opinions or ideas to the public".[253] Moreover, against the backdrop that partial or total commercialization of the speaker does not naturally compromise the pursuit for public interests entailed in the activi-

---

252 ECtHR, Magyar Tartalomszolgáltatók/Hungary, Application No. 22947/13; CJEU, Satamedia, C-73/07, para. 56. In this case, the plaintiffs were two companies who collected and published information on the income and tax of 1.2 million natural persons in Finland, first through newspapers and later through an SMS service where people could receive tax information on another person by sending his or her name to one of the companies. After this service was prohibited by Finnish data protection authority, plaintiffs raised the lawsuit, which was subsequently referred to the CJEU by the Finnish court for an interpretation about, inter alia, processing for solely journalistic purposes. The CJEU answered that "activities may be classified as 'journalistic' if their sole object is the disclosure to the public of information, opinions or ideas, irrespective of the medium used to transmit them." *Oster,* Media Freedom as a Fundamental Right, 249 et seq.; *Weberling and Bergann*, AfP, 2019, 293 (297). The term *Bürgerjournalismus* was forwarded by the Australian DPA in its notification to the Commission to indicate an expensive reading for journalistic purposes. Österreichische Datenschutzbehörde DSB-D123.077/0003-DSB/2018 v. 13.8.2018, S. 5-6.

253 CJEU, Satamedia, C-73/07, para. 56, 61.

ties,[254] it is well argued that most cases regarding the right to one's image shall still be regulated by §§ 22, 23 KUG.[255] For instance, the platform of YouTube compensates YouTubers automatically according to the view number. This business model should not and does not undermine the journalistic purpose of a YouTuber because contributions of the processing of data in disclosure to the public of information, opinions or ideas are decisive in relation to journalistic purposes.[256] In this sense, the valid concern raised by *Ohly* that personality intrusions through acts of communication on the Internet should not be forced into the Procrustean bed of data protection[257] can be addressed since the "back door" is closed by the GDPR itself through a liberal reading of journalistic purposes in Art. 85 (2) GDPR.

Nevertheless, merchandising defined in this dissertation serves the commercial interests of merchandisers exclusively. Borderline cases such as satirical advertising and self-promotion of newspapers that contribute to the formation of public opinion are excluded. Therefore, the Member States shall not make derogation or exemption of the GDPR in merchandising cases pursuant to Art. 85 (2) GDPR.

---

254 See ibid., para. 60. "it…is not determinative as to whether an activity is undertaken solely for journalistic purposes".

255 BGH, GRUR 2021, 100 - Bildberichterstattung über ein Scheidungsverfahren, para 11; OLG Köln ZD 2018, 434 OLG Köln, ZUM-RD 2018, 549 - Anwendbarkeit des KUG neben der DSGVO; VG Hannover, 27.11.2019 - 10 A 820/19 - Fanpage einer Partei bei Facebook, para. 35; *Bienemann,* Reformbedarf des Kunsturhebergesetzes im digitalen Zeitalter, S. 245; *Gramlich and Lütke*, MMR, 2020, 662 (666); *Reuter and Schwarz*, ZUM, 2020, 31; *Lauber-Rönsberg*, AfP, 2019, 373 (375f.); *Weberling and Bergann,* AfP, 2019, 293 (295); *Krüger and Wiencke*, MMR, 2019, 76 (78); *Raji*, ZD, 2019, 61(64); *Ziebarth and Elsaß*, ZUM, 2018, 578 (585);*Hansen and Brechtel*, GRUR-Prax, 2018, 369; *Hildebrand*, ZUM, 2018, 585 (589); *Sundermann*, K&R 2018, 438 (442); *Lauber-Rönsberg and Hartlaub*, NJW, 2017, 1057 (1062); *Specht*, MMR, 2017, 577. In this sense, a notification to the Commission with the KUG should be made pursuant to Art. 85 (3) GDPR. See Specht-Riemenschneider, in *Dreier/Schulze,* Urheberrechtsgesetz, vor § 22 KUG, para. 6a.

256 See CJEU, Sergejs Buivids, C-345/17, para. 57; Vgl. Pötters, in *Gola,* DSGVO, Art. 85 Rn. 8; Buchner/Tinnefeld, in *Kühling/Buchner,* DSGVO/BDSG, Art. 85 Rn. 25; Vgl. BGH, NJW 2009, 2888 - Spickmich. para. 10; *Rombey*, ZD, 2019, 301 (303); Dix, in *Simitis, et al.,* Datenschutzrecht, Art. 85, Rn. 14; *Spindler,* DB, 2016, 937 (939).

257 *Ohly*, AfP, 2011, 428 (437).

Noteworthy, some scholarly literature argues for more discretion for national laws resorting to Art. 85 (1) GDPR.[258] This proposal may seem difficult to accept at first glance, as it is so disruptive that it could allow the Member States to adapt the entire regulation of the GDPR for reconciliation between freedom of expression and personal data protection. Out of this concern, the validity of this proposal is not explored here but placed in Part IV Solutions.

2.4 Conclusions

As merchandising involves processing of personal data as always, the GDPR is applicable. It was not a problem under Directive 95/64/EC because it provided more extensive discretion for the Member States and the BDSG gave precedence to the KUG according to the principle of *lex speicilas*. However, after the GDPR came into effect in May 2018, German legislators have been evasive on this issue in sharp contrast to the heated academic debate. Moreover, they have not yet notified the Commission about the KUG but merely the state laws in Germany on press privilege pursuant to Art. 85 (3) GDPR.[259]

The expanded territorial applicability of the GDPR is problematic. Stemming from the political imperative anchored in the Charter, the EU data protection law is purported to permeate legal orders worldwide with the influence of the EU (market).[260] This goal premises that data controllers/processors are located or represented in the EU. When models are represented by themselves instead of agencies and cooperate with foreign companies outside the EU, the GDPR faces significant implementation difficulties. Though a teleological reduction of Art. 3 (2) GDPR is forwarded

258 For instance, *Bienemann*, Reformbedarf des Kunsturhebergesetzes im digitalen Zeitalter, S. 71f.; *Lauber-Rönsberg*, AfP, 2019, 373 (377); *Krüger and Wiencke*, MMR, 2019, 76 (78); *Ziebarth and Elsaß*, ZUM, 2018, 578 (581f.); *Lauber-Rönsberg and Hartlaub*, NJW, 2017, 1057 (1062); *Specht*, MMR, 2017, 577.

259 EU Member States notifications to the European Commission under the GDPR, see „Notifizierungspflichtige Vorschriften Deutschlands gemäß der Verordnung (EU) 2016/679 des Europäischen Parlaments und des Rates vom 27. April 2016 zum Schutz natürlicher Personen bei der Verarbeitung personenbezogener Daten, zum freien Datenverkehr und zur Aufhebung der Richtlinie 95/46/EG (Datenschutz-Grundverordnung) Gesetze des Bundes", at https://ec.europa.eu/info/sites/default/files/de_notification_articles_49.5_51.4_83.9_84.2_85.3_88.3_90.2_publish.pdf.

260 Reidenberg, 52 STAN. L. REV. 1315 (2000) (1347).

when an offshore company concludes a one-time contract with one certain data subject in the EU, it does not prejudice the general applicability of the GDPR in merchandising because these are rare cases as models are usually represented by local agencies which account for the responsibilities assigned by the GDPR.

Moreover, merchandising – using one's likeness to influence consumers' decisions via image-transfer or attention-grabbing – does not fall under the scope of Art. 85 (2) GDPR because neither is it intended to nor factually does it contribute to a debate of general interest in society or aesthetical expression.[261] The controversy around the nature of Art. 85 (1) GDPR may bring some problems for the application of the GDPR in merchandising, but they are dealt with late. Therefore, the GDPR takes precedence over the KUG in merchandising due to the primacy of the EU law.

3. *Unauthorized merchandising under the GDPR*

3.1 The unlawfulness of unauthorized merchandising cases under the GDPR

3.1.1 Applying Art. 6 (1) (f) GDPR in unauthorized merchandising cases

(1) The principle of accountability regarding the "test grid" of Art. 6 (1) (f) GDPR

Before starting the analysis of the substance of Art. 6 (1) (f) GDPR, the principle of accountability proclaimed in Art. 5 (2) GDPR must be mentioned first. It consolidates two requests for data controllers. They shall not only be held responsible for fulfilling the GDPR-compliance obligations but, more importantly, be able to demonstrate that they have fulfilled the obligations.[262] As failure to comply with the principle leads to an upgraded administrative penalty according to Art. 83 (5) (a) GDPR, the principle raises the awareness (and cost) of compliance for data controllers and reduces the burden on oversight authorities.[263] In addition, controllers bear (civil) liability if "it is not in any way responsible for the event giving rise to the damage" (Art. 82 (3) GDPR). It is hence necessary for them to keep

261 *Tavanti*, RDV, 2016, 295 (233).
262 Vgl. Herbst, in *Kühling/Buchner*, DSGVO/BDSG, Art. 5 Rn. 77.
263 Vgl. Schantz, in *Brink/Wolff*, BeckOK Datenschutzrecht, Art. 5 Rn. 38-39.

proper documentation regarding data processing. Against this backdrop, controllers in unauthorized merchandising cases must demonstrate the lawfulness of data processing before or at least at the timepoint they begin to process the personal data according to the principle of accountability. Otherwise, even if their processing is legal, they may still face administrative penalties.

One may wonder how far the controller should go to demonstrate its compliance because, unlike consent, the GDPR does not specify the conditions for other legitimate grounds in Art. 6 (1) GDPR. The risk-based approach may be relevant here in assessing the burden of proof. The greater the impact of data processing on the rights and freedoms of the data subject, the more careful and cautious the controller should be in weighing interests in light of Art. 24 GDPR. It also echoes the requirement of the GDPR that the controller shall hire professionals to weigh the interests of both parties if data processing poses significant risks.[264] In this sense, if the data processing is rather conventional and brings minor risks on the rights and freedoms of the data subject, such as the bakery in the corner issuing membership cards, it may be sufficient for the controller to demonstrate that he has recognized the impinged rights and freedoms of the data subject, but the legitimate interest he pursued prevails. Although it appears from the wording of Art. 6 (1) (f) GDPR that the data subject should demonstrate that his or her interest overwhelms, but according to the principle of accountability and the wording of Art. 21 (1) GDPR,[265] the mainstream opinion still holds that the controller must provide documentation about the balancing of interests.[266]

Art. 6 (1) GDPR requires that data controllers must have a lawful ground to process personal data. The most relevant one in unauthorized merchandising cases is the alternative (f) since the data subject (the person depicted) has not given consent. Art. 6 (1) (f) GDPR reads,

---

264 Art. 37-39 GDPR require data controllers to designate a data protection officer to, for instance, monitor compliance with this Regulation in some events.

265 If the lawful ground for processing is Art. 6 (1) (f) GDPR, Art. 21 (1) GDPR obliges the controller to stop processing when the data subject claims the right to object, "unless **the controller demonstrates** compelling legitimate grounds for the processing which override the interests, rights and freedoms of the data subject" (stressed by the author).

266 See Schantz, in *Simitis, et al.*, Datenschutzrecht, Art. 6 Rn. 87; *Robrahn and Bremert*, ZD, 2018, 291 (294); *Voigt and Bussche,* The EU General Data Protection Regulation (GDPR): A Practical Guide, 31.

processing is necessary for the purposes of the legitimate interests pursued by the controller or by a third party, except where such interests are overridden by the interests or fundamental rights and freedoms of the data subject which require protection of personal data, in particular where the data subject is a child.

It provides a "test grid" (*Prüfraster*) that contains three cumulative conditions for lawful data processing:

1) legitimate interests pursued by the controller or by a third party through the processing of personal data, and
2) the necessity between the processing and the pursuit of the legitimate interests, and
3) legitimate interests in (1) outweighing the interests or fundamental rights and freedoms of the data subject harmed by data processing.

It is largely agreed upon in literature and courts that the legitimate interests of controllers should be widely understood in light of recital 47 of the GDPR and the working papers of the WP29.[267] The commercial interests in promoting business pursued by merchandisers are protected by the fundamental freedom to conduct a business anchored in Art. 16 of the Charter and partially by the freedom to choose an occupation and right to engage in work in Art. 15 of the Charter. These interests are generally legitimate under the GDPR.[268]

Admittedly, public figures may contain some information that is interesting to the public. The "infotainment" is also covered by the freedom of expression irrespective of editorial control,[269] as who would not be interested to see Naomi Campbell's popping out to the shops for a bottle of milk,[270] to know celebrities' lifestyles,[271] or to judge the solidarity between members of royal families.[272] After all, deeming the curiosity about

267 See WP29, Opinion 06/2014 on the notion of legitimate interests of the data controller under Article 7 of Directive 95/46/EC, WP 217, 844/14/EN, 25-26.

268 Vgl. Ehmann, in *Simitis, et al.*, Datenschutzrecht, Anhang 3 zu Art. 6 Rn. 25.

269 BVerfG, GRUR 2000, 446 - Caroline von Monaco II, para. 58; BVerfG, NJW 2001, 1921 - Prinz Ernst August von Hannover, the 4th Guideline; BVerfG, NJW 2006, 2836 - Luftaufnahmen von Prominentenvillen II.

270 Naomi Campbell v MGN Limited House of Lords, 6 May 2004 [2004] UKHL 22, para. 154.

271 BGH, GRUR 2007, 527 - Winterurlaub, para. 26; BGH, GRUR 2009, 584 - Enkel von Fürst Rainier; BGH, GRUR 2008, 1024 - Shopping mit der Putzfrau auf Mallorca, para. 20; ECtHR, Zu Guttenberg v. Germany, Application No. 14047/16, para. 13,

272 BGH, GRUR 2007, 523 - Abgestuftes Schutzkonzept I, para. 14.

celebrities' privacy inferior seems rather condescending.[273] However, informational value lacks in merchandising cases because controllers neither make contribution to a debate on matters of general interest nor intend to.[274]

(2) The necessity between data processing and the pursuit of the interests

The term "necessary" in Art. 6 (1) (f) GDPR deserves more attention since it is one of the gatekeepers to prevent the balancing of interest from becoming an "argumentative Façade" for data controllers.[275] Stemming from the principle of data minimization in Art. 5 (1) (b) GDPR and the jurisprudence of the CJEU, the majority opinion in the literature understands the term "necessary" as no less intensive data processing possible to achieve the legitimate interests to a similar extent.[276] In this wise, one must scrutinize the contents, means, and duration of the specific processing operations.

From a practical perspective, identification is the key to image transfer or attention grabbing in celebrity merchandising. In addition, dentification of ordinary people is also necessary for in users' merchandising that enables the advertising to spread in a ripple pattern and possibly go viral via interactions with "friends". Moreover, there is no need to distinct celebrity merchandising from users' merchandising in assessing the necessity in Art. 6 (1) (f) GDPR. The emergence of internet influencers whose job is to make other people interested in their images and thus influence followers' patterns of consumption,[277] blurs the distinction between celebrities and non-celebrities to some extent as many microcelebrities are

273 ECtHR, von Hannover v Germany (no 2), Application No. 40660/08 and 60641/08, § 109; Vgl. *Ohly*, GRUR Int, 2004, 902 (911).

274 ECtHR, von Hannover v Germany (no 2), Application No. 40660/08 and 60641/08, § 109, with further references.

275 Frenzel, in *Paal and Pauly*, DS-GVO BDSG, Art. 6 Rn. 26.

276 Recital 39 of the GDPR; CJEU, Volker und Markus Schecke, Joined Cases C-92/09 and C-93/09, para. 74, 76, 77; CJEU, Digital Rights Ireland and Others, Joined Cases C-293/12 and C-594/12, para. 56; Roßnagel, Pfitzmann and Garstka, Modernisierung des Datenschutzrechts, 2001, S. 101; *Roßnagel*, ZD, 2018, 339 (344); *Robrahn and Bremert*, ZD, 2018, 291 (292); Plath, in *Plath*, DSG-VO/BDSG, Art. 6 Rn. 17, 56; Buchner/Petri, in *Kühling/Buchner*, DSGVO/BDSG, Art. 6 Rn. 147a.

277 OLG München, 25.6.2020 – 29 U 2333/19 - Blauer Plüschelefant, 1. Guideline.

active online.[278] There are too many factors to assess publicity, such as the number of followers, the degree of internet influences' liquidity, and the impact of the platform. After all, it is not only impractical but also presents an antiquated understanding of merchandising in the online environment.

More importantly, by denying the necessity in merchandising cases from the outset, pictures on the internet for commercial interests would need to be pixeled in general unless controllers have obtained consent of the data subjects or a public interest according to Art. 6 (1) (e) GDPR exists. Consent would be inflated.[279] It would behoove controllers to obtain blanket consent from data subjects for any subsequent processing to avoid violation of the GDPR.[280] A more liberal proposition is argued in merchandising cases that public exposures of clearly identifiable photos/videos are usually necessary to promoting and advertising one's legitimate business. It does not mean that the court's conclusion that consent must be obtained for ads involving ordinary people is incorrect. Rather, the lawfulness of data processing in the case should not be rejected at the requirement of necessity.

(3) The interfered interests of data subjects

The interests or fundamental rights and freedoms of data subjects must also be understood broadly to ensure a high level of data protection for data subjects (recital 6 GDPR).[281] Possible interfered interests, rights and

278 Microcelebrities are "ordinary Internet users who accumulate a relatively large following on blogs and social media through the textual and visual narration of their personal lives and lifestyles……and monetize their following by integrating "advertorials" into their blogs or social media posts and making physical paid-guest appearances at events." See Abidin, 2 Social Media + Society 3 (2016).

279 Vgl. *Engeler*, PinG, 2019, 149 (152).

280 Thinking about the emails sent by LinkedIn, Instagram, and so on, they all use their users' images and names for promotion and advertainments. This practice is in fact appalling to many users even though it appears that they have given their consent. See lawsuits in this regard, Fraley v. Facebook, Inc. 830 F. Supp. 2d 785, 808 (N.D. Cal. 2011); Perkins v. LinkedIn Corp. 53 F. Supp. 3d 1190 (2014); Parker v. Hey, Inc. Case No. CGC-17-556257, 2017 Cal. Super. LEXIS 609. Given the fact that people usually give their consent without reading the terms due to limited capacity of time and cognition, and other structural problems. Without citing many, see Solove, 126 Harvard Law Review 1880 (2013), 1883-1889.

281 Schantz, in *Simitis, et al.*, Datenschutzrecht, Art. 6 Rn. 101.

freedoms in unauthorized merchandising are the data subject's fundamental rights to privacy according to Art. 7 of the Charter and Art. 8 ECHR as a result of exposure (*die Bloßstellung*) to the public,[282] and the right to the protection of personal data enshrined in Art. 8 of the Charter as the control of the data subject over personal data would be essentially deprived.[283] Moreover, it is uncontested that celebrities' images have substantial goodwill if they participate personally in merchandising business.[284] Thus, the commercial interests embodied in their icons should also be protected by the fundamental freedom to conduct a business anchored in Art. 16 of the Charter.

Therefore, even though the privacy of celebrities is not interfered with by merchandising, the commercial interests embedded in their control over images can be included t into the equation that awaits balancing against the commercial interests pursued by the controller.

(4) The balancing of conflicting interests

Some constructive methods for interests-balancing have been proposed in literature.[285] The distilled guideline is that the more interests and rights in terms of quantity and quality are impaired by data processing, the more substantial the legitimate interests pursued by the controller must be to sustain the processing.[286] More specifically, one should apply an overall assessment by taking the expressive contents of the personal data, the nature of the data controller, the purpose, means, consequences as well as

282 Nemitz, in *Ehmann and Selmayr*, DS-GVO, Art. 82 Rn. 13; See, *Bieker and Bremert*, ZD, 2020, 7 (10).

283 Schantz, in *Simitis, et al.*, Datenschutzrecht, Art. 6 Rn. 101.

284 Goodwill is presented when a distinctive connection between the goods or services provided by the depicted person and his or her indicia has been established in the mind of the purchasing public. See Robyn Rihanna Fenty v Arcadia Group Brands Ltd (T/A Topshop) [2015] EWCA Civ 3.

285 For instance, *Bieker* and *Bremert* made contributions to identifying the fundamental rights and freedoms of individuals that may be hindered and threatened at different stages of data processing, and how the risks manifest. See *Bieker and Bremert*, ZD, 2020, 7 (8); *Herfurth* forwarded a "3x5 – model" in the form of a matrix that comprehensively lists 15 essential criteria for measuring the riskiness of data processing operations. See *Herfurth*, ZD, 2018, 514 (515).

286 See *Herfurth*, ZD, 2018, 514 (515); See Schantz, in *Simitis, et al.*, Datenschutzrecht, Art. 6 Rn. 105f.

the impacts of the processing into account. Among the factors, the means and purpose of the data processing are foremost important.[287]

In addition, it must examine the role played by online communication as to whether it establishes a "more or less detailed profile" of the data subject,[288] or leads to *de facto* uncontrollability and incalculably high risk of recombination and long-term storage of personal data as *VG Hannover* stressed.[289]

On the one hand, Internet communication allows information to spread faster and wider. At almost zero-cost, information can be accessed, copied, extracted (from the original context), redistributed and stored. It is almost impossible for data subjects to make information that is already on the web disappear.[290] As the BVerfG proposed almost half a century ago, unlimited use, and storage of personal data posed high risks of profiling and making everyone a "hollow man" based on the construction of integrated information systems (*Aufbau integrierter Informationssysteme*).[291] On the other hand, risks posed by data technologies such as big data must be distinguished from the ones brought up by the internet as a means of communication.[292] If the view adopted by the *VG Hannover* is followed, then risk impact assessments and other higher requirements in the GDPR would become a routine for controllers who use the internet as a mean of communication. Consequently, risk impact assessments would be reduced to a dead letter because the risks posed by the Internet are abstract and general,[293] and most data controllers would shed online communication because of the high cost of compliance.

Thus, the internet can quantitatively magnify the impact on the rights and freedoms of data subjects but not necessarily triggers the so-called big

---

287 Buchner/Petri, in *Kühling/Buchner*, DSGVO/BDSG, Art. 6 Rn. 152.

288 See CJEU, Google Spain, C-131/12, para. 37.

289 Ibid., para. 87; BGH, GRUR 2014, 1228 - Ärztebewertungsportal, para.40; BVerfG, GRUR 2020, 74 - Recht auf Vergessen I, para. 147; VG Hannover, 27.11.2019 - 10 A 820/19 - Fanpage einer Partei bei Facebook, para. 36; Schantz, in *Simitis, et al.*, Datenschutzrecht, Art. 6 Rn. 107.

290 Not only is the effectiveness of de-searching results limited to the EU (CJEU, Google LLC v CNIL, C-507/17), but the media blitz would also make it more likely that what the data subject wants to be forgotten remains in the web forever.

291 BVerfG, NJW 1984, 419 - Volkszählung, para. 159.

292 Ibid., para. 91.

293 BVerfG, GRUR 2020, 74 - Recht auf Vergessen I, para. 104.

data risks for data subjects.[294] This understanding is also in the line with the CJEU. In both the *Google Spain* case and *GC* case, the Court found the structured overview of one's information enabled by the list of results based on name searches, instead of the online communication, particularly risky for the freedoms and rights of individuals because it can thereby "establish a more or less detailed profile of him."[295] Therefore, the CJEU's argument in the *Google Spain* case that the commercial interests of data controllers are generally inferior to the right of privacy and the right to the protection of personal data of data subjects cannot be directly applied here because that case was involved with an additional risk for a "more and less detailed profile" of the data subject.

As the notion of "reasonable expectations" adopted by the GDPR requires a mixed subjective and objective standard,[296] it invites an evaluation from the social perspective that enables a certain margin of appreciation for the Member States in this regard.[297] Noteworthy, the "reasonable expectations" in the GDPR has to be differentiated from the notion "reasonable expectation of privacy" referred by the ECtHR in a series of privacy cases.[298] Whereas the latter serves to delineate the protective scope of Art. 8 ECHR from the public sphere,[299] the GDPR's notion is merely one criterion to weigh against the interests pursued by the data controller.[300]

---

294 OLG München, NJW 1982, 244 - Löschung von Negativmerkmalen einer Kartei, 245.

295 CJEU, Google Spain, C-131/12, para. 35; CJEU, GC and Others, C-136/17, para. 36.

296 Schulz, in *Gola,* DSGVO, Art. 6 Rn. 57; *Tavanti*, RDV, 2016, 295 (299).

297 Vgl. Schantz, in *Simitis, et al.*, Datenschutzrecht, Art. 6 Rn. 108.

298 See ECtHR, von Hannover v. Germany, Application No. 59320/00, para. 51; ECtHR, Halford v. the United Kingdom, Application No. 20605/92, para. 45. This consideration is also valid in the German judiciary. See BGH, GRUR 2021, 100 - Bildberichterstattung über ein Scheidungsverfahren. The plaintiff has been photographed during her divorce lawsuit in front of the court building. The BGH relied on the term "the reasonable expectation of privacy" to argue for the protection of personality rights.

299 See the concurring opinions of Judge Cabral Barreto and Judge Zupančič in the case of ECtHR, von Hannover v. Germany, Application No. 59320/00; ECtHR, Copland v the United Kingdom, Application no. 62617/00, para. 42; ECtHR, Peev v. Bulgaria, Application no. 64209/01, para. 37 et seq.

300 The 4th sentence of recital 47 of the GDPR, "[a]t any rate the existence of a legitimate interest would need careful assessment including whether a data subject can reasonably expect at the time and in the context of the collection of the personal data that processing for that purpose may take place"; WP29,

In balancing the interests specified above, courts could argue through a "German lens" (*Deutsche Brille*)[301] by using the notion of "reasonable expectations" to introduce the national law. In merchandising, the German judiciary has been reinforcing the perception that merchandising requires permission from the person depicted irrespective of his or her social role ever since the *Paul Dahlke* case. This practice not only shapes the commercial practice of merchandising but also profoundly affects the "reasonable expectations" of the German people and the public. Consequently, a data subject should not reasonably expect that his or her data would be processed for advertising purposes if a contractual relationship between him/her and the controller is absent. This conclusion raises a weighty indication that the interests of the data subject outweigh the legitimate interests of the controller.[302]

Thus, one can reasonably argue that the interests, and rights of data subjects in unauthorized merchandising cases in general outweigh the data controller's legitimate advertising interests in accord with the reasonable exceptions of data subjects irrespective of their social roles. As some German courts have already dealt with merchandising under the GDPR, it is imperative to review the judgments and the new "harmony approach" adopted by courts.

3.1.2 Case analysis of Art. 6 (1) (f) GDPR

(1) Evaluation of the German decisions

i. Lack of legal basis

After the GDPR came effective, German courts have already delivered some judgments about merchandising cases but surprisingly, they have not referred any cases to the CJEU yet.[303] Noteworthy, the courts have developed a quasi "harmony approach", i.e., since the result of applying

Opinion 06/2014 on the notion of legitimate interests of the data controller under Article 7 of Directive 95/46/EC, WP 217, 844/14/EN, 33, 40, 60 and 63.

301 *Kühling*, NJW, 2020, 275 (278).

302 Vgl. Heberlein, in *Ehmann and Selmayr*, DS-GVO, Art. 6 Rn. 28; Albers/Veit, in *Brink/Wolff*, BeckOK Datenschutzrecht, Art. 6 Rn. 53.

303 OVG Niedersachsen, MMR 2021, 593 - Veröffentlichung eines Fotos auf einer Facebook Fanpage; LG Frankfurt am Main, 3.09.2018 - 2-03 O 283/18 - Friseursalon,.

§§ 22 and 23 KUG would be the same as the application of Art. 6 (1) (f) GDPR there is no need to solve the concurrence issue of the KUG and the GDPR. However, this approach is questionable in many respects.

Above all, the direct application of §§ 22 and 23 KUG is only permissible if the GDPR allows the Member States to make derogations or exemptions from the GDPR in scenarios regarding commercial data processing. In these cases, while the courts admitted that merchandising was not covered by Art. 85 (2) GDPR, they applied §§ 22 and 23 KUG directly without stating any legal basis. Though Art. 85 (1) GDPR could arguably be an independent opening clause that would delegate competence to the Member States, the courts left this controversy open.[304] Therefore, the courts implied Art. 85 (1) GDPR as an independent opening clause without giving any conclusive opinion.[305] As it is not *acte clair*, the validity of this premise should be brought up to the CJEU. In any case, it is not appropriate to imply the application of Art. 85 (1) GDPR vaguely as now.

ii. Some main requirements in the GDPR omitted

Some main requirements in the GDPR were left out in the judgments because the courts mainly relied on the KUG. For instance, the requirement of the GDPR for the controller to demonstrate that he has fulfilled the obligations according to Art. 6 (1) (f) GDPR was fully omitted by the court in the *hair salon* case.[306] Furthermore, the review of the "test grid" stipulated in Art. 6 (1) (f) GDPR is overly simplistic as the court resorted to the German jurisprudence on the KUG in balancing the conflicting interests, even though it later stated that this analysis could provide effective assistance in understanding Art. 6 (1) (f) GDPR. For instance, the court jumped to the conclusion that the fundamental rights and freedoms of the data subject outweighed the interests of the data controller, and thus the processing was unlawful only after its examination of the unlawfulness of the publication under the German legal regime.[307]

---

304 OVG Niedersachsen, MMR 2021, 593 - Veröffentlichung eines Fotos auf einer Facebook Fanpage, Rn. 42f.; LG Frankfurt am Main, 3.09.2018 - 2-03 O 283/18 - Friseursalon, para. 30.

305 The same conclusion, see *Jangl*, ZUM, 2021, 103 (106).

306 LG Frankfurt am Main, 3.09.2018 - 2-03 O 283/18 - Friseursalon.

307 The court argued that, on the one hand, the video clip did not belong to contemporary history and probably with some privacy implications, and on the

iii. Inaccurate understanding of the terminology in the GDPR

Because of the over-reliance on the case law of the KUG, courts lacked the incentive to adopt and learn the GDPR's narrative. Some understandings of the terminology in the GDPR is inaccurate, such as the direct marketing purpose and the necessity between the data processing and the purposes. More importantly, the rights and civil remedies prescribed in the GDPR were completely ignored, even though the courts validated the unlawfulness of the data processing under the GDPR. Only the injunctive relief according to §§ 823 and 1004 BGB were confirmed.[308]

For instance, *VG Hannover* in a case concerning advertising on a fan page considered that a less intrusive means existed for merchandising purposes, i.e., pixilation or a mosaic depiction of one's facial features.[309] A possible reason might be that blurring of the data subject in the advertisement would not dismiss its authenticity or creditability. However, this idea is objectionable in several aspects as argued in Section 3.1.1 (2). The main flaw of the court's argument is that it did not compare the data processing with the subjective purpose of the controller in the case but rather assumed an objective purpose instead. This renders this conclusion conservative. Both the *VG Hannover* and its higher instance probably recognized the weakness of this argument by not stopping here but discussing the balancing of interests further.[310]

---

other, the publication was in a purely commercial context, which rendered the consent of the person depicted indispensable. Ibid., para. 57.

308 It can be argued that plaintiffs only claimed remedies in the BGB against the unlawful data processing, so the court did not need to review the rights under the GDPR, such as the right to information. However, *Hoeren* suggests that an elaboration for the right to information and its exception would be needed because the court tried to argue that the consent, even if existed, was invalid since the obligation to inform the data subject has not been fully fulfilled. See *Hoeren*, ZD, 2018, 587 (588).

309 In that case, a member of a political party published several meeting photos on his fan page on Facebook to promote the achievements of his party in local affairs. In some photos of the gathering, the data subjects could be identified and thus sought help from the local DPA to ask that member of the political party (the data controller) to remove the photos. The *VG Hannover* has addressed that the identification of the data subjects was not necessary for the promotional purposes pursued by the controller. See VG Hannover, 27.11.2019 - 10 A 820/19 - Fanpage einer Partei bei Facebook, para. 50.

310 Ibid., para. 51f.; OVG Niedersachsen, MMR 2021, 593 - Veröffentlichung eines Fotos auf einer Facebook Fanpage, para. 27f.

In addition, the court in the *hair salon* case wrongfully qualified the data processing by the hair salon as direct marketing. Consequently, the impinged interests and rights of the data subject, and eventually, the balance between the countervalues from both sides, were incorrect. Direct marketing describes a series of means of marketing that directly communicates with customers who have been selected in advance.[311] In other words, it focuses on the relationship between the advertising company and the targeted consumers, whose preferences and behaviors are generally tracked and profiled via cookies, like-buttons on social platforms, etc.[312] Thus, the GDPR attaches great importance to the impact and threat of direct marketing on the rights and freedoms of data subjects and obliges data controllers an unconditional duty to stop processing for direct marketing when the data subject claims the right to object in Art. 21 (2) and (3) GDPR.[313] However, in the *hair salon* case, the dispute revolved around the advertiser and the person depicted instead of being targeted by the advertising. Although the advertisement on the company's fan page enabled the company to directly communicate with customers who have already "befriended" the company, it was merchandising instead of direct marketing.

Therefore, it was incorrect for the court to argue that the interest pursued by the controller was legitimate because the data processing was direct marketing with reference to recital 47 of the GDPR. A more detrimental result was that this incorrect qualification unduly exaggerated the impact of typical merchandising for the data subject because it fabricated the risks triggered by tracking and profiling. It would further exert influence on the balance of interests required by Art. 6 (1) (f) GDPR. Practically, the wrong qualification for direct marketing would also lead to a peculiar consequence. The data controller who chooses the Internet

311 The definition of direct marketing, see *Dallmer,* in: *Dallmer, Das Handbuch Direct Marketing & More*, S. 7-8.

312 Recitals 41, 42, 43,45, Art. 13 (1), (2) and (4) of the ePrivacy Directive; Art. 4 (3) (f) and recital 32 of the Proposal for the ePrivacy Regulation; Vgl. Ehmann, in *Simitis, et al.,* Datenschutzrecht, Anhang 3 zu Art. 6 Rn. 18; Also in this direction, Martini, in *Paal and Pauly,* DS-GVO BDSG, Art. 21 Rn .47ff. It excludes the online display of advertisements; Vgl. *Barth,* Der Kampf um die Werbung im Internet, S. 208.

313 While Art. 21 (1) GDPR requires other indicators such as balancing of interests or "profiling" to sustain an objection, Art. 21 (2) states that "the data subject shall have the right to object at any time" to direct marketing. Vgl. *Spindler/ Schuster,* Recht der elektronischen Medien, Art. 21 Rn. 4 and 9.

as the communication tool must cease the advertisements immediately as the data subject claims the right to object according to Art. 21 (3) GDPR, whereas the controller who uses television/magazine – the seemingly outdated communication tools – does not have to.

Moreover, the court did not explain the term "necessary" either.[314] Since the court misidentified the interest pursued by the controller in the case, the measurement of necessity between its operations and the pursuit of the legitimate interest would be incorrect either. However, according to the court's logic, the court should not be skeptical about the requirement of necessity as the hair salon processed the plaintiff's data for direct marketing. As argued by some scholars, in pursuit of direct marketing, obtaining the addresses of customers (data subjects), be them physical or online, are necessary, while other personal indicia, such as age, sex, and consumer preference would be arguable.[315] Following this line, processing of data subjects' likenesses for publicity was completely unnecessary for direct marketing. Thus, the assessment of the court should stop here because the conditions prescribed in Art. 6 (1) (f) GDPR are cumulative.

Without specifying the infringed interests or fundamental rights and freedoms of the data subject, the court simply relied upon the notion of "reasonable expectations" in recital 47 of the GDPR to argue that the interests of the data subject outweighed those of the controller. It seems convincing that "it is contrary to the reasonable expectations of a customer in a hair salon that the visit is recorded and used for advertising on the internet".[316] However, the court seemed to misconstrue the "reasonable expectations" in the GDPR and the notion "reasonable expectation of privacy" referred by the ECtHR.

All in all, the approach adopted by German courts in applying Art. 6 (1) (f) GDPR to merchandising cases has some critical flaws besides its lack of justification. The overlooked principle of accountability, the wrongful understanding of direct marketing, and the overly abbreviated application of Art. 6 (1) (f) GDPR intertwined with too many national initiatives increase the risk of being challenged by the CJEU significantly. In other words, using the GDPR's narrative in applying it should be borne in mind to preclude forming a self-contained German system.

---

314 LG Frankfurt am Main, 3.09.2018 - 2-03 O 283/18 - Friseursalon, para. 58.

315 Vgl. Ehmann, in *Simitis, et al.*, Datenschutzrecht, Anhang 3 zu Art. 6 Rn. 29.

316 LG Frankfurt am Main, 3.09.2018 - 2-03 O 283/18 - Friseursalon, para. 58.

(2) To apply Art. 6 (1) (f) GDPR rightfully

Case studies of Art. 6 (1) (f) GDPR present here to make the comparison between the regulation of the GDPR and the German legal regime in merchandising more vivid and concrete.

At the outset, the court should examine whether the controller has provided documentation to prove that he has properly followed the "test grid" of Art. 6 (1) (f) GDPR to demonstrate the lawfulness of its data processing. An omission of this obligation would constitute a violation of the principle of accountability in Art. 5 (2) GDPR and lead to fines. In this wise, before data processing, the controller has to list the legitimate interest in advertising his business, and the interests, rights and freedom of the data subject, which were likely to be harmed by the data processing. Then, he should weigh the conflicting interests and demonstrate that his legitimate interests prevail. In the *clickbait* case, it could be argued that as the controller believed that certain public interests in knowing the information existed in addition to the commercial interest, he was convinced that the data processing was legitimate according to Art. 6 (1) (f) GDPR.

Against this background, one can focus on the substantial issues regarding Art. 6 (1) (f) GDPR. After denying the public interests of the clickbait, it is recommended for the court to specify the impinged interests and rights of the data subject due to the processing. While the control over personal data was deprived by the unlawful data processing, damages resulting in intrusions into privacy were not visible in this case. The *hair salon* case needs to be mentioned here for comparison. On the contrary, ideal interests like the mental distress suffered by the long-term display of the video online and the intrusion into privacy were prominent whereas commercial interests were not mentioned by the data subject.[317] This difference may make an impact on the remedies. These interests, as argued above, should be considered in balancing the interests, or precisely, to examine the weighing of interests conducted on the initiative of the data controller.

Noteworthy, unlike direct marketing, making advertainments online available does not amount to a game-changer that introduces a different or upgraded form of personality infringement. While the commercial purpose and online communication for merchandising do not have an impact on the data subject as significant as other purposes such as profiling and

---

317 One could also argue that the data subject was embarrassed by the fact of having hair extended, but the data subject did not address this issue.

scoring, the right to the protection for personal data enshrined in Art. 8 of the Charter is infringed not insignificantly since the data subjects were deprived of control over personal data and the informational self-determination from the outset. In other words, online communication was able to cause quantitative, not qualitative changes compared to merchandising in TV or magazines in both cases. Thus, the main competing values in the *hair salon* case were commercial interests in promoting the business on the one side,[318] and the rights to privacy according to Art. 7 of the Charter and Art. 8 ECHR, and the right to the protection for personal data enshrined in Art. 8 of the Charter on the other side. In the *clickbait* case, the most impinged right was the right to informational self-determination regarding the commercial interests in personal data.

Moreover, against the prevalent new logic of merchandising in social platforms, identifying ordinary people is necessary for advertisers who would like to make customers become advertisers. The necessity of being identified is unequivocally clear in the *clickbait* case. In balancing the interests, the German jurisprudence in merchandising scenarios is referential as the "reasonable expectations" of the data subjects mandates. In the *hair salon* case, by comparing the "reasonable expectations" of a consumer for having a service in a hair salon with the fact in the case, one can argue that the privacy of the data subject has been largely invaded according to the theory of sphere (*die Sphärentheorie*). It thus triggered *prima facie* protection against intrusion since having a hair extension is normally a private matter for a person.[319] Nevertheless, this case reminds one of users' merchandising on social platforms. As ordinary internet users are increasingly participating in exploiting their likenesses to promote or endorse local bistros or public events, it is possible that data subjects would not feel mentally disturbed by such merchandising. In other words, data subjects' "reasonable expectations" are prone to changes over time. It motivates one to wonder whether data subjects in similar cases to the *hair salon* case would increasingly become like the moderator in the *clickbait* case. Nevertheless, it would not compromise the argument's validity here in light of the "reasonable expectations" of the data subject because they would expect to be compensated from merchandising.

---

318 It could be argued that the video clip in the *hair salon* case might have some informational value if it shared some knowledge about hair extension. However, it was not obvious in the case.

319 Götting, in *Götting/Schertz/Seitz*, Handbuch Persönlichkeitsrecht, § 1 Rn. 5; For an elaboration about the theory of sphere see *Degenhart*, JuS, 1992, 361.

Therefore, the data processing in the *hair salon* case and the *clickbait* case were both unlawful in strict accordance with the GDPR. It is consistent with the conclusion of the previous analysis of the framework of Art. 6 (1) (f) GDPR in unauthorized merchandising in general.

3.2 Civil damages under the GDPR

3.2.1 Art. 82 GDPR as the legal basis

(1) Statutory conditions and contested application in Germany

Given the primacy of EU law, Art. 82 GDPR that mandates an independent civil liability for data controllers (and processors) based on violations against GDPR's provisions shall directly apply in the Member States.[320] According to its first paragraph,[321] infringement, material or non-material damages, and the causality between the infringement and damages are the conditions to sustain a claim.[322] It is uniformly agreed that infringements refer not only to violations of the legality of data processing (Art. 6 and 9 GDPR) but also the principles, the data subject's rights, and the obligations of data controllers, etc.[323]

The German judiciary seems to reach the consensus that damages under the GDPR should be broadly interpreted including "discrimination, identity theft or fraud, financial loss, damage to the reputation, loss of confidentiality of personal data protected by professional secrecy, unauthorized reversal of pseudonymization, or any other significant economic or social disadvantage" (recital 75 GDPR). Material damages refer not only to the loss of property but also to the loss of interests with property value, for instance, non-employment due to false information, credit or insurance

320 LG Karlsruhe, 02.08.2019 - 8 O 26/19 - Negative Bonitätsscore in Wirtschaftsauskunftei, para. 20; ArbG Düsseldorf, NZA-RR 2020, 409 - Unvollständige DSGVO-Auskunft, para. 104; Vgl. Frenzel, in *Paal and Pauly*, DS-GVO BDSG, Art. 82 Rn. 1; Boehm, in *Simitis, et al.*, Datenschutzrecht, Art. 82 Rn. 1.

321 "Any person who has suffered material or non-material damage as a result of an infringement of this Regulation shall have the right to receive compensation from the controller or processor for the damage suffered."

322 Vgl. Nemitz, in *Ehmann and Selmayr*, DS-GVO, Art. 82 Rn. 7; Becher, in *Plath*, DSGVO/BDSG, Art. 82 Rn. 4.

323 Instead to cite many, see Boehm, in *Simitis, et al.*, Datenschutzrecht, Art. 82 Rn. 10.

agreements with worse conditions.[324] However, in the practice, plaintiffs are more inclined to claim for immaterial damages instead of material ones.[325] It is controversial whether fictive license fees can be deployed to compute the actual loss suffered by data subjects when their data have been exploited unlawfully by controllers.[326] While some scholars are in favor of this proposition as the commercial interests of personal data become prominent, and data subjects can benefit from these,[327] the German judiciary is equivocal in this regard.[328] In a case concerning account blocking on Facebook, the plaintiff claimed a fictive license fee as Facebook blocked her account while keeping pushing ads.[329] In her arguments, Facebook should compensate her with at least a portion of the revenue from advertising campaigns by using her data when it blocked her account. The *OLG München* rejected this claim by denying the synallagmatic relationship between the provision of services and consent given by the data subject: As Facebook violated neither the GDPR nor its contractual obligations, its use of personal data during the block was lawful.[330]

It is an innovation of the GDPR is to specify immaterial damages in the liability clause.[331] Since recital 146 of the GDPR requires a broad interpretation in terms of damage to ensure that data subjects receive "full and

---

324 See Moos/Schefzig, in *Taeger, Gabel and Arning,* DSGVO - BDSG - TTDSG, Art. 82 Rn 29; Nemitz, in *Ehmann and Selmayr,* DS-GVO, Art. 82 Rn. 17; Laue, in *Laue, Nink and Kremer,* Das neue Datenschutzrecht in der betrieblichen Praxis, § 11 Rn. 5; Gola/Piltz, in *Gola,* DSGVO, Art. 82 Rn. 11; Becker, *Plath,* DSGVO/BDSG, Art. 82 Rn. 4a; Kreße, in *Sydow,* DSGVO: Handkommentar, Art. 82 Rn. 5; Bergt, in *Kühling/Buchner,* DSGVO/BDSG, Art. 82 Rn. 19; *Neun and Lubitzsch,* BB, 2017, 2563 (2567).

325 Material damages for lost profits could be traceable when a loan was denied due to allegedly wrongful data processing. See LG Karlsruhe, 02.08.2019 - 8 O 26/19 - Negative Bonitätsscore in Wirtschaftsauskunftei, para. 18.

326 Nemitz, in *Ehmann and Selmayr,* DS-GVO, Art. 82 Rn. 17; *Herberger,* NZFam, 2021, 1088 (1092); *Strittmatter, Treiterer and Harnos,* CR, 2019, 789 (793-794).

327 *Peitz and Schweitzer,* NJW, 2018, 275; Gola/Piltz, in *Gola,* DSGVO, Art. 82 Rn. 11; Becker, in *Plath,* DSGVO/BDSG, Art. 82 Rn. 4a f. Boehm, in *Simitis, et al.,* Datenschutzrecht, Art. 82 Rn. 28. *Wybitul, et al.,* ZD, 2018, 202 (205); *Paal,* MMR, 2020, 14 (17); *Neun and Lubitzsch,* BB, 2017, 2563 (2567); Kosmides, in *Forgó, Helfrich and Schneider,* Betrieblicher Datenschutz, Teil XIII Rn. 45; *Dickmann,* r+s, 2018, 345 (351-352).

328 See the list of German judgments according to Art. 82 GDPR up to March, 2021, see *Leibold,* ZD-Akutell, 2021, VI.

329 OLG München, GRUR 2021, 1099 - Klarnamenpflicht bei Facebook, para.17f.

330 Ibid., para. 108-110.

331 Spindler, in *Spindler/Schuster,* Recht der elektronischen Medien, Art. 82 Rn. 1.

effective compensation for the damage they have suffered", the literature in Germany presents an attitude towards a more flexible interpretation for moral damages.[332] Courts also waive the German condition for serious mental damages in sustaining a non-material claim based on personality rights when the data subject claims non-material damages pursuant to Art. 82 GDPR.[333] However, the judiciary practice is contested about how specific and substantial the damages should be to get protection. For instance, some courts found the uneasy feeling and a constant state of distress non-material damages as the data subjects lost control over personal data due to data breaches or unlawfully disclosure.[334] In contrast, other courts stated that mere fear of misusing personal data after a data

---

332 Boehm, in *Simitis, et al.,* Datenschutzrecht, Art. 82 Rn. 11; Frenzel, in *Paal and Pauly,* DS-GVO BDSG, Art. 82 Rn. 10; Gola, in *Gola,* DSGVO, Art. 82 Rn. 13; Quaas, in *Brink/Wolff,* BeckOK Datenschutzrecht, Art. 82 Rn. 28; Becher, in *Plath,* DSGVO/BDSG, Art. 82 Rn. 4c; Bergt, in *Kühling/Buchner,* DSGVO/BDSG, Art. 82 Rn. 18a; *Wybitul, Haß and Albrecht*, NJW, 2018, 113 (114); *Klein*, GRUR-Prax, 2020, 433 (434 f.).

333 OLG Köln, 26.03.2020 - 15 U 193/19 - Geldentschädigung Rn. 87; LG Karlsruhe, 09.02.2021 - 4 O 67/20 - Mastercard; LG Landshut, 06.11.2020 - 51 O 513/20 - Anspruch auf Schadensersatz aus Datenschutzverletzungen; LG Mainz, 12.11.2021 - 3 O 12/20 - Schadensersatz wegen falscher Negativmeldung an Wirtschaftsauskunftei; LG Düsseldorf, ZD 2022, 48 - Bloße Verletzung keinen immateriellen Schaden; LG Essen, ZD 2022, 50 - Immaterieller Schaden, Verlust USB-Stick; LG Bonn, ZD 2021, 652 - Lange Wartezeit für Datenauskunft; LG Hamburg, K&R 2020, 769 - Verstoß gegen die DSGVO allein begründet keinen Schadensersatzanspruch; LG Lüneburg, ZD 2021, 275 – Datenübermittlung an Schufa; LG Karlsruhe, 02.08.2019 - 8 O 26/19 - Negative Bonitätsscore in Wirtschaftsauskunftei; AG Pfaffenhofen MMR 2021, 1005, - 300 EUR DSGVO-Schadensersatz für unerlaubte E-Mail; AG Hannover, ZD 2021, 176 (Ls.) - Kein Schadensersatz nach DSGVO für Bagatellverstoß; AG Diez, ZD 2019, 85 - Kein Schadensersatz nach DSGVO bei bloßen Bagatellverstößen.The opposite opinion, see OLG Dresden, MMR 2021, 575 - Posten eines Bilds mit Symbolen einer „Hassorganisation", Rn. 14; A "comparably serious mental damage" required, see LG München I ZD 2022, 52 - Voraussetzungen des Anspruchs auf immateriellen Schadensersatz nach der DSGVO, Rn. 31.

334 Courts recognize the fear of loss of control caused by a data breach or unlawfully disclosure as (moral) damages, see LG Darmstadt, 26.05.2020 - 13 O 244/19 - Schadensersatz wegen fehlgeleiteter Mail mit Bewerberdaten (the defendant inadvertently sent the email containing the plaintiff's non-sensitive personal information in the sense of the GDPR to a wrong recipient); ArbG Lübeck, 20.06.2019 - 1 Ca 538/19 - Mitarbeiterfotos im Facebook (unauthorized use of an employee photo on the company's own Facebook page); ArbG Dresden, 26.08.2020 - 13 Ca 1046/20 - unberechtigte Weitergabe von Gesundheitsdaten durch Arbeitgeber (the defendant unlawfully disclosed the plaintiff's sick leave

breach was either trivial or not concrete enough to sustain a claim.[335] In a case where the name, date of birth, gender, email address, and phone number were lost in the course of a data breach for a MasterCard, the court addressed that risks for identity theft claimed by the plaintiff were abstract and not particularly probable; the court went even further finding that even if the transaction data had been stolen, it would not have had a significant impact since the data only concerned small purchases.[336]

Nevertheless, some parallel practices are discernable in calculating the amount of non-material damages regarding certain violations, for instance, the violation of the obligation to provide information regarding data processing.[337] In two cases, in failing to respond promptly, controllers were required to pay 500 EUR after a month when data subjects claimed for the right of information, and from the 3rd month after the request, the monthly compensation upgraded to 1,000 EUR.[338] Besides, there are some similarities in quantifying the damages resulting from data breaches and failure to delete data in a timely manner. For instance, failure to withdraw photos and information from official websites within a reasonable time after the employee has left the company led to a compensation of 300 EUR.[339] This compensation upgraded to 1,000 EUR when the post

---

time); AG Pforzheim, 25.03.2020 - 13 C 160/19 - Psychotherapeut (a psychotherapist violated the GDPR by disclosing the sensitive data of a patient unlawfully).

335 See AG Frankfurt/Main, 10.07.2020 - 385 C 155/19 (70) - DSGVO-Schadensersatz setzt ernsthaften Verstoß voraus (due to an internal error, the personal data of customers being freely accessible on the Internet); AG Bochum, 11.03.2019 - 65 C 485/18 - Kein Ersatzanspruch nach DSGVO ohne konkreten Schadensnachweis (the defendant sent the judicial appointment document to another individual via unencrypted email); See LG Hamburg, K&R 2020, 769 - Verstoß gegen die DSGVO allein begründet keinen Schadensersatzanspruch (due to an error setting, the plaintiff's reservation information on the defendant's website was made available to the public for approximately 6 weeks).

336 LG Karlsruhe, 09.02.2021 - 4 O 67/20 - Mastercard.

337 It is well argued that inconsistency remains in this respect. See *Franck*, ZD, 2021, 680. This, however, makes the parallel practices more prominent.

338 ArbG Düsseldorf, NZA-RR 2020, 409 - Unvollständige DSGVO-Auskunft, followed by ArbG Neumünster, 11.08.2020 - 1 Ca 247 c/20 - Schadenersatz für verspätete Auskunft, and LAG Hamm, 11.05.2021 - 6 Sa 1260/20 - Schadensersatz bei nicht erteilter Auskunft nach DSGVO.

339 LAG Köln, 14.09.2020 - 2 Sa 358/20 - Foto des früheren Arbeitnehmers auf Webseite; ArbG Köln, 12.03.2020 - 5 Ca 4806/19 - vergessene Online-PDF-Datei.

was on Facebook.[340] For data breaches, the damage was 1,000 EUR and upgraded to 4,000 EUR when sensitive data were involved.[341]

More importantly, in none of these decisions did the courts require the plaintiffs to prove the specific number of damages they suffered. Instead, it took upon themselves the calculation of the appropriate amount. The underlined logic could be that mental damages were typical results of such torts and foreseeable for data controllers,[342] and the damages ordered by courts echoed the principle of effectiveness and dissuasiveness. These parallel practices effectively reduce the burden on data subjects to demonstrate their damages. On the contrary, there are also courts taking a strict approach to determining moral damages and causation. In this wise, data subjects suffering mental distress were unlikely to get compensated because they could not demonstrate the causality between their deteriorating position and the misbehavior of controllers as well as the justification for the amount of damages.[343] Given the difficulty for data subjects to prove the causality between infringements and damages, especially in the context of big data, it is a promising judiciary attempt to allow data subjects to receive some compensation without having to prove specific damage and causation after specific torts occurred.[344] Also, the final amount of compensation is subjected to fine tuning in light of the principle of effectiveness and dissuasiveness.

In assessing the number of damages, in particular non-material ones, scholarly literature suggests taking the factors listed in Art. 83 (2) GDPR, in particular the financial strength and subjective fault of the controller into account to ensure "full and effective" compensation.[345] If the violation

340 ArbG Lübeck, 20.06.2019 - 1 Ca 538/19 - Mitarbeiterfotos im Facebook. Compensation for 1,000 EUR was the maximal.

341 LG Darmstadt, 26.05.2020 - 13 O 244/19 - Schadensersatz wegen fehlgeleiteter Mail mit Bewerberdaten; AG Pforzheim, 25.03.2020 - 13 C 160/19 – Psychotherapeut.

342 Bergt, in *Kühling/Buchner*, DSGVO/BDSG, Art. 82 Rn. 44.

343 See LG Frankfurt/Main, 18.01.2021 - 2-30 O 147/20 - Datenleck (the court has denied the causal link between the data breach and the harassing phone calls received by the data subject thereafter); LAG Baden-Württemberg, 25.02.2021 - 17 Sa 37/20 - Kein immaterieller DSGVO-Schadensersatz bei US-Transfer (the causal link between illegal transfer of data to the United States and the damage has been denied).

344 In the same direction, *Franck*, ZD, 2021, 680 (683f.).

345 See *Wybitul, et al.*, NJW, 2018, 113 (115); *Wybitul, et al.*, ZD, 2018, 202 (205); Bergt, in *Kühling/Buchner*, DSGVO/BDSG, Art. 82 Rn. 18; Frenzel, in *Paal and Pauly*, DS-GVO BDSG, Art. 82 Rn. 10; *Kremer, Conrady and Penners*, ZD, 2021,

is caused by structural problems such as the data controller reduces the level of protection for profit, or the violation renders many people at stake, the amount of compensation should be effective and deterrent for the controller.[346] However, the function of administrative penalties must be distinguished from civil damages. It is currently under discussion whether a GDPR/EU standard for calculation is necessary.[347] Hopefully, the assessment of moral damages and causality will be clarified by the CJEU shortly since the BVerfG has forwarded a request for a preliminarily ruling.[348]

By stating that "*[a] controller or processor shall be exempt from liability under paragraph 2 if it proves that it is not in any way responsible for the event giving rise to the damage*", Art. 82 (3) GDPR asserts a presumption of fault instead of a liability without fault.[349] However, it is questionable how a data controller can be exempt from liability because it must be "not in any way responsible". On the one hand, the occurrence of damages cannot prove the liability. On the other, the data subject cannot be required to demonstrate where the controller has not done enough to claim damages.[350] It would be a clear violation against *lex non cogit and impossibilia* since data subjects cannot know the factual and supposed technical and organizational measures taken by the controller. Rather, the controller bears the burden to demonstrate that it has implemented appropriate technical and organizational measures to prevent the risks that are likely to arise by taking "into account the nature, scope, context, and purposes of processing" according to the risk-based approach according to Art. 24 (1) GDPR. This requirement is somewhat abstract and difficult to provide effective practical guidance in the absence of detailed industry standards. As a result, some controllers have turned to the argument that there is no causal relationship between the violation and the damages.[351] As this is the point that the data subject needs to prove according to the

---

128 (131); *Paal,* MMR, 2020, 14 (17); Holländer, in *Brink/Wolff,* BeckOK Datenschutzrecht, Art. 83 Rn. 31.

346 Becker, in *Plath,* DSGVO/BDSG, Art. 82 Rn. 4 d).

347 *Wybitul, et al.*, ZD, 2018, 202 (206).

348 BVerfG, NJW 2021, 1005 - DSGVO-Schadensersatzanspruch.

349 Boehm, in *Simitis, et al.*, Datenschutzrecht, Art. 82 Rn. 6.

350 A German court held that the principle of accountability is only applicable when the data controller is being challenged by a data protection authority instead of a data subject for the fulfillment of Art. 24 (1) GDPR. See OLG Stuttgart, 31.03.2021 - 9 U 34/21 - Mastercard-Priceless-Datenleck, para. 56.

351 LAG Baden-Württemberg, 25.02.2021 - 17 Sa 37/20 - Kein immaterieller DSGVO-Schadensersatz bei US-Transfer (the causal link between illegal transfer of data to the United States and the damage has been denied).

general rule on the allocation of the burden of proof and it is difficult,[352] the attempt mentioned above makes more sense to provide some standard compensation after specific violations occurred.

(2) Evaluation

Art. 82 GDPR is envisaged to allow data subjects easier access to recourse through the explicit provisions for moral damages and the reversed burden of proof in lability. Reading in entirety with the compliance rules in the GDPR, Art. 82 GDPR expands the scope of claims that data subjects can make. Controllers must strictly adhere to the GDPR's rules to avoid possible civil liabilities because an objective violation can trigger the claim of Art. 82 (1) GDPR for data subjects in the first place. However, the lack of an EU standard in interpreting the damages, causality and quantifying compensation undermines the practical importance of Art. 82 GDPR. The execution of Art. 82 GDPR remains ambiguous and contested to some extent in Germany.

It is thus not a surprise that the German judiciary is inclined to grant national remedies even though infringements of the GDPR have been established.[353] Admittedly, plaintiffs also tend to invoke the GDPR to prove illegality but assert damages under German law based on §§ 823, 1004 BGB in connection with §§ 22 and 23 KUG. The supremacy of the GDPR over national laws requires the application of Art. 82 GDPR provided on a violation of the GDPR.

As current cases mostly focus on moral damages, and so does the scholarly literature,[354] it is a pity that the *OLG München* forewent an opportunity to explore the attribution of the economic benefits of personal data. In

352 The causality between material damages and infringements is difficult to prove, not to mention the non-material ones. See *Paal,* MMR, 2020, 14 (17); Gola/Piltz, in *Gola,* DSGVO, Art. 82 Rn. 11; *Neun and Lubitzsch,* BB, 2017, 2563 (2567); *Dickmann,* r+s, 2018, 345 (351-352).

353 OVG Niedersachsen, MMR 2021, 593 - Veröffentlichung eines Fotos auf einer Facebook Fanpage; LG Frankfurt am Main, 3.09.2018 - 2-03 O 283/18 - Friseursalon; OLG Köln, ZUM-RD 2018, 549 - Anwendbarkeit des KUG neben der DSGVO.

354 There are more articles focusing on moral damages since it is the first time the EU data protection law entitled natural persons to compensation for moral damage. Even when material damages are mentioned in the articles, the examples and calculations are rather brief. Vgl. *Geissler and Ströbel,* NJW, 2019, 3414 (3415). Nevertheless, a noteworthy elaboration on the importance and connota-

that case, the underlying business logic of social platforms revolves around the commercial interests of personal data.[355] Thus, even though Facebook did not guarantee the continuity of its services in its privacy policy (which is certainly not an appropriate place to stipulate), it seemed to have some validity to claim for restitution based on the unlawful appropriation by continuously using data processing to push ads for revenue when it did not provide the service.

It is also interesting to note that civil damages are virtually trivial compared to the sky-high fines issued by data protection authorities. In an Austrian case, the Austrian Post was fined 18 million euros by the Austrian Data Protection Authority for unlawful processing of sensitive data (political orientation) of Austrian citizens.[356] On the contrary, the controller was liable to the infringed data subject for 800 euros.[357] Admittedly, the legal mechanisms and purposes of administrative penalties and civil damages are distinctly different and cannot be compared directly. Nevertheless, the principle of effectiveness and dissuasiveness also steers the measurement of damages to render infringements no longer profitable for controllers.[358] More importantly, generous civil compensation can incentivize data subjects to proactively exercise their rights under the GDPR. Such a huge discrepancy between administrative penalties and civil damages undermines the proactive pursuit of legal remedies by data subjects and shift all the responsibility of vetting and prosecuting to the data protection supervisory authority. It would be a huge waste of public power and tax as it can be solved entirely by data subjects on their initiative. After all, the huge administrative costs, and the use of enforcement in the "whack a mole" style are questionable.

All in all, by facilitating a more data subjects-friendly recourse mechanism, Art. 82 GDPR provides an impetus for enhanced protection for data subjects but is in dire need of guidance at the EU level. The motivation

tions of material damage see *Dickmann*, r+s, 2018, 345 (348f.); *Strittmatter, et al.*, CR, 2019, 789 (792).

355 The data controller generates revenue from processing personal data for ad distribution, which subsidizes the "free" social services it offers, and the "free" social services, in return, provide a constant flow of personal data.

356 See Datenschutzbehörde, Strafverfahren gegen Österreichische Post AG, OTS0095, at https://www.ots.at/presseaussendung/OTS_20191029_OTS0095/strafverfahren-gegen-oesterreichische-post-ag.

357 OGH Wien, ZD 2019, 72.

358 Boehm, in *Simitis, et al.*, Datenschutzrecht, Art. 82 Rn. 26; *Schantz*, NJW, 2016, 1841 (1847); *Strittmatter, et al.*, CR, 2019, 789 (791).

of data subjects to protect themselves proactively is, however, weakened by the contested application of Art. 82 GDPR and the ambiguity of the attribution of commercial interests contained in personal data.

3.2.2 Remedies for data subjects in unauthorized merchandising cases

(1) Infringements of Art. 6 (1) (f) GDPR

As explored above, unauthorized merchandising generally violates Art. 6 (1) (f) GDPR as the interests and rights of data subjects outweigh the data controller's legitimate advertising interests. Thus, data subjects only have to demonstrate damages resulting from the unlawful data processing in order to claim remedies based on Art. 82 GDPR. According to the scholarly literature and judgments in Germany, damages must be genuine and substantial. A not yet materialized risk does not suffice.

In merchandising cases, moral damages are hardly conceivable as German jurisprudence consistently addresses: No privacy infringement but free-riding on publicity. As the right to one's image confers both moral and property interests embodied in the autonomous decision of one's portrait to the person depicted, the typical remedy is restitution for the fictive license fee that the person would have received if his images had been used lawfully. Through the lens of the GDPR, moral damages of data subjects in typical merchandising cases are not visible either. Moreover, an actual financial loss of data subjects such as the diminished market value of their image and publicity due to the illegal data processing is, if any, difficult to prove. In fact, data subjects in merchandising cases are cut off from the value chain of data processing without any legal basis, and the commercial interests resulting from the processing flow to the controller exclusively. Therefore, the decisive question is whether data subjects can claim material damages drawn on the analogy with fictive license fees under the GDPR.

Though material damages are widely understood, and some scholars suggest an analogy with fictive license fees,[359] one may claim damages computed on the fictive license fee in a comparable situation upon two conditions. First, the EU personal data protection law attributes the commercial interests encompassed in personal data to data subjects. Second, a

---

359 Nemitz, in *Ehmann and Selmayr*, DS-GVO, Art. 82 Rn. 17; *Herberger*, NZFam, 2021, 1088 (1092); *Strittmatter, et al.*, CR, 2019, 789 (793-794).

market of commercial exploitation of personal data is recognized, at least, not objected to by law. The latter also supports the causality between the damage and infringement. If one cannot prove that he was able to get remuneration without the illegal data processing, then he cannot claim compensation.[360] Moreover, a lawful market is indispensable because the value of the commercial interests is a fact and determined by the market. Without a market, it is difficult to calculate the damage.

While the GDPR is elusive regarding the first condition,[361] it is arguable whether a market for personal data is admissible as the EDPB frowns upon it. The opinion of the EDPB, albeit not decisive at all, is referential in interpreting the GDPR. If the GDPR were to adopt the EDPB's opinion and prohibit any form of commercialization of personal data, the fact that a lawful market for licensing portraits exists in Germany (and possibly in all the Member States) should not be able to be an argument against it. Recital 146 GDPR would not serve as an argument either as it addresses that national law of the Member State could be applied in apportioning responsibility between joint controllers instead of quantifying (material) damages. Thus, both conditions are in question. A combination of Art. 6 (1) (f) GDPR and §§ 812 and 818 II BGB is not possible either, if the commercial interests embodied by the right to informational self-determination are not attributed to data subjects under the regime of the EU data protection law.

Therefore, besides the costs of establishing the infringements of the GDPR, expenses for inquiry, attorney's fees, and litigation costs,[362] it is questionable whether data subjects in merchandising cases can be well compensated. The real issues are whether the GDPR protects the pecuniary interests encompassed by personal data and whether the market for exploiting personal data is not legally objectionable.

---

360 In this direction, Moos/Schefzig, in *Taeger, et al.*, DSGVO - BDSG - TTDSG, Art. 82 Rn. 30.

361 Duch-Brown, Martens and Mueller-Langer, The economics of ownership, access and trade in digital data, 2017, 17, arguing that "the GDPR de facto (but not *de jure*) assigns property rights on personal data to the data controller, however limited they may be due to his fiduciary role."

362 ArbG Dresden, 26.08.2020 - 13 Ca 1046/20 - unberechtigte Weitergabe von Gesundheitsdaten durch Arbeitgeber; LG Darmstadt, 26.05.2020 - 13 O 244/19 - Schadensersatz wegen fehlgeleiteter Mail mit Bewerberdate; *Wybitul, et al.*, NJW, 2018, 113 (114); Laue, in *Laue, et al.*, Das neue Datenschutzrecht in der betrieblichen Praxis, § 11 Rn. 5; *Neun and Lubitzsch*, BB, 2017, 2563 (2567); *Wybitul, et al.*, ZD, 2018, 202 (205); Bergt, in *Kühling/Buchner*, DSGVO/BDSG, Art. 82 Rn. 19.

However, when mental damages are present in unauthorized merchandising cases, the outcome is very different. Data subjects also have to demonstrate that some concrete mental damages have resulted from the unlawful data processing in claiming moral damages under Art. 82 GDPR. It should include all damages that occur in all phases of data processing including recording, uploading, and possibly long-term storage of personal data. Taking the *hair salon* case as an instance, the filming of the hair extension constituted annoying harassment, and the online publication making her non-public information to the public presented a server intrusion into her privacy and caused fear and distress. Since the video clip was uploaded on Facebook and was visible to all, the data subject could not control or even know who knew her personal information.

Moreover, one may wonder whether data subjects could claim more moral damages if online communication takes place since it would render control over personal data virtually impossible. It seems reasonable to contend that the possibility of uncontrollability, (re)combination, and re(use) resulting from the free accessibility would escalate moral damages.[363] However, this argument would make large moral compensation a routine consequence of illegal online communication irrespective of other factors. In other words, such a risk in online communication always exists and it is too general and abstract (see 3.2.1). Therefore, it is suggested here to judge the magnitude of the impact in terms of the number of times the video is played and retweeted. The greater the number of plays and retweets is, the higher the degree of moral damage is, and the less likely it is that the data subject will make the information disappear from the web altogether. At the same time, this criterion is consistent with the principle of accountability. On the one hand, the controller wants the promotional video to be widely disseminated and thus always takes active measures to increase its spread. On the other hand, the controller is also capable of taking technical measures to restrict the spread of the video, such as rendering it visible only to friends, prohibiting downloads, etc. Hence, data subjects have to substantialize the exacerbated risks due to the online communication by demonstrating, for instance, the mass distribution of the video, the futility of stopping it.

In assessing the amount of damages, one can deploy the factors listed in Art. 83 (2) GDPR as suggested by some scholars and courts. It may seem contradictory to the role of civil damages, which is designed to fill damages rather than condemnation and punishment. However, the principle

363 *Korch*, NJW, 2021, 978 (979).

of effectiveness and dissuasiveness stipulated in the GDPR has to be noted here. Some fine-tuning of the number of damages is suggested taking account of the controller's financial strength because it is a prominent indicator of the dissemination range and influence. As noted above, some German courts held that an employer who forgot to delete an employee's data from a website after the employee left the company needed to pay damages of 300 to 1,000 euros. The difference in amount was largely dependent on the content of the data (whether the profile was detailed or not) and the extent of dissemination (on an intranet or Facebook).[364]

In this line, moral damages for more than 1,000 euros seem reasonable in unauthorized merchandising cases like the *hair salon* case. Firstly, the unlawful uploaded video was a severe invasion of the privacy of the data subject. Secondly, the controller has done nothing to limit the dissemination of the video on Facebook that was accessible by everyone. If data subjects want more compensation because they are concerned about further misuse resulting from the online communication, they must demonstrate the actual moral injury in a concrete way than just raising the concern. This also applies to the situation where they want to claim grave damages due to the loss of control over personal data.

(2) Infringements of the principles of data processing?

As the first material rule in the GDPR, Art. 5 sets out the basic requirements for data processing in response to the objectives of the Regulation. Art. 83 (5)(a) GDPR provides that a violation of the principles constitutes a ground for escalating administrative penalties to address the importance of these fundamental rules. However, since the manifestation of Art. 5 GDPR is in the form of principles, its general and abstract formulation coupled with flexible, yet ambiguous terms do not lend the principles to easy execution.[365] It creates difficulties in determining infringement and the ensuing damages. For instance, how to assess "fairness"? To what

364 While ArbG Lübeck has considered compensation of 1,000 EUR appropriate (the upper limit) when an employer uploaded a photo of an employee on Facebook without authorization, LAG Köln has implied that 300 EUR was a little too much for a university that did not take down an employee's resume in a timely manner after the end of employment. See ArbG Lübeck, 20.06.2019 - 1 Ca 538/19 - Mitarbeiterfotos im Facebook; LAG Köln, 14.09.2020 - 2 Sa 358/20 - Foto des früheren Arbeitnehmers auf Webseite.

365 *Roßnagel*, ZD, 2018, 339 (342).

extent are the amount, content, and storage of personal data "adequate" and "necessary" for processing under the data minimization and storage limitation principles?

Nevertheless, principles have been substantialized in the following provisions of the GDPR. As the first and probably the most important principle in Art. 5 (1) GDPR, the principle of lawful processing has been materialized in Art. 6 (1) GDPR and Art. 9 GDPR when it involves the processing of sensitive data. The intricate and all-embracing principle of fairness is guaranteed in numerous rules of the GDPR. For instance, it constitutes the core justification for the necessity test embedded in Art. 6 (1)(b) GDPR, which would otherwise be free of restriction due to freedom of contracts. In light of the principle of fairness, the EDPB requires "a combined, fact-based assessment of the processing for the objective pursued" by the contractual service instead of a subjective and contractual terms-based assessment.[366] Besides, even though the consent is obtained lawfully according to Art. 6 (1) (a) and 7 GDPR, the principle of fairness warns against the abuse of consent by data controllers since it has an independent meaning of the principle of legality to avoid redundancy.[367] The principle of transparency is embodied in the right to information in Art. 12, 13, 14, and 15 GDPR as well as the specific requirements for the validity of consent in Art. 7 (1) and (2) GDPR. Art. 25 and 32 GDPR are manifestations of data integrity and confidentiality principles. This principle requires controllers to conduct adequate technical and organizational management commensurate with the damage and risk it incurs.[368] The principle of accountability in Art. 5 (2) GDPR guides the understanding of Art. 25 (privacy design and default), 30 (records of processing activities), and 35 GDPR (data protection impact assessments) as well as at the same time relies on them to be more feasible for controllers.

Since civil damages under the GDPR require the existence of an infringement and substantial harm according to Art. 82 GDPR, decisive issues remain whether the conduct of the data controller constitutes a violation of provisions of the GDPR and whether such a violation causes damages. In this sense, the examination of a violation against principles still relies on the scrutiny of the terms in which they have been specified

366 EDPB, Guidelines 2/2019 on the processing of personal data under Article 6(1)(b) GDPR in the context of the provision of online services to data subjects, 4 and 8.

367 See Herbst, in *Kühling/Buchner*, DSGVO/BDSG, Art. 5 Rn. 17.

368 Art 25 (1) and 32 (1) GDPR.

in most cases. It is noteworthy that the principle of accountability can serve as a basis for infringement for providing specific obligations for controllers.[369] Nevertheless, it is questionable whether failure in keeping proper documentation would cause damages to the data subject. Thus, without dismissing the mandatory nature of the principles of the GDPR,[370] civil damages stemming from a violation against principles are normally difficult to establish in terms of proving infringements and damages.

(3) Infringements of the data subject's rights

The data subject's rights granted by the GDPR from Art. 12 to 22 are remarkable. On the one hand, they are not limited by a pre-existing relationship of rights and obligations between the data subject and controller. By making the rights flow with personal data, any data controller that processes the personal data is obliged to respond to the data subject's rights. On the other hand, the rights are not "absolute" rights in the sense that controllers must fulfill any claim forwarded by a data subject. Some conditions must be met for a data subject to claim the rights. For instance, an alternative in Art. 17 (1) must present for the data subject to claim the right to be forgotten rather than the controller needing to delete all traces of the data subject on the network at any time as some media touted.[371] Moreover, there are exceptions for controllers to not to enforce the claim of data subjects. In terms of the right to be forgotten, the freedom of expression and information is a good cause to continue processing personal data.[372] Nonetheless, controllers must be responsive when a data subject raises a claim based on the GDPR according to Art. 12 (1) GDPR stemming from the principles of transparency and accountability.[373]

---

369 *Alexy,* Theorie der Grundrechte, S. 74.

370 *Roßnagel,* ZD, 2018, 339 (344).

371 Art. 18 (1), 20 (1) and (2), 21 (1) and (2), and 22 (1) GDPR all set specific conditions for claiming the right to restriction of processing, data portability, object, and not to be subject to automated individual decision-making, including profiling.

372 Exceptions are also available in Art. 13 (4), 15 (4), 17 (3), 20 (4), 21 (6) and 22 (2) GDPR for the respective data subject's right.

373 Art. 12 (1) GDPR reads, "the controller shall take appropriate measures to provide any information referred to in Articles 13 and 14 and any communication under Articles 15 to 22 and 34 relating to processing to the data subject in a concise, transparent, intelligible and easily accessible form, using clear and plain language, in particular for any information addressed specifically to a child.

i. The right to information

Art. 12 GDPR requires data controllers to provide information concerning data processing considering the principle of transparency. Accordingly, data subjects are harnessed with the right to information anchored in Art. 13 and 14 GDPR. The CJEU regards the provision of information by controllers as a prerequisite for the legality of data processing.[374] Otherwise, the possibility for a data subject to control personal data would be deprived from the outset. This standpoint is convincing because an autonomous decision (consent or concluding a contract) rests on transparent, and sufficient information, and errors or incompleteness of information would affect the validity of that decision.[375] More convincingly, the right to information is an enabling right that facilitates other data subject's rights and ultimately the control over personal data by the data subject.

In unauthorized merchandising, controllers usually do not notify the data subject, but there may be a difference in where they get the personal data from. For instance, in the *hair salon* case, the controller collected the data directly from the data subject, and thus it should provide the information "at the time when personal data are obtained" (Art. 13 (1) GDPR). In the *clickbait* case, the controller who did not obtain the data directly from the data subject should conduct its obligation to inform "at the latest when the personal data are first disclosed" on the internet according to Art. 14 (3)(c) GDPR. This would have no effect on the outcome of the infringement but only on the legal basis.

When controllers fail to fulfill the obligation to inform promptly, they may invoke the exceptions in Art. 13 (4) or 14 (5) (a) GDPR to exempt from this obligation if the data subjects have already possessed the relevant information including their contact information and the description of the content, purpose, manner, and consequences of data processing. This excuse remains doubtful if controllers fail to prove that the data subject

---

The information shall be provided in writing, or by other means, including, where appropriate, by electronic means. When requested by the data subject, the information may be provided orally, provided that the identity of the data subject is proven by other means."

374 CJEU, Bara and Others, C-201/14, para.43.

375 Vgl. Dix, in *Simitis, et al.*, Datenschutzrecht, Art. 13 Rn. 26; Bäcker, in *Kühling/Buchner*, DSGVO/BDSG, Art. 14 Rn. 44.

has the information stemming from the principle of accountability.[376] Moreover, data subjects in unauthorized merchandising are probably unaware of all the information listed in Art. 13 (1) and Art. 14 GDPR. More specifically, controllers would certainly fail to inform the lawful basis for data processing, and, if the lawful basis is Art. 6 (1) (f) GDPR, the legitimate interests pursued by the controllers according to Art. 13 (1) (c) and (d), and 14 (1) (c) and (2) (b) GDPR. In addition, notification regarding storage, further exploitation of personal data as well as available remedies for data subjects according to Art. 13 (2) and 14 (2) GDPR are probably also omitted here. Another excuse claimed by a German court – disproportionate effort in providing information in recital 62 of the GDPR – is not applicable anyway.[377] Hence, controllers in unauthorized merchandising cases would violate the right to information according to Art. 13 or 14 GDPR significantly.

Damages might be alleviated by an active and timely response to the data subject's request according to Art. 12 (3) in combination with 15 GDPR. As noted in Section 3.2.2, German courts only hold controllers liable for damages when they have not responded to the data subject's request for more than a month. Against the backdrop that the omission of the obligation for information by controllers amounts to significant disadvantages for data subjects, damages of 500 to 1,000 EUR per month are also discernable from the practice.[378] The underlined rationale is self-explanatory. Without prompt and duly notification, data subjects would not be able to invoke protections provided by the GDPR to defend human rights. More importantly, in the cases, data subjects did not prove the damages and causality besides the fact that they made a request.

It is the starting point for a data subject to control personal data by knowing which personal data is processed how by whom, and for what purposes. Hence, the review of the controller's compliance with the obligation for information should be rigorous. As an enabling right, damages

376 Dix, in *Simitis, et al.*, Datenschutzrecht, Art. 13 Rn. 22. It argues that every exception for the data subject's right should be proved by the controller who would like to invoke the exception.

377 LG Heidelberg, 21.02.2020 - 4 O 6/19 - Kein DSGVO-Auskunftsanspruch bei zu hohem Aufwand. In this case, the information was not necessary since it was already 10 years old.

378 ArbG Düsseldorf, NZA-RR 2020, 409 - Unvollständige DSGVO-Auskunft; ArbG Neumünster, 11.08.2020 - 1 Ca 247 c/20 - Schadenersatz für verspätete Auskunft; LAG Hamm, 11.05.2021 - 6 Sa 1260/20 - Schadensersatz bei nicht erteilter Auskunft nach DSGVO.

resulting from infringements thereof are difficult to calculate. In this sense, the parallel practices of German courts in ruling the damages are beneficial in urging controllers to actively provide information. It is thus also welcomed in merchandising cases where controllers deliberately fail to provide the necessary information without any legitimate reasons such as impairment to trade secrets or intellectual property.[379] Since damages are only awarded after one month, data subjects are recommended to claim the right to information as soon as possible.

ii. The right to object

Art. 21 GDPR provides the right to object allowing the data subject to object to the processing of personal data based on Art. 6 (1) (f) GDPR at any time "on grounds relating to his or her particular situation". When receiving the claim of this right, the controller shall stop the contested processing and delete the personal data according to Art. 17 (1) (c) GDPR unless it can demonstrate "compelling legitimate grounds for the processing which override the interests, rights and freedoms of the data subject".[380] If the verification about the legitimate grounds of the controller is pending, the controller shall nevertheless restrict data processing pursuant to Art. 18 (1) (d) GDPR.

It is questionable whether a data subject can object to unlawful processing based on Art. 21 (1) GDPR. On the one hand, the wording of Art. 21 (1) GDPR seems to suggest that this right is only applicable in scenarios of lawful processing. The obligation for demonstrating personal or special reasons by data subjects to contest the processing is suitable for scenarios where a data controller processes a large volume of data and evaluates competing interests in a general and abstract manner. Therefore, the "corrective function" served by Art. 21 (1) GDPR helps the controller to value the particular situation of a data subject and thus promises data subjects comprehensive protection.[381] More importantly, the data subject should seek remedies instead of the right to object when his or her data has been unlawfully processed.[382]

379 Recital 63 GDPR.
380 Vgl. Caspar, in *Simitis, et al.*, Datenschutzrecht, Art. 21 Rn. 19.
381 Braun, in *Ehmann and Selmayr*, DS-GVO, Art. 21 Rn. 10; Martini, in *Paal and Pauly*, DS-GVO BDSG, Art. 21 Rn. 30.
382 Herbst, in *Kühling/Buchner*, DSGVO/BDSG, Art. 21 Rn. 15.

On the other hand, some scholars contend that this consideration restricts the applicable scope of the right to object too much.[383] Recital 69 indicates that "a data subject should, nevertheless, be entitled to object to the processing where personal data might lawfully be processed". The "corrective function" of this right should thus not prejudice its applicability in unlawful processing. In addition, it expects too much of normal people by requiring them to first judge (rightfully) the lawfulness of data processing and then to select the correct data subject's right.[384] In this sense, the "grounds relating to his or her particular situation" should be regarded as no more than a procedure condition.[385]

Following this seemingly mainstream opinion, data subjects in unauthorized merchandising cases can claim the right to object with reference to some personal reasons, such as invasion of privacy and encroachment on goodwill. Consequently, as they fail to demonstrate compelling legitimate grounds for the processing, controllers ought to stop processing. When this right is claimed together with the right to be forgotten discussed below, controllers in unauthorized merchandising cases shall delete the personal data that they collected immediately.

iii. The right to erasure (to be forgotten)

The right to be forgotten emerged in the high-profile *Google Spain* case and became famous even before it has been codified in the GDPR. It originates in the right to erasure in Art. 17 GDPR and is characterized by the deletion of personal data or blocking access to them.[386] As envisaged by the Council,[387] the right to be forgotten was born to be a data subject's right with great adaptability and many manifestations in the digital age.[388] The right to erasure needs to be fulfilled if the processing is unlawful

383 *Spindler/Schuster*, Recht der elektronischen Medien, Art. 21 Rn. 5.
384 Martini, in *Paal and Pauly*, DS-GVO BDSG, Art. 21 Rn. 21f.
385 Caspar, in *Simitis, et al.*, Datenschutzrecht, Art. 21 Rn. 7.
386 Dix, in *Simitis, et al.*, Datenschutzrecht, Art. 17 Rn. 5.
387 Council of the EU, Position of the Council at first reading with a view to the adoption of the General Data Protection Regulation, 5419/1/16 REV 1 ADD 1, 16.
388 As the right to be delisted by search engines, see CJEU, Google Spain, C-131/12, para. 88; CJEU, GC and Others, C-136/17, para. 52. As the right to request pseudonymization in news reports, web archives, Dix, in *Simitis, et al.*, Datenschutzrecht, Art. 17 Rn. 35

(Art. 17 (1) (d) GDPR) unless the controller can demonstrate that the processing is necessary "for exercising the right of freedom of expression and information" pursuant to Art. 17 (3) (a) GDPR.

The data subjects in unauthorized merchandising cases so far have not claimed this right in Germany. Instead, they requested the controllers to take down the personal picture/the video clip from the internet relying on German law (§§ 1004, 823 BGB and the KUG). The injunction here is very similar to the right to be forgotten in the GDPR's narrative because they both intend to block access to personal data in the internet environment.

If controllers stop the data processing without delay, the data subject cannot claim damages because there is no infringement of the right to be forgotten. Although since it has already made the personal data public, the controller shall inform other controllers who are processing the personal data, this obligation is on the condition of reasonableness pursuant to Art. 17 (2) GDPR.[389] However, if controllers refuse to stop the data processing and continue for a rather long time, they are liable for damages resulting from the infringement since the processing of personal data by no means contributes to public debate in merchandising scenarios. The decisive question for claiming Art. 82 GDPR is, once again, contingent on whether the data subject has suffered damages from the omission of this obligation. The data subject has to prove that due to the refusal, additional damages occur. Therefore, it is recommended that data subjects monitor the number of times a video is played and retransmitted in real time after they claimed the right to be forgotten.

It is highly recommended for data subjects to claim the right to erasure according to Art. 17 (1) (c) in combination with the right to object under Art. 21 (1) GDPR right after they discover the violation. In this way, controllers shall cease the processing and take down the personal data right after it receives the claim and would be liable for damages resulting from any omissions.

389 It reads, "the controller, taking account of available technology and the cost of implementation, shall take reasonable steps, including technical measures, to inform controllers which are processing the personal data that the data subject has requested the erasure by such controllers of any links to, or copy or replication of, those personal data".

iv. Other rights?

The other data subject's rights including the right to rectification, the right to restriction of processing, and the right to data portability are either inapplicable or ill-suited for unauthorized merchandising cases.

The right to rectification in Art. 16 GDPR grants the data subject the right to rectify inaccurate personal data concerning him or her against the controller. Moreover, "the data subject shall have the right to have incomplete personal data completed, including by means of providing a supplementary statement." Taking the *clickbait* case as an example, the right to rectification would not be supported since the commercial exploitation of the data subject's data concerned speculation aiming at attracting internet flow instead of misrepresentation. However, the right to rectification would be applicable if the advertising concerns a depiction in false light or a wrongful endorsement since the personal data/information is inaccurate.

It is, nonetheless, questionable whether this right is suitable for these kinds of unauthorized merchandising cases. A counterargument or a supplementary statement indicating the inaccuracy of the advertisement and requesting the rectification would be ineffective unless it has been made public. However, in this wise, the controller would get nothing but more exposure. The claim of the right to rectification would hence eventually encourage merchandising involving false light and wrongful endorsements. The right to restriction of processing in Art. 18 (1) GDPR is nonapplicable here because it purports to provide a middle ground for a *temporary truce* between the data subject and the controller where there is a dispute. According to Art. 18 (2) GDPR, the data controller can still process personal data within a minimum degree including storing when the data subject claims the right to restriction. Yet, the illegality of unauthorized merchandising is so obvious that the data subject needs not put up with data processing anymore despite the minimum degree but can simply claim the right to object and to erasure.

While it seems that a data subject might benefit from the right to data portability in Art. 20 GDPR in merchandising cases because he or she may ask the controller to transmit all personal data to a competitor of the controller in order to get higher remuneration, it is legally infeasible according to the conditions listed in Art. 20 (1) GDPR (discussed in the next Part regarding authorized merchandising). Furthermore, the right to data portability is useless in prohibiting data processing of the controller since it is an independent right from the right to object and to be forgotten pursuant to Art. 20 (3) GDPR.[390]

3.3 Preliminary conclusions

Unauthorized merchandising is unlawful according to Art. 6 (1) (f) GDPR. The pure commercial interests pursued by the controller, albeit legitimate, still need to yield to the right to informational self-determination in accord with the reasonable exceptions of data subjects irrespective of their social roles. However, the current "harmony approach" in merchandising cases adopted by some German courts is flawed. For one, the direct reliance on the jurisprudence of the KUG needs a clear legal basis in the GDPR. As the reasonable expectations of the data subject would be the appropriated one, German courts should not apply §§ 22 and 23 KUG at the beginning in the ruling. For another, by resorting to the jurisprudence of the KUG German courts tend to ignore the specificity of the provisions in the GDPR, such as the principle of accountability and the "test grid" of Art. 6 (1) (f) GDPR. Furthermore, adopting the narrative of the EU data proception law does not mean quoting terms from the GDPR in any case. Exploration of their correct meaning, such as direct marketing, is indispensable to avoid exaggeration of the risks and harms of data processing in online communication.

Both advantages and disadvantages of the strict accordance with Art. 82 GDPR are highlighted in unauthorized merchandising cases. On the one hand, Art. 82 GDPR provides an impetus for enhanced protection for data subjects by facilitating a more data subjects-friendly recourse mechanism. For one, the principle of accountability and the data subject's rights increase the obligations of controllers both qualitatively and quantitatively. For another, Art. 82 GDPR not only expands the scope of damages but also indicates a high level of compensation following the principle of effectiveness and dissuasiveness. Yet the contested practice of assessing the damages undermines the importance of Art. 82 GDPR for data protection. The tendency towards some standard compensation for some typical infringements of the GDPR, such as infringements to the right to information, is beneficial for data subjects and expected to be recognized at the EU level.

On the other, the equivocal attitude of the GDPR towards the attribution of the commercial interests contained in personal data significantly

390 Vgl. Dix, in *Simitis, et al.*, Datenschutzrecht, Art. 20 Rn. 16.

devalues the material damages that the data subject can claim. Furthermore, the strong resistance of the EDPS towards the idea that personal data can be commercialized makes it more difficult to calculate the amount of compensation even when a data market exists factually. In this sense, the material damages cover the expenses for inquiry, evidence collection, and litigation but probably not the commercial interests contained in personal data exploited unlawfully by the controller according to Art. 82 (1) GDPR. Therefore, if the data subject suffers moral damages from the data processing, it is more likely he or she would be better-off at a smaller cost than the data subject who suffers merely material damages in merchandising. In this wise, faced with unauthorized merchandising, average data subjects would get more compensation than celebrities because the latter usually do not feel morally violated, unlike the former.

As a result, celebrities who are used to merchandising probably cannot be compensated properly under the GDPR, and there is a high probability that they will even receive nothing, even though their data are worth more proved by the established merchandising market.

4. *Authorized merchandising under the GDPR*

4.1 The applicability of Art. 9 GDPR in merchandising cases?

4.1.1 Specific protection for sensitive data

(1) The statutory requirements in Art. 9 GDPR

Rooted in Convention 108,[391] the GDPR distinguishes between (normal) personal data and "special categories of personal data" (sensitive data) and, in general, prohibits the processing of the latter from the outset (Art. 9 (1) GDPR).[392] Data controllers are allowed to process sensitive data if they meet one of the specific requirements listed in Art. 9 (2) GDPR as well as other requirements in the GDPR "in particular as regards the conditions for lawful processing".[393]

---

391 Art. 6 in Convention 108.

392 Art. 9 GDPR is born out of Art. 8 of the Directive 95/46.

393 Recital 51 of the GDPR clarifies the relation between Art. 9 (2) and 6 (1) GDPR by stating that "in addition to the specific requirements for such processing, the general principles and other rules of this Regulation should apply, in particular

Seemingly, conditions for processing sensitive data are more rigorous than normal personal data. For instance, Art. 9 (2) GDPR lacks a general clause like Art. 6 (1) (f) that allows private entities to process personal data for compelling legitimate interests after a balancing test.[394] A free pass deriving from contracts between data subjects and controllers under Art. 6 (1) (b) GDPR is also absent in Art. 9 (2) GDPR. Moreover, Art. 9 (2) (a) GDPR imposes higher requirements for the validity of consent. Besides the principle of lawfulness, obligations imposed on data controllers who systematically process sensitive data are intensified in quality and quantity. For instance, regulation of automated individual decision-making processing is stricter when sensitive data are involved (Art. 22 (4)), the obligation to conduct data protection impact assessments is seemingly mandatory (Art. 35 (3) (b)), and, of course, penalties for violations are aggravated (Art. 84 (5) (a)).

This higher-standard protection flows from the acknowledgment that processing of sensitive data is more likely to create substantial risks to fundamental rights and freedoms of individuals.[395] An expansion of the types of sensitive data is thus foreseeable as data technology advances.[396] For instance, genetic data is evaluated as sensitive data per se in Art. 8 of Directive 95/46 after more than a decade of Convention 108, while biometric data emerge in the list of sensitive data in Art. 9 (1) GDPR after another decade of Directive 95/46.

To strike a balance between flexibility and certainty, types of sensitive data prescribed in the EU data protection law are, albeit exhaustive, with elusive boundaries. It leads to the question of whether personal photos are considered sensitive data since sensitive information about the person

---

as regards the conditions for lawful processing." The opposing view advocates an exclusion of the application of Art. 6 (1) GDPR based on the principle lex speicilas, see Kampert, in *Sydow*, DSGVO: Handkommentar, Art. 9 Rn. 1.

394 Although Art. 9 (2) (g) provides an open-ended clause irrespective of fields, it specifically requires that the purpose of processing must be of public interest. Thus, it is in general inapplicable for private data controllers. Vgl. Weichert, in *Kühling/Buchner*, DSGVO/BDSG, Art. 9 Rn. 89.

395 The first sentence of recital 51 of the GDPR states, "Personal data which are, by their nature, particularly sensitive in relation to fundamental rights and freedoms merit specific protection as the context of their processing could create significant risks to the fundamental rights and freedoms"; Petri, in *Simitis, et al.*, Datenschutzrecht, Art. 9 Rn. 1.

396 Cullagh, 2 Journal of International Commercial Law and Technology 190 (2007) (191).

depicted, including race (mental or physical), health status, etc., can be inferred from one's facial and physical appearance.

Two categories of sensitive data are contained in Art. 9 (1) GDPR. One refers to genetic and biometric data resulting from specific technical processing, which are per se sensitive data.[397] The other describes "data sources", from which sensitive information about racial or ethnic origin, political opinions, religious or philosophical beliefs, or trade union membership, health, sex life, or sexual orientation can be inferred directly or indirectly, independently or in combination.[398] For instance, one's dressing accessories such as kippah, hijab or glasses, one's behaviors including participating in political, religious or LGBT social movements, or engaging in extreme sports are not informative about health or religious beliefs per se, but rather are considered sensitive data because they can reveal such information.[399]

Personal pictures are not biometric data in the first category. Although Art. 4 (14) GDPR lists "facial images" as an example of biometric data, they are not personal photos taken by normal cameras but rather special photos generated through a specific technical means in the sense of Art. 4 (14) GDPR, such as the facial image used in ID cards, passports, etc.[400] However, a personal photo can still be considered sensitive data in the second category if sensitive information about the person depicted can be revealed by his or her facial or physical features or even the context in the photo.[401]

---

397 *Weichert, DuD, 2017, 538 (540).*

398 Some scholars argue that the data "concerning" health, sex life, or sexual orientation builds another category of sensitive data, or is subjected to the same category of biometric data because it also refers to data that directly shows that information. See *Schneider*, ZD 2017, 303 (304); Albers/Veit, in *Brink/Wolff*, BeckOK Datenschutzrecht, Art. 9 Rn. 19. However, the definition of these data provided in Art. 4 (15) eliminates the semantic distinction between the terms "concerning" and "revealing". See *Matejek and Mäusezahl*, ZD, 2019, 551 (553); *Schneider/Schindler*, ZD, 2018, 463 (467); Ernst, in *Paal and Pauly*, DS-GVO BDSG, Art. 4 Rn. 109; Schulz, in *Gola,* DSGVO, Art. 9 Rn. 14; Schild, in *Brink/ Wolff,* BeckOK Datenschutzrecht, Art. 4 Rn. 143.

399 *Reuter*, ZD, 2018, 564 (565); *Schneider/Schindler*, ZD, 2018, 463 (466f.).

400 Recital 51 of the GDPR; See Perti, in *Simitis, et al.*, Datenschutzrecht, Art. 4 Nr. 14 Rn. 9; *Klein,* Personenbilder im Spannungsfeld von Datenschutzgrundverordnung und Kunsturhebergesetz, S. 5.

401 WP29, Advice paper on special categories of data ("sensitive data"), Ref. Ares (2011)444105, 8.

(2) the academic controversy over the criteria

Scholarly literature agrees on a case-by-case analysis about the sensitivity of a photo.[402] However, the pivotal question lies in the details of the judgment inquiring about which factors play a role in concrete cases. Some scholars focus on the subjective purpose (*Auswertungsabsicht*) of data controllers.[403] According to this subjective approach, personal photographs are only regarded as sensitive data if the controller's purpose is to analyze sensitive information from them. However, in the view of the proponents of an objective evaluation, personal photographs reflecting facial features are normally considered sensitive data because they are objectively capable of revealing sensitive information.[404]

(3) Evaluation

Advantages and flaws in both propositions are evident. The subjective approach can effectively exclude data processing that poses no particular risk for data subjects by examining the purpose of the processing. At the same time, it lacks prominent legal support and is difficult to assess.[405] The objective approach enables the GDPR to intervene at an early stage, which is in line with the intention of the EU data protection law. From its inception, the EU data protection law has been cast widely to cope with technologies.[406] However, stemming from the blurred boundaries of "data sources", the objective approach would extend too far that it virtually provides a borderless pool so that non-sensitive data can trigger the stringent precautionary measures and renders the distinction between sensitive data and normal data obsolete.[407]

Based on the characteristics of data processing, the purpose of the data controller should not be excluded from assessing the capabilities of data processing in any case. One's skin color revealing the race is a thinking process conducted by human beings, which is not processing in the sense

402 *Matejek and Mäusezahl*, ZD, 2019, 551 (552).
403 Schulz, in *Gola*, DSGVO, Art. 9 Rn. 13; *Matejek and Mäusezahl*, ZD, 2019, 551 (552).
404 Schiff, in *Ehmann and Selmayr*, DS-GVO, Art. 9 Rn. 10.
405 Perti, in *Simitis, et al.*, Datenschutzrecht, Art. 9 Rn. 12.
406 Erdos, 26 International Journal of Law and Information Technology 189 (2018) (194).
407 *Matejek and Mäusezahl*, ZD, 2019, 551 (552).

of the GDPR. Data and processing cannot be conceptualized separately. A machine cannot "see" through pictures unless it has been mandated to and provided with the necessary assistance of manual tagging and persistent "learning". In other words, a machine, or an Artificial intelligence (AI) system can only identify and record the "hidden" sensitive information from the photo when it is programmed to do so.[408] The objective approach ignores the gap between data processing and human cognition.[409] Thus, the purpose of data processing cannot be left aside to determine whether the "data sources" are sensitive or not. It is true that "there is no trivial data", but this statement has a premise, namely, data processing technologies are making it easier and easier to analyze, integrate and store data, thereby significantly increasing the risk of people being exposed to unrestricted data collection.[410] Therefore, an overall assessment not only regarding data but also taking account of the context including the purposes, means, and impact of the processing is warranted.[411]

While the GDPR places great importance on the objective factors in terms of data processing technologies,[412] official documents of the EU data protection law and its legal resources consistently emphasize the rationale

---

408 Opposite opinion See *Reuter*, ZD, 2018, 564 (565). She argues that surveillance footage should be generally categorized as sensitive data. An introduction to how AI systems work through combining large sets of data with intelligent, iterative processing algorithms, See *Posner and Weyl*, Radical Markets: Uprooting Capitalism and Democracy for a Just Society, 214 et seq.

409 Vgl. *Bull*, Sinn und Unsinn des Datenschutzes, S. 13; *Lenk*, Der Staat am Draht, S. 33f.

410 BVerfG, NJW 1984, 419 - Volkszählung, para. 159.

411 Some scholars support a more radical teleological reduction by retrieving the fundamental rights and freedoms that provide the basis for the stringent protection for specific sensitive data. Thereby, the ambit of sensitive data would not extend too far. For instance, *Petri* suggests limiting the racial and ethnic origins in Art. 9 (1) GDPR in ethnic and racial minorities, such as Eskimo, to respond and guarantee its breeding human right against discrimination. See Petri, in *Simitis, et al.*, Datenschutzrecht, Art. 9 Rn. 16. This approach is not followed based on three main reasons among others. First, no official documents indicate such restrictive understanding that would substantially undermine the effectiveness of the GDPR. Secondly, this view is likely overly conservative, since profiling, social-sorting, and discrimination in employment, admissions, and price are not only among minorities. Finally, it does not solve the core issue in Art. 9 (1) GDPR, which revolves around a general understating of a whole category of data, namely the "sources data".

412 See Recital 26 of the GDPR: "To ascertain whether means are reasonably likely to be used to identify the natural person, account should be taken of all objective factors, such as the costs of and the amount of time required for

under the specific protection of sensitive data: processing thereof poses significant risks and harms to the fundamental rights and freedoms of individuals.[413] On the one hand, since the development of data analytical technology is still in an embryonic stage, and even data controllers might not be fully aware of the capabilities of data processing technologies, their purposes could be elusive and thus the nature of personal data provides a definite and fixed criterion for judgment. On the other hand, the GDPR is not concerned with the protection of sensitive data per se, but with the impacts of data processing on human beings. This rationale is reflected more evidently in the risk-based rules in the GDPR, which directly employ the risk brought up by data processing as a benchmark to increasing the controller's responsibility instead of using the term sensitive data per se.[414] Thus, the category of sensitive is a sign of the existence of high risk, and if in fact the processing of sensitive data does not entail high risk, then exclusion becomes necessary.[415]

4.1.2 Conclusions

Here argues for a subjective approach to Art. 9 (1) GDPR. As the concern arising from the difficulty of determining the purpose of data controllers is

---

identification, taking into consideration the available technology at the time of the processing and technological developments."

413 WP29, Advice paper on special categories of data ("sensitive data"), Ref. Ares (2011)444105; *Council of Europe, Explanatory Report to the Convention for the Protection of individuals with regard to automatic processing of personal Data, Nr. 38, para. 43, "while the risk that data processing is harmful to persons generally depends not on the contents of the data but on the context in which they are used, there are exceptional cases where the processing of certain categories of data is as such likely to lead to encroachments on individual rights and interests"; OECD, The Explanatory Report The explanatory memorandum of the OECD Guidelines on the Protection of Privacy and Transborder Flows of Personal Data, No. 50 - 51, "the Expert Group discussed a number of sensitivity criteria, such as the risk of discrimination, but has not found it possible to define any set of data which are universally regarded as sensitive".*

414 For instance, Art. 24 (1), 25, 32, 33 and 35 (1) GDPR.

415 *Spies, ZD, 2020, 117; Fazlioglu, 46 Fordham Urban Law Journal 271 (2019); Ohm, 88 Southern California law review 1125 (2015); Simitis, Revisiting Sensitive Data, 1999;* Weichert, in *Kühling/Buchner,* DSGVO/BDSG, Art. 9 Rn. 23; Schulz, in *Gola,* DSGVO, Art. 9 Rn. 13; Different opinion See Schiff, in *Ehmann and Selmayr,* DS-GVO, Art. 9 Rn. 13, with a mere focus on the data per se.

not unreasonable, it further argues for an emphasis on the reverse burden of proof stemming from the principle of accountability.[416]

The reverse burden of proof stemming from the principle of accountability can effectively prevent circumvention of obligations when data controllers process personal images that might pose higher risks to data subjects. Possible measures are detailed documentation proving that no sensitive data is being collected, analyzed, or stored.[417] Plausible circumstantial evidence is also supported here; For instance, the processing of sensitive data is inconsistent with the business objectives. Also, controllers must take effective measures including privacy by default or design, such as separated storage and timely deletion to prevent and forbid further processing.

The subjective approach of Art. 9 (1) GDPR with an emphasis on the reverse burden of proof is already reflected in some German cases. In one case, the judgment excluded the surveillance footage from sensitive data despite the personal data recorded by the camera being at a high resolution and could reveal racial and ethnic origin (skin color, hair). The argument was that the controller was not interested in collecting the special category of personal data.[418] The other case was about a data controller who owns an online pharmacy. The court ruled that the controller must prove that it had neither the purpose nor the ability to process sensitive data to exclude the application of Art. 9 GDPR.[419]

In merchandising cases, the data processing regarding personal portraits generally attracts attention and resonates with consumers instead of collecting and analyzing sensitive information of the person depicted. As discussed in Part II Section 3.1.2 (1), the difference between merchandising and direct marketing is evident: photos are used to increase publicity, while the data processing concerned by the GDPR is purported to generate

416 The emphasis on the reverse burden of proof is often ignored, see *Schneider/Schindler*, ZD, 2018, 463 (467f.); Vgl. BVerfG, NJW 2008, 1505 - Automatisierte Kennzeichenerfassung, para. 66; Weichert, in *Kühling/Buchner*, DSGVO/BDSG, Art. 9 Rn. 22f.; *Matejek and Mäusezahl*, ZD, 2019, 551 (553).

417 For instance, Art. 24 GDPR orders the controllers to take reasonable and proportionate responsibilities when they adopt some new data technology aiming at analyzing data subjects, and creating significant risks for individuals. Vgl. *Veil*, ZD, 2015, 347.

418 VG Mainz, ZD 2021, 336 - DSGVO bei Kameras am Monitor, 337.

419 LG Dessau-Roßlau (3. Zivilkammer), GRUR-RS 2018, 14272 - Speicherung personenbezogener Daten beim Vertrieb apothekenpflichtiger Arzneimittel über Handelsplattform, para. 40f.

more information from photos. Taking the *landlady* case as an example, the magazine used erotic photos of the model to increase sales. Racial information may be inferable, but the magazine is not aimed at or even interested in this sensitive information.[420] It would not collect, analyze, or store sensitive information. Interestingly, despite the photos in the *landlady* case being pornographic and might be sensitive in daily life, they were hardly considered sensitive in Art. 9 (1) GDPR because they were staged photos and related to occupation.[421] Conversely, information regarding consumption of these magazines is likely sensitive data because it might tell one's sexual orientation.[422]

Following the subjective approach of Art. 9 (1) GDPR with an emphasis on the reverse burden of proof, merchandisers can exclude the application of Art. 9 GDPR by demonstrating that no sensitive information about the data subject's race, ethnic origin, or health status that could be revealed from the stage photos is processed in the sense of the GDPR. Feasible measures include detailed documentation concerning the content, means of processing, and business purpose. However, if the controller cannot convincingly prove that it does not process such information, or that sensitive information is already recorded, then it must find a legitimate justification from Art. 9 (2) GDPR.

For instance, when a party member uploaded pictures onto his fan page showing the data subjects' appearance in a political campaign, the *VG Hannover* should scrutinize the data processing under Art. 9 GDPR since the data subjects' political attribute was directly recorded online.[423] It also holds in users' merchandising scenarios concerning feedbacks of pregnancy products and drugs. As a result, when sensitive information is explicitly processed – collected, stored, made available online – in the meaning of the GDPR, Art. 9 GDPR and other relevant precautionary obligations should be applied to provide a high-level protection for individuals

420 In the same direction, see Schulz, in *Gola,* DSGVO, Art. 9 Rn. 15, stating that the processing of food and drinks in delivery services does not possess the intention to evaluate one's eating habit and drug addictions.

421 *Ehmann*, ZD, 2020, 65 (68).

422 Weichert, in *Kühling/Buchner,* DSGVO/BDSG, Art. 9 Rn. 42; Schiff, in, *Ehmann and Selmayr,* DS-GVO, Art. 9 Rn. 31; The opposite opinion without reason see, Schulz, in *Gola,* DSGVO, Art. 9 Rn. 14. Probably because a data processing operation or a clear intention to process such information lacks here.

423 Schnabel has expressed his concern for merchandising under the GDPR by forwarding a similar hypothetical case. See *Schnabel,* ZUM, 2008, 657 (661).

since the processing thereof is risk-prone as regards fundamental rights and freedoms of individuals.

4.2 Consent as the lawful ground for data processing under the GDPR

4.2.1 The collision of norms (Normenkollision) between the GDPR and the KUG

Although both the KUG and the GDPR use consent (*Einwilligung*) as a legitimate basis for merchandising/data processing, their understanding of consent diverges significantly. Under the KUG, consent can indicate non-binding acts of friendship (*Gefälligkeiten*) and binding promises in synallagmatic contracts.[424] As shown in Part I Section 3.1, German jurisprudence generally considers consent in a merchandising contract a legal act that cannot be withdrawn freely. Consent in the GDPR, however, is deemed to be freely revocable. Consent of the GDPR is only one connotation of consent according to German doctrine, and thus it cannot replace the various senses of consent under the KUG.

The supremacy of the EU law only indicates a precedence of the GDPR over the KUG when their application overlaps. Therefore, there is no basis for a comprehensive substitution of legal concepts.[425] In other words, the indication of the depicted person's wish needs to be judged according to the specific scenario, and the GDPR is authorized to determine whether such a disposal of personal data is permitted or not. After all, life is not performed according to the law; on the contrary, law needs to be adjusted to the needs of reality. Furthermore, the GDPR also agrees to determine whether the definition of consent is met based on the true meaning of the data subject, rather than focusing only on the term consent as such. According to the definition of consent in Art. 4 (11) GDPR, consent can be presented in various manifestations, such as a statement, a clear affirmative action, or a signed agreement. Thus, even if the data subject does not use the word consent, it does not automatically lead to the conclusion that

424 *Dasch*, Die Einwilligung zum Eingriff in das Recht am eigenen Bild, 68f.; Specht, in *Dreier/Schulze*, Urheberrechtsgesetz, § 22 KUG Rn. 19a.

425 About the collision of norms, see *Bienemann*, Reformbedarf des Kunsturhebergesetzes im digitalen Zeitalter, S. 103f.; Specht, in *Dreier/Schulze*, Urheberrechtsgesetz, Art. 22 KUG Rn. 16a und 35.

their intention to allow the data controller to process personal data is not revocable at any time in the sense of the GDPR.

Finally, this finding does not discriminate against the interests of the data subject because the controller bears the burden to inform the data subject about the legal consequence of her or his action according to the principle of accountability. In case of doubt, the data controller must demonstrate that the data subject wants to and agrees to conclude a contract rather than giving consent. Furthermore, the GDPR considers that contracts can only provide legitimacy for necessary data processing. If it goes beyond what is necessary, then the data subject can revoke their consent at any time.

4.2.2 Consent as the lawful ground in merchandising

(1) Conditions for the validity of consent and the consequence of omissions

As the "central hinge" of private data protection law,[426] consent is the "indication of the data subject's wishes", which can be given by "a statement or by a clear affirmative action" according to Art. 4 (11) GDPR. In this sense, consent is a unilateral declaration of the data subject that legitimizes the data processing conducted by the controller.

The GDPR imposes stringent requirements on consent to ensure that the data subject genuinely executes the right of informational self-determination.[427] Art. 4 (11) GDPR requires consent to be "freely given, specific, informed, and unambiguous". While Art. 7 (2), recitals 32 and 42 prescribe detailed conditions for "specific" and "unambiguous", Art. 13 (1) and (2) GDPR have listed the information the controller shall provide when it collects the personal data from the data subject directly to facilitate the requirement of "informed". Furthermore, Art. 7 (3) GDPR requires that consent must be freely revocable. The free revocability of consent is one of the major innovations in the EU data protection law to make data controllers always walk on thin ice. Data subjects can thus "vote with their feet" and render future processing operations unlawful.

Moreover, it can also mitigate the adverse consequences of wrong choices to some extent because data subjects can withdraw consent freely when

426 Vgl. Stemmer, in *Brink/Wolff*, BeckOK Datenschutzrecht, Art. 7 Rn. 19.
427 Buchner/Petri, in *Kühling/Buchner*, DSGVO/BDSG, Art. 6 Rn. 17.

they become aware of their cognitive deficiencies. It means that the revocability of consent must be free from negative consequences for the data subject and can be executed anytime. Some scholars argue it is because of the bound cognition of human beings, especially in the face of big data but refuse to confine its application within this scenario.[428] While the cognitive problems might constitute partly the justification, it is still necessary to look at the source of law. Art. 8 of the Charter places high value on data subjects' the control over personal data. Thereby, the free revocability of consent is devised to render the lawfulness of data processing entirely contingent on data subjects' willingness in permitting or objecting data processing.

The GDPR ensures the voluntariness of consent through the so-called prohibition of coupling (*Kopplungsverbot*) in Art. 7 (4) GDPR. It requires that the performance of a contract, especially the provision of a service, should not depend on the consent to which the data processing is not necessary for the provision of that service. For instance, if an App for flashlight makes the consent to read the data subject's contact book indispensable for using that app, it violates the prohibition of coupling. However, it is rightfully argued the name of the prohibition is exaggerated because Art. 7 (4) GDPR only requires taking "utmost account" instead of prohibiting coupling entirely.[429] As suggested by recital 43, the coupling issue acquires more attention when there is structural inequality between the data subject and controller because it is more likely that the data subject would fail to express his or her genuine wishes due to dependency on the service.

Seemingly clear, these requirements are particularly problematic in practice, coupled with the legal consequence.[430] Art. 7 GDPR is of particular importance in evaluating the consequences for failing to meet the conditions for valid consent because it prescribes the conditions and the consequence flowing from a violation – (partial) invalidation of the consent according to Art. 7 (2) GDPR.[431] The prevailing view in the academic community argues for differentiation according to the type of the omitted

428 Ibid., Rn. 34 und 38.

429 Vgl. *Engeler*, ZD, 2018, 55 (58f.); Schulz, in *Gola*, DSGVO, Art. 7 Rn. 26; *Sattler*, in: *Pertot, Rechte an Daten*, 49 (75). However, some judiciary judgments tend to recognize an absolute prohibition of coupling, See OGH Wien, ZD 2019, 72, Rn. 47; *Pertot*, Zeitschrift für das Privatrecht der Europäischen Union, 2019, 54.

430 *Brink/Wolff*, BeckOK Datenschutzrecht, Rn. 94.

431 Stemmer, in ibid.Art. 7 Rn. 93.

information.[432] If the missing information is so important that it would affect the right to self-determination of the data subject seriously, then consent is invalid. Otherwise, invalidation of consent is uncalled for because it exceeds the protective purpose of Art. 7 (2) GDPR since the data subject would exercise the informational self-determination in the same way. Nevertheless, it must be distinguished from the possible administrative fines for controllers due to incompliance.

Among all, two requirements are deserving special attention in the context of merchandising. One is the voluntariness of data subjects, and the other is the omission of the notification about the revocability of consent.

Some indicators address the voluntariness of consent under the GDPR including the pre-relationship between the data subject and controller,[433] the consequence for refusing to consent,[434] and the notification of the anytime revocability of consent.[435] For instance, if the data subject is dependent on the controller or the data processing conducted by the controller as in an employment relationship, the controller must formulate the declaration in a written and independent form from the employment contract to facilitate the evaluation of the voluntary nature of consent.[436] Moreover, the controller shall prove that consent is not coerced in any sense if a structural inequity exists.[437]

The most decisive indicator is that there is no adverse consequence for refusing to consent.[438] Some scholars further demand that there should not be any beneficial consequences either.[439] However, this approach is too

---

432 Buchner/Kühling, in *Kühling/Buchner*, DSGVO/BDSG, Art. 7 Rn. 59; Schiff, in *Ehmann and Selmayr*, DS-GVO, Art, 7 Rn. 58; *Ernst*, ZD, 2017, 110 (112).

433 Recital 43 GDPR; *Gola and Schulz*, RDV, 2013, 1(6); *Pötters*, RDV, 2015, 10 (15).

434 See WP29, Guidelines on consent under Regulation 2016/679, 17/EN, 7.

435 WP29, Opinion 8/2001 on the processing of personal data in the employment context, WP48, 3.

436 Ibid., 3. It makes a strict distinction between data processing that is necessary for the establishment, continuation, and termination of the employment relationship and confines consent solely to the latter scenario.

437 It is noteworthy that the provision was originally envisaged in Art. 7(4) GDPR-E that consent is *per se* invalid if there is a "significant imbalance" between the data subject and the controller, such as in an employment relationship. However, this *proviso* has been deleted because the EU Parliament feared that this exclusion would be too broad. See European Commission, Proposal for a General Data Protection Regulation, COM(2012) 11 final, recital 34.

438 See WP29, Guidelines on consent under Regulation 2016/679, 17/EN, 7. It gives an example that the employees who refuse to consent are provided with necessary assistance so that their work would not be affected.

439 *Ernst*, ZD, 2017, 110 (112).

general to agree with. Admittedly, it might make sense when the benefit is career-related such as promotions. But monetary consideration for merchandising in a situation like the *company-advertising* case is reasonable and cannot be used as a reason to deny voluntariness. Otherwise, it virtually demands that all employees be completely altruistic for the company's commercial interests in merchandising scenario. Lastly, the WP29 also emphasizes the notification of the anytime revocability of consent to sustain "a genuine free choice" of an employee.[440] All in all, the more prominent the structural inequity between the data subject and controller is, the more additional measures the controller needs to take to demonstrate the voluntary nature of the data subject.[441]

It is questionable whether the omission of the notification about the revocability shall lead to the invalidation of consent. Some scholars find the compulsory notification incompatible with everyday life scenarios. They argue that it seems preposterous that a photographer must have a sign on him stating all necessary information about data processing and the revocability of consent to take pictures at a party.[442] This argument has some merit because the context of data processing imaged by the GDPR is most likely to be data processing in a network environment where anytime revocable consent has substantial practical implications. Foremost importantly, data subjects relying on consent shall no longer be intimidated by the complexity and length of the privacy policy drafted by controllers, as they can withdraw consent whenever they change their minds. However, this counterargument seems superfluous.

In practice, official organizers acquire attendees' consent in advance for data processing (for taking photographs) in writing with the information including the purpose, means of processing, and revocability of consent. Admittedly, this is a change based on the GDPR compliance requirements, but such a change is progress in light of the data protection law and does not give rise to peculiar consequences. Moreover, the household exception in the GDPR is applicable to private parties. Secondly, according to the

440 WP29, Opinion 8/2001 on the processing of personal data in the employment context, WP48, 3.

441 It is noteworthy that the provision was originally envisaged in Art. 7(4) GDPR-E that consent is *per se* invalid if there is a "significant imbalance" between the data subject and the controller, such as in an employment relationship. This *proviso* has been deleted because the EU Parliament feared that this exclusion would be too broad. See European Commission, Proposal for a General Data Protection Regulation, COM(2012) 11 final, recital 34.

442 The instance and the argument for the incompatibility, see *Ernst*, ZD, 2020, 383.

explicit wording of Art. 7 (3) GDPR, the notification regarding the revocability of consent must be "prior to giving consent".[443] While it has been argued that the information about the revocability of the consent is only needed when it is necessary "to ensure fair and transparent processing" according to Art. 13 (2) (c) GDPR,[444] this interpretation is uneasy to apply due to tautology and the inherent abstractness of the concept of "fair". Moreover, Art. 13 (2) (c) GDPR puts more emphasis on the notification about the *ex-nunc* effect of a withdrawn consent instead of the notification about the revocability per se. Finally, limiting the scope of the GDPR to the online environment or large data controllers lacks a legal basis.

Furthermore, it is essential to notice that either the consent can be withdrawn at any time or withdrawal is allowed (similar to a binding contract). When the revocability of consent is informed, the data subject can exert his or her control over the operations of data processing; when the binding nature of the contract is made clear, it warns the data subject to think carefully before he or she gives a binding commitment. Against this backdrop, without any reference to the revocability of consent, the data subject is deprived of either the control over personal data or the opportunity to think carefully. Given the imbalance of power in employment relationships, there is a clear risk that the data subject would be hoodwinked into a situation where they thought the consent was revocable at any time, but it is not in reality. Consequently, the central factor of the judgment regarding the consequence of failing to notify the revocability is contingent on whether the omission has led the data subject to a wrongful perception that ultimately affects the execution of the right to informational self-determination.

(2) Applying Art. 6 (1) (a) GDPR in authorized merchandising cases

i. Merchandising contracts no longer binding

The most obvious and troublesome issue in merchandising is the free revocability of consent anchored in Art. 7 (3) GDPR. In this sense, mer-

---

443 Vgl. Stemmer, in *Brink/Wolff*, BeckOK Datenschutzrecht, Art. 7 Rn. 55.
444 Kamlah, in *Plath*, DSGVO/BDSG, Art. 13 Rn. 16.

chandising contracts are no longer binding since data subjects can revoke consent at any time and must be exempt from liability.[445]

When controllers remain equivocal about the revocability of consent by neither excluding nor including it in merchandising cases, it constitutes a violation of Art. 7 (3) GDPR, and the legal consequence of this violation is dependent on how serious the self-determination of the data subject is harmed. While one would argue that since a data subject signs such a contract while mistakenly thinking it was "binding", the data subject would have carefully examined the situation before making the decision. If the voluntariness of the choice can be established, the fundamental right of the data subject in Art. 8 of the Charter to make informed decisions about data processing did not seem to be undermined. In short, a violation existed but no harm was done. However, this argument is ill-grounded. Consent is known to enhance control of the data subject as it makes the legality of data processing always dependent on the willingness of the data subject. The data subject can revoke consent anytime and renders data processing void *ex nunc.* Without notification, the data controller "tricked" the data subject into a situation where they wrongly relinquished the control they could have achieved during the processing. Even though the data subject has carefully considered his choice, depriving the right to withdrawal under the guise of a contract was illegal from the outset. In other words, upon deliberate silence, the controller misguided the data subject from the choice that is beneficial for him but undesirable for the controller.

The notification is even more indispensable as the anytime revocability of consent is a rather innovative concept forwarded by the EU data protection. Furthermore, as disclosed in Part I Section 3.1, consent in merchandising scenarios may be binding in Germany. The German court has rejected the data subject's request for withdrawal of consent resorting to balancing interests under § 241 BGB.[446] It was the exact opposite of the GDPR, according to which the execution of the withdrawal of consent should not be contingent on a balancing of interests,[447] and be as simple as the grant of consent and at any time freely (Art. 7 (3) GDPR). Thus,

445 *Westphalen and Wendehorst*, BB, 2016, 2179 (2185f.) Langhanke and Schmidt-Kessel, 4 Journal of European Consumer and Market Law 218 (2015) (221f.); *Sattler*, JZ, 2017, 1036 (1038f. und 1043f.); *Specht*, JZ, 2017, 763 (766ff.).

446 BAG, GRUR 2015, 922 - Veröffentlichung von Arbeitnehmer-Bildnissen zu Werbezwecken, Rn. 38

447 Vgl. Klement, in *Simitis, et al.,* Datenschutzrecht, Art. 7 Rn. 91, mentioning the exact case here and arguing for a different result than the BAG; *Spelge*,

the emphasis on the duty to inform stemming from the principle of transparency according to the GDPR is indispensable to implementing the high-level protection for personal data.

Without highlighting the notification of the unique characteristic of consent under the GDPR, it virtually allows the controller to benefit from its ambiguity. Even though the controller fails to address the revocability of consent, the controller could argue that no confusion has been aroused by its omission as long as the data subject claims revocability. As a result, the controller can enjoy a *de facto* stable position as if it relied on a contract. Lastly, it is the controller's burden to prove that the data subject is not confused by its wrongdoings, which could hardly be met in this situation because the data subject suffered from confusion. Thus, the declaration given by the data subject is likely invalid when the controller fails to notify the revocability of consent at the outset in merchandising cases, and the data processing is thus unlawful according to Art. 7 (2) and (3) GDPR.[448]

ii. Agency-merchandising contracts at issue

Besides, it is arguable whether consent given by a model in an agency-merchandising contract can legitimize merchandising by companies who have not negotiated with the model but the agency. Regarding the data protection law, it concerns the ambit of consent: Can consent be declared to one controller extent to data processing conducted by third controllers who may or may not be explicitly mentioned in the consent?

Under the GDPR, companies who process the personal data to advertise their products are not processors who outright implement the agency's instructions (Art. 4 (8) GDPR). Instead, they are joint controllers with the agency because they make joint decisions with the agency about when, how, and for what purpose to process the personal data of the data subject (Art. 4 (7) GDPR). Thus, third controllers also need to rely on Art. 6 (1)

DuD, 2016, 775 (781); Laue, in *Laue, et al.*, Das neue Datenschutzrecht in der betrieblichen Praxis, § 2 Rn. 14.

448 Art. 88 GDPR provides the margin of appreciation for the Member States in the employment context, but it aims to "ensure the protection of the rights and freedoms in respect of the processing of employees' data". Thus, rules reducing the controller's (employer's) duty to inform do not suit the purpose of Art. 88 GDPR. Vgl. Riesenhuber, in *Brink/Wolff*, BeckOK Datenschutzrecht, Art. 88 Rn. 1.

(a) GDPR, though they are usually not explicitly mentioned in the consent according to an agency-merchandising contract.

On the one hand, the wording of Art. 6 (1) (a) GDPR – the "data subject has given consent to the processing of his or her data for one or more specific purposes" – suggests that the recipient of the consent is not necessarily the controller. This neglect of the recipient is not a mistake of legislators for several reasons. Firstly, Art. 22 (2) (a) GDPR that explicitly requires the counterparties indicates that legislators do give clarity when they need to limit the boundaries of lawful grounds.[449] Secondly, Art. 9 (2) (e) GDPR even provides that active and manifest disclosure by the data subject is a legitimate reason for any controller to process sensitive data. Therefore, the specification of identities of third controllers in merchandising cases is not decisive for them to invoke the consent stated in agency-merchandising contracts according to the verbatim reading of Art. 6 (1) (a) GDPR. On the other hand, this reading would lead to a borderless application of Art. 6 (1) (a) GDPR because the possibility of not knowing the identity of third controllers is not surreal. This fear is even more justified in scenarios of processing sensitive data as any controller can invoke Art. 9 (2) (e) GDPR to justify their processing.

The wording of Art. 6 (1) (a) GDPR leaves room for its application of third controllers. However, the high-level data protection objective may need to be achieved by implementing a relatively strict interpretation of the consent in light of the principles of transparency and data minimization in the GDPR. Therefore, how the consent is drafted in an agency-merchandising contract is vital. Above all, the consent must specify that the data subject agrees to further data processing in terms of collecting, editing, granting sub-licenses, and transmitting for advertising, endorsement, etc., for business partners according to the agency's arrangement. Moreover, to prove that the processing does not exceed the ambit of the consent, try to clarify the business partners if possible, or state the type and area if not. For instance, in the *landlady* case where an agency-merchandising contract was concerned, the data subject gave explicit consent to processing her images by magazines without their identities being determined. Furthermore, she considered the identity information unimportant by stating on the telephone that she was willing to authorize any publications as long as the remuneration reached a certain threshold. In other words, the data subject actively and voluntarily gave up the right to information granted by the

449 Art. 22 (2) (a) GDPR specifies "a contract between the data subject and a data controller".

GDPR to some extent. Though the act was invalid under the GDPR as data subject's rights are not waivable,[450] one could argue that as a professional model, the data subject had a general understanding of the identities of third controllers in the industry. Thus, the lack of such information would not affect her exercise of the right to informational self-determination.

Nevertheless, it is highly recommended and almost imperative for the agency and third controllers to notify the data subject when personal data has been transmitted, according to Art. 14 (1), (2) and (3) (a) GDPR. Failure in the notification would constitute a violation that may not invalidate the consent but lead to an administrative fine under Art. 83 GDPR or damages according to Art. 82 GDPR.

iii. Rigorous conditions for validity of consent

The issue above implies another problem in applying Art. 6 (1) (a) GDPR in merchandising, i.e., data processing for merchandising is likely to be unlawful because of these rigorous conditions for validity prescribed by Art. 4 (11) and 7 GDPR. It holds for both merchandising contracts, namely the standard merchandising agreement and the agency-merchandising agreement.

While scholars argue that insufficient information does not automictically lead to invalidation of consent that renders the processing unlawful *ex tunc*, it is mainly contingent on the nature and content of the information omitted. Business practices do not welcome great uncertainty. Nevertheless, the omission of the obligation to provide information is not uncommon in merchandising because it is a mature business, and thus some information is self-explanatory or not crucial to both parties so that it would not be included in contracts. For instance, one may find that no information about the presentation and duration of the publication in the *landlady* case was discussed by the data subject – the model and the controller – the photographer.[451]

Similarly, in the *company-advertising* case, the content, means, and duration of data processing in the declaration drafted by the controller were stated abstractly according to Art. 13 (2) (a) and (b) GDPR, especially considering that the company's website was not online at the time of the data

450 Dix, in *Simitis, et al.*, Datenschutzrecht, Art. 12 Rn. 6.
451 OLG München, NJW-RR 1990, 999 - Wirtin.

subject's signature.[452] They were not an issue under the German law[453] but is controversial under the GDPR. It can be submitted in the *landlady* case that the insufficiency was not detrimental because the data subject implied those conditions by requesting relatively high royalties and thus would not exercise the right to information self-determination oppositely because of the lack of such information.[454] In the *company-advertising* case, the online distribution neither exceeded the scope of the declaration literally nor was beyond the reasonable expectation of the data subject. The company's promotion had clear relevance to the establishment of the company's website, and the data subject did not bring any question about the means or purposes of the data processing before, during, and after the production of the footage. Nevertheless, administrative fines are conceivable. The lack of clarity regarding data storage could arguably constitute a significant problem according to the principle of storage limitation in Art. 5 (1) (e) GDPR because an indefinite data storage increases the risk of data leakage and thereby poses significant risks to the fundamental rights and freedoms of data subjects. Art. 34 GDPR also requires a default rule on (semi-)automatic deletion of data when the processing is no longer necessary in honor of the default privacy.

iv. The voluntariness of consent given by young models?

In addition to the insufficiency of notification, the solid structural inequity between young models and powerful agencies is another issue related to the voluntariness of consent. Models are not stars when they start their ca-

452 See BAG, GRUR 2015, 922 - Veröffentlichung von Arbeitnehmer-Bildnissen zu Werbezwecken, Rn. 2.

453 For instance, it is well established in a similar case in Germany that the presentation of erotic photos should not be in a manner that would violate the personality of the model unless the model gives explicit consent. See LG Frankfurt/Main, 30.05.2017 - 2-03 O 134/16 - Stinkefingers.

454 One may argue that the storage of her data was necessary because the publication was likely to get that much remuneration. Consequently, if high payouts are only possible in the first 5 years according to the commercial practice, then the permissible duration should be limited to 5 years. Deleting the data after five years is advisable in accord with the GDPR. The ambiguity of the agreement did not lead to the invalidation of the contract because the data subject has already known the information that belongs to common knowledge in that practice, and thus the omission of such information does not affect the rational judgment of the data subject.

reers. However, like the aforementioned "*stink fingers*" case demonstrates, many young models would take (nude) photos for exposure against no remuneration. Their voluntariness in giving consent to such data processing is not beyond doubt.

It is noteworthy that models voluntarily choose the lifestyle to embrace publicity and glamour, and data processing is the inevitable cost. The necessity of data processing for merchandising precludes the application of the prohibition of coupling. Moreover, the competition among agencies and photographers is also intensive, making information asymmetry less prominent. Therefore, it argues that while the dependency of (young) models on agencies should not be underestimated, it should not be overestimated. After all, none of the data subjects challenged this point even in the "*stink fingers*" case and the *company-advertising* case where an employment relationship existed.

Nevertheless, the voluntariness of especially young models against powerful agencies in some agency-merchandising contracts requires a particular examination. As briefly mentioned in Part I Section 3.2.2 (4), the quasi "slave contracts" between young molders who are mainly teenagers and agencies speak strongly for deploying the indicators proposed above for assessing the voluntariness of an employment relationship here to ensure the voluntariness of data subjects. Therefore, it seems important for controllers to prove that no negative consequence follows the refusal of the data subject, and they have notified the revocability of consent to sustain a genuine free choice of the data subject.

However, these two indicators are hardly applicable in merchandising business because the data processing is necessary for their publicity, and once again, the revocability of consent is troublesome in merchandising.

4.2.3 Conclusions

Art. 7 and 4 (11) impose rigorous conditions for validity of consent in Art. 6 (1) (a) GDPR. It enhances the protection of data subjects coupled with the principle of accountability. Controllers must comply with the obligation to provide sufficient and precise information and enable data subjects to withdraw consent at any time. Failure to meet the conditions puts the validity of consent in question. Through the sword of Damocles hanging over controllers, the revocability of consent warns of the unstable legal status and urges controllers to safeguard the rights and interests of the data subject adequately.

Consent in Art. 6 (1) (a) GDPR can legitimize the data processing in authorized merchandising cases but raises many difficulties that seem insoluble.

The most significant one is its free revocability in Art. 7 (3) GDPR contradicts the principle of *pacta sunt servanda* in merchandising contracts. Seemingly, it might enhance the controller of the data subject over personal data by withdrawing consent anytime. It is a deterrent for data controllers as they lose the stable legal status for data processing. Merchandisers would not make significant and long-term investments, which would, in return, affect the career development of the data subject in merchandising. Moreover, merchandisers are obligated to notify the free revocability of consent before the data processing because they have to prove that the data subject was not misguided by the declaration. Otherwise, merchandisers are likely liable for seriously affecting the exercise of the right to information self-determination of the data subject. The omission of this notification would possibly render consent invalid under Art. 7 (2) and (3) GDPR.

Furthermore, the application of consent in agency-merchandising agreements is problematic. While the wording of Art. 6 (1) (b) GDPR leaves room for its application to third controllers that have not been stated in the consent, the agreements must be carefully drafted to include the further data processing into the ambit of the consent. Some ambiguity in consent regarding the duration and presentation of personal images would not be a significant problem for the legitimacy of data processing as it is not detrimental to the exercise of the right of informational self-determination of the data subject. Lastly, the indicators suggested by the WP29 to assess the voluntariness of consent can hardly be supported in merchandising cases even when a severe structural inequity between young models and powerful agencies exists.

It concludes that the consent envisioned by the GDPR brings insoluble difficulties for authorized merchandising. It not only deviates from models' expressed willingness to establish a binding contract with merchandisers but is also likely to invalidate their genuine willingness due to the strict conditions for validity. More importantly, the legal regulation of consent in the GDPR cannot effectively protect models, including the young and powerless ones, even though it advocates a high level of data protection. Nevertheless, controllers are strongly advised to specific contractual terms to avoid unnecessary legal disputes. Moreover, they must ensure that they have informed every detail listed in Art. 13 (1) and (2) GDPR to be exempt from administrative fines according to Art. 83 GDPR.

4.3 Contracts as the lawful ground?

4.3.1 Contracts as the lawful ground in merchandising

(1) The ambit of Art. 6 (1) (b) GDPR

Art. 6 (1) (b) GDPR presents a mixture of private autonomy and legal obligation.[455] Whereas contracts amount to the most critical and common manifestation of private autonomy in civil law,[456] data subjects are obliged to provide personal data for processing according to the contract. Thereby, Art. 6 (1) (b) GDPR allows the controller to obtain a stable data processing position while respecting the autonomy of the data subject's willingness.

Since Art. 6 (1) (b) GDPR legitimizes data processing that "is necessary for the performance of a contract to which the data subject is party", two requirements are imposed to limit its ambit: The necessity between the data processing and the performance of a contract, and the data subject as a party to the contract. The performance of a contract is broadly understood as including primary performance obligations, secondary contractual obligations related to the primary performance and processing in the context of the conclusion, amendment, and performance of a contract.[457] The mainstream opinion is to limit the requirement of necessity only to accessory types of data processing for the performance of a contract, such as collecting and using a buyer's address to perform a delivery service.[458] In other words, Art. 6 (1) (b) GDPR is applicable only if the data subject and

---

455 *Metzger*, AcP, 2016, 817 (825f.).

456 Buchner/Petri, in *Kühling/Buchner,* DSGVO/BDSG, Art. 6 Rn. 26.

457 Instead to cite many, see Albers/Veit, in *Brink/Wolff,* BeckOK Datenschutzrecht, Art. 6 Rn. 43

458 KG Berlin, DuD 2019, 301 - Zahlreiche Datenschutz-Klauseln von Apple rechtswidrig (303). It ruled that data processing for purposes, such as product improvement or advertising was not necessary for the performance of a contract within the meaning of Art. 6 (1) (b) GDPR; BKartA, BeckRS 2019, 4895 - Marktbeherrschung, Facebook, Rn. 671f.; *Wendehorst and Graf v. Westphalen*, NJW, 2016, 3745 (3747); *Westphalen and Wendehorst,* BB, 2016, 2179 (2184f.); *Tavanti,* RDV, 2016, 295 (296); *Bräutigam*, MMR, 2012, 635 (640); *Funke,* Dogmatik und Voraussetzungen der datenschutzrechtlichen Einwilligung im Zivilrecht, S. 271; Schantz, in *Simitis, et al.,* Datenschutzrecht, Art. 6 Rn. 32f.; Buchner/Petri, in *Kühling/Buchner,* DSGVO/BDSG, Art. 6 Rn. 39f.; Plath, in n *Plath,* DSGVO/BDSG, Art. 6 Rn. 25; Heberlein, in *Ehmann and Selmayr,* DS-GVO, Art. 6 Rn 13; Schulz, in *Gola,* DSGVO, Art. 6 Rn. 38, and especailly 40; Probably, Frenzel, in *Paal and Pauly,* DS-GVO BDSG, Art. 6 Rn. 14.

the controller have entered into or are about to enter into a contract whose primary performance is not data processing.

In this wise, Art. 6 (1) (b) GDPR is notably excluded from application in scenarios where personal data has been commercialized to some extent, such as the model of "data against service": It mainly describes the situation where data subjects allow controllers to process personal data in order to get "free" services provided by controllers with the cost of being exposed to targeted ads.[459] This conclusion is also drawn in the EPDB's *Guidelines* in interpreting the applicability of Art. 6 (1) (b) GDPR in the online environment. While the EPDB's *Guidelines* do not confine Art. 6 (1) (b) GDPR to accessory types of data processing, such as electronic archiving, collection of payments, etc., it does argue that data subjects can only give revocable consent to data-driven controllers, such as YouTube, for "free" services because their pursuit of free-of-charge does not belong to the genuine purpose of the service required by data subjects.[460]

One of the reasons argued by scholars is that since personal data is treated as quasi-consideration for the use of such service, and users may also pay monetary consideration, the choice to collect personal data is simply a choice of the controller/service provider, and is thus by no means necessary; The more far-reaching reason is the reduction of the applicable scope of Art. 6 (1) (b) GDPR is decisive to prevent circumvention of Art. 6 (1) (a) GDPR.[461]

Conceivably, if Art. 6 (1) (b) GDPR would legitimize the data processing as the primary performance of a contract, the data-driven controllers who collect and exploit personal data in large quantities would be encouraged

---

459 See EDPB, Guidelines 2/2019 on the processing of personal data under Article 6(1)(b) GDPR in the context of the provision of online services to data subjects, para. 53. Instead to cite many, see *Schmidt,* Datenschutz als Vermögensrecht: Datenschutzrecht als Instrument des Datenhandels, 58f.; Abundant examples and analysis, see *Voigt,* Die datenschutzrechtliche Einwilligung, „Datenfinanzierte Geschäftsmodelle" (Data-financed business models), 171f.

460 See EDPB, Guidelines 2/2019 on the processing of personal data under Article 6(1)(b) GDPR in the context of the provision of online services to data subjects, para. 53.

461 For instance, Schantz, in *Simitis, et al.,* Datenschutzrecht, Art. 6 Rn. 33; *Westphalen and Wendehorst,* BB, 2016, 2179 (2184); Langhanke and Schmidt-Kessel, 4 Journal of European Consumer and Market Law 218 (2015) (220); *Sattler,* JZ, 2017, 1036 (1040); Buchner/Kühling, in *Kühling/Buchner,* DSGVO/BDSG, Art. 7 Rn. 16; Schulz, in *Gola,* DSGVO, Art. 6 Rn. 10; Heckmann/Paschka, in *Ehmann and Selmayr,* DS-GVO, Art. 7 Rn. 17; Plath, in *Plath,* DSGVO/BDSG, Art. 6 Rn. 5; *Piltz,* K&R, 2016, 557 (562).

to include the commercial use of personal data in the standard contracts drafted by themselves. Thereby, data-driven controllers, such as Facebook, Alphabet, Tiktok, Baidu, etc., could replace the anytime revocable consent with binding contracts signed by data subjects. As these controllers always present commercial purposes independent from the data subject's purpose in processing personal data, they would make the data processing stated in the contract as borderless as possible (in terms of content, manner, purpose, and time).[462] Coupled with the facts that data subjects seldom read the privacy policy provided controllers and controllers always take advantage of data subjects' inattentiveness or lack of time,[463] the high-level data protection promised by the GDPR by enhancing the control over personal data would be an illusion. Moreover, as Art. 6 (1) (b) GDPR does not require the data processing must be conducted by the controller who concluded the contract with the data subject, it is well argued that its application in contracts containing sub-licensing terms would render the lawful ground borderless.[464]

Moreover, one can make a clear distinction between the applicability of Art. 6 (1) (a) and (b) GDPR. Some scholars convincingly argue that the contract in the GDPR should also include unilateral legal acts *(einseitige Rechtsgeschäfte)*, for instance, the promise of a reward for the performance of an act *(Auslobung)*,[465] even though the EU legislation, ECJ decisions as well as Art. 4:102 (1) ACQP understand contract must contain an offer and an acceptance of that offer.[466] In this scenario, it seems unreasonable that the data subject, on the one hand, expressed his willingness to offer a

462 See *Westphalen and Wendehorst,* BB, 2016, 2179 (2184).

463 *Solove,* The digital person, 44 et seq.

464 See *Sattler, in: Pertot, Rechte an Daten,* S. 69f. More details about this argument see Part IV Section 4.

465 For the application in unilateral legal acts, see Schulz, in *Gola,* DSGVO, Art. 6 Rn. 29; Schantz, in *Simitis, et al.,* Datenschutzrecht, Art. 6 Rn. 16. Despite the contract being an autonomous concept, the GDPR does not impose any rules on the formulation of contracts. See Schiff, in *Ehmann and Selmayr,* DS-GVO, Art. 7 Rn. 29; *Schantz* argues that the conclusion of a contract thus has to be answered by national contract law in the absence of unified contract law at the EU level. Schantz, in *Simitis, et al.,* Datenschutzrecht, Art. 6 Rn. 21.

466 CJEU, Rudolf Gabriel, C-96/00, para. 48-49; *Schulze and Zoll,* European Contract Law, Chapter 3, para. 64-65. However, from another angle, one could argue that the declaration given by the data subject is an offer, and the contract concludes when the controller accepts the offer. See *Ohly,* "Volenti non fit iniuria": die Einwilligung im Privatrecht, S. 171f. Binding consent to a certain recipient is the same as a contract based on doctrinal arguments in German law.

reward to anyone who has achieved the result but, on the other hand, does not allow the person to carry out the corresponding data processing.[467] However, in this wise, the distinction between contract and the anytime revocable consent in Art. 6 (1) (a) in combination with Art. 7 (3) GDPR would be blurring. For this precise reason, some scholars contest this reading of the contract in Art. 6 (1) (b) GDPR,[468] but they cannot solve the aforementioned unreasonable result. If the data subject intends to improve the legal position of the public by expressing a binding will, there is little reason to deny the resulting reliance interest in holding the improved legal position.[469] The dominant opinion solves this problem. By confining Art. 6 (1) (b) GDPR within the data processing that is auxiliary to the performance of the contract, Art. 6 (1) (b) GDPR is applicable regardless of whether the contract consists of a unilateral commitment or bilateral declaration of will, as long as its primary performance is not data processing.[470]

(2) Art. 6 (1) (b) GDPR inapplicable to authorized merchandising

Merchandising contracts are, in essence, a form of commercialization of personal data. The main performance of the person depicted in that contract is to give consent under the KUG to the merchandiser regarding the exploitation against license fees. Thus, it is impossible to apply Art. 6 (1) (b) GDPR to merchandising contracts according to the mainstream opinion.[471]

---

467 Vgl. Schantz, in *Simitis, et al.*, Datenschutzrecht, Art. 6 Rn. 15; *Buchner*, Informationelle Selbstbestimmung im Privatrecht, S. 257.

468 See Buchner/Petri, in *Kühling/Buchner*, DSGVO/BDSG, Art. 6 Rn. 28.

469 Vgl. *Ohly*, "Volenti non fit iniuria": die Einwilligung im Privatrecht, S. 174.

470 Conditional denial of its application in unilateral acts, see Albers/Veit, in *Brink/Wolff*, BeckOK Datenschutzrecht, Art. 6 Rn. 42.

471 The view that Art. 6 (1) (b) GDPR cannot be applied to merchandising contracts, or at least it is highly questionable, see *Sattler, in: Lohsse/Schulze/Staudenmayer, Data as Counter-Performance – Contract Law 2.0?*, 225 (237); *Schnabel*, ZUM, 2008, 657 (661). On the contrary, *Bunnenberg* argues for an unobjectionable application of Art. 6 (1) (b) GDPR in merchandising scenarios because, under the dogmatics of the civil law, the merchandiser has a protected reliance interest in holding a binding nature and stability of the legal relationship, which overrides the data subject's interest in revocation. While this result is agreeable, it ignores the EDPS' s resistance to the commercialization of personal data and seems to omit a necessary explanation about why consideration

Nevertheless, it is important to note that the data processing for merchandising is necessary for the performance of merchandising contracts. An agency-merchandising agreement, including sub-licensing, serves as an example to examine whether the data processing meets the requirement of necessity as it is more complex and welcomed by professionals in practice.

The purposes of an agency-merchandising agreement for an average data subject are evident: to acquire (as much as possible) consideration and publicity by licensing the use of personal photos while saving the time and expense of contacting business partners. Consequently, there is no less intrusive way of processing data to achieve this purpose than concluding an agency-merchandising agreement. It also holds for exploitation of erotic photos, given that it is the exact lifestyle the data subject chooses, and erotic photos are not sensitive data from the perspective of the GDPR. Thus, the publication of normal photos would be neither the purpose of the data subject nor less intrusive from his or her perspective. After all, the publication of normal photos and erotic photos belong to different professional fields. In terms of data transmission, there is no less intrusive way either because without transmitting the data to third controllers, the contract's main purpose – receiving remuneration from publications would fall through. Moreover, a standard merchandising agreement between the model and third controllers cannot provide professional and efficient management of the personal images/data of the data subject, including sub-licensing. In short, they serve different purposes and are thus irreplaceable.

In summary, operations concerning data processing including sub-licensing and transmitting in merchandising are necessary to the performance of agency-merchandising contracts. If Art. 6 (1) (b) GDPR would apply to merchandising contracts, a more stable status for both parties than the anytime revocable consent could be provided. The form of merchandising contract does not affect its validity under the GDPR since Art. 6 (1) (b) GDPR does not restrict the form of contracts.

On the one hand, the high-level data protection envisioned by the GDPR should not be exaggerated to stifle private autonomy as the data subject in merchandising also wishes to establish a long-term and stable

---

of personality protection under German civil law can provide a basis for the interpretation of necessity under EU data protection law. See *Bunnenberg*, Privates Datenschutzrecht: über Privatautonomie im Datenschutzrecht, S. 59-60, 265-266; *Golz and Gössling*, IPRB, 2018, 68 (71f.), while no argumentation is provided.

cooperative relationship with the agency. On the other hand, the narrow ambit of Art. 6 (1) (b) GDPR would lead to a deviation from the genuine meaning of the data subject. Even in the *company-advertising* case, the declaration given by the data subject by signing his name on the name list (*Namensliste*) is intended to be binding.[472] Moreover, the wording of Art. 6 (1) (b) GDPR – "processing is necessary for the performance of a contract to which the data subject is party" – also suggests that it can legitimize data processing of third parties not mentioned in the contract.

On the other, the EDPS holds a solid resistance to commercializing personal data as it compares a market for personal data with a market for live human organs.[473] In addition, agency-merchandising agreements might increase the risk of data subjects losing control of personal data if consent is not the compulsory lawful ground for the first controller and the second controllers (sub-licensees).[474] Last but not least, if an agency-merchandising agreement qualifies the application of Art. 6 (1) (b) GDPR, the data subject needs to terminate the contract under domestic law even if he or she has not been notified about the second controllers when that contract is concluded. The strength of the protection is thus significantly weaker than the readily revocable consent. The right to object or restrict processing due to challenges to the legal basis for processing would not be very supportive either if the data processing is necessary for the performance of that contract.

Following the mainstream opinion in literature, Art. 6 (1) (b) GDPR does not apply to authorized merchandising as the main performance of merchandising contracts is data processing. Though the data processing including sub-licensing is absolutely necessary to the performance of merchandising contracts, the commercialization of personal data in light of such contracts is strongly objected to by the EDPS, and, more importantly, the relatively broad reading of Art. 6 (1) (b) GDPR would circumvent the pivotal lawful ground of consent and thereby cause data subjects to lose control of personal data.

---

472 BAG, GRUR 2015, 922 - Veröffentlichung von Arbeitnehmer-Bildnissen zu Werbezwecken, Rn. 27.

473 EDPS, Opinion 4/2017 on the Proposal for a Directive on certain aspects concerning contracts for the supply of digital content, para. 17.

474 *Sattler, in: Pertot, Rechte an Daten,* 49 (69~70); *Westphalen and Wendehorst,* BB, 2016, 2179 (2187); Wendehorst, Verbraucherrelevante Problemstellungen zu Besitz und Eigentumsverhältnissen beim Internet der Dinge, Rechtgutachten für BMJV, 201611/2016, S. 51 ff.

4.3.2 Any other possibilities to conquer the revocability of consent?

(1) Cumulation of lawful grounds

The GDPR does not oppose a cumulation of lawful grounds as Art. 6 (1) and 17 (1) (b) GDPR suggest.[475] While the WP29 rejects the idea that processing for one purpose could be based on several legal bases,[476] many scholars express opposition to this interpretation for legal and practical reasons.[477] Admittedly, the practical consequence of the free revocability of consent is prevented by other lawful grounds. It thus might be misleading to data subjects who thought they would be able to call off the processing at any time.[478] However, the GDPR prepares two cumulative measures to address this concern.

First, the duty to inform as an *ex-ante* precaution ensures that data subjects would not be misled in cases of a cumulation of lawful grounds. Furthermore, subsequent modifications/additions to legitimate grounds shall be prohibited because the data subject's informational self-determination would be compromised.[479] The duty of information is enhanced when the controller relies on both consent and Art. 6 (1) (f) GDPR to ascertain that it processes personal data even if the data subject withdraws consent. Art. 13 (1) (d) GDPR requires the data controller to name the specific legitimate interests it pursues when it rests on the balancing of interests; Art. 21 (1) grants the data subject the right to object at any time when his or her data has been processed based on Art. 6 (1) (f) GDPR. Until the controller can demonstrate an overwhelming legitimate interest, it shall suspend processing according to Art. 18 (1) (d) GDPR. This rigorous duty to inform is referential for the cumulation of consent and contract because

---

475 Art. 6 (1) states that: "Processing shall be lawful only if and to the extent that at least one of the following applies." (Stressed by the author); Art. 17 (1) (b) GDPR states that the controller shall erase personal data when the data subject withdraws consent, "and where there is no other legal ground for the processing".

476 WP29, Guidelines on consent under Regulation 2016/679, 17/EN, 22. According to it, a cumulation of lawful grounds is only possible if the data processing is carried out for several purposes.

477 Vgl. Plath, in *Plath*, DSGVO/BDSG, Art. 6 Rn. 5; Buchner/Petri, in *Kühling/Buchner*, DSGVO/BDSG, Art. 6 Rn. 22f.; Schulz, in Gola/Schulz Art. 6 Rn. 11; Albers/Veit, in *Brink/Wolff*, BeckOK Datenschutzrecht, Art. 6 Rn. 24.

478 Vgl. Buchner/Petri, in *Kühling/Buchner*, DSGVO/BDSG, Art. 6 Rn. 23.

479 See also *Krusche*, ZD, 2020, 232 (233f.).

the data subject cannot stop the processing when he or she withdraws consent either.

Imagine if a controller invokes both consent and a contract to process personal data, its instructions to the data subject need to satisfy the respective notification requirements for legitimate reasons and be unambiguous. Moreover, this duty of information must be exercised prior to the data processing, and any subsequent change is prohibited. More specifically, the controller must meet the conditions listed in Art. 7 and 4 (11) GDPR to construct the validity of consent. Therefore, to demonstrate compliance with Art. 6 (1) (b) GDPR, the fulfillment of the requirement of necessity is indispensable. Noteworthy, the requirement of necessity is not contradictory to the prohibition of coupling in Art. 7 (4) GDPR because the latter only "prohibits" the coupling of consent with unnecessary data processing in relation to the performance of a contract. Most importantly, the data subject must be notified that he or she has to effectively terminate the contract to stop the data processing due to the existence of that contract.

Second, the principles of lawfulness and accountability require data controllers to be responsible for the accuracy of their duty to inform. Therefore, if the controller asserts a contract that does not meet the requirements of the GDPR, then it needs to take responsibility for the misstatements. If the controller's declaration is mistake-free, the data subject could easily call off the data processing by withdrawing consent, but instead, he or she needs to first terminate the contract following domestic law. This mistake is not insignificant because the difficulty of exercising the control of the data subject has been significantly increased due to the controller's unintentional/intentional misinformation. Thus, it is warranted that Art. 83 (5) (a) GDPR prescribes the provision of a wrongful lawful ground as one of the circumstances for aggravated fines and probable damages.

In summary, the information provided by the controller must be extremely elucidative and comprehensive provided on a cumulation of lawful grounds. Given the heavier obligations in notification when the controller needs to process personal data based on contractual obligations, the declaration must become extremely long and complicated. It will, in return, affect the data subject's understanding of the content.[480] In

480 Solove, 126 Harvard Law Review 1880 (2013), 1885. He argues that the privacy notice is complex and needs to be explained in detail. A "visceral notice" like the powerful graphic warnings on cigarettes is likely to be inherently incompatible with privacy notices.

addition, the more legitimate reasons there are, the more likely they are to be challenged.

Therefore, contrary to what scholars envision, a cumulation of the contract and consent is not necessarily a better approach.[481] While it is acceptable in theory, it raises more obligations and concerns than what it can benefit in merchandising scenarios. Moreover, since the applicability of Art. 6 (1) (b) GDPR in merchandising contracts is under question, the notification about this lawful ground could lead to liability and fines for misleading information. If Art. 6 (1) (b) GDPR cannot be applied, it is both misinformation and a severe limitation on the right to self-determination of the data subject when the statement drafted by the controller declares that the withdrawal of consent shall not render the merchandising unlawful because the contract is still valid.[482] If Art. 6 (1) (b) GDPR is applicable in merchandising cases, the controller must be very cautious in drafting the declaration to avoid any confusion of the data subject.

It is thus advised here that data controllers choose only the legitimate reason they are most confident rather than relying solely on quantity.[483]

(2) Any other alternatives?[484]

To prevent the principle of *pacta sunt servanda* in merchandising contracts from being overridden by the anytime revocability of consent,[485] some scholars propose to treat the contracts as the legal basis for data subjects

481 Some scholars argued that it would suffice when the data subject is informed that "the processing is not prohibited when the data subject withdraws the consent because Art. 6 (1) (b) GDPR also applies in this case." See Schulz, in *Gola*, DSGVO, Art. 6 Rn. 12; Buchner/Petri, in *Kühling/Buchner*, DSGVO/BDSG, Art. 7 Rn. 39a.

482 Since the termination of the contract shall rely on national law, the "consent" (authorization) in merchandising is only revocable under exceptional circumstances with a due cause like the change of beliefs of the data subject as German courts consistently found.

483 Different opinion, see *Krusche*, ZD, 2020, 232 (234f.).

484 There are also other possibilities in interpreting Art. 6 (1) (b) GDPR by scholars and the EDPB. They are introduced and evaluated in Part IV as one of the solutions.

485 Albers/Veit, in *Brink/Wolff*, BeckOK Datenschutzrecht, Art. 6 Rn. 44; Klement, in *Simitis, et al.*, Datenschutzrecht, Art. 7 Rn. 92.

to give consent in the sense of Art. 6 (1) (a) GDPR.[486] In this wise, consent here is still anytime revocable according to Art. 7 (3) GDPR, but the withdrawal without reason could be regarded as a breach of contract and thus compensation for data controllers is possible based on the principle of fairness. In other words, the provision of consent under the data protection law, i.e., revocable consent, is a contractual obligation, and it cannot be refused without legitimate reasons.[487] However, this proposal would be a deterrent for data subjects to withdraw consent at any time, which seems to defeat the purpose of Art. 7 (3) GDPR. While one may argue that controllers would be more willing to make significant and long-term investments that are beneficial for data subjects, too, the scholars admit that their proposal presupposes strict scrutiny of the validity of contracts. Otherwise, it becomes a cover for circumventing the high-level data protection provided by the GDPR.

Another interesting opinion is to consider the lawful ground based on the balancing of interests pursuant to Art. 6 (1) (f) GDPR.[488] As argued in Part II Section 3.1, merchandisers cannot invoke Art. 6 (1) (f) GDPR as the lawful ground for data processing for merchandising purposes because the interests and rights of the data subject override the commercial interests of the controller. However, in the case of commercial cooperation in merchandising, the balance of interests may be slightly different because the data controller acquires additionally legally protected reliance interests derived from the contract signed by the data subject. The possibility of this alternative is explored in detail as one of the solutions in Part IV.

---

486 Vgl. Klement, in *Simitis, et al.*, Datenschutzrecht, Art. 7 Rn. 92; Schulz, in *Gola*, DSGVO, Art. 7 Rn. 57; *Specht*, JZ, 2017, 763 (769); Ronellenfitsch, Siebenundvierzigster Tätigkeitsbericht zum Datenschutz und Erster Bericht zur Informationsfreiheit, 2018, § 4.9.1.; *Riesenhuber*, RdA, 2011, 257

487 This consideration is very similar to how German courts and scholars understand the consent in merchandising under the KUG, namely, it is neither irrevocable nor free revocable. See Part I Section 3.1.1.

488 Enlighted by the judgments delivered in German courts. BAG, GRUR 2015, 922 - Veröffentlichung von Arbeitnehmer-Bildnissen zu Werbezwecken, Rn. 34f. and 38; LG Köln, AfP 1996, 186 - Model in Playboy; OLG München, NJW-RR 1990, 999 - Wirtin.

4.4 Preliminary conclusions

Personal images are not biometric data of Art. 4 (14) GDPR. Moreover, since the processing defined in the GDPR is different from human cognition, the purpose of data processing is an indispensable factor in invoking the protection for sensitive data as a machine cannot "see" through pictures unless it is programmed to do so. The processing of images for merchandising does not fall under the scope of Art. 9 GDPR according to the subjective approach of Art. 9 (1) GDPR with an emphasis on the reverse burden of proof if the data controller can demonstrate that no sensitive information about the data subject's race, ethnic origin, or health status that could be revealed from the photo is processed. Feasible measures include detailed documentation concerning the purpose, content, and means of processing as well as the business model.

The lawful grounds of consent and a contract under the GDPR are effective ways to implement private autonomy. In merchandising scenarios, the collision of norms between the GDPR and the KUG does not mean that consent in the KUG must be understood per GDPR. Rather, the indication of the depicted person needs to be judged based on facts. This finding does not unduly discriminate against the interests of the data subject because it, by virtue, respects the self-determination of the data subject, and the controller bears the burden of proof that the data subject intends to conclude a contract rather than a simple consent according to the principle of accountability. However, consent and a contract both present insoluble difficulties for authorized merchandising.

Above all, merchandising contracts are no longer binding as consent is free revocable pursuant to Art. 7 (3) GDPR. Art. 6 (1) (b) GDPR cannot legitimize the data processing that is the primary performance of the contract as in merchandising scenarios according to the prevailing opinion. Secondly, given the rigorous conditions of validity for consent in Art. 4 (11) and 7 GDPR, controllers are obliged with a strict duty of notification. Failure to meet these conditions probably results in damages and administrative fines, and if the failure seriously affects the right to informational self-determination of the data subject, the data processing would be regarded as unlawful from the outset. Furthermore, the absence of notifying the revocability of consent is argued to render the consent invalid because it leads to confusion on the part of the data subject and deprives the data subject's rights including the right to withdraw consent at any time. In addition, although the emphasis on the voluntariness of consent in light of the GDPR is warranted and welcomed, especially in case of a severe structural inequity between young models and powerful agencies, the assessment supported by the WP29 is ill-suited in merchandising as it ignores the essence of merchandising: data processing against money and exposure.

The consequences are two folded. On the one hand, merchandisers are dissuaded from making significant and long-term investments in merchandising as their investments would not be protected anymore. On the other hand, it, in return, affects models significantly and contradicts their genuine willingness. As reiterated, both parties in authorized merchandising wish to have a binding cooperative relationship. However, it is further argued that the enhanced protection for data subjects facilitated by the rigorous conditions of validity for consent is not ideal for them, either. The outcome of applying Art. 6 (1) GDPR to the *company-advertising* and the *landlady* case is a good example. While the data processing in the former case was unlawful from the beginning despite the data subject's explicit consent to advertising for the company, the data subject in the latter would probably end up without a job because no magazine would be willing to accept the condition that all data processing regarding photos must stop immediately as soon as she withdrew consent.

Some scholars note the conflict between the principle of pacta sunt servanda and the anytime revocable consent; some suggest a combination of consent in the sense of GDPR and a contract under German law. However, despite all their apparent benefits, counterarguments abound. Among others, the most decisive ones are: the possible circumvention of the revocable consent, the accompanying compromise of the enhanced control over personal data envisaged by the GDPR, and the strong resistance of the EDPS and EDPB against the commercialization of personal data.

4.5 Data subject's rights in merchandising

4.5.1 Mandatory rights under the GDPR

The GDPR is not a single rule that determines the lawfulness of the processing. Instead, it is a complete regulatory system for compliance evaluation of the entire process of data processing. Thus, full compliance with the GDPR also requires a responsive mechanism for data subject's rights. In Chapter 3 of the GDPR, data subjects are granted numerous rights including the right to information and its associated rights (Art. 12-15), the right to rectification (Art. 16), the right to erasure ("right to be forgotten") (Art. 17), the right to restriction of processing (Art. 18), the right to data portability (Art. 20) and the right to object (Art. 21) and not to be subject to a decision based on automated processing (Art. 22).

The right to information and its associated rights are highlighted in the GDPR because they are the foundation of transparency and guarantee the genuine execution of informational self-determination of the data subject. Based on explicit knowledge about data processing, Art. 16-22 GDPR further provide rights for data subjection to control data processing. Since the GDPR pursues dual objectives – data protection for data subjects and free flow of data (within the EU), these rights to control data processing naturally have conditions and exceptions, which have been concretized in their respective provisions and some general clauses such as Art. 85 GDPR.

Since there is no legal text in the GDPR stating that these rights are indispensable, it is questionable whether the data subject can give up the rights voluntarily or if the controller can restrict the application or execution of these rights through consent or contract.[489] The compelling consensus in the literature is that the data subject's rights are indispensable and not negotiable. Thus, any declaration given by the data subject or contractual terms suggesting a derogation or exclusion of the data subject's rights are void.[490] Justifications proceed as follows.

Above all, the rights in Chapter 3 of the GDPR are corollaries of "effective protection of personal data throughout the Union".[491] Both the rights guaranteeing transparency and ones enhancing the control of data subjects undergird the protection of personal data anchored in Art. 8 of the Charter – fair and lawful data processing with specified purposes and, in particular, the self-determination of the data subject.[492] Rendering them disposable would significantly undermine the high-level data protection enabled by the compliance rules and virtually deprive the control of data subjects over personal data.

Secondly, while the rights seem to present uneven protection towards data subjects at the expense of controllers, the GDPR provides a two-tier framework to strike a fair balance between the competing interests of the

---

489 Franck, in *Gola,* DSGVO, Art. 12 Rn. 31.

490 Schmidt-Wudy, in *Brink/Wolff,* BeckOK Datenschutzrecht, Art. 15 Rn. 34; Dix, in *Simitis, et al.,* Datenschutzrecht, Art. 12 Rn. 6.

491 See recital 11 of the GDPR.

492 Dix, in *Simitis, et al.,* Datenschutzrecht, Art. 12 Rn. 6.

data subject, controller, and third party.[493] In the highest tier, the opening clauses in the GDPR allow the Member States to make derogations and exemptions from Chapter 3 for some critical countervalues, such as the freedom of expression in four exclusive fields listed in Art. 85 (2) GDPR, public interests in accessing official documents pursuant to Art. 86, and public interests regarding scientific, historical research, or statistical purposes in Art. 89 (2) GDPR.

The second level involves the handling of details. For example, in Art. 12 (5) GDPR, the controller is allowed to charge a reasonable fee or refuse to act on the request if the claims from a data subject are "manifestly unfounded or excessive".[494] This provision is devised to prevent abuse of rights derived from the principle of good faith. Moreover, concerning the rights to control data processing – be it the right to erasure, objection, or portability – the GDPR sets forth detailed conditions for their validity and exceptions to mandate an interests-balancing in a case-by-case fashion. For instance, according to Art. 17 (3) (a) GDPR, the right to erasure shall not apply, if "processing is necessary for exercising the right of freedom of expression and information".

Lastly, given the conditions and exceptions of the data subject's rights, they are not "absolute" rights that the controller must satisfy if the data subject requests.[495] Rather, the GDPR emphasizes the responsiveness of the controller in compliance with the requirements forwarded by Art. 12 GDPR. Therefore, these rights have some value in upholding procedural justice for the data subject by granting them a protectable legal stand over which to exert control on personal data.[496]

To shape a data processing architecture that is fair, transparent, and compliant with fundamental rights requirements,[497] more reasons for why these rights cannot be waived by contract or consent are needed.

---

493 Vgl. *Benedikt and Kranig*, ZD, 2019, 4 (7).

494 CJEU, Google Spain, C-131/12; Dix, in *Simitis, et al.*, Datenschutzrecht, Art. 12 Rn. 30f.

495 *Gusy*, in: *Knopp and Wolff, Umwelt - Hochschule - Staat : Festschrift für Franz-Joseph Peine zum 70. Geburtstag*, 423 (432ff.). It argues that the recognition of the individual's control over personal data is partly a (mere) political postulate.

496 *Worms and Gusy*, DuD, 2012, 92.

497 *Bull*, Sinn und Unsinn des Datenschutzes, S. 6.

4.5.2 The execution of the data subject's rights

(1) The right to information and its associated rights (Art. 12-15)

The GDPR provides detailed rules to implement the principle of transparency in Art. 12-15 GDPR. A cording to Art. 12 GDPR, the data controller is obliged to provide information regarding data processing (Art. 12 (1) GDPR) and convenience and the executions of rights listed in Art. 15-22 GDPR for the data subject (Art. 12 (2) GDPR). More specifically, Art. 12 (1) GDPR specifies how to fulfill the obligation to inform, while Art. 12 (3) and (4) GDPR set the time limit for fulfilling that obligation. Under the principle of fairness, Art. 12 (5) provides exceptions where the controller may charge or refuse to provide information. The last two paragraphs of Art. 12 GDPR present expectations for "iconization" of the duty to inform.[498]

Art. 13 and 14 GDPR specify the content, manner, and time frame in which the controller shall fulfill the duty to inform when it collects data directly from the data subject or elsewhere, respectively. Mainly, the information concerns the controller's identity and contact information, data processing, including its content, means, purpose, and the remedies and rights of the data subject. Although the provision of such information is mandatory according to the principle of transparency, Art. 13 (4) and 14 (5) (a) GDPR offer a way to soften the legal consequence for omissions, if the data controller can prove that the data subject has already acquired that information. After that, the provision would no longer be necessary.

The right to access in Art. 15 GDPR guarantees the principle of transparency from the side of the data subject. Moreover, Art. 15 (3) GDPR grants data subjects the right to obtain "a copy of the personal data undergoing processing" by the controller. The relationship between this

498 Originated in the Creative Commons, the expression of icons for licensing agreements has inspired a discussion of whether and how privacy agreements can be expressed iconically (standardized) in the privacy protection field. Besides Art. 12 (7) GDPR, Recitals 60 and 166 have also encouraged attempts to iconify privacy policies at the legal level. There has also been much useful academic discussion of this issue and suggestions for iconographic standards: Edwards and Abel, The Use of Privacy Icons and Standard Contract Terms for Generating Consumer Trust and Confidence in Digital Services, CREATe Working Paper 2014/15, at https://www.create.ac.uk/publications/the-use-of-privacy-icons-and-standard-contract-terms-for-generating-consumer-trust-and-confidence-in-digital-services/.

right and the right to information is controversial because the scope of the information they request appears to be different.[499] While the right to information is concerned more about the legality of data processing, the right to obtain a copy focuses on the data possessed by the controller.[500] In qualifying the content of the right to obtain a copy, some scholars argue that the categories of information specified in Art. 15 (1) GDPR are sufficient and that no more data are needed.[501] Conversely, others attach more value on the verbatim reading of Art. 15 (3) GDPR. It indicates that personal data undergoes processing by the controller instead of the information listed in Art. 15 (1) GDPR.[502] In this regard, it is not enough for controllers to provide a copy of the data actively provided by the data subject; They also need to provide a copy of personal data collected from elsewhere and already edited with inputs of the controller, such as examination reviews, assessments by treating physicians, etc.

It is convincing that the data subject can inquire about the legality of data processing and invoke specific claims, such as the right to rectify or delete obsolete data only by knowing exactly what data is in the controller's possession. Therefore, one could argue that the principle of legitimacy is undergirded by the right to obtain a copy to a more extensive extent. The view that the right to obtain a copy is needed only for documentation for data subjects is largely dismissive of the potential of this right in enabling data subjects. Moreover, this actual reading is compatible with the exception for this right in Art. 15 (4).[503] If the content of Art. 15

499 Schmidt-Wudy, in *Brink/Wolff,* BeckOK Datenschutzrecht, Art. 15 Rn. 85; *Wybitul and Brams*, NZA, 2019, 672.

500 LAG Baden-Württemberg, NZA-RR 2019, 242 - DSGVO-Auskunftsanspruch gegen Arbeitgeber, para. 104; *Kremer*, CR, 2018, 560 (563f.); Franck, in *Gola,* DSGVO, Art. 15 Rn. 23 und 27; Bäcker, in *Kühling/Buchner,* DSGVO/BDSG, Art. 15 Rn. 40; Dix, in *Simitis, et al.,* Datenschutzrecht, Art. 15 Rn. 28; *Riemer*, ZD, 2019, 413 (414); Schmidt-Wudy, in *Brink/Wolff,* BeckOK Datenschutzrecht, Art. 15 Rn. 87.1; Paal, in *Paal and Pauly,* DS-GVO BDSG, Art. 15 Rn. 33.

501 *Dausend*, ZD, 2019, 103 (106f.); Paal, in *Paal and Pauly,* DS-GVO BDSG, Art. 15 Rn. 33 und 33a; *Wybitul and Brams,* NZA, 2019, 672 (676).

502 CJEU, YS, Joined Cases C-141/12 and C-372/12; Recital 63 of the GDPR; Franck, in *Gola,* DSGVO, Art. 15 Rn. 23; Bäcker, in *Kühling/Buchner,* DSGVO/BDSG, Art. 15 Rn. 39a.

503 Art. 15 (4) GDPR states that the right to obtain a copy "shall not adversely affect the rights and freedoms of others".

(3) GDPR is merely the categories of personal data according to Art. 15 (1) GDPR, such an extensive exception seems unconvincing.[504]

Regarding the legal consequence of failing to meet these obligations, as consistently argued above, the core issue is whether the data subject has wrongly exercised control over personal data based on misinformation. On the one hand, the right to information is the fundamental and enabling right of the data subject. In the absence of information, the data subject cannot effectively implement the right to information self-determination. On the other hand, not all lack of information would affect the data subject's execution of the right to self-determination. Therefore, one should carefully distinguish the nature of the information and check whether its absence could result in the data subject wrongly exercising control over personal data.

Against this backdrop, the controller in a merchandising case must provide information regarding its contact information, data processing, and the remedies and rights available for the data subject prior to data processing "in a concise, transparent, intelligible and easily accessible form, using clear and plain language". However, the controller does not bear the obligation to provide the data subject with the accounting since the accounting information about the distribution and revenue is in general not personal data, though the remuneration for the data subject is computed on the revenue.

In practice, it is advised to list the information prescribed in Art. 12-15 GDPR in an appendix as an indispensable component of the written merchandising contract for compliance. In addition to storing the personal data volunteered by the data subject separately (also in response to the data portability right in Art. 20 GDPR), it is recommended for merchandisers to store the final advertising artwork separately to respond to the right to obtain a copy of personal data as well. When other person's data is also included in the final presentation of the artwork, some scholars argue for pixilation of other's images in response to the right to obtain a copy.[505]

---

504 Vgl. Dix, in *Simitis, et al.*, Datenschutzrecht, Art. 15 Rn. 33; Vgl. *Härting*, CR, 2019, 219 (221f.).

505 Dix, in *Simitis, et al.*, Datenschutzrecht, Art. 15 Rn. 33.

(2) The right to rectification (Art. 16)

According to the first sentence of Art. 16, the data subject is entitled to request the data controller to correct inaccurate personal data. Stemming from the principle of accuracy in Art. 5 (1) (d) GDPR, the awareness of the inaccuracy does not necessarily depend on the notification of the data subject. In other words, the controller carries the duty to review its data processing operations to assure that personal data are accurate and to erase or rectify the inaccurate data without delay. Therefore, the decisive condition for claiming this right is to demonstrate that the personal data the controller processed is inaccurate. While it is the unanimous outlook in the academic literature that personal data is inaccurate if it does not correspond to reality,[506] it comes into a debate when it involves opinions and value judgments.[507] The seemingly mainstream opinion is that the pure value judgments are exempted from the obligation to rectification due to freedom of speech, but one should carefully distinguish pure value judgments and judgments based on wrong facts.[508] The right to rectification is, in any event, feasible in the latter scenario.

The second sentence of Art. 16 GDPR grants the data subject the right to have incomplete personal data completed. This right might play a crucial role in fields concerning profiling and automated decision-making, where the accuracy of the analysis is based on the integrity of personal data. In this sense, the right to complete personal data is also derived from the principle of accuracy. While it might be elusive for the data subject to sense when his or her data is incomplete, scholars tend to postulate that personal data processed by the controller is "never comprehensive", thus a risk-based approach is advocated here.[509] The more risks are posed to the rights and freedoms of the data subject by processing, the more data are needed to achieve the purpose agreed on by the data subject, and the stronger the reason is to complete personal data.

In authorized merchandising scenarios, these two rights aimed at guaranteeing the accuracy of personal data are not as useful as expected. Taking the *company-advertising* case as an example, the data subject might be able

---

506 Reif, in *Gola,* DSGVO, Art. 16 Rn. 11; Peuker, in *Sydow,* DSGVO: Handkommentar, Art. 16 Rn. 7; BVerwG, NVwZ 2004, 626 - Personalaktendaten; Dix, in *Simitis, et al.,* Datenschutzrecht, Art. 16 Rn. 11 f.

507 Worms, *Brink/Wolff,* BeckOK Datenschutzrecht, Art. 16 Rn. 53f.; Reif, in *Gola,* DSGVO, Art. 16 Rn. 10.

508 Dix, in *Simitis, et al.,* Datenschutzrecht, Art. 16 Rn. 14f.

509 Worms, *Brink/Wolff,* BeckOK Datenschutzrecht, Art. 16 Rn. 57.

to request the right to rectification because the video displayed on a company's website presented a false narrative of him; specifically, that he was still working for the company. Therefore, according to the rights in Art. 16 GDPR, the controller might have to pixilate his facial images, remove the video, or write a statement next to the video saying the data subject named *XX* and depicted in the video (concrete position) is no longer working here. However, even though this claim may be sustained, it does not satisfy the claim of the data subject in the case.

Firstly, even though the German court has argued that the commercial produced by the company did not necessarily generate the idea that the characters in the video were current employees,[510] it is contested here that the personal data processed in the commercial was no longer accurate after the data subject has left the company in light of the purposes of data processing when the controller has collected the personal data.[511] In other words, the controller is obliged to guarantee the accuracy of data up to update. If the purposes of producing the video were to show the friendly and family-like working atmosphere in the company, the participants should be real employees of the company. Therefore, the data subject could claim the right to rectification in the case. Secondly, one might argue that the take-down of the video would affect the rights and freedoms of the other people shown in the commercial since they choose to exercise their right to self-determination positively. However, unlike other rights such as the right to erasure, the rights to rectification and complete incomplete data do not have specific exceptions.[512] The objection based on the harmed rights and freedoms of third parties thus cannot find a legal basis in the GDPR.

Lastly, to make a counterstatement to set the record right may be influential and effective in (automated) decision-making seems absurd in merchandising scenarios. In doing so, the data subject virtually makes him highlighted in the commercial and gives more personal data to the public. All in all, the right to rectification presents a resemblance to the claims for correction, and publication of a counterstatement in Germany discussed in Part I Section 2.2.2. They are effective in protecting the person from distortion or misunderstanding but cannot be used to reduce exposure of

---

510 BAG, GRUR 2015, 922 - Veröffentlichung von Arbeitnehmer-Bildnissen zu Werbezwecken, Rn. 39.

511 Dix, in *Simitis, et al.*, Datenschutzrecht, Art. 16 Rn. 12.

512 Ibid., Rn. 19.

the advertisement and combat the motivation of the merchandiser to use the portrait illegally.

Nevertheless, if the data subject becomes aware of the inaccurate information before making it available to the public and exercises the right to rectification promptly, it might be useful to prevent wrongful endorsements.[513] The data subject could thus rely on this right to correct the statements about him or her in controlling the presentation of the final product. However, it is noteworthy that the right to rectification limits its application within inaccurate data per facts.

The right to rectification, albeit showing both *ex ante* and *ex post* characters, is not quite useful in merchandising cases. For one, rekindling old issues is not a desirable outcome for the data subject who would not want to draw people's attention again to the inaccurate merchandising. This holds especially true in celebrity merchandising. Moreover, this right is governed by the facts instead of the wish of the data subject. This significantly narrows the scope and effectiveness of the right to rectification from the data subject's perspective.

(3) The right to erasure (Art. 17)

The right to erasure under the GDPR is a manifestation of the principles of lawfulness and data minimization.[514] If the data processing is no longer lawful, the deletion of personal data is a proper and necessary consequence flowing from the right to protection for personal data in Art. 8 of the Charter. Reflected in the *Google Spain* case, "erasure" in the provision does not only cover physical deletion in the conventional sense but is supposed to be a term that should keep up with the technology (see the discussion in

---

513 An interesting case in China shows the importance of the right to rectification. The pianist Lang Lang and his wife make endorsements for milk powder coming from two brands and state that my baby only drinks XX brand of milk powder. Since this advertisement is clearly at odds with the facts, it would not have caused consumers to wonder about the creditability of this couple, if they would have noticed the tagline before the ad was released and asked for a correction.

514 Some scholars consider that this right stems from the principles of necessity and accuracy. See Dix, in *Simitis, et al.,* Datenschutzrecht, Art. 17 Rn. 1. However, the principle of necessity, albeit reflected in the principle of data minimization, is not explicitly anchored in the GDPR. The principle of accuracy seems remote since Art. 17 GDPR does not regard inaccurate data as a reason for deleting.

Part II Section 3.2.3 (3)). Thus, considering the technical limitations, it is conceivable to blur an actor's face to render him unrecognizable in a film or TV program, for example, since it is often impossible to delete the scene or sequences composited by several other actors/actresses.[515]

Art. 17 (1) GDPR states six alternative conditions for which the data controller shall timely delete the personal data upon the request of the data subject. The most important ones in authorized merchandising are Art. 17 (1) (b) and (d) GDPR. When the processing relies on the consent of the data subject, the controller needs to delete the data when the consent is withdrawn by the data subject according to Art. 17 (1) (b) GDPR.[516] For instance, the data subject in the *company-advertising* case could invoke Rt. 17 (1) (d) GDPR in combination with the withdrawal of consent to guarantee the right to erasure since he was confused about the binding nature of his "consent" due to the ambiguous declaration drafted by the controller.

It is thus discernable that the exercise of the right to erasure is closely linked to the legitimate grounds for data processing by the data controller. If the lawful ground is consent, a long and costly collaboration between the controller and data subject seems inconceivable. If the data subject withdraws consent, subsequent investments will cease, and previous investments made by the controller will be futile because of the *ex nunc* effect of the withdrawal of consent and the semi-automatic consequence of data deletion according to Art. 17 (1) (b) GDPR. Even though Art. 17 (3) (a) GDPR provides some relatively wide exceptions for the right to erasure, it is questionable whether the exclusive commercial interests pursued by the controller could be regarded as necessary "for exercising the right of freedom of expression and information". No contribution to public discussion or formation of public opinions has been made in typical merchandising cases such as the *landlady* case and the *company-advertising* case. In this sense, only some borderline cases mentioned in Part I Section 2.1.3, such as the *Rücktritt des Finanzministers* case, might be able to invoke this exception.

A due cause, such as a changed belief to withdraw consent to terminate the merchandising contract is required in Germany. Art. 17 (1) (a) GDPR, which requires the controller to delete the personal data that are no longer necessary in relation to the purposes for which they are processed, may

515 *Reuter and Schwarz*, ZUM, 2020, 31 (37).

516 However, this obligation can be suspended if there is another legal ground for the processing.

also be relevant when the processing exceeds the reasonable expectation of the data subject. As discussed in the *landlady* case in association with the *"stink fingers"* case, many details of merchandising may not be specified in the contract for efficiency against the background of mature business practices in the industry. Thus, some excessive processing activities like the editing in the *"stink fingers"* case, or the long-term storage of personal data can be challenged by the right to erasure according to Art. 17 (1) (a) GDPR. Noteworthy, the claim does not affect the validity of the consent but the specified processing operation(s).

In summary, the right to erasure is effectively coupled with the anytime revocable consent.

(4) The right to portability (Art. 20)

As an innovative data subject's right in the GDPR,[517] the right to portability is envisaged to be the "disruptive" right in tackling the lock-in effect of online social platforms.[518] By virtue of this right, the data subject shall request the controller to transmit personal data to data subject self (Art. 20 (1)) or directly to another controller designated by the data subject (Art. 20 (2)), unless the exception in Art. 20 (4) GDPR is applicable. The aim of the transmission directly to another controller is clear: by enabling data subjects to smoothly switch from one controller to another, a competitive environment for data controllers is encouraged for a higher protection level for personal data.[519]

Despite the seemingly strong potential, the fact is that the right to portability has many constraints apart from the exception for protection of the rights and freedoms of others. On the one hand, the right to portability merely covers the data provided by the data subject's initiative or that the controller was collected based on the open-access permitted by the data subject, namely the observation data.[520] In this wise, as long as

---

517 Vgl. *Albrecht and Jotzo,* Das neue Datenschutzrecht der EU, S. 293, 299f.

518 *Kühling and Martini*, EuZW, 2016, 448 (450); WP29, Guidelines on the right to "data portability", wp242 rev.01, 6.

519 Vgl. *Drexl,* in: *Franceschi and Schulze, Digital Revolution - New Challenges for Law: Data Protection, Artificial Intelligence, Smart Products, Blockchain Technology and Virtual Currencies*, 28.

520 WP29, Guidelines on the right to "data portability", wp242 rev.01, 9 et seq.; Dix, in *Simitis, et al.,* Datenschutzrecht, Art. 20 Rn. 8; Herbst, in *Kühling/Buchner,* DSGVO/BDSG, Art. 20 Rn. 11. Some scholars consider this theme contro-

the personal data collected by the controller are not based on consent or contract, or have been processed by the controller with inputs from other sources, and thus become the so-called "inferred data or derived data", the right to portability is no longer applicable.[521] Therefore, the ambit of the right to portability is narrower than the one of the right to obtain a copy of data in Art. 15 (3) GDPR. On the other hand, the GDPR mitigates the impact of the right to portability by introducing a "not very concrete legal concept" (*wenig konkrete Rechtsbegriff*).[522] In Art. 20 (2) GDPR, a data controller must transmit data directly to another controller only if it is technically feasible to do so.

In merchandising scenarios, while information regarding the identity of the data subject in the contract is subject to the right to portability as it is actively provided by the data subject, the photographs of the data subject taken by the controller are in question. For one, it may belong to observation data because the controller collects the data by recording only upon the authorization and cooperation of the data subject. Second, the photos require editorial processing conducted by the controller to become advertisements. Varied aesthetic assessments and alterations have been taken to serve publicity and commercial interests. Therefore, the edited data processed by the controller are more likely to be derived data rather than observed data and thus do not fall under the scope of Art. 20 GDPR.

Against the backdrop, the data subject can claim the right to portability to transmit his or her identification data and perhaps unedited photographs, but not the processed data combined with inputs from the controller. According to Art. 20 (2) GDPR, the data subject may also ask the controller to transmit those data directly to another controller designated by the data subject. However, since the pictures are taken by virtue of aesthetic assessments of the photographer, copyright would be a legitimate reason to limit any further exploitation of the photos in this scenario. Trade secrets would be perceivable if the merchandising relationship between the data subject and the controller has not been disclosed, or information about new products that are being merchandised is confidential.

---

versial and argue for a differentiation based on the type of the services, see *Strube*, ZD, 2017, 355 (359f.); *Gierschmann*, ZD, 2016, 51 (54); Kamann/Braun, in *Ehmann and Selmayr*, DS-GVO, Art. 20 Rn. 13.

521 WP29, Guidelines on the right to "data portability", wp242 rev.01, 10 et seq.

522 von Lewinski, in *Brink/Wolff*, BeckOK Datenschutzrecht, Art. 20 Rn. 88.

4.5.3 Preliminary conclusions

The data subject's rights are essential manifestations of the dual-objectives and the principles of the GDPR. They are applicable and indispensable in merchandising scenarios but not well-tailored to the data subject's expectations who opt for this lifestyle. The right to information and its associated rights in Art. 12-15 GDPR concretize the controller's obligation to inform and provide a new type of right to enable the data subject to obtain a copy of personal data undergoing processing. As cumbersome as it may seem, the merchandiser in an authorized case can meet compliance requirements through programmatic measures. It is recommended that the merchandiser stores personal data about the data subject's identity, the raw data about original photos, and the data of the final advertising image separately, as well as keep proper documentation.

The right to rectification in Art. 16 GDPR is not valuable in merchandising cases because the data subject must prove inaccuracy in data processing. Thus, the data subject cannot require the data controller to modify the data following his or her preferences. An *ex post* claim of this right would again draw people's attention to the wrongful merchandising, whereas an *ex ante* claim would be hardly needed because the presentation of the data subject's likeness is supposed to be appealing as a device for attention-grabbing and image-transfer. The right to erasure in Art. 17 GDPR is a corollary of unlawful or unnecessary data processing stemming from the principles of lawfulness and data minimization. Therefore, as data processing for merchandising relies on the anytime revocable consent of the data subject, this right is impactful in eliminating records of the data processing. The data subject may claim the right to portability in Art. 20 (1) GDPR to transmit the identification data and raw data for photographs, but not the data concerning edited photos, information relating to the merchandiser, or the goods/services being advertised. The data subject may also ask the controller to transmit these personal data to another controller designated, but any further use of the original photographs is prohibited due to copyright. Trade secrets would be a possible objection if information about the cooperation or new products has not been disclosed yet.

5. Conclusions

Following the subjective approach of Art. 9 (1) GDPR with an emphasis on the reverse burden of proof, merchandisers who use personal photos as a device for attention-grabbing or image-transferring can be excluded from Art. 9 GDPR by demonstrating that no sensitive information is being processed under the GDPR. The underlined rationale here is that merchandising differs from the data processing concerned by the GDPR because merchandising is to increase publicity of the data subject and ultimately the goods/service advertised by the data subject. In contrast, data processing aims to extract more information from the photo.

Nevertheless, the high-level data protection facilitated by rigorous conditions of lawful grounds and the mandatory data subject's rights is generally very costly and unfriendly to authorized merchandising and likely to make it unsustainable.

Against the backdrop that Art. 6 (1) (b) GDPR is not appliable in merchandising scenarios as data processing is the main performance of these contracts, the anytime revocable consent according to Art. 6 (1) (a) in combination with Art. 7 (3) GDPR renders merchandising contracts not binding anymore. Reflected in the *landlady* case, merchandising contracts as licensing agreements regarding personal data are in general at risk of being disregarded under the GDPR. In practice, long-term cooperation between the data subject and the controller, as well as the first controller and the second one (sub-licensee), would be hardly feasible because controllers would lack a reliable legal status to invest. Efforts are made to mediate the conflict between the principle of *pacta sunt servanda* and the anytime revocable consent under the GDPR. However, they all suffer from several flaws, including strict and overly narrow prerequisites, compromising the GDPR's high-level data protection, and ignoring the EDPB and EDPS's objections to commercialization of personal data.

Moreover, the rigorous conditions for validity are likely to render consent voluntarily given by data subjects invalid and consequently, the data processing. It deviates from the genuine will of the individual. *Vice versa*, Controllers in authorized merchandising cases are facing insurmountable obstacles. Besides the free revocable consent that would discourage them from making a significant and sustained investment in merchandising, it is almost impossible for agencies to prove that the consent given by young models is genuine and voluntary provided on the strong structural inequity. The *company-advertising* case is a prime example of how the strong protection offered by the GDPR could make ordinary merchandising very costly. Since the controller failed to notify the revocability of consent according to Art. 7 (3) GDPR, consent given by the data subject was invalid as his control over personal data was compromised in a significant way.

Apart from compliance requirements for the legality, the GDPR requires data controllers to establish mechanisms for responding to the rights of data subjects including the right to information and its associated rights, the right to rectification, the right to erasure ("right to be forgotten"), and the right to data portability. Although they are applicable and non-negotiable in merchandising contracts, there are significant questions about their suitability and effectiveness in relation to the expectations of the data subject who chooses the publicity voluntarily.

As a result, while the cost for compliance is transferred to controllers, the uneven protection for data subjects is not necessarily ideal for them. It is conceivable that data controllers would rely on their *de facto* capacity and power to weaken the negative impact of revocable consent. In other words, the more the data subject relies on the services the controller provides, the more difficult it is to withdraw consent and the more *de facto* similar to a contractual relationship.

Part III The comparison between the German legal regime and the GDPR regarding merchandising

1. Introduction

Both unauthorized and authorized merchandising have been scrutinized under the German legal regime and the GDPR. Divergent legal consequences regarding both tortious infringements and a contractual relationship validate the assumption of this thesis: The GDPR would cause a disruption of the right to one's image in Germany.

A problem-oriented comparison presents in Chapter 2. As it focuses on the divergences between the German legal regime and the GDPR in regulating merchandising, similarities such as the unlawfulness of unauthorized merchandising and the construction of consent in light of the principle of purpose limitation are omitted unless necessary. Section 2.1 identifies the problems emerging in unauthorized merchandising cases. While it seems that onerous compliance rules in the GDPR would lead to overprotection for data subjects in unauthorized merchandising, the real and urgent issue is that professional models and celebrities are not likely to be compensated under the GDPR as they seldom suffer from moral damages in merchandising. Issues in authorized merchandising are explored in Section 2.2, including the fact that merchandising contracts are no longer binding, the impact of the autonomous and rigorous conditions of validity of consent under the GDPR, and the consequences of the mandatory data subject's rights. Finally, based on the identified problems and negative long-term consequences, Section 2.3 concludes that the application of the GDPR in merchandising cases is inappropriate as it neither does a good job of curbing unauthorized merchandising nor serves the interest of data subjects. Furthermore, it contradicts the self-determination of data subjects.

Chapter 3 attempts to find possible explanations for the incompatibility of the GDPR in merchandising. Section 3.1 introduces the approach of one size fits for all, reasons for the reticence toward the commercial value of personal data and the resistance held by the EDPS, as well all the data paternalism reflected in the GDPR. After a comparison between merchandising and the data processing envisioned by the GDPR in light of the working papers by its authorities, Section 3.2 concludes merchandising is forgotten by the GDPR, and the application of the GDPR to merchandising is unreasonable.

Chapter 4 concludes the application of the GDPR to merchandising is inappropriate and unreasonable in light of the consequences flowing from the application of the GDPR in merchandising in contrast with the German legal regime as well as the divergences between merchandising and the data processing envisioned by the GDPR.

2. *The GDPR's regulation in merchandising in contrast with the German legal regime*

2.1 Problems arising from the application of the GDPR in unauthorized merchandising

2.1.1 Overprotection for data subjects?

(1) More moral damages under the GDPR?

As discussed in Part II Section 3.2, the civil liability for data controllers according to the GDPR is regulated independently in Art. 82 GDPR. The detailed and extensive compliance rules in the GDPR facilitate for a more friendly and robust recourse mechanisms for data subjects.

Above all, the GDPR applies to every production link in merchandising, from photographing over editing and disseminating to storing and deleting – as long as the operations are digitalized to some extent. In contrast, the right to one's image merely regulates the publication and dissemination of personal images according to § 22 and 23 KUG. Against this backdrop, the data subject, like the one in the *hair salon* case, is entitled to claim damages occurred in all phases of the data processing, while she could only be protected against publication under the KUG.

Secondly, data subjects who are neither famous nor seriously hurt by unauthorized merchandising are likely get more immaterial damages under the GDPR. The GDPR's threshold for claiming immaterial damages is lower than that of the German legal regime. Data subjects shall no longer demonstrate grave mental damages to sustain the claim for compensation. Furthermore, some parallel decisions in Germany tend to reward immaterial damages ranging from 500 to 1,000 EUR for violations of the rights to information and erasure without onerous burden of proof on the side of data subjects, such as proving concrete damages and causation. As presented in Part II Section 3.2.1, data subjects were rewarded 500 to 1,000 EUR per month for a delay in fulfilling the right to information and 300 to 1,000 EUR for omissions of Art. 17 GDPR when the data processing relates to the online environment

Notably, the interpretation in assessing the damage and quantifying the compensation by the CJEU is still pending. It partially undermines the importance of Art. 82 GDPR for data protection. That is probably why the German civil law still plays a significant role in unauthorized merchandising cases right now instead of the independent remedy clause in the GDPR, even though data subjects have argued for the unlawfulness of processing based on the GDPR. Thus, albeit not yet apparent, the generous attitude of the GDPR in the field of moral compensation needs to be taken seriously, and its impact on the German law regarding moral damages should not be underestimated.

Nevertheless, the highlight of moral interests due to the emphasis on protecting human rights is not particularly problematic. Firstly, the principle of compensation for tort remedies is unchanged: compensation is used to fill the damage, and double compensation is to be avoided. Therefore, data subjects must prove damages at first, and the number of compensation is in accord with the damages. The trend for damages increases the cost of compliance for merchandisers, but it does not raise concerns about overcompensation or violations of the rationale of national tort law. The amount of the damages is only several hundred and should be assessed according to the capacity of the controller. Moreover, it is only rewarded after a delay of one month. Finally, the compliance rules do not order the controller to act as the data subject asks but merely respond to the claim. It is reasonable to encourage controllers to fulfill their obligations in light of the principle of effectiveness and dissuasiveness of the GDPR.

Therefore, though the GDPR gives *vires* for ordinary people without severe ideal damages due to unauthorized merchandising to claim more damages than the German legal regime, it is not particularly problematic.

(2) Overpowering data subject's rights?

The non-monetary remedies under German law are premised on illegal acts. In contrast, data subjects can exercise the data subject's rights to any controller who processes their data, and the unlawfulness of data processing is not the prerequisite. It raises the concern as to whether the data subject's rights are overpowering since they do not depend on the unlawfulness of data operations.

However, most of the data subject's rights share the same condition with the German remedies including injunction, claim for destruction, correction and publication of a counterstatement, and the auxiliary claim for information and accounting as discussed in Part II Section 3.2.3 (3). In addition, some rights in the GDPR, albeit legally available, are impractical and not preferred for data subjects in merchandising cases, such as the rights to data portability and rectification. In practice, the person depicted is still addressing remedies available in German law, including injunctions and the auxiliary claim for information and accounting while arguing for the unlawfulness of processing personal data under the GDPR. Moreover, the situation that controllers have to respond to claims for data subject's rights promptly in compliance with the GDPR is not a valid argument when problematizing the strength of data subject's rights. To get a response is guaranteed as a fundamental right in Art. 8 of the Charter and further materialized in the principles of transparency and accountability and Art. 12 (1) - (4) GDPR. Thus, the concretization of the right to the protection of personal data is instead an advancement that has not been explicated in German law.[523]

Thus, the concern that the data subject's rights granted by the GDPR are overpowering is superfluous.

2.1.2 Under-protection for professional models and celebrities

(1) Lack of non-monetary remedies in the GDPR?

Since Art. 82 GDPR only grants damages for data subjects who suffer from a violation of the GDPR, it is questionable whether there is a lack of non-monetary remedies for data subjects from the perspective of the GDPR. However, this concern is unrealistic.

On the one hand, some of the data subject's rights, including the right to object, the right to rectification, and the right to erasure, have a similar protective effect on non-monetary remedies in Germany. For instance, the right to erasure, characterized by the deletion of the personal data or the blocking of access to them, can be regarded as an adaption of injunction in § 1004 BGB aimed at eliminating interference in the online environment.

523 Vgl. *Schneider*, ZD, 2021, 1.

Moreover, the right to information and its associated rights is an enabling right in the GDPR and thus highly practical. Although it does not cater to the needs of data subjects in unauthorized merchandising cases like the auxiliary claim for information and accounting, it is purported to obtain information about the data processing itself to determine whether it is legal/compliant with the GDPR. Furthermore, the data subject can claim further rights or damages based on incompliance. On the other hand, the German non-monetary remedies are not prejudiced by the recourse mechanism of the GDPR under recital 146 of the GDPR. For instance, the auxiliary claim for information and accounting to investigate the profitability of the data processing is also available for the person depicted in an unauthorized merchandising case.

Therefore, to achieve a function such as an injunction deriving from § 1004 BGB, the data subject can choose from the GDPR or the German legal regime as they are interchangeable. Moreover, it is recommended that the data subject invoke both the auxiliary claim for information and accounting as well as the right to information in the GDPR because they serve different purposes. The rule of thumb is to adopt the GDPR's narrative in claiming the data subject's rights as much as possible due to timely response and the principle of effectiveness in compensation.

(2) Incomparable material damages under the GDPR to German law

As illustrated in Part II Section 3.2.2 (1), professional models and celebrities who suffer no immaterial damages but only prominent material ones in unauthorized merchandising cases only be compensated for actual losses such as expenses for inquiry, attorney's fees, and litigation costs. The claim for material damages computed on fictive license fees probably falls short under the GDPR. For one, unlike the KUG, it is not clear in the GDPR whether the commercial interests in personal data belong to data subjects. For another, while celebrities can effortlessly demonstrate the existence of a licensing market for their images, it is questionable whether this market belongs to the licensing market of personal data repined by the EDPS. If it is, then the calculation of the commercial interests in personal data is problematic.

Against this backdrop, in contrast with the German practice, where a reward for a fictive license fee for professional models and celebrities in unauthorized merchandising is very much one of the standard claims, professional models and celebrities have far less protection under the

GDPR in terms of material damages. The main reason is that German law recognizes the commercial interests contained in personal pictures and attributes these interests to the person depicted.

Noteworthy, as the 4th sentence of recital 146 GDPR states that the Art. 82 GDPR "is without prejudice to any claims for damage deriving from the violation of other rules in Union or Member State law", the prevailing opinion among scholars is that claims for damages under national law including § 823 BGB are permissible provided that the violation is not against rules in the GDPR, such as contractual obligations, the general personality right beside the right to informational self-determination.[524] In this wise, it seems possible to adapt some national law to solve the under-protection problem for professional models and celebrities, such as § 823 II BGB in combination with the KUG. However, it is contested because the "other rules" in the Member State law stated in recital 146 GDPR should not be broadly understood so that it undermines the supremacy of the GDPR. In this sense, one cannot maintain that the GDPR takes precedence over the KUG in merchandising on the one hand, but on the other hand, applies the claim for damages based on § 823 BGB in combination with the GDPR.

Nevertheless, the claim for restitution according to the law of unjust enrichment seems applicable to improve the situation for professional models and celebrities, as he claim according to § 812 BGB is not a claim for damages but gratuitous gain by the infringer.[525] One may argue that the data subject could claim the law of unjust enrichment to restore the commercial interests gratuitously gained by the controller through the unlawful data processing since Art. 82 GDPR only regulates the civil liability

524 Nemitz, in *Ehmann and Selmayr*, DS-GVO, Art. 82 Rn. 7; *Kühling, Martini and al.*, Die DSGVO und das nationale Recht, 2016, S. 351 ff.; Frenzel, in *Paal and Pauly*, DS-GVO BDSG, Art. 82 Rn. 20; Moos/Schefzig, in *Taeger, et al.*, DS-GVO - BDSG - TTDSG, Art. 82 Rn 105; Quaas, in *Brink/Wolff*, BeckOK Datenschutzrecht, Art. 82 Rn 8; Bergt, in *Kühling/Buchner*, DSGVO/BDSG, Art. 82 Rn. 12; Gola/Piltz, in *Gola*, DSGVO, Art. 82 Rn. 25ff.; Laue/Kremer, *Laue, et al.*, Das neue Datenschutzrecht in der betrieblichen Praxis, § 11 Rn. 17; Boehm, in *Simitis, et al.*, Datenschutzrecht, Art. 82 Rn. 6; Piltz, in *Gola*, DSGVO, Art. 82 Rn 20. It is stressed that Art. 82 GDPR shall not be circumvented through claims based on § 823 II BGB in combination with rules in the GDPR. See Boehm, in *Simitis, et al.*, Datenschutzrecht, Art. 82 Rn. 32. The opposite opinion, see Kreße, in *Schwartmann, Jaspers, Thüsing, Kugelmann and Leutheusser-Schnarrenberger*, DS-GVO/BDSG, Art. 82 Rn. 27.

525 Vgl. Bergt, in *Kühling/Buchner*, DSGVO/BDSG, Art. 82 Rn. 67

of controllers.[526] However, this proposition is questionable. According to the law of unjust enrichment regarding *Eingriffskondiktion* explained in Part I Section 2.2.1, the restitution presupposes that the economic benefits of personal data should be attributed to the subject. Once again, as the GDPR is equivocal about the attribution of the commercial interests encompassed by personal data, this claim would fall short. Nevertheless, the person depicted could claim the law of unjust enrichment to restore the commercial interest gratuitously gained by the infringer through the unauthorized merchandising under German law since the GDPR does not touch upon the question about the commercial value of personal data, either.

This pure German claim based on the law of unjust enrichment may be contestable under the EDPS's opinion that *a market for personal data is as tragical as a market for live human organs*. However, the influence of this opinion should not be overestimated due to its flaws in many aspects (see below). As long as the GDPR does not reject the attribution of the commercial interests encompassed by personal data to data subjects, the claim for restitution based on the law of unjust enrichment can solve the under-protection problem because it does not resort to any rules in the GDPR.

(3) The long-term consequences of the reticence

Although the application of the law of unjust enrichment in national law can improve the compensation for professional models and celebrities in unauthorized merchandising cases significantly, this "outside the box" solution would hide some serious problems in the long run.

Firstly, the effectiveness of civil damages granted by the GDPR would be undermined due to the lack of economic incentives for data subjects to bring such claims. As more and more data subjects tend to value the commercial value of personal data, the inadequacy of the GDPR for material compensation would become apparent. While it is true that some data subjects, such as the one in the *hair salon* case, might feel morally offended by merchandising, it is also true that some people do not feel distressed about the processing of personal data but only exploited and thus want to claim a fair share of the controller's advertising revenues. Therefore,

---

526 Thüsing/Pötters, in *Thüsing and Forst,* Beschäftigtendatenschutz und Compliance, § 21 Rn. 40.

it would be questionable why the preference of the EDPS should hinder them.

In this wise, if data subjects would like to claim more monetary damages, they would either deploy national remedies as they do right now so that they can get pecuniary damages that controllers have yielded from the unlawful data processing, or they have to pretend to be morally offended to get moral compensation. The latter solution is of course not feasible. As a result, the solution provided by national law instead of finding solutions within the recourse mechanism offered by the GDPR itself would undermine the effectiveness of the GDPR in civil practice.[527]

Another consequence is related to the deficiency of Art. 82 GDPR in terms of material damages. Though the law of unjust enrichment would improve the situation for professional models and celebrities, ordinary data subjects would not be able to benefit from this because they cannot demonstrate the value of their images. Of course, they are likely to have more moral damages, but this builds on their good comprehension of the GDPR's provisions, especially the data subject's rights. Take the *hair salon* case as an example, the data subject only claimed injunction based on German law even though she addressed the GDPR to argue for the unlawfulness of data processing. As mentioned, damages for a violation of the right to information without proving concrete damages or causality are only available for more than a month after the request for information, and damages for omission to the right to erasure presuppose the request.

Therefore, until there is sufficient education about the GDPR, data subjects would suffer from continuous exploitation despite the seemingly generous moral compensation as unauthorized merchandising of ordinary people is lucrative for controllers, unless DPAs start to intervene by conducting investigations and imposing fines, according to Art. 83 (5) (a) GDPR. One may argue that even if the GDPR assigns the commercial value of personal data to data subjects, it will not change the fact that data from ordinary people is not worth much,[528] and they still find it difficult to demonstrate the value of their data. However, no matter how cheap the data is, forcing the controller to surrender the money it saved from the violation is an effective way to stop the violation, as the *Herrenreiter* case demonstrates. Moreover, if a licensing market for personal data would be

527 Frenzel, in *Paal and Pauly*, DS-GVO BDSG, Art. 82 Rn. 21. It warns not to devalue Art. 82 GDPR regarding the dogmatics in national laws, thus leaving it empty.

528 See *Lewinski*, in: *Datenschutz, Dateneigentum und Datenhandel*, 209 (210).

facilitated by acknowledging the attribution of the commercial value of personal data, then there would be a basis for calculating fictive license fees.[529]

Thirdly, the antipathy to the commercialization of personal data held by the EDPS would lead to the general insensitivity of data subjects to the commercial value of their data. Without the emphasis on compensation for the commercial value of personal data from the EU level, ordinary data subjects would not realize that their data is worth money. This problem would be more prominent in authorized merchandising scenarios as they give consent for free not because they do not want remuneration but simply because they do not know there could be remuneration, or they do not know how to ask for reasonable remuneration.[530]

2.1.3 Interim summary

If data subjects in unauthorized merchandising are knowledgeable about the GDPR and correctly assert Art. 82 GDPR in combination with data subject's rights, they will get more compensation for moral damages than those under the KUG. Undoubtedly, this premise is not easy to meet. In addition, the mandatory data subject's rights are powerful in the context of the principles of accountability, and effectiveness and dissuasiveness for compensation. However, both changes in contrast with the German legal regime are not problematic. As the principle of compensation for tort remedies is unchanged: Compensation is used to fill the damage, the enforcement of the right to the protection of personal data by breaking down into data subject's rights and lowering the threshold for moral damages is rather a legal advancement than overprotection. Moreover, the data subject's rights that are suitable in unauthorized merchandising are similar to the non-monetary remedies under German law.

The difficulty of professional models and celebrities in obtaining adequate material compensation under the GDPR needs to be addressed urgently. This resistance to the commercialization of personal data held

---

529 Paal/Piltz, in *Gola*, DSGVO, Art. 82 Rn. 11; *Plath*, DSGVO/BDSG, Art. 82 Rn. 4.

530 OLG München, GRUR 2021, 1099 - Klarnamenpflicht bei Facebook, para.17f. The lack of an established merchandising market (transparency) is detrimental for data subjects to claim restitution because they cannot demonstrate the market value of personal data.

by the EDPS is reminiscent of the *Zeppelin* case.[531] During that time, the German court had to fabricate mental distress to grant adequate compensation. Though the German legal regime solved this issue as early as the middle of the last century, its application is questionable after the GDPR came into force. A significant drawback in merchandising scenarios presents itself by dragging people back to a half-century-old debate: Whether celebrities can be compensated without moral damages when the right to control the commercial use of their likeness is infringed.

The law of unjust enrichment in German law may be a suitable solution here, but it is questionable whether it is reasonable and desirable to look outside the framework of the GDPR to solve a systemic problem within the GDPR itself, especially given its long-term consequences. For instance, the circumvent of Art. 82 GDPR as well as the substantial protection offered by the GDPR, and increased pressure on the public sector. More importantly, the GDPR's reticence and the EDPS's resistance toward the commercial value of personal data would contribute to the negligence of data subjects in understanding and controlling these interests. After all, failing to protect the identified person simply because the harmed interest is pecuniary would encourage data controllers to have endless exploitation of (commercial interests of) personal data.[532]

In summary, the overprotection is a pseudo-question, while the underprotection for models is a real problem and the reliance on the national remedy based on the law of unjust enrichment would present more long-term consequences.

531 From a century ago, America also tended to stress moral damages more than material ones. See Roberson v Rochester Folding Box Co 171 NY 538 (NY 1902). In the case, the plaintiff claimed to be teased by her friends because her (beautiful) back was used to advertise the flour, and she was also called the "flour of the family" in the advertisement. However, the *Zeppelin* case is more noteworthy because the court made up Mr. Zeppelin's moral damages since he had also authorized another tobacco company to use his name and images.

532 Bietti, 40 Pace law review 310 (2020), 377.

2.2 Prominent challenges to merchandising contracts in contrast with German law

2.2.1 From pacta sunt servanda to the anytime revocability

In light of the theory of the *ladder of permissions*, consent specified in § 22 KUG is subject to different conations except for assignment. This interpretation gives dogmatic support for German rulings that consistently indicate the binding nature of merchandising contracts, and the consent given by the person depicted is only revocable for due cause (*supra* Part I Section 3.1.1). By doing so, it not only accords to the will of the person depicted but also protects the reliance interests of the merchandiser who needs a stable legal position to encourage investments in time and money in a not insignificant manner to facilitate merchandising. Consent in merchandising is revocable under exceptional circumstances to protect the ideal interests encompassed by the right to one's image. Based on the analogy of the German Copyright Law, consent is revocable when a changed belief of the person depicted is demonstrated regarding the commercial exploitation, and the right to self-determination must be executed in a contradictory way to protect the core personality interests (see Part I Section 3.1.1 (2))

In contrast, data processing prescribed in merchandising contracts can only resort to Art. 6 (1) (a) GDPR as its lawful ground. The ambit of Art. 6 (1) (b) GDPR, according to the mainstream opinion, does not extend to the data processing that is the main performance of the contract. Otherwise, controllers would flee from the anytime revocable consent to Art. 6 (1) (b) GDPR. As a consequence, merchandising contracts are no longer binding because consent given by data subjects shall be free revocable pursuant to Art. 7 (3) GDPR (see Part II Section 4.2.3). One can convincingly argue that data processing is absolutely necessary for contractual purposes and voluntarily agreed upon by data subjects in merchandising. However, the EDPB maintains that independent commercial purposes of the controller would undermine the protective objective of the GDPR for data subjects and objects to the idea of commercializing personal data, while merchandising contracts are virtually commercializing personal data (see Part II Section 4.3.1 (2)).

Consequently, the data subject's control over personal data is enhanced at the expense of a stable legal position for merchandisers. Furthermore, since the GDPR appears to limit the manifestation of consent only in the anytime revocable form, controllers are obliged to cease data processing and delete personal data when data subjects claim Art. 17 (3) GDPR at the same time when they withdraw consent. Moreover, controllers are not compensated when data subjects withdraw consent without reason. As a consequence, controllers would likely shy away from making extensive and substantial investments because the relationship between them and data subjects is too volatile. This result also falls foul of the willingness of data subjects as they wish to increase publicity and get income by allowing others to commercialize personal data.

2.2.2 Stricter conditions for valid consent under the GDPR

Failure to meet the requirements for voluntariness or adequate clarification could result in the invalidity of consent and thus render data processing unlawful, even though the data subject wants personal data to be processed. Furthermore, the excessive pursuit of formality increases the burden on the data subject and controller in expressing their will and drafting the contract. In addition, the legal regulation of consent in the GDPR cannot effectively protect models including the young and powerless even though it advocates a high-level of data protection.

As argued in the *company-advertising* case, the omitted notification of the revocability of consent invalidated the consent and the whole data processing, even though the data subject supported the data processing during the employment but merely wanted to withdraw consent after he quit the job. Instead of inquiring about the indication of the data subject, the GDPR negates the lawfulness of the data processing outright. The GDPR incurs additional costs for the controller (communicating one-on-one with data subjects and documenting, asking lawyers to review statements, etc.) to produce a simple commercial promotion for the company. On the contrary, without imposing many requirements for validity, German courts analyze the true meaning of the parties based on facts and balance the conflicting interests. In the same case, the German court saw the real issue here, i.e., a misunderstanding regarding the duration of consent due to the equivocal declaration. Thus, the merits of the dispute were whose understanding and interests were more worthy of legal protection, and in no case, it should affect the validity of the previous data processing since the agreement to advertise the company (free of charge) was completely voluntary.

Therefore, merchandisers not only have to accept that data subjects may withdraw consent at any time but also the risk that the validity of consent may well be invalidated by its somewhat defective duty to inform. Given that merchandising concerns an equal partnership, these mandatory and protective measures in the GDPR neither consider the reliance interests of the controller nor faithfully fulfill the data subject's will. Moreover, the principles of transparency, data minimization, and accountability pose serious challenges to contract-drafting, and the execution of the principles themselves is still unclarified. Thus, controllers need to explicate every detail in contracts, even though this is self-explanatory among professionals. Minor flaws would put the cooperation in danger. For instance, in the *landlady* case, even though the ambiguity about the means and duration of the merchandising was innocuous, it qualified as a violation of the compliance rules in the GDPR, and repeated violations on a systematic and large scale are likely to result in huge fines. Thus, an additional annex of the merchandising contract seems in need. *Vice versa*, data subjects also need to read more of the terms and be extra careful about the terms that deviate from business practices because explicit consent to data processing that touches the core interests of personality is valid based on the *"stink fingers"* case.

Thus, it is likely to lead the jurisprudence established in that case to the opposite of what it sought – to help the controller "ambush" the data subject when the data subject signs the unconventional exploiting acts without reading. After all, overly complex and lengthy information reduces the comprehension of data subjects and the efficiency of collaboration.[533] In other words, complete reliance on contracts without trusting the experience and self-sufficiency of professionals in proven business practices does not always lead to results that meet the expectations of the parties. In doing so, it significantly reduces efficiency and considerably increases the burden on both sides in the established merchandising business. Thus, data subjects would find it more difficult to establish cooperation or get lower income due to the higher compliance costs taken by the controllers. Neither result is desirable for data subjects because it does not fulfill their merchandising needs.

Compared with German law, high-level data protection is generally very costly and ill-suited to authorized merchandising and likely to make it unsustainable.

533 Solove, 126 Harvard Law Review 1880 (2013), 1885. He argues that more granularity in drafting privacy policies creates a greater risk of confusion.

2.2.3 The excessive burden for merchandisers imposed by the data subject's rights

Since the data subject's rights in Art. 12-22 GDPR are indisposable in merchandising contracts, controllers shall take these rights seriously with the help of professionals. For instance, a merchandiser is suggested to store personal data about the identity of the data subject, the raw data about original photos and the data of the final advertising image separately from its management and accounting data to meet requirements for the right to information with the right obtain a copy, the right to rectification, the right to erasure and the right to data portability.

Admittedly, some of these rights do not make sense in merchandising scenarios. However, the right to erasure in Art. 17 GDPR, coupled with the free revocable consent, is too powerful in a merchandising relationship. Although the withdrawal of consent does not affect the legality of the previous data processing, the merchandiser should delete all personal data when the data subject revokes the consent. Consequently, all advisements, except for printed ones, must be taken down because it is detrimental to the investments of the controller.

Therefore, it is a compelling illustration of how the mandatory data subject's rights are excessive and unnecessary in a merchandising contract. Nevertheless, the data subject's rights require no small compliance costs but are not well-tailored to the specific expectations of the data subject in authorized merchandising scenarios. Moreover, it is conceivable that the controller would share the costs with data subjects who seek cooperation.

2.2.4 Interim conclusion

The challenges brought by the GDPR in merchandising present themselves in two main aspects compared to the German legal regime. First, the inapplicability of Art. 6 (1) (b) GDPR and the anytime revocability of consent in Art. 7 (3) GDPR renders merchandising contracts no longer binding. Secondly, the mandatory protective measures, including the rigorous conditions for validity of consent and data subject's rights in the GDPR, place a significant burden on both sides.

As models must be allowed to opt out from the relationship at any time without restrictions or compensation to merchandisers, it is difficult, if not impossible at all, for them to establish a partnership because no merchandisers as data controllers would risk a massive administrative penalty under the GDPR to enter into a contract that excludes the data subject's right of withdrawal. Not only would this deadlock harm merchandisers' legitimate business interests, but it also deals a devastating blow to the development of models' careers and even affects the operation of the market and people's entertainment life.

In summary, the mandatory protective measures in the GDPR deviate from the genuine wish of data subjects and do not do an excellent job of protecting data subjects. Thus, the acute and detrimental incompatibility aroused by the GDPR with merchandising needs a solution urgently.

2.3 Inappropriate application of the GDPR in merchandising

Based on the comparison, it is argued that the direct application of the GDPR in merchandising is not appropriate and likely to make merchandising unsustainable.

Under the German legal regime, the genuine wish of the individual in a merchandising scenario – to get profits by granting the controller a relatively stable legal status to exploit the commercial value of his or her data by exhibiting and sometimes sub-licensing – is recognized and respected. Upon this premise, varied monetary and non-monetary remedies have been developed to help the person depicted curb unauthorized merchandising by recovering the license fees he or she is entitled to and thus make the infringer unprofitable. On the flip side, by interpreting consent, German law provides the model with varied tools for disposition of his or her rights including establishing a binding, cooperative (and long-term) relationship through a legal act. Thus, the merchandiser with a stable status shall combine its image with the model's image to increase sales, and simultaneously the model is allowed to use the merchandiser's social and pecuniary resources to gain higher exposure and career development opportunities. At the same time, the law intervenes only when it is necessary to defend the core personality interests. The analogies with the German Copyright law regarding revocability of consent and the construction of consent in case of doubt strike a fair balance between the person depicted and the merchandiser without dismissing the inalienability of personality rights.

However, under the GDPR, the high-level protection for data subjects deviates from the genuine wish of the individual in a merchandising scenario. As the attribution of personal data for data subjects is not clear under the GDPR, professional models and celebrities are challenged to obtain adequate material compensation under the GDPR. By the same token, merchandising contracts do not bind data subjects. Instead, they are "forced" to enhance the position in controlling personal data by making the lawfulness of data processing by the controller dependent on their anytime revocable consent. The data subject's autonomy is restricted because the GDPR deprives the data subject of the possibility to express willingness to be bound by his or her commitments to merchandising. Hence, it becomes increasingly difficult for the data subject to find partners willing to invest consistently in a state without protection. Moreover, even if the data subject finds a partner, the mandatory protective measures, including the rigorous conditions for validity of consent and the data subject's rights, make the partner assume all risks arising from the cooperation to enforce uneven protection for the data subject. The controller needs to account for any ambiguities in the agreement. Furthermore, any trivial incompliance with the GDPR is eligible for civil damages and administrative fines, not to mention how excessive and unnecessary the data subject's rights are in a merchandising contract.

Before diving into the solutions, here is the right place to explore the reasons for the main divergences. In doing so, it can prove whether the direct application of the GDPR in merchandising is reasonable, on the one hand, and provide starting points for solutions to address the inappropriate results deriving from the severe discrepancies between the German legal regime regulating merchandising and protection provided by the GDPR, on the other.

3. *Possible explanations for the incompatibility*

3.1 Possible reasons for the high-level data protection of the GDPR

3.1.1 The approach of one size fits for all

One of the reasons is that the GDPR treats all forms of data processing for varied purposes equally. By conceptualizing varied operations regarding personal data by the term "processing", not only are legal overlaps emerging hand in hand as automated processing technologies become widespread, but challenges also as individuality and characteristics in different scenarios regarding the claims of data subjects, the interests of data subjects and controllers, and data processing are all ignored.

Such a mindset of an integrated view for data processing has its roots in the history of the data protection law in the EU as well as the Council of Europe. As discussed in Part II Section 2, the need for personal data protection stemmed from the concern about the risks that automated data processing technologies might pose to individual freedoms and rights. Automated data processing technology is perceived as particularly risky as it facilitates the construction of integrated information systems for individual persons through an integration of data collection, recording, analysis, combination (transmission), and storage.[534] Thus, the GDPR, from its inception, was intended to control every aspect of the processing of personal data and to treat every processing method and link equally. Its reason resides in the consideration that fundamental rights, particularly the right to informational self-determination, are affected by all forms of data processing regardless of its material and territorial characteristics; and the risks posed by data processing are so great that they warrant some preventive protection norms.[535] For this precise reason, the GDPR leans on compliance requirements and the accountability of controllers.

On the contrary, the KUG has been able to regulate merchandising for more than a century effectively because its regulatory purposes are catering to the need of the right holders in light of the specific scenarios. The KUG always provides suitable protection without fabricating or neglecting damages, be it economic or moral interests, celebrities or ordinary people, celebrities or ordinary people. The enrichment of the connotation and disposability of the right to one's image rights is facilitated by constant refinement of norms and legal development (*Rechtsfortbildung*) by differentiation. In this sense, the risk-based approach adopted by the GDPR could be a tool to alleviate tensions arising when the obligations are disproportional to the data processing. However, the equivocal description of risks and their assessment under the GDPR does not lend it to easy execution.

---

534 BVerfG, NJW 1984, 419 - Volkszählung, para. 145; Council of Europe, Convention for the Protection of Individuals with regard to Automatic Processing of Personal Data, European Treaty Series (ETS) No. 108, Art. 2 (b); Evans, 29 THE AMERICAN JOURNAL OF COMPARATIVE LAW 571 (1981) (578); Zech, 11 Journal of Intellectual Property Law & Practice 460 (2016) (461); OECD, Exploring the Economics of Personal Data: A Survey of Methodologies for Measuring Monetary Value, OECD Digital Economy Papers, No. 220, 10-13.

535 BVerfG, NJW 2000, 55 - Telekommunikationsüberwachung I, the 4th Guideline; *Roßnagel*, in: *Hill, E-Transformation. Veränderung der Verwaltung durch digitale Medien*, 79 (89).

Thus, the jurisprudence of the KUG is acclaimed because it has already paved the way in concretizing some contexts of data processing in light of the risk-based approach.

3.1.2 Reasons for the reticence towards the commercial value of personal data

The focus of the EU data protection law is consistently on the damages and threats that digitalization might pose to individual freedoms and rights instead of noticing what digitalization might bring to individuals. The starting point for data protection – the rights and freedoms of individuals anchored in Art. 8 ECHR and Art. 7 and 8 of the Charter – further supports the empowerment of data subject with substantial defensive rights, such as the right to erasure, rectification, object, portability, and the enabling right – the right to information. One can only ask to delete personal data upon the right to erasure or to withdraw consent according to Art. 7 (3) GDPR (i.e., negative consequences based on negative rights).[536] On the flip side, the person can decide when personal data do not need to be deleted and under what conditions he or she would not withdraw consent. However, the GDPR is reticent about this positive aspect of the rights of data subjects. Though recital 7 of the GDPR states that "natural persons should have control of their own personal data", it is achieved through negative rights. Some scholars even argue that "the GDPR *de facto* assigns property rights (the "residual right") on personal data to the data collector",[537] since the GDPR only carves out some (moral) rights such as the right to information and erasure for data subjects and does not mention economic rights at all.

Yet, it would be a misconstruction that the EU data protection law overlooks the commercial value of personal data. From the inception of the 108 Convention, the omnibus approach to governing both public and private sectors alike became the principle of the subsequent legislation in the EU. In recital 6 GDPR, private companies are mentioned before public

536 Vgl. *Dickmann*, r+s, 2018, 345 (350).

537 Duch-Brown, et al., The economics of ownership, access and trade in digital data, 2017, 17.

authorities in respect of making use of personal data.[538] As the commercial value of personal data is indisputably the core, if not the only, reason to drive private companies in collecting, processing, and storing data,[539] the precautions against the use of data by private companies at the EU level is a clear indication of the importance the GDPR places on the economic benefits of personal data.

Moreover, even those scholars who argue that the GDPR has assigned the commercial value of personal data to controllers *de facto* admit that the GDPR by law *(de jure)* does not assign property rights on personal data to the data controller.[540] Reading from the context, the gist of their argument would rather be that since personal data are easily transferred to data collectors the absence of defined ownership right regarding personal data in the GDPR may be beneficial in avoiding anti-common problems in data among controllers.[541] Furthermore, the intrinsic value of personal data is the natural person identified or identifiable.[542] Thus, any exploitation of that value, be it financial or spiritual, will inevitably pass on the harm to the identified person. Given the fact that one's consent is increasingly used as a tool to exploit the commercial value of personal data,[543] the denial that individuals can protect the commercial value of personal data is

538 It states, "technology allows both private companies and public authorities to make use of personal data on an unprecedented scale in order to pursue their activities".

539 In an enterprise environment, personal data have always been likened to the "new oil" because they are raw material to conduct digital transformation in respect of developing customer networks, building platforms, keeping innovating, etc. Instead of citing many, see *Schefzig*, K&R Beihefter, 2015, 3; *Rogers*, The Digital Transformation Playbook: Rethink Your Business for the Digital Age, 89 et seq.

540 Duch-Brown, et al., The economics of ownership, access and trade in digital data, 2017, 17; Cf. Körner, GDPR – boosting or choking Europe's data economy?, 2018, at https://www.dbresearch.de/servlet/reweb2.ReWEB?rwnode=NAVIGATION&rwsite=RPS_EN-PROD&rwobj=ReDisplay.Start.class&document=PROD0000000000470381.

541 Duch-Brown, et al., The economics of ownership, access and trade in digital data, 2017, 31.

542 Art. 1 (1) GDPR states, "This Regulation lays down rules relating to the protection of natural persons with regard to the processing of personal data and rules relating to the free movement of personal data"; BVerfG, NJW 1984, 419 - Volkszählung, para. 94; Hornung/Speicker gen. Döhmann, in *Simitis, et al.*, Datenschutzrecht, Art. 1 Rn. 3; *Büchler*, AcP, 2006, 300 (324).

543 *Rogosch and Hohl*, Data Protection and Facebook: An Empirical Analysis of the Role of Consent in Social Networks, 63.

virtually to turn a blind eye to the data market that exists.[544] To recognize and protect the commercial interests encompassed by the right to the protection of personal data can thus better protect data subjects from exploitation by controllers driven by commercial motives.

The free flow of personal data, as one of the dual objectives of the GDPR, may be used to make some interpretations in light of the commercialization of personal data since a functioning market is purported to allocate recourses efficiently.[545] However, the materialization of the free flow of personal data in specific provisions is difficult to find.[546] A fortiori, the free flow of personal data is suggested to be understood as guaranteed as the GDPR has harmonized data protection laws across the Member States at a higher level.[547]

Against this background, a possible reason for the reticence on behalf of GDPR can be deduced from the history of the regulation based on the KUG over merchandising. After the recognition of the commercial value of personal data, the next logical step is to alienate personal data from the person identified to some extent.[548] Otherwise, people would wonder why they could only be compensated when the third party illegally exploits their data but cannot legally profit from letting the third party exploit actively. Therefore, one should be very cautious in opening the floodgate because the consequences for data subjects are not as certain, established, and obvious as the ones of merchandising. Even though personal data *per se* could be non-transferable without prejudicing the tradability of its ma-

---

544 Most data brokers have already traded data since the 1970s for direct marketing. See Ramirez, Brill, Ohlhausen, Wright and McSweeny, Data Brokers: A Call For Transparency and Accountability, 2014, 1 and 12 et seq.; Simonite, MIT Technology Review (2014)at https://www.technologyreview.com/2014/02/12/174259/sell-your-personal-data-for-8-a-month/; Abraham and Oneto, Berkley School of Information W231-1 (2015)1 et seq, at https://www.ischool.berkeley.edu/sites/default/files/projects/abraham-oneto-final-paper.pdf.

545 Vgl. Radin, 15 Journal of Law and Commerce 509 (1996) (514-516).

546 See *Sattler, in: Lohsse/Schulze/Staudenmayer, Data as Counter-Performance – Contract Law 2.0?*, 225 (233).

547 Recital 10 of the GDPR; CJEU, Lindqvist, C-101/01, para. 96; CJEU, European Commission v. Germany, C-518/07, para. 20; CJEU, ASNEF, Joint cases C-468/10 and C-469/10, para. 29; Schantz, in *Brink/Wolff*, BeckOK Datenschutzrecht, Art. 1 Rn. 3.

548 An example, see the right to one's image Part I Section 3.1.1. BGH, GRUR 1956, 427 - Paul Dahlke,429; BGH, GRUR 2000, 709 - Marlene Dietrich, para. 31. The pecuniary components of personality rights are not indissolubly linked to the person in the same way as the ideal ones. See *Sattler*, JZ, 2017, 1036 (1045).

terial interests, the serious power and informational asymmetry between controllers and average data subjects would easily distort the licensing of data that is supposed to be fair.[549]

Thus, the focus of the entire regulatory complexity of the GDPR is on passive defense rather than being active in elucidating the commercial value of personal data.

The EDPS further highlights the concerns about the consequences of the commercialization of personal data because it contends that internet users are fraught with cognitive deficiency and tend to give (access to) their data for trivial benefits.[550] By illustrating the situation in which users of web services allow the operators to collect personal data in return for (free) services, the EDPB shares similar opinions.[551]

Upon this conception, the GDPR takes the priority to guarantee the data subject's unbreakable control over data rather than facilitating a property right that would be transferred to the controller ultimately and easily.[552] Thereby, the GDPR limits the ability of data subjects to dispose of personal data by fixing their consent as revocable anytime. In other words, the GDPR establishes a system analogous to moral rights that are inalienable from the data subject yet can break through the relative relationship of

549 Cf. *Lanier, Weyl and McQuaid*, Harvard Business Review, 2018, 2 (5 et seq.), at http://eliassi.org/lanier_and_weyl_hbr2018.pdf. Out of similar concerns, it advocates establishing MIDs (mediators of individual data) to help ordinary people assert their economic rights vis-à-vis large data-driven companies.

550 *Preibusch, Kübler and Beresford*, Electronic Commerce Research, 2013, 423. Verified by experiments, most consumers would give up privacy for 1 dollar discount; Solove, 126 Harvard Law Review 1880 (2013) (1883-1893), with further references.

551 EDPB, Guidelines 2/2019 on the processing of personal data under Article 6(1) (b) GDPR in the context of the provision of online services to data subjects, para. 4.

552 There is an American case to demonstrate that the alienability shall not be attributed to interests or rights that "constitute the person and the general essence of his or her self-consciousness" (*welche meine eigenste Person und das ihr allgemeine Wesen meines Selbstbewusstseins ausmachen*). See *Hegel,* Grundlinien der Philosophie des Rechts, § 66. In the case, Brooke Shields, an American actress, sought to dissolve a contract for the transfer of her right of publicity regarding nude photographs signed by her mother when Brooke was a teenager. The New York court held that the right of publicity was freely transferable as a property right, and thus that once the holder transferred it, he or she had no right of withdrawal because promises must be kept. See Shields v Gross 58 N.Y.2d 338 (N.Y. 1983).

contracts.[553] Thus, even though data subjects do not possess any negotiation power in the face of data-driven companies, they can walk away with their data at any time felicitated by flanking measures including the data subject's rights, the principles of data processing, and some default privacy rules to ensure the high level of data protection.[554] This protection is effective and reasonable because data subjects are *de facto* not given any possibility to negotiate with controllers. In practice, pre-drafted, standard contracts filled with legal and technical jargon prevail in the online environment aiming to collect as much data as possible, profile individuals for targeted advertising, and store data for future needs.

3.1.3 Protective provisions stemming from the data-paternalism

Paternalism, albeit lacking legal definition, has two significant characteristics: To protect people for their good by (partially) negating their decisions.[555] Restricting private autonomy to protect the fundamental rights and freedoms of individuals is not a new legal phenomenon. *Dworkin* has even summarized a list of legal provisions in different legal areas that protect people from being harmed by their own decisions.[556] Specified in the legal area of personality rights, the boundary of legal paternalism seems to be the eternal theme,[557] which outlines the boundary of the disposition of personality rights.[558] Therefore, as the history of the development of the jurisprudence of the KUG shows, the requirements of protecting personal images change with the conception and moral values of people that are underpinned by advancements of economy and technology. In this sense, one should always ask why his or her dispositive power should be limited.

Under the data protection law, there has been a growing acceptance of "data paternalism" (*Datenpaternalismus*) in the face of data-driven

553 Calabresi and Melamed, 85 Harvard Law Review 1089 (1972), 1111 et seq.

554 See *Lauber-Rönsberg*, AfP, 2019, 373 (376).

555 *Eidenmüller*, Effizienz als Rechtsprinzip, S. 359.

556 *Dworkin*, The Monist, 1972, 64 (65 et seq.)

557 Vgl. BGH, GRUR 2000, 709 - Marlene Dietrich, para. 34; *Götting*, Persönlichkeitsrechte als Vermögensrechte, S. 7f.; *Ohly*, AfP, 2011, 428 (431).

558 *Eidenmüller*, Effizienz als Rechtsprinzip, S. 385f. He addresses that a series of problems come up when the untransferable and indispensable part of the personality is immaterial and ideal instead of a pound of flesh like Shylock asked from Antonio.

practices.[559] Reasons in economic and political aspects are briefly introduced as follows:[560]

Sometimes, data subjects are unable to make a true and rational judgment because of structural problems.[561] In practice, long, complex, and obscure privacy policies hinder data subjects from making knowingly and rational judgments – if they had enough information and time to deliberate their decisions concerning the processing, their choices would be different.[562] It nudges data subjects to give their data freely to data controllers for unnecessary purposes and to be fed up with profiling, targeted advertising, etc. Thus, data subjects cannot and shall not self-incriminate for the decisions that they would not make if they had the choice and information.[563] Moreover, as people are more attempted toward short-term preferences over long-term ones, they would give up their data for trivial benefits, though they know privacy is important and valuable.[564]

---

559 *Krönke*, Der Staat, 2016, 319.

560 A comprehensive and thorough discourse on this issue is neither possible nor necessary for this dissertation (the data paternalism reflected in the GDPR would amount to another dissertation). This part only briefly introduces the ones that are relevant for making a distinction between the data processing envisioned by the GDPR and merchandising. A general elucidation for the legitimacy of legal partialism in terms of efficiency and politic policy as well as the respective counterarguments, see *Eidenmüller,* Effizienz als Rechtsprinzip, S. 365-373.

561 Solove, 126 Harvard Law Review 1880 (2013), 1888 et seq.

562 Another study reckons that if people read the privacy policies of the websites they visit verbatim over a year, the lost productivity is worth $781 billion. See McDonald and Cranor, 4 A Journal of Law and Policy for the Information Society 543 (2008), 564. These studies, despite revolving around privacy policies online, reveal the common problems raised by the stricter duty to inform under high-level protection for data subjects: in addition to higher compliance costs, a more transparent policy, while beneficial for the data subject to have sufficient information, also requires more effort and time on his or her part. Thus, effective self-management/determination is difficult to achieve with transparent policies alone if there is a lack of proactive participation by the data subject.

563 This justification must be distinguished from the one for prescribing default rules in the GDPR, such as the default-privacy and design-privacy model in Art. 25 GDPR. In short, the latter requires a stronger rationale than guaranteeing the voluntariness of self-decisions, such as to protect third parties, social welfare, and the public interest, because the law needs to justify why it needs to "nudge" the data subject into choosing something for the sake of a better outcome he or she would not otherwise choose voluntarily. See *Krönke,* Der Staat, 2016, 319 (329).

564 *Acquisti and Grossklags,* in: *Acquisti, Digital Privacy: Theory, Technologies, and Practices*, 363 (372); The contradiction between short-term and long-term prefer-

Pricing (the consideration for personal data) cannot be left to the market either because data subjects themselves would largely underestimate the commercial value of personal data.[565] Some scholars have likened the production of personal data to domestic work (often performed by women), arguing that they both contribute significantly to productivity but are grossly undervalued.[566] Moreover, even if the valuation of the data is accurate, there is still a risk that price inequities between the poor and rich exists, and the former are more vulnerable in becoming "data slaves" catering to all needs of controllers including those not yet determined.[567] In this scenario, what being called as the external moral cost, proposed by *Calabresi*, plays a non-negligible role in assessing the cost of legislation; if it is large enough, there is more reason to argue that the protection for personal data shall not be alienated from the data subject.[568]

Anchored in the text of the GDPR, the protection for personal data is inalienable from data subjects due to the imperative of fundamental rights including personality as well as the right to privacy (recital 1 GDPR).[569] Based on the *categorical imperative (Kategorischer Imperativ)*, the assignment of personality rights is forbidden. For one, the protection of personal data is so treasured that the loss of it would undermine the dignity and personality of a human being. Secondly, the controller over personal data should be warranted because data subjects should be given an opportunity to learn from their mistakes regarding disposing of their data.[570] Another

---

ences as one of the justifications for legal paternalism, see Cooter, 64 Notre Dame Law Review 817 (1989) (825).

565 While people tend to give their data for 1 dollar or discounts for pizza, Google (Alphabet), Amazon, Facebook, Apple, as well as Alibaba, Tencent and ByteDance are becoming monopiles or oligopolies relying on large datasets of personal data. See *Posner and Weyl,* Radical Markets: Uprooting Capitalism and Democracy for a Just Society, 234-235.

566 *Jarrett,* in: *David and Christian, Digital Objects, Digital Subjects: Interdisciplinary Perspectives on Capitalism, Labour and Politics in the Age of Big Data*, 103 (107); Cf. Bruni, 41 CARDOZO LAW REVIEW 2203 (2020) (2233); *Posner and Weyl,* Radical Markets: Uprooting Capitalism and Democracy for a Just Society, 209 with further references.

567 *Posner*, Regulation: the Cato review of business and government, 1978, 19 (20).

568 *Calabresi,* The Future of Law and Economics: Essays in Reform and Recollection, 46-48.

569 *Oostveen and Irion,* in: *Bakhoum, Personal Data in Competition, Consumer Protection and IP Law - Towards a Holistic Approach?* , 7 (9); Bietti, 40 Pace law review 310 (2020) (368).

570 *Eidenmüller,* Effizienz als Rechtsprinzip, S. 384-385; If it is foreseeable from the outset that the lender is unlikely to be free from the burden of the debt

reason that has recently received increasing attention is that personal data have a collective value and thus the disposal of personal data is beyond the capabilities of individuals.[571] Reflected in the Cambridge Analytica scandal,[572] a person's decisions regarding privacy settings not only affect other people (his or her "friends") directly but also indirectly affect society due to their contribution of the data analysis results. In summary, the constitutive value of personal data to society speaks for their market-inalienability.

3.2 Unreasonable direct application of the GDPR in merchandising

3.2.1 Merchandising is forgotten by the GDPR

Leaving the question of whether the high-level protection in the GDPR can be justified by the reasons aside,[573] there are significant differences between merchandising and the envision that the EU legislator holds in deploying data protection.

Both the EDPB's and the EDPS' opinions revolve around the model of "data against service" in the online environment. The foundation of this business model is the well-developing two-sided market. In the market of service providers versus web users, providers attract more users by offering more appealing services (collecting more data to build a more accurate profile), whereas users are increasingly locked in by service providers while enjoying free digital services and (inadvertently) providing data; in the market between service providers and advertisers, providers are paid to "introduce" users' characteristics to advertisers and provide them with ad

assumed for the rest of her life, the preconditions and reasons for entering into the contract need to be carefully examined, see BVerfG, NJW 1994, 36 - Bürgschaftsverträge, 39.

571 Janger and Schwartz, 86 Minnesota Law Review 1219 (2002) (1247); Schwartz, 52 Vanderbilt Law Review 1609 (1999), 1613.

572 Badshah, Facebook to contact 87 million users affected by data breach, The Guardian, at https://www.theguardian.com/technology/2018/apr/08/facebook-to-contact-the-87-million-users-affected-by-data-breach.

573 For instance, some scholars have convincingly argued that the high standard of consent required by the GDPR (encompassing ready revocability and a high degree of transparency) is hardly effective to ensure that the data subject's right to informational self-determination is not distorted by the power asymmetry with platforms; In essence, the attention of the question should enhance platform justice instead of the revocability and disclosure of information of consent. See Bietti, 40 Pace law review 310 (2020) (349).

space (on the platform), while advertisers have a higher chance of success by placing targeted ads.[574]

The data processing consented by average internet users in light of the model of "data against service" differs from merchandising significantly. Above all, the lack of a two-sided market in merchandising makes the agreement between models and advertising agencies on the commercial use of personal data unmistakable, while such an expression of intent is hardly ever seen in privacy agreements.[575] Furthermore, the two-sided market leads to severe information asymmetry, which makes it almost impossible to obtain a transparent market to assess the value of personal data.[576] On the contrary, the market for merchandising is relatively clear so that it is always used as the criterion to compute the fictive license fee. Lastly, the purpose of data collection and exploitation of service providers are multi-layered. Profiting from advertisers is one essential purpose to make the free services on the internet sustainable after the tech bubble cooled down in the late 20th century.[577] The other is to increase the number of users and the attractiveness of services to achieve a monopoly.[578] These aims are facilitated by unrestricted collection and profiling, which is completely absent in merchandising. Significant differences in terms of the content, volume, method, and duration of data processing are extant, which also indicate different levels of risks and impacts of data subjects.

Admittedly, an imbalanced structural relationship due to power asymmetry may exist in scenarios like time-for-print contracts. The market dictates that their images are not as valuable as those of a supermodel, and thus allowing free use of their photos for photographs might be the only opportunity for new models to get free photographs by professionals. Newcomers to the show business including models, actors, singers,

---

574 Metzger, 8 JIPITEC 2 (2017); Duch-Brown, et al., The economics of ownership, access and trade in digital data, 2017, 40; *Dewenter and Rösch,* Einführung in die neue Ökonomie der Medienmärkte, S. 115; Dewenter, Rösch and Terschüren, Abgrenzung zweiseitiger Märkte am Beispiel von Internetsuchmaschinen, 2014, Diskussionspapier, No. 151, Hamburg, S. 3.

575 See *Hacker*, ZfPW, 2019, 148 (169f.); *Wendehorst and Graf v. Westphalen,* NJW, 2016, 3745 (3748).

576 *Jentzsch,* in: *Datenschutz, Dateneigentum und Datenhandel*, S. 177 (179).

577 *Posner and Weyl,* Radical Markets: Uprooting Capitalism and Democracy for a Just Society, 212 and 213; *Buchner*, DuD, 2010, 39.

578 The education about the monopoly brought about by the lock-in effect in internet companies, see Ewald, in: *Wiedemann,* Handbuch des Kartellrechts, § 7, Rn. 70; *Bunnenberg,* Privates Datenschutzrecht: über Privatautonomie im Datenschutzrecht, S. 267-268.

and internet influencers who are not as successful as Cathy Hummels[579] are undoubtedly subjected to powerful merchandisers. They are relatively young and inexperienced, and their comprehension of merchandising contracts, especially agency-merchandising contracts as well as voluntariness of making binding decisions may be impaired.[580] Since this seems to be a necessary path for professionals, it cannot be claimed to be an extreme case.[581]

This may raise concerns about inequality, but such concerns are dissipated by many factors. Above all, although young models do not have strong negotiating power, they enter the industry voluntarily. More or less, they understand the basic rules of merchandising given the wealth of information available on the Internet. Even in several controversial cases regarding pornographic photos, the models were not tricked into the business but willingly engaged.[582] Second, models who are new to the business are also very cautious about their authorization. They would fight against unwittingly commercial use,[583] disgraceful presentation and equivocal contracts.[584] More importantly, there are also flanking measures developed in jurisprudence and practice, such as the theory of purpose transfer in constructing the authorization, the contractual rights and privileges for the person depicted ensuring an appropriate level of personality protection. They stem from the practice rather than legislation. Conceivably, they are targeted and useful. Last but not least, as argued consistently in Part II Sections 4.2, 4.3, and 4.5, the rigorous conditions for the validity of consent, the restricted ambit of Art. 6 (1) (b), and the mandatory data subject's rights are neither effective nor necessary for even young models who are a disadvantaged position. This intervention is too much

579 OLG München, 25.6.2020 – 29 U 2333/19 - Blauer Plüschelefant.

580 See Part I Section 3.2.2 (4). For instance, "idol trainees" in Korea as well as in China and Japan are teenagers. Their contracts are signed by their parents who are usually not well educated. Many lawsuits have been filed in China by idol trainees and their parents claiming that the contract is invalid based on their insufficient knowledge.

581 TV shows like "Germany's Next Topmodel", "America's Next Top Model, "Australia's Next Top Model", etc. are vivid illustrations of how young models who might be easily manipulated become top models who are significantly more professional and experienced.

582 OLG München, NJW-RR 1990, 999 - Wirtin; LG Köln, AfP 1996, 186 - Model in Playboy, 188.

583 See LG Düsseldorf, AfP 2003, 469 - Veröffentlichung von Fotografien einer Modenschau.

584 See LG Frankfurt/Main, 30.05.2017 - 2-03 O 134/16 - Stinkefingers.

and unwelcomed in merchandising because it deprives models of career developments. After all, no one needs to be forced to improve his or her protection status.[585]

Perhaps a spectrum can be used to illustrate the level of awareness of data subjects of the purpose, means, and consequences of the data processing they are facing. The average web users acquire the least knowledge, while professional models are self-sufficient and often businessmen by themselves. Young models who are new in the business are somewhere in between.

Moreover, the discrepancy in the attitude of the persons depicted in these two scenarios is prominent. It roots in the different expectations and purposes of data processing between celebrities and ordinary internet users. As the bulk of celebrity income, at least a large portion, comes from what is referred to in this article as merchandising, they wish to maximize the profits from their images in a sustainable way. Therefore, they have a specific vision for the content and purpose of merchandising so that their images would not be misrepresented or distorted. It is hardly possible that professionals would inadvertently authorize others to exploit their data. More likely than not, they would fight for an adequate licensee fee as long as the exploitation exceeds their expectation.[586] This differs from ordinary internet users fundamentally. Their data are valuable only viewed from the big data perspective,[587] and they do not make a living by exploiting personal data. These factors determine that ordinary internet users usually do not understand how data processing should be reasonable in terms of content, purpose, and time, and they usually do not take such trifles to heart. Furthermore, the purpose of the permission for data processing is different. It is unusual for a user to allow a controller to use data for commercial benefits. Normally, it is for other reasons such as socializing, watching videos, surfing the web, etc. Even if it is for some commercial benefit, such as a free pizza, the user is usually unaware of what his or her consent means.[588]

---

585 Vgl. *Ohly*, "Volenti non fit iniuria": die Einwilligung im Privatrecht, S. 173.

586 For instance, BGH GRUR 1992, 557 - Talkmaster.

587 Vgl. *Riemensperger and Falk*, in: *StiftungDatenschutz, Dateneigentum und Datenhandel*, S. 261.

588 Buchner/Petri, in *Kühling/Buchner*, DSGVO/BDSG, Art. 6 Rn. 26. They use the scenario regarding a smart TV to illustrate the integration of different contracts in one purchase to get as many permissions of the data subject as possible. It is also a prime example showing that users of the smart TV neither allow the

Against this backdrop, reasons for data paternalism rooting in the imperative of fundamental rights are not so pertinent in merchandising as they are for the data processing for average internet users.

Human dignity especially protection for core and ideal interests of personality rights is indispensable and inviolable. The freedom of personality development and autonomy cannot be exercised in an irreversible way that they are completely abandoned by the individual.[589] These freedoms and rights are crucial to individuals as an opportunity must be given to people to learn from their mistakes and to make improvements from mistakes.[590] However, some emancipation of certain personal data from the data subject for certain purposes does not necessarily deploy an assignment. Merchandising of personal indicia including images, names, voices and even secrecy is an established market.[591] The soft-licensing model in merchandising based on the monistic approach in the German Copyright Law is well acknowledged by scholars and implied by courts (see Part I Section 3.1.1). In light of the *ladder of permissions* that visualizes all possibilities of disposition of rights and interests with corresponding preconditions and results, there are varied forms of commercialization of personal data. The market-inalienability of personal data can be fully warranted by, for instance, the soft-licensing model as it allows models to commercialize personal data to some extent without dismissing the control over his or her likeness.

In summary, the self-sufficiency of models in merchandising differs significantly from the general insensitivity of internet users in disposing of their data. The soft licensing model is the genuine choice of models because both they and merchandisers need a stable relationship to develop their careers and business. Moreover, the established market for merchandising regarding celebrities further guarantees the fairness of the consideration for data licensing. Likewise, the mature market reduces the cost of legal estimation of compensation amounts. Thus, the development of the

---

processing for money nor do they know exactly what they have authorized to the controller.

589 *Mill,* On Liberty, 212.

590 That is also the reason why Mill, on the one hand, argues against paternalism because it deprives people of the opportunity to make mistakes and thus prevents them from learning from their mistakes and growing up so that they will always be children in a paternalist society; but, on the other hand, supports the restriction of freedom in some specified situations like voluntary slavery. See

591 A factual and legal discourse, see *Götting/Schertz/Seitz,* Handbuch Persönlichkeitsrecht, Teil 7 Das Persönlichkeitsrecht im REchtscerkehr S. 644~705.

KUG in respect of merchandising is not a surrender of one's personality to commercialization, but rather a concession of paternalism to individual autonomy.

3.2.2 Unsuitable explanations for merchandising

Against the differences between merchandising and online services including direct marketing, it is argued here that the explanations for the high-level data protection in the GDPR are not suitable for merchandising.

Above all, cognitive problems for data subjects and structural problems between data subjects and controllers are persuasive to confine the private autonomy of data subjects in agreements concerning the commercialization of personal data. In response, important information is required to be presented in a simple, clear, and conspicuous manner, non-necessary data processing must be distinguished from necessary data processing, and most importantly, contract-related data processing is restricted to auxiliary types, while consent must be revocable.[592] In contrast, professional models and celebrities generally have deep background knowledge of merchandising and take their rights and obligations seriously. Merchandising contracts stem from negotiation between the parties on an individual basis which is distinct from the privacy policies that internet users usually "check" the box without reading.

Secondly, the soft-licensing model in merchandising is consistent with the long-term preferences of the data subject, and the pricing is fair. The efficiency consideration apart from the cost of moralism is ill-founded. Admittedly, the cost for estimation of personal data could be too high,[593] but it is the exact reason why legal scholars/courts should not take the cost but rather leave it to the market.[594] The analogy with the women's chore is

592 See EDPB, Guidelines 2/2019 on the processing of personal data under Article 6(1)(b) GDPR in the context of the provision of online services to data subjects, para. 16 and the examples.

593 See OECD, Exploring the Economics of Personal Data: A Survey of Methodologies for Measuring Monetary Value, OECD Digital Economy Papers, No. 220, 18. It proposes 6 methods to estimate the economic value of personal data but admits that all these methods are pre-mature and not able to capture all aspects of the economic value of personal data. Vgl. *Lewinski, in: Datenschutz, Dateneigentum und Datenhandel,* 209 (212f.).

594 Calabresi and Melamed, 85 Harvard Law Review 1089 (1972) (1109-1110).

creative and leads to this result as well.[595] Though the external psychological cost of people by letting poor people be subordinated to the economic interests of the platform must be warranted in the scenario of merchandising, it is inapplicable to celebrity merchandising.[596] In essence, the inadequacy of economic interpretation stems from its deliberate avoidance of value judgments, while legal paternalism is emblematic of the efforts of legislators to "nudge" or "push" people towards a life that conforms to the objective value order (*objektive Wertordnung*) consistent with fundamental rights.[597] Thus, the changed mentality and improved knowledge about merchandising of professional models cannot support the application of efficiency reasons for data paternalism.

Thirdly, it is well acknowledged that selling personal data is prohibited by the fundamental right in Art. 8 of the Charter because it would lead to an ultimate deprivation of protection, which defeats the very purpose of allowing individuals the freedom to dispose of their personal data.[598] Personal data shall not be reduced as freely tradeable money *per se*. However, it does not an exclusion of any active use of personal data (commercialization). In merchandising, one is not selling personal data but disposing of them by licensing, granting binding permission, or giving an anytime

595 According to *Engels* in 1884, it was the emancipation of women from home into social production that gave real value to women's labor in both terms of housework and social production. See *Engels*, The Origin of the Family, Private Property and the State, 104-105; In this direction, see *Posner and Weyl*, Radical Markets: Uprooting Capitalism and Democracy for a Just Society, 209; Bruni, 41 CARDOZO LAW REVIEW 2203 (2020) (2233). Even data controllers successful in exploiting personal data are beginning to advocate the marketization of data to increase the quality of personal data. They argue that given the importance of personal data to AI, a family of four in the US should receive $20,000 annually by providing personal data. See *Lanier, et al.*, Harvard Business Review, 2018, 2 (16).

596 Also, the efficiency reason for the moral cost is questionable in general. It does not explain how this externality emerges and why it should be shared by all people at the cost of diminishing the free choice of the poor.

597 See *Thaler and Sunstein*, Nudge: improving decisions about health, wealth, and happiness, 5 and 6; With reference to the critical comments that despite the best efforts of the advocates of liberal paternalism to avoid it, the value judgment – the appeal to the maintenance of an objective value order – is still necessary, i.e., the substance of health, wealth, and happiness. See *Eidenmüller*, JZ, 2011, 814 (820); BVerwG, NJW 1982, 664 - Peep-Shows.

598 Cf. *Mill*, On Liberty, 257-258; Feinberg, 1 Canadian Journal of Philosophy 105 (1971)(120).

revocable consent as Art. 6 (1) (a) GDPR described. These patterns all preserve the control of data subjects over personal data to some extent.

In essence, celebrities are using personal data in the same way as they are using their labor to make money instead of treating data as money *per se*. Moreover, since the parties of merchandising contracts are usually professionals, consumer protection is not a relevant topic here. When considering the *quid pro quo* relationship between the licensing of personal data and the "free" service provided by a professional photographer in a time-for-print contract, the similarity with the business model "data against services" might be more evident. Compared with celebrities, the personal data of the models in time-for-print contracts are more like money. However, they are not consumers, either.

Last but not least, if personal data has some collective value that does not belong to the identified or identifiable natural person by that data, then not only is commercialization impermissible but all disposition including consent shall be prohibited. In other words, over-reliance on the collective value of personal data suggests an outright prohibition of individual disposition, which would destabilize the self-autonomy in the EU data protection law. However, the GDPR sets forth numerous requirements to guarantee a free flow of personal data in a fair and reasonable manner. The data subject's rights and the principles of data processing guarantee that data subjects do not exercise the right to information self-determination at the expense of losing it. Not only are the conditions of disposing of personal data under the scrutiny of the GDPR, but the principle of accountability also obliges the controller to bear the negative consequences including remedies and fines when it fails to prove its legitimacy or to be responsive to the data subject's rights. Against this consideration, though the collective value of personal data deserves more attention and deeper exploration, it exceeds the scope of this dissertation. Moreover, anonymized data that fall outside the scope of the GDPR are normally sufficient to draw a demographic analysis. One may argue that personal data are usually not necessary for controllers in a big data scenario like the one in the Cambridge Analytica case, which is, however, the prime case presenting the collective value of personal data. In this sense, the consideration that personal data contain collective values is more helpful in explaining why individuals must provide data in certain situations – even against their will. After all, if the data collection is important for society, such as the census, individuals are obliged to provide data.

In summary, the EU data protection law primarily uses the scenario between data subjects and platforms in the online environment as the starting point for interpreting and guiding the application of the GDPR. Notwithstanding the effectiveness of these restrictions on data subjects, the rationale is untenable in a merchandising scenario where the data processing is, in general, a genuine result of the private autonomous decision stemming from free negotiations between two equal parties.[599] Rather than arguing that the EDPS and EDPB deny the binding effect of merchandising contracts under the GDPR, it seems more compelling to contest that they overlook merchandising scenarios at all.

4. Conclusions

In light of the divergences between the KUG and the GDPR in regulating merchandising, serious challenges need to be addressed urgently, and less significant ones that only require the attention of merchandisers in practice for compliance. The more generous moral damages under the GDPR and the compliance requirements for merchandisers in delivering data subject's rights belong to the latter category. They are tolerable and justified. Nevertheless, there is a caveat for merchandisers in practice: to ensure compliance in the organizational structure and business operations, especially concerning the principle of transparency and the data subject's rights. It is meaningful for avoiding unnecessary litigation and administrative fines.

Based on the findings in the previous chapters, it is argued that the application of the GDPR in merchandising is inappropriate because the GDPR is subject to problems including under-protection for celebrities and the negation of the binding force of merchandising contracts. While the reliance on the national remedy based on the law of unjust enrichment would fix the first problem, the reticence for the commercial value of personal data would lead to some meaningful problems in the long term. The restitution for the fictive license fee in the German legal regime regarding merchandising, which is effective in combating unauthorized merchandising, is based on a mature and relatively transparent licensing market for personal images. The valuation of merchandising is objectively determined and accepted by both parties as well as the court. Without such a market, the valuation of data processing is troublesome and might be infeasible. In this wise, the lack of sufficient financial incentives will not only reduce the incentive for data subjects to proactively assert their rights

599 Vgl. Petri, in *Kühling/Buchner*, DSGVO/BDSG, Art. 6 Rn. 26.

and increase pressure on the public sector but will also likely fail to curb illegal data processing by private controllers effectively. More importantly, it will result in data subjects being negligent in understanding and controlling these interests.

The failed binding effect of merchandising contracts is an acute and detrimental incompatibility aroused by the GDPR with merchandising. After all, no businessman would want to invest time, money, and other resources into a relationship that is not protected by law without *publicity* (leave charity aside). Yet, a direct application of the GDPR in merchandising is unappreciated.

The approach of one size fits for all, the reticence of the commercial value of personal data, and data paternalism are possible reasons for the regulation of the GDPR. However, while they may be imperative and efficient in restoring the unbalanced relationship between data subjects and data controllers in big data scenarios, they do not offer a self-explanatory application in merchandising.

The EDPB and EDPS may well treat the business model "data against service" prevailing between internet users and platforms differently because of the insufficient information, excessive data use, unfair consideration, etc.[600] However, merchandising differs from the situation the EU data protection law envisaged in contents, means, purposes, and risks. Models in merchandising are also distinct from average internet users in terms of knowledge, attitudes, purposes, and negotiation power. More importantly, the market-inalienability of personal data cannot lead to an outright prohibition of any forms of commercialization of personal data, and this imperative can also be guaranteed by the soft-licensing model prevailing in merchandising business in Germany. While the merchandising law aims to prevent one's images from unexpected/unremunerative exploitation due to publicity, the high-demanding requirements in the GDPR are devised to enhance the control of data subjects over personal data to prevent data subjects from becoming the object of opaque and unfair data processing. Thus, the fears of commercialization of personal data,

600 Some scholars have convincingly argued that the high standard of consent required by the GDPR (encompassing ready revocability and a high degree of transparency) is hardly practical to ensure that the data subject's right to informational self-determination is not distorted in his or her significantly unequal relationship with platforms; In essence, the attention of the questions of power and platform justice instead of focusing on the voluntariness and disclosure of information of consent should be called upon. See Bietti, 40 Pace law review 310 (2020) (349).

devaluation of personality, and the necessity of data-paternalism tend to lose their conditions and exceed their boundaries in merchandising. More importantly, the market-inalienability of personal data cannot lead to an outright prohibition of any forms of commercialization of personal data, and this imperative can also be guaranteed by the soft-licensing model prevailing in merchandising business in Germany. Therefore, it validates the idea of this dissertation that the GDPR forgets merchandising, and the direct application of the GDPR in merchandising is unreasonable.

In short, the direct application of the GDPR in merchandising is neither appropriate nor reasonable. Solutions must be sought to address the lack of material remedies for celebrities and the "dysfunctionality" (*Dysfunktionalität*)[601] of transactional relationships in merchandising under the GDPR.

601 Vgl. Albers/Veit, in *Brink/Wolff*, BeckOK Datenschutzrecht, Art. 6 Rn. 29.

Part IV Solutions to settle the inconsistencies

1. *Direct application of the KUG in merchandising cases based on Art. 85 (1) GDPR*

1.1 Art. 85 (1) GDPR as a stand-alone opening clause

An extensive reading of journalistic purposes in Art. 85 (2) GDPR cannot support a direct application of the KUG in merchandising defined in this dissertation (see Part II Section 2.3.2). Accordingly, some scholars postulate that Art. 85 (1) GDPR being a stand-alone opening clause would solve the awkward situation of the KUG after the GDPR came into effect.[602]

Art. 85 (1) GDPR reads, "*Member States shall by law reconcile the right to the protection of personal data pursuant to this Regulation with the right to freedom of expression and information, including processing for journalistic purposes and the purposes of academic, artistic or literary expression*".

At first glance, this paragraph appears to be an independent opening clause from Art. 85 (2) GDPR since Art. 85 (1), by its wording, also allows ("*shall*") the Member States to reconcile the GDPR with freedom of speech by law. In this sense, the Member States' discretion is no longer limited to processing data for journalistic purposes, etc., exclusively enumerated in Art. 85 (2) because Art. 85 (1) GDPR uses the term "including" instead of exclusively. In this wise, if the German legal regime for merchandising meets the two requirements, namely the need for the freedom of speech and in the form of law,[603] Germany can advocate the application of the

602 *Lauber-Rönsberg and Hartlaub*, NJW, 2017, 1057 (1062); *Ziebarth and Elsaß*, ZUM, 2018, 578 (583f.); *Golz and Gössling*, IPRB, 2018, 68 (72); *Nettesheim*, AfP, 2019, 473 (479); *Lauber-Rönsberg*, AfP, 2019, 373 (377); *Krüger and Wiencke*, MMR, 2019, 76 (78); Frey, in *Schwartmann, et al.*, DS-GVO/BDSG, Art. 85 Rn. 33; von Strobl-Albeg, in *Wenzel, et al.*, Das Recht der Wort- und Bildberichterstattung, § 7 Rn. 124; Lauber-Rönsberg, in *Götting/Schertz/Seitz*, Handbuch Persönlichkeitsrecht, § 22 Rn. 45; *Bienemann*, Reformbedarf des Kunsturhebergesetzes im digitalen Zeitalter, S. 43f. with further references in the footnote 95.

603 Leaves the questions of whether the jurisprudence of the KUG can be regarded as law from the EU perspective, and whether merchandising falls under the scope of the freedom of speech aside.

KUG as a principle on the one hand, and not relinquish protection provided by the GDPR in certain aspects on the other.

According to *Bienemann*, who explores this issue in her dissertation and reaches the conclusion that Art. 85 (1) GDPR is an independent opening clause with a sweeping (*pauschal*) effect, the overall assessment of four methods of interpretation – wording, systematics, history, and telos – of Art. 85 (1) GDPR speaks for an "optional general opening clause" (*fakultative allgemeine Öffnungsklausel*):[604] The most powerful argumentation for the wider reading of Art. 85 (1) GDPR is that the word "including" suggests that its applicable scope is wider than the processing for "journalistic purposes and the purposes of academic, artistic or literary expression";[605] According to the systematic interpretation, Art. 85 (1) GDPR would be redundant if it is not an "optional general opening clause". *Lauber-Rönsberg* and *Hartlaub*, who also support this idea, have forwarded another pragmatical argument: The legal fragmentation as a result of the opposing interpretation would ultimately lead to serious legal uncertainty and delimitation problems.[606] Moreover, unlike the GDPR, the KUG rests on abundant case law developed for more than a century to reconcile personality rights including the right to privacy and the right to freedom of expression and information. The cost of abandoning this precious heritage would take years or even decades to make up for.[607]

In addition, the German Federal Parliament (*Bundestag*) and the Federal Ministry of the Interior (*BMI*) also supported this solution by stating that the KUG continues to apply after the GDPR came into force based on Art. 85 (1) GDPR despite the lack of argumentation.[608] Noteworthy, as

---

604 *Bienemann,* Reformbedarf des Kunsturhebergesetzes im digitalen Zeitalter, S. 43f.; Similar argumentation see *Ziebarth and Elsaß,* ZUM, 2018, 578 (583f.); Vgl. *Krüger and Wiencke,* MMR, 2019, 76 (79).

605 *Bienemann,* Reformbedarf des Kunsturhebergesetzes im digitalen Zeitalter, S. 49; *Krüger and Wiencke,* MMR, 2019, 76 (78); Frey, in *Schwartmann, et al.,* DS-GVO/BDSG, Art. 85 Rn. 2.

606 *Lauber-Rönsberg and Hartlaub,* NJW, 2017, 1057 (1062).

607 Ibid. It has been argued that "it would probably take several years or even decades until a consolidated case law of the ECJ on specific cases would have developed."

608 The German Federal Parliament (*Bundestag*) and the Federal Ministry of the Interior (*BMI*) have stated that the KUG continues to apply after the GDPR came into force based on Art. 85 (1) GDPR without thorough argumentationBT-Drs. 19/4421, Antwort des Parlamentarischen Staatssekretärs Dr. Günter Krings vom 20. September 2018, S. 47 f.; FAQs zur Datenschutz-Grundverordnung, "Unter welchen Voraussetzungen ist das Anfertigen und Verbreiten personenbezogen-

mentioned in Part II Section 3.1.2, some German courts also implicitly share this view.

Pragmatically, this proposal is appealing as the self-contained regulation of merchandising based on the established jurisprudence of the KUG would remain unchanged, and the problems identified above would disappear. The under-protection issue for lacking material damages for celebrities in unauthorized merchandising cases can be resolved. Moreover, data subjects affected by unauthorized merchandising can still invoke the non-monetary remedies that they are familiar with such as injunctive relief, the auxiliary claims for information and accounting, etc. As noted above, they have more benefits for the data subjects in unauthorized merchandising scenarios compared to the scenarios concerning data subject's rights. Besides, the soft-licensing model adopted in merchandising agreements would remain according to the KUG and its jurisprudence. Merchandising contracts are binding, while the assignment of the right to one's image is prohibited. Moreover, the construction of the ambit of authorization in case of doubt is still limited to what is necessary for relation to the purposes of that contract. The data subject's rights are not available in the German legal regime. While omissions of granting such rights would lead to a notable under-protection issue, the rights are either inapplicable or ill-suited for merchandising cases because they are primarily designed to combat the risks posed by untransparent data processing or the lock-in effect aroused by platforms, such as the right to portability, and the right to not be subject to automated decisions.[609] After all, as argued above, Art. 85 (1) GDPR provides the Member States with flexibility in reconciliation within its law with the GDPR: German courts can freely decide to what extent they should deploy the rules in the GDPR to strike a fair balance between the protection of personal data and the freedom of speech in respect of merchandising.

It is important to note that the German legal regime by recognizing the commercial value of personal images and assigning this value to the person depicted offers more thorough protection for data subjects against unau-

---

er Fotografien künftig zulässig?" (Under what conditions is the taking and dissemination of personal photographs permissible in the future?), The Federal Ministry of the Interior, at https://www.bmi.bund.de/SharedDocs/kurzmeldungen/DE/2018/04/faqs-datenschutz-grundverordnung.html.

609 WP29, Guidelines on the right to "data portability", wp242 rev.01, 3; See Hert, Papakonstantinou, Malgieri, Beslay and Sanchez, 34 Computer Law & Security Review 193 (2018) (194-196); EDPS, Meeting the challenges of big data, Opinion 7/2015, 7-8, and 11.

thorized merchandising. Take the *hair salon* case as an example. In this typical case of users' merchandising, the economic interests attached to the processing of personal data are the main motive driving the controller to conduct users' merchandising. If, the data subject in this scenario feels no more humiliated like the girl called "*flour of the family*" did more than a century ago,[610] but only commercially exploited like Mr. Zeppelin felt and thus would like to claim reasonable material damages from the social platform,[611] the GDPR is restrained. On the contrary, the German legal regime can offer different compensation catering to the depicted person's needs.

1.2 Counterarguments for the independent nature of Art. 85 (1) GDPR

Many scholars argue that Art. 85 (1) GDPR is a mere *Anpassungsauftrag* (an instruction to adjustments) that specifies the purpose and means of the derogations or exemptions by the Member States.[612] Thus, the direct application of the KUG in merchandising cannot base on Art. 85 (1) GDPR after the GDPR became effective.

Except for the wording of Art. 85 (1) GDPR, the argumentation based on the historical, systematic, and teleological interpretation can also be used to support the opposite conclusion that Art. 85 (1) should not be a stand-alone opening clause. From an intra-systematic view, if Art. 85 (1) GDPR is an independent opening clause, the conditions, and limitations in Art. 85 (2) would be meaningless; Moreover, Art. 85 (3) GDPR only addresses "paragraph 2" as the legal basis for derogations or exemptions from the GDPR, and the omission in Art. 85 (3) of mentioning the first paragraph should not be qualified as a "legislative error"(*fehlerhaft*)[613] as the scholars suggest.[614] From an inter-systematic view, the overstretching

---

610 Roberson v. Rochester Folding Box Co. 171 N.Y. 538, 64 N.E. 442 (N.Y. 1902)

611 Cf. Fraley v. Facebook, Inc. 830 F. Supp. 2d 785, 808 (N.D. Cal. 2011)

612 *Dregelies*, AfP, 2019, 298; Pauly, in *Paal and Pauly*, DS-GVO BDSG, Art. 85 Rn. 4; *Benedikt and Kranig*, ZD, 2019, 4 (5); *Kahl and Piltz*, K&R, 2018, 289 (292); *Klein*, Personenbilder im Spannungsfeld von Datenschutzgrundverordnung und Kunsturhebergesetz, S. 201ff.; *Assmus and Winzer*, ZD, 2018, 508(512); Buchner/Tinnefeld, in *Kühling/Buchner*, DSGVO/BDSG, Art. 85 Rn. 12; *Benecke and Wagner*, DVBl, 2016, 600 (602f.); *Raji*, ZD, 2019, 61 (64).

613 *Bienemann*, Reformbedarf des Kunsturhebergesetzes im digitalen Zeitalter, S. 63.

614 Vgl. *Dregelies*, AfP, 2019, 298 (303).

of Art. 85 (1) GDPR would sabotage the fine-tuned Art. 6 GDPR.[615] The teleological interpretation is even more so because the dual objectives of the GDPR, especially the free flow of personal data within the EU cannot be achieved if the authority of the Member States is so extensive in reconciling the GDPR and the freedom of speech. The same problem arises for having multiple meanings in the arguments based on historical interpretation. In the Communication from the Commission to the European Parliament and the Council, Art. 85 (1) GDPR is rather an instruction specifying the purpose and means of derogations or exemptions instead of a mandate itself.[616]

Against its pragmatic advantages, some scholars contend that regarding Art. 85 (1) GDPR as a stand-alone opening clause is, in essence, an appeal of "it cannot be what it is not allowed to be" (*es kann nicht sein, was nicht sein darf*).[617] In addition, the limited applicable scope of the KUG would undermine the advantages.[618] Since the KUG does not entail regulations against unauthorized production and storage of photographs, these activities would be governed by the GDPR if they are not operated wholly manually.[619] Thus, a complete exploitation process of personal photos (data) would be artificially divided into many parts and subject to completely dif-

615 Vgl. *Kühling, et al.*, Die DSGVO und das nationale Recht, 2016, S. 287.

616 The EU Commission, Communication from the Commission to the European Parliament and the Council, Stronger protection, new opportunities - Commission guidance on the direct application of the General Data Protection Regulation as of 25 May 2018, 8. It states, "in accordance with the Regulation, Member States have to take the necessary steps to adapt their legislation by repealing and amending existing laws, ... and laying down the rules for the reconciliation of freedom of expression and data protection" according to Art. 85 (1) GDPR.

617 *Krüger and Wiencke*, MMR, 2019, 76 (79).

618 *Klein*, Personenbilder im Spannungsfeld von Datenschutzgrundverordnung und Kunsturhebergesetz, S. 180 ff.; *Benedikt and Kranig*, ZD, 2019, 4 (5); *Kahl and Piltz*, K&R, 2018, 289 (292); *Assmus and Winzer*, ZD, 2018, 508 (512). The opposite opinion that the KUG is compliant with GDPR and can continue to apply since the KUG is a stricter law. See *Remmertz*, MMR, 2018, 507 (509). This opinion is not followed here because neither the logic of its arguments nor the arguments are tenable. Moreover, even the adherent to the idea that the KUG still applies after the GDPR came into effect advocates a profound reform for the KUG to delineate it from the otherwise intertwined applicable scope of the GDPR. See *Bienemann*, Reformbedarf des Kunsturhebergesetzes im digitalen Zeitalter, S. 244f.; Frey, in *Schwartmann, et al.*, DS-GVO/BDSG, Art. 85 Rn. 39.

619 However, if the album constitutes or is intended to constitute a filing system structured according to specific criteria, it might fall under the scope of the GDPR. See Recital 15.

ferent laws, It would be far more complex than admitting the precedence of the GDPR. Moreover, it would be questionable whether the case law about "apron protection" (*Vorfeldschutz*)[620], based on the general personality right, fulfills the requirements underscored in Art. 85 (1) GDPR. If not, legal fragmentation and uncertainty because of the production chain of personal photos would be inevitable and might bring far more serious problems than not being able to apply the KUG. Moreover, the numerous and extensive regulatory differences between the GDPR and the KUG remain and await balancing depending on concrete assessments.

There are some pragmatic solutions in Germany being sought to tackle this controversy. The concern that new provisions in the GDPR, in particular, Art. 6 (1)(f) GDPR would not be supported by sufficient case law, can be addressed by introducing German jurisprudence in weighing adversarial interests. Against the backdrop that the German casuistry has succeeded in striking a fair balance between the personality rights and the freedom of expression following the case law of the ECtHR in the field of §§ 22, 23 KUG, the BVerfG has interpreted the GDPR in compliance with the European fundamental rights anchored in the Charter through a "German lens". In doing so, it respects the primacy of EU law on the one hand, and on the other incorporates considerations of German jurisprudence in the areas covered by EU law.

1.3 Evaluation

Based on a reflection of the literature, Art. 85 (1) GDPR is a rather typical, yet deliberately ambiguous norm created by the EU legislator. There is some validity to the arguments of both opposing sides. On the one hand, a too restrictive interpretation of the maneuver space of the Member States granted by Art. 85 GDPR would create the risk that the EU law would achieve full harmonization with respect to the balance between freedom of expression and the right to privacy and personality through the "back door" of data protection.[621] Not that it is impossible or unimagined be-

620 Before the GDPR, even when the KUG had been given the special law status over the BDSG, the photo production phase, i.e., before disclosure and publication, had not uniformly treated

621 Schulz/Heilmann, in *Gierschmann, Schlender and al.*, Kommentar Datenschutz-Grundverordnung, Art. 85 Rn. 10.

fore,[622] the balance in this respect depends and shall depend greatly on national culture, history, and values. On the other hand, the GDPR is devised to fully harmonize "the level of protection of the rights and freedoms of natural persons with regard to the processing of such data" for the dual objectives (recital 10). A wide and flexible leeway for the Member States without substantial restrictions prescribed in Art. 85 (2) GDPR is hardly conceivable. Moreover, the continued validity of the KUG cannot be denied for the reason that Germany has only notified the Commission about its state laws on press privilege pursuant to Art. 85 (3) GDPR without mentioning the KUG at all.[623] Because firstly, the obligation for notification laid down in Art. 85 (3) is not a constitutive condition for derogations or exemptions, and secondly, Art. 85 (3) GDPR does not mention Art. 85 (1) GDPR. Therefore, even if it is an independent opening clause, the Member States do not have the obligation to notify the Commission about the adopted national pursuant to Art. 85 (1) GDPR.

Nevertheless, one must be very cautious and refrained in interpreting the opening clauses to avoid preemption of the regulation provided by the GDPR. In addition, this relatively narrow reading of Art. 85 GDPR can be compensated by the liberal understanding of journalistic purposes in the light of "citizen journalism" (see Part II Section 2.3.2). Moreover, even if Art. 85 (1) GDPR is understood as an independent opening clause, it is doubtful whether the KUG can join hands with the GDPR to govern the controversy about (digital) personal portraits. Among other reasons, issues of legal fragmentation and the growing dominance of platforms in users' merchandising scenarios would highlight the incompetence of the KUG in the online environment. Thus, the postulation of Art. 85 (1) GDPR as an independent opening clause fails in its feasibility.

In Germany, a broad understanding of Art. 85 (1) GDPR is rejected by the German highest courts in constitutional law and civil law. Similar to *Recht auf Vergessen I*,[624] the BVerfG only recognized Art. 85 (2) GDPR as

---

622 *Ohly*, GRUR Int, 2004, 902.

623 EU Member States notifications to the European Commission under the GDPR, see „Notifizierungspflichtige Vorschriften Deutschlands gemäß der Verordnung (EU) 2016/679 des Europäischen Parlaments und des Rates vom 27. April 2016 zum Schutz natürlicher Personen bei der Verarbeitung personenbezogener Daten, zum freien Datenverkehr und zur Aufhebung der Richtlinie 95/46/EG (Datenschutz-Grundverordnung) Gesetze des Bundes", at https://ec.europa.eu/info/sites/default/files/de_notification_articles_49.5_51.4_83.9_84.2_85.3_88.3_90.2_publish.pdf.

624 BVerfG, GRUR 2020, 74 - Recht auf Vergessen I, para. 74.

the opening clause: As activities conducted by search engines are not serving journalistic purposes, the BVerfG rejected the application of domestic law deviating from the GDPR in this constellation.[625] This consideration also held in the case of *Recht auf Vergessenwerden* ruled by the BGH.[626]

Specified in merchandising scenarios, the replacement of the recourse mechanism in the GDPR by the German remedies is superfluous in solving the under-protection problem. In essence, this proposal offers no more benefit than the assistance of the law of unjust enrichment that coexists with the recourse mechanism of the GDPR. However, the substitution of German remedies would result in data subjects being placed at a disadvantage relative to the GDPR in terms of moral compensation. For one, moral damages must be severe to receive compensation in Germany. For another, the person depicted loses the protection facilitated by the data subject's rights and thus the damages due to the failure to respond to rights in time. In this case, a reverse-discrimination for celebrities is conceivable. Merchandisers are also likely to be free from damages when they are negligent in fulfilling the GDPR-compliant requirements. Even though these would not make a huge difference in merchandising cases as mental impairment is very rare in some residual unauthorized merchandising cases, the discrepancy between the German legal regime and the GDPR in terms of mental damages seems unjustified. Given the inferior position of commercial speech in the freedom of speech,[627] there seems to be no legitimate reason for controllers not to provide sufficient information to the data subject promptly.

As many regulations in the regime of the right to one's image rely on both the BGB and the case law. A conclusion that they all strike a fair balance between the freedom of speech and information and the protection for personal data pursuant to the GDPR can neither be drawn in principle nor without a careful evaluation based on detailed comparisons. Therefore, a well-reasoned application of the KUG in merchandising would be indispensable because courts must demonstrate that the specific law/case law reconciles the GDPR and the freedom of speech. In this wise, a full account of the motivation and significance of the data processing must be taken in applying the KUG and its jurisprudence based on Art. 85 (1)

625 BVerfG, NJW 2020, 314 - Recht auf Vergessen II, para. 41.
626 BGH, GRUR 2020, 1331 - Recht auf Vergessenwerden, para. 36.
627 *Peers, Hervey, Kenner and Ward,* The EU Charter of Fundamental Rights: A Commentary, Art. 11 paras. 11.28 and 11.40; *Harris, O'Boyle and Warbrick,* Law of the European Convention on Human Rights, 461 et seq.

GDPR. Issues about legal uncertainty would probably take place because no one knows when exemptions and derogations from the GDPR would be made.

The high degree of legislative freedom enjoyed by member states based on Art. 85 (1) GDPR can seriously affect the harmonization of data protection within the EU. This broad understanding of freedom of expression, and in particular the inclusion of purely commercial advertising in the scope of what needs to be considered, runs the risk of circumventing the entire regulation of the GDPR. It would bring uncertainty at the EU level because every Member State would form a self-contained system of merchandising. After all, opening clauses should be restrictively understood as a principle to guarantee the harmonization of data protection within the EU.

At the micro-level within one Member State, the high degree of flexibility enjoyed by courts in deciding to what extent is the application of the KUG or the GDPR reasonable presents, from the other side of the coin, legal uncertainty. More importantly, this problem is almost unsolvable because the reconciliation between data protection and freedom of speech relies on the weighing of interests in individual cases. As mentioned above, the application of certain provisions in the GDPR is also necessary in merchandising cases, but the reasonableness lies in the detail.

2. *Art. 6 (1) (f) GDPR as an additional lawful ground for authorized merchandising*

2.1 The significance of this proposal

2.1.1 The application of Art. 6 (1) (f) GDPR in a contractual relationship

As argued in Part II Section 3.1, merchandisers cannot invoke Art. 6 (1) (f) GDPR as the lawful ground for data processing for merchandising purposes because the interests and rights of the data subject override the commercial interests of the controller. However, in the case of commercial cooperation in merchandising, the balance of interests may be slightly different because the data controller acquires additionally legally protected reliance interests derived from the contract or consent given by the data subject based on the contract.

Though it may seem odd to rely on a legal ground rather than on the autonomous decision of the data subject to legitimize data processing that has been approved and desired by that data subject,[628] Recital 47 of the GDPR does not preclude the application of Art. 6 (1) (f) GDPR in a contractual relationship.[629] In this wise, in addition to the purpose of promoting its products, the reliance interest of the controller arising from the commercial cooperation with the data subject, as a legally protected commercial interest, could also constitute a legitimate interest prescribed in Art. 6 (1) (f) GDPR. Against this backdrop, it might be possible for the controller to rely on Art. 6 (1) (f) GDPR to legitimize its data processing for merchandising on the premise of a valid merchandising contract between the controller and the data subject. One of the questions is, nonetheless, whether the lawful ground at this point is Art. 6 (1) (f) GDPR alone or a cumulation of consent (Art. 6 (1) (a)), the contract (Art. 6 (1) (b)) and the balance of interests (Art. 6 (1) (f)). For the same reasons mentioned in Part II Section 4.3.2 (2), it is argued here that the balance of interests should be relied upon alone.[630] As long as the merchandising contract has not been invalidated or withdrawn under the national law, the controller has the protected interests in the data processing.

The other question is more substantial as to whether the legitimate interests of the controller outweigh the rights, freedoms, and interests of the data subject in this context. The reliance interest of the controller derives from the commitment of the data subject in the freely negotiated merchandising contract. Upon the reliance interest in the binding contract, the controller usually invests not insignificant money and time to increase sales or brand exposure for a relatively long period (during the duration of the contract).

German courts have consistently ruled that the revocation of consent in merchandising contracts requires a weighing of interests following the

---

628 According to Art. 8 (2) of the Charter, lawful grounds for data processing are distinguished between autonomy (consent and arguably the contract) and heteronomy. The first sentence of Art. 8 (2) of the Charter states, "such data must be processed fairly for specified purposes and on the basis of the consent of the person concerned or some other legitimate basis laid down by law". Also considering Art. 6 (1) (f) GDPR as a foreign body (*Fremdkörper*) for the partnership, see *Bunnenberg*, Privates Datenschutzrecht: über Privatautonomie im Datenschutzrecht, S. 61, 64.

629 The second sentence of Recital 47 suggests that legitimate interests of the controller for data processing could exist "where there is a relevant and appropriate relationship between the data subject and the controller in situations such as where the data subject is a client or in the service of the controller".

630 Simply put, it is mainly to avoid causing misunderstandings of the data subject, and the cumulation does not bring more guarantee to the data controller.

principle of good faith in § 241 (2) BGB, even though the conflicting interest is the right of self-determination in the image of the person depicted.[631] In other words, the person depicted must demonstrate convincingly that why he or she has to exert the right of self-determination in a contrary way to override the reliance interests of the merchandiser. Although the interests-balancing according to Art. 6 (1) (f) GDPR should be observed from the perspective of the EU data protection in light of the fundamental rights and freedoms, the reasonable expectations of the data subject introduce the possibility of reflection based on the (legal) culture and traditions of the Member States (see Part II Section 3.1.1 (4)). Moreover, as German cases show, the balance of interests in assessing the revocability of consent has already taken the fundamental rights and freedoms anchored into account.

Therefore, it is possible to argue that upon a valid merchandising contract under national law, the controller may invoke Art. 6 (1) (f) GDPR to legitimize its data processing for merchandising, and the reliance interest of the controller overrides as it also falls under the scope of the reasonable expectations of the data subject in Germany, at least. The controller should make it clear to the data subject that the contract between them is not the lawful ground for data processing under the perspective of the GDPR. In this sense, the data subject is unable to withdraw consent at any time according to Art. 7 (3) GDPR because the lawful ground for data processing is not the consent under Art. 6 (1) (a) GDPR. However, if the contract expires, or the consent in the contract law is successfully withdrawn by the data subject according to national law, then Art. 6 (1) (f) GDPR alone cannot support further data processing because the reliance interest of the controller would no longer be extant.

2.1.2 Conducive for the bindingness of a merchandising relationship

The advantages of this solution are obvious. First, Art. 6 (1) (f) GDPR provides a more stable legal position for the data controller compared to the anytime revocable consent. Since this lawful ground derives from heteronomy instead of autonomy, the control of personal data does not lie in the hand of the data subject. Second, by relying purely on the balancing

631 See BAG, GRUR 2015, 922 - Veröffentlichung von Arbeitnehmer-Bildnissen zu Werbezwecken, Rn. 34f. and 38; LG Köln, AfP 1996, 186 - Model in Playboy; OLG München, NJW-RR 1990, 999 - Wirtin.

test coupled with merchandising contracts under German law, controllers do not have to worry about consent and contracts, which have strict yet controversial conditions for validity, such as the requirement of necessity. Third, controllers (merchandisers) hardly need to make changes to the existing business operations in the context of Art. 6 (1) (f) GDPR. In addition to the documentation of the merchandising contract (as controllers used to do before the GDPR), they merely need to keep documentation about the assessment of the conflicting interests of both sides according to the principle of accountability. Lastly, the risk-based approach seems to favor a lightened interests-balancing for the data controller in authorized merchandising cases.

2.2 Limitations of this proposal

2.2.1 Legal uncertainty and overpressure on the general clause

Disadvantages of Art. 6 (1) (f) GDPR as the lawful ground for a relatively long-term relationship valuing trust and cooperation are at hand.

The balance of interests is by nature uncertain. It closely depends on concrete facts. In merchandising cases, details of the contract, professionality of the data subject and his or her power in relation to the controller, and ways of presentation are all capable of changing the result of the balancing test. For instance, as some scholars stated, if the merchandiser in a time-for-print contract has taken unfair advantage of the informational and power asymmetry of the model, then the validity of that contract should be questioned.[632] In this wise, the legitimacy of the controller is still uncertain because it is dependent of the validity of the merchandising contract. It is therefore almost unrealistic for merchandising companies to tie their entire business model to the lawful ground that is both subject to rejection at any time and dependent on the balance of interests.

Even though the controller is confident about the outcome of the balancing of interests, it must stop processing until the "verification whether the legitimate grounds of the controller override those of the data subject" whenever the data subject claims the right to restriction in Art. 18 (1) (d) in combination with Art. 21 (1) GDPR. Thus, the merchandiser must take down the advertising online or stop the circulation of the prospects or magazines (Art. 18 (2) GDPR). While the GDPR seems to hold the

632 *Vogler*, AfP, 2011, 139 (141).

opinion that the verification should be carried out by the controller itself, scholars argue that the courts have the final decision.[633] Thereby, the legitimacy of the controller is in a position that it can be challenged at any time. It is unthinkable for a businessman as a degree of certainty and predictability are fundamental to business operations.[634]

Another flaw originates from the nature of general clauses. Extensive use of a general clause contradicts its purpose of being an "overpressure relief valve" for vastly developing technology and society.[635] The general clause, always in the tension of legal flexibility and uncertainty, is the last resort for guaranteeing the principle of fairness in concrete cases.[636] Since the questioned binding effectiveness of merchandising contracts under the GDPR is a systematical problem created by the overarching data paternalism in the EU data protection law, it would be better to seek a systematical solution instead of applying the general clause of the lawfulness of data processing in the GDPR systematically.

2.2.2 Fundamentally incompatible in authorized merchandising scenarios

Apart from the drawbacks, the most detrimental disadvantage derives from the fundamental incompatibility between the rationales underlining Art. 6 (1) (f) GDPR and authorized merchandising. In Germany, the right to one's image takes a long journey from a defensive right that only focuses on moral interests to a positive right that is licensable to some extent. The analogy of the soft licensing model of one's portraits with the copyright in Germany is an elegant dogmatical solution to enhance instead of undermining human dignity and the free development of personality by legitimatizing the practical development of self-determination without dismissing the market-inalienability of personality. It has been acclaimed both in academia and practice.

Admittedly, the freely negotiated merchandising contract is the central hinge of this solution under the guise of balance tests according to Art. 6 (1) (f) GDPR. However, from the surface, the decision has once again been

---

633 Dix, in *Simitis, et al.*, Datenschutzrecht, Art. 18 Rn. 9; Herbst, in *Kühling/Buchner*, DSGVO/BDSG, Art. 18 Rn. 27.

634 See *Beale*, in: *de Elizalde, Uniform Rules for European Contract Law?: A Critical Assessment*, 9 (23).

635 *Sattler, in: Lohsse/Schulze/Staudenmayer, Data as Counter-Performance – Contract Law 2.0?*, 225 (243).

636 *Ohly*, AcP, 2001, 1 (7).

taken from the hand of the data subject to the court and, essentially, the controller. Against this backdrop of the GDPR, the heteronomy facilitated by this lawful ground takes place of the autonomy in merchandising scenarios, and the contract between the data subject and the controller is reduced to the accompaniment of the balance test.[637] In this sense, it would not amount to an elegant solution for merchandising scenarios. The reliance on the heteronomy would also restrict the rights granted by the GDPR for the data subject. For instance, the right to portability is merely applicable for the data processing based on the autonomous decision of the data subject, although the restriction would be harmless as the right to portability would not have made much sense in merchandising cases.

2.2.3 Unable to address the long-term consequences

Leaving the objections aside, Art. 6 (1) (f) GDPR focuses merely on lawful data processing i.e., authorized merchandising. Even though the under-protection problem per se is innocuous because the restitution for a fictive licensee fee based on unjust enrichment in Germany can be smoothly applied in unauthorized merchandising cases, it cannot address the long-term consequences of the under-protection problem. The general insensitivity of data subjects to the commercial value of their data would still be the case. To make matters worse, Art. 6 (1) (f) GDPR helps in covering these problems by replacing the autonomous decision of the data subject with the objective interests-balancing. It seems that the data subject is being decided by the controller and the court instead of being the decider for merchandising.

---

637 *Veil*, NJW, 2018, 3337 (3343). It addresses the highly different connecting factors for self-determination (consent) and the balance of interests as lawful grounds for data processing.

3. *Recalibrating the application of Art. 6 (1) (b) GDPR in the B2B merchandising*

3.1 Other possibilities of the interpretation of Art. 6 (1) (b) GDPR

3.1.1 The EDPB's Guidelines and some scholars' proposition

There are two other noteworthy points of view, both of which tend to interpret the ambit of Art. 6 (1) (b) GDPR broadly for their own agenda.

Besides some similarities, the EDPB's *Guidelines*' interpretation of Art. 6 (1) (b) GDPR in the online environment have major differences to the mainstream opinïon discussed in Part II Section 4.3.1. Likely, this interpretation lends Art. 6 (1) (b) GDPR to applying to merchandising contracts, though it is merely aimed at online services.

The EDPB's *Guidelines* do not confine the applicability of Art. 6 (1) (b) GDPR within accessory types of data processing to the performance of a contract; Rather, it maintains that the requirement of necessity means that Art. 6 (1) (b) GDPR can legitimize data processing that is absolutely necessary to achieve the (objective) purpose of the contract.[638] In the first step, the EDPB inquiries about the objective expectations of the contracting parties and categorizes the contract according to the nature and specific characteristics of the service provided by controllers;[639] Subsequently, the EDPB compares the objectively determined purpose with the data processing envisioned by the controller and assesses objectively whether there is a less intrusive operation of data processing.[640] The approach to confine data processing to the least intrusive operation stems from the interpretation of CJEU regarding Art. 7 and 8 of the Charter.[641]

---

638 See EDPB, Guidelines 2/2019 on the processing of personal data under Article 6(1)(b) GDPR in the context of the provision of online services to data subjects, para. 15 and 25.

639 See ibid., para. 30, 33, 36. It encourages finding out the expectation of average data subjects by asking questions, such as "what is the nature of the service being provided to the data subject", "what is the exact rationale of the contract", and "what are the mutual perspectives and expectations of the parties to the contract".

640 See ibid., para. 25.

641 See CJEU, Volker und Markus Schecke, Joined Cases C-92/09 and C-93/09, para. 74, 76 and 77; CJEU, Digital Rights Ireland and Others, Joined Cases C-293/12 and C-594/12, para. 56; CJEU, Rīgas, C-13/16, para. 30; Recital 39 of the GDPR; *Bygrave,* Data Privacy Law: An International Perspective, S. 150.

As a result, while the EDPB's interpretation and the prevailing opinion both reject the application of Art. 6 (1) (b) GDPR in the commercialization of personal data, their reasons are different. The EDPB does not consider the commercialization of personal data meets the genuine wish of average data subjects, whereas scholars holding the prevailing opinion fear that it would circumvent the enhanced protection for data subjects facilitated by the anytime revocable consent. In other words, the majority opinion does not base on the wish of the data subject. Hence, one would argue that a deviation from the free choice of the data subject is observed in the dominant opinion in respect of the commercialization of personal data, while the EDPB's approach respects the data subject's self-determination but negates the commercialization for other reasons.

Therefore, the difference between this opinion and the leading one in the literature emerges in those scenarios where the data processing is primary performance of the contract as well as absolutely necessary to achieve the objective contractual purpose. For instance, as the EDPB reckons, data processing for the provision of personalized content may invoke Art. 6 (1) (b) GDPR as it may be necessary for the performance of the contract.[642] While it is arguably that the main performance of such contracts is data processing, this service is on top of a large amount of personal data and profiling. The data processing in this context is by no means an accessory type.

Against this backdrop, it motivates one to wonder the standpoint of the EDPB for merchandising. First of all, as drawn in Part II Section 4.3.1 (2), the requirement of (absolute) necessity is in general fulfilled in merchandising contracts since there is no less intrusive means to achieve the contractual purpose agreed upon by the data subject has freely and prudently.[643] Secondly, it motivates one to wonder the standpoint of the EDPB for merchandising since it considers that the data processing for the provision of personalized content might meet the necessity requirement, and clearly, merchandising needs significantly less personal data and is less risky than it. Therefore, one may argue that merchandisers may invoke Art. 6 (1) (b) GDPR to legitimize the data processing according to the rela-

642 See EDPB, Guidelines 2/2019 on the processing of personal data under Article 6(1)(b) GDPR in the context of the provision of online services to data subjects, , para. 57.

643 Vgl. Ettig, in *Koreng and Lachenmann*, Formularhandbuch Datenschutzrecht, J. Datenschutz und Personenbildnisse, III. Model-Release-Vereinbarung, S. 1317.

tively conservative opinion of the EDPB, while an official interpretation by the CJEU stalls.

3.1.2 A relatively liberal reading of the ambit of Art. 6 (1) (b) GDPR by some scholars

Stemming from the principle of private autonomy, some scholars propose a relatively liberal reading of the ambit of Art. 6 (1) (b) GDPR.[644] Just as the mutual understanding of data subjects and controllers in implementing their willing should be respected, so too should the construction of the contract regarding data processing.[645] Data processing is thus *prima facie* "necessary for the performance of a contract" if it has been specified, anticipated and desired by the data subject to achieve the purposes pursued by both parties; thereby, the rejection to provide personal data by the data subject would be considered as in bad faith.[646] After all, the literal interpretation of Art. 6 (1) (b) GDPR also leaves room for this interpretation. Moreover, this approach would not compromise the fundamental rights of data subjects – the right to the protection for personal data because the compliance rules in the GDPR including the principles of data processing and the contractual and consumer protection laws in the Member States are also applicable.[647]

This premise for this proposition is relatively narrow as the free negotiation between data subjects and controllers must be present.[648] Otherwise, data controllers would exploit personal data unrestrictedly under the guise of contracts without being subject to the anytime revocable consent by merely including the data processing in the contract.[649] In this sense, this approach shares several commonalities with the mainstream opinion. They

644 Vgl. *Engeler*, ZD, 2018, 55 (57f.); Albers/Veit, in *Brink/Wolff*, BeckOK Datenschutzrecht, Art. 6 Rn. 44f.; *Bunnenberg*, Privates Datenschutzrecht: über Privatautonomie im Datenschutzrecht, S. 53 ff.

645 *Heinzke and Engel*, ZD, 2020, 189 (192).

646 See Schantz, in *Simitis, et al.*, Datenschutzrecht, Art. 6 Rn. 32; Schulz, in *Gola*, DSGVO, Art. 6 Rn. 37; *Bunnenberg*, Privates Datenschutzrecht: über Privatautonomie im Datenschutzrecht, S. 57.

647 See *Engeler*, PinG, 2019, 149 (152f.); *Rott*, GRUR Int., 2018, 1010 (1012).

648 Schantz, in *Simitis, et al.*, Datenschutzrecht, Art. 6 Rn. 32.

649 Vgl. Albers/Veit, in *Brink/Wolff*, BeckOK Datenschutzrecht, Art. 6 Rn. 32; Buchner/Petri, in *Kühling/Buchner*, DSGVO/BDSG, Art. 6 Rn. 39; Schulz, in *Gola*, DSGVO, Art. 6 Rn. 39.

both agree to prohibit the commercialization of personal data through standard contracts. In addition, both approaches require a direct connection between the data processing and the specific purpose of the contract by ordering the processing must be "adequate, relevant and limited to what is necessary" for that purpose.[650]

Another scholarly view chooses the term "necessary" in Art. 6 (1) (b) GDPR as the dogmatic starting point to distinguish the applicable scope of Art. 6 (1) (a) and (b) GDPR and thus to reconcile the national contract law and the GDPR.[651] By considering that the free revocable consent is less intrusive than a binding contract for the data subject, it assesses whether the free revocability of consent as an alternative for the binding contract is objectively reasonable for the controller.[652] In this wise, the requirement of necessity, on the one hand, is not stretched too much to exclude data processing as the main performance of the contract in general, and on the other, does not allow every data processing prescribed in the contract to enter the gate.

Both scholarly opinions offer a hint of breathing space for merchandising contracts to apply Art. 6 (1) (b) GDPR when the contracts are not pre-drafted standard contracts that models/data subjects cannot insert any influences in the terms.

3.2 The objections to these interpretation

3.2.1 Criticism of the EDPB's Guidelines and evaluation

The approach taken by the EDPB is criticized by scholars for many reasons. The most convincing one is that the purely objective assessment is, in essence, a balancing of interests anchored in Art. 6 (1) (f) GDPR and thereby ignores the protection of personal autonomy advocated by Art. 6

650 Recital 39 of the GDPR; EDPB, Guidelines 2/2019 on the processing of personal data under Article 6(1)(b) GDPR in the context of the provision of online services to data subjects, 8; See also Recital 44; Albers/Veit, in *Brink/Wolff*, BeckOK Datenschutzrecht, Art. 6 Rn. 32; *Plath*, DSGVO/BDSG, Art. 6 Rn. 12; Buchner/Petri, in *Kühling/Buchner*, DSGVO/BDSG, Art. 6 Rn. 38; Schulz, in *Gola*, DSGVO, Art. 6 Rn. 38; In this direction, see Schantz, in *Simitis, et al.*, Datenschutzrecht, Art. 6 Rn. 33.

651 *Bunnenberg*, Privates Datenschutzrecht: über Privatautonomie im Datenschutzrecht, S. 54.

652 Ibid., S. 56f.

(1) (b) GDPR.[653] By forbidding "artificially" expanding the scope of data processing by the controller, this approach cannot find its support in the GDPR and also poses risks in reshaping national contract law.[654] The categorization of contracts to explore the "*essentilia negotii*" of that contract is subject to criticism of being willful.[655] Moreover, its feasibility is also rightfully challenged because of the trend toward convergence in the variety of web services.[656] Large platforms try to combine all services, which makes it increasingly difficult to judge the necessity of the approach by distinguishing the different purposes of data processing. Lastly, as the EDPB rejects the application of Art. 6 (1)(b) GDPR in justifying the commercialization of personal data,[657] it is difficult to explain the application of Art. 6 (1)(b) GDPR to free personalized service prevailing on platforms. Last but not least, the proposal of the EDPB is relatively conservative compared with the prevailing opinion as it confines itself within the business model "data against service".[658] This business model is quite limited in application in the dawn of big data, machine learning and AI.[659] Conceivably, controllers will come up with new business models to harvest personal data. It thus would make more sense not aim at a particular business model but a business logic.

Besides, it is also contended here that the argumentation drawn by the EDPB suffer from some flaws that render its application untenable.

At the outset, the EDPB argues that because data subjects usually do not know that targeted advertising based on profiling is used to monetize the so-called "free" services, there is no intention of data subjects to con-

653 Critics on the ambiguity and uncertainty of the objective assessment adopted by the EDPB's *Guidelines,* see *Engeler,* PinG, 2019, 149 (151-152); Schantz, in *Simitis, et al.,* Datenschutzrecht, Art. 6 Rn. 32; Buchner/Petri, in *Kühling/Buchner,* DSGVO/BDSG, Art. 6 Rn. 45.

654 *Indenhuck and Britz,* BB, 2019, 1091 (1094f.).

655 Vgl. Schulz, in *Gola,* DSGVO, Art. 6, Rn. 37.

656 See *Engeler,* ZD, 2018, 55 (57).

657 See EDPB, Guidelines 2/2019 on the processing of personal data under Article 6(1)(b) GDPR in the context of the provision of online services to data subjects, para. 53 and 54.

658 *Sattler, in: Pertot, Rechte an Daten,* S. 70.

659 *Posner and Weyl,* Radical Markets: Uprooting Capitalism and Democracy for a Just Society, 213 et seq. It explains how "factories for thinking machines" work based on the neural networks.

clude such a contract for "data against services".[660] Therefore, on the flip side, it can be deduced that if the data subject is aware of the *quid pro quo* relationship between the processing of personal data and the "free" services, his or her will – be it revocable consent or binding permission – shall be respected. The EDPB's second argument is that Art. 21 (2) GDPR supports the exclusion of data licensing agreement for profiling: A special opt-out right for direct marketing indicates the cautious and restrictive mentality of the GDPR towards personal profiling.[661] However, it cannot lead to the conclusion that the data subject is prohibited to agree on behavioral advertising as remuneration. Rather, the controller who opts in this business model is subject to this special opt-out right of data subjects. Lastly, the examples and argumentation advanced in the EDPB's *Guidelines* imply another reason for deviating from the choice of the data subject, i.e., the voluntariness of data subjects is endangered due to power asymmetry since data objects always face a "take it or leave it" situation.[662]

Hence, these arguments cannot lead to a general exclusion of Art. 6 (1) (b) GDPR in scenarios of "data against service". It could be argued that if the data subject knows and requests the data processing voluntarily, even if it concerns profiling as the necessary tool for providing personalized content, which is deemed significantly risky for the rights and freedoms of data subjects, the will of that data subject may still be considered within the EDPB's framework.[663]

Therefore, the EDPB's *Guidelines* are not followed because of its flaws and more importantly, its inapplicability to merchandising.

3.2.2 Possible counterarguments

The most convincing argument against the relatively liberal reading of Art. 6 (1) (b) GDPR is advanced by the scholars with the mainstream opin-

---

660 EDPB, Guidelines 2/2019 on the processing of personal data under Article 6(1) (b) GDPR in the context of the provision of online services to data subjects, para. 4.

661 Ibid., para. 52.

662 It revolves around "contracts for online services, which typically are not negotiated on an individual basis." Moreover, the examples it listed focus on digital service scenarios, which are often triggered by the user's consent to standard contracts unilaterally drafted by the data controller. See ibid. para. 16, and the examples.

663 Vgl. *Indenhuck and Britz*, BB, 2019, 1091 (1092).

ion. The wider reading of the ambit of Art. 6 (1) (b) GDPR would result in an escape from the consent (*"Flucht vor der Einwilligung"*),[664] because controllers as big platforms can easily apply professional contract writing skills to meet the requirement of necessity. To use an online service, internet users are used to signing the privacy policy provided by the digital service provider. Although most privacy policies today are templates written by controllers, it is easy for them to argue, with some fine-tuning, that many of the conditions are subject to negotiation with data subjects. If this argument is supported, then the anytime freely revocable consent would not be used anymore. This is the exact situation the GDPR aims to prevent by emphasizing the free revocable consent.[665]

Moreover, difficulties in assessing the mutual expectations of the parties are undeniable given the increasingly complex contract designs.[666] One would reasonably argue that even in a freely negotiated contract, the data subject does not well comprehend the purpose, content, and means of the data processing (See examples about the relationship between "idol trainees" and powerful agencies in Part II Section 3.2.2 (4)). Thus, a loophole according to the systematic interpretation of Art. 6 (1) GDPR surfaces not because the anytime revocable consent must be applied in preference,[667] but because the GDPR's objective of deploying the ready revocability of consent to protect data subjects would fall short.[668]

The emphasis on the concept of "necessary" as a normative correction (*normatives Korrektiv*)[669] according to *Bunnenberg* is a commendable solu-

---

664 Frenzel, in *Paal and Pauly*, DS-GVO BDSG, Art. 7, Rn. 26; Also in Langhanke and Schmidt-Kessel, 4 Journal of European Consumer and Market Law 218 (2015) (221).

665 Buchner/ Kühling, in *Kühling/Buchner*, DSGVO/BDSG, Art. 7 Rn. 39; *Tinnefeld and Conrad*, ZD, 2018, 391 (396).

666 *Heinzke and Engel*, ZD, 2020, 189 (192).

667 Buchner/Kühling, in *Kühling/Buchner*, DSGVO/BDSG, Art. 7 Rn. 16; Schulz, in *Gola*, DSGVO, Art. 6 Rn. 10; Heckmann/Paschka, in *Ehmann and Selmayr*, DS-GVO, Art. 7 Rn. 17; Plath, in *Plath*, DSGVO/BDSG, Art. 6 Rn. 5; *Piltz*, K&R, 2016, 557 (562); In this direction, see Schanz, in *Simitis, et al.*, Datenschutzrecht, Art. 6 Rn. 11 The opposite opinion, see Frenzel, in *Paal and Pauly*, DS-GVO BDSG, Art. 7 Rn. 1; *Sattler*, JZ, 2017, 1036 (1040).

668 Stemming from the purpose of emphasizing individuals' control over personal data, consent in Art. 6 (1) (a) GDPR shall be prevented from restrictive interpretation. Moreover, compared to other legitimate grounds, Art. 8 of the Charter focuses on the data subject's consent specifically.

669 Albers/Veit, in *Brink/Wolff*, BeckOK Datenschutzrecht, Art. 6 Rn. 44; A similar term "evaluative corrective" (*wertendes Korrektiv*) stems from *Bunnenberg*, Privates Datenschutzrecht: über Privatautonomie im Datenschutzrecht, S. 59.

tion because it chooses the path of data protection law rather than contract law.[670] It is more warranted compared to the EDPB's *Guidelines* as it inquires the "the motives of the parties behind the conclusion of the transaction" (*die hinter der Geschäftseingehung stehende Motivlage der Parteien*).[671] However, at the second point, the approach of absolute necessity deployed by the EDPB is directly adopted in private sector without further explanation. Free revocable consent is indeed less intrusive than a binding contract for the data subject. This is also illustrated by *the ladder of permission*, of which free revocable consent is at the bottom due to its weakest binding effect on the subject. Nonetheless, the question that the author does not address is why, in the realm of private autonomy, data subjects do not have the freedom to choose to climb one rung higher – the binding contract.

Admittedly, the principle of data minimization may play a role in interpreting the concept of "necessary",[672] but it mainly concerns the content of personal data and the necessity to process personal data at all.[673] The CJEU also adopted the approach of absolute necessity in data processing conducted by public authorities.[674] The EDPB's *Guidelines* focus merely on online services where the contracts are generally pre-drafted standard contracts that are typically signed by the users without looking. It cannot

670 The distinction between solutions based on data protection law and contract law, see *Funke,* Dogmatik und Voraussetzungen der datenschutzrechtlichen Einwilligung im Zivilrecht, , S. 271f.; The solutions on the basis of contract law centering on the consumer protection and the content control of contracts pursuant to the BGB, see Schulz, in *Gola,* DSGVO, Art. 6, Rn. 27 und 37; *Engeler,* ZD, 2018, 55 (58); *Indenhuck and Britz,* BB, 2019, 1091 (1094 f). The approval of this solution, see Albers/Veit, in *Brink/Wolff,* BeckOK Datenschutzrecht, Art. 6 Rn. 44.

671 The author describes it as the "objective purpose of the contractual relationship" in line with the EDPB's *Guidelines* though. See *Bunnenberg,* Privates Datenschutzrecht: über Privatautonomie im Datenschutzrecht, S. 58.

672 EDPB, Guidelines 2/2019 on the processing of personal data under Article 6(1) (b) GDPR in the context of the provision of online services to data subjects, , para. 15; Roßnagel, in *Simitis, et al.,* Datenschutzrecht, Art. 5, Rn. 116.

673 "The personal data should be adequate, relevant and limited to what is necessary for the purposes for which they are processed". "Personal data should be processed only if the purpose of the processing could not reasonably be fulfilled by other means." See Recital 39 of the GDPR.

674 CJEU, Volker und Markus Schecke, Joined Cases C-92/09 and C-93/09, para. 77; CJEU, Rīgas, C-13/16, para. 30; see EDPS, Assessing the Necessity of Measures that limit the fundamental right to the protection of personal data, 7.

lead to the conclusion that the approach of absolute necessity should be followed in all types of contracts.

It is even more questionable when *Bunnenberg* finally argues that Art. 6 (1) (b) GDPR is applicable if the reliance interest of the controller overrides the interest of the data subject to revoke consent at any time.[675] In this wise, since the readily revocable consent is not reasonable for a merchandiser,[676] the data subject seems to be prohibited to choose consent in Art. 6 (1) (a) GDPR even if the controller agrees. This outcome would be unreasonable in users' merchandising scenarios. Considering the *hair salon* case, if the data subject agrees with the use of her photos on the fan page of the hair salon for some discount, would she not be allowed to withdraw her consent at any time and thus ask the controller to take down her photos? Based on the theory of *the ladder of permission*, there are a variety of conditions that need to be considered for the rightful holder to have more binding dispositional power upward, but downward extensions usually do not require justification.[677] Therefore, the assessment of the concept "necessary" presents an evident resemblance with the application of Art. 6 (1) (f) GDPR in contractual relationship (see above Chapter 3), which rests on a balance of interests instead of an advocation of personal autonomy anchored in by Art. 6 (1) (b) GDPR.

The main issue is that it seems to overlook the fundamental differences between merchandising and the model of "data against service". The EU data protection legislator tacitly acknowledges that in the context of data exploitation the data subject cannot actively choose as the choices he or she makes are predetermined by controllers. Data subjects are hence "nudged" to the lowest step of *the ladder of permission* to protect themselves, and if they want to be binding by contracts, an objective weighing of interests including the requirement of necessity is required.[678] Using the concept "necessary" to distinguish the applicable scope of consent and a

675 In the book, the author argues that Article 6(1) (b) GDPR is only applicable if the controller cannot reasonably be expected to obtain the consent of the data subject; and unreasonableness is indicated when the controller can claim a special interest in the binding nature of the legal relationship, which takes precedence over the data subject's interest in revocation in the given case. See *Bunnenberg*, Privates Datenschutzrecht: über Privatautonomie im Datenschutzrecht, S. 57.

676 Ibid., S. 59-60.

677 *Ohly*, "Volenti non fit iniuria": die Einwilligung im Privatrecht, S. 144 und 146.

678 Brinkmann, in *Gsell, Weller and Geibel*, GROSSKOMMENTAR zum Zivilrecht: BeckOGK, § 307 Datenschutzklausel Rn. 16.

contract within the scenario envisaged by the legislator may be warranted, but it would be inappropriate to use this normative correction stemming from the principle of proportionality without justification to regulate civil transactions.[679]

3.3 Applying Art. 6 (1) (b) GDPR to merchandising in the B2B context

3.3.1 Arguments and advantages of this solution

(1) The legal basis for this solution

It is argued here to make an exception from the leading opinion of Art. 6 (1) (b) GDPR by considering merchandising contracts in the B2B (Business to Business) context a special contract type, and as it fulfills the two requirements in the provision literally Art. 6 (1) (b) GDPR is applicable.

First of all, the application of Art. 6 (1) (b) GDPR to merchandising in the B2B context does not prevent circumvention of Art. 6 (1) (a) GDPR as the anytime revocable consent is not dodged by controllers to compromise the objective of the GDPR in protecting data subjects from data exploitation. Rather, it is to guarantee contract law is not replaced or overturned by the GDPR.[680] This reading has its support in the GDPR.[681] By advocating an understanding of the requirement of necessity "in the context of a contract", recital 44 GDPR requires the respect to autonomous contracts.[682]

Moreover, the control of data subjects over personal data is not only materialized in the free revocability of consent but also the principles of data fairness, transparency, and accountability as well as the data subject's

---

679 *Rüpke, Lewinski and Eckhardt,* Datenschutzrecht, S. 172-175; Schantz, in *Brink/Wolff,* BeckOK Datenschutzrecht, Art. 5, Rn. 26. The problem of applying the principle of proportionality in horizontal relationship has also been noticed by the proposer of this solution, see *Bunnenberg,* Privates Datenschutzrecht: über Privatautonomie im Datenschutzrecht, S. 55.

680 Albers/Veit, in *Brink/Wolff,* BeckOK Datenschutzrecht, Art. 6 Rn. 44.

681 It is argued that the general restriction of the applicability of Art. 6 (1) (b) GDPR in auxiliary data processing cannot find a legal basis in the GDPR. See *Indenhuck and Britz,* BB, 2019, 1091 (1095f.).

682 It states, "processing should be lawful where it is necessary in the context of a contract or the intention to enter into a contract."

rights. After all, the GDPR is not a single provision regarding lawfulness but a legal system to guarantee high-level data protection.

Thirdly, the restrictive ambit of Art. 6 (1) (b) GDPR may go too far in merchandising in the B2B context. All the opinions including the mainstream one focus on the pre-drafted standard contracts prevailing in the "data against services" model because data subjects are likely to inadvertently enter a binding relationship, and data controllers from using contracts to take (permanent) possession of personal data and make them serve their business purposes exclusively.[683] Given the fact that digital contracts in standard forms are complex, lengthy, and ubiquitous, and "the duty to read" a contract is both impractical and inefficient,[684] data subjects probably do not understand the contracts even if they try, they cannot afford the cost not to be contracting or to negotiate at every time of contracting. Thus, an exclusion of this kind of contracts from Art. 6 (1) (b) GDPR seems plausible. As reiterated, this situation differs from merchandising in the B2B context significantly.[685] Professional models and celebrities value their rights and are able to negotiate with agencies about specific terms and conditions. Some pre-drafted standard contracts exist due to efficiency,[686] but they are subject to negotiation on an individual basis.[687] When parties have freely decided the purpose, contents, and duration of the data processing, strong justification is needed to deviate from the principle of private autonomy in the civil law.

In addition, an independent commercial purpose of the controller is highlighted to support the exclusion of Art. 6 (1) (b) GDPR according to the mainstream opinion as it suggests that the data processing is unnecessary and likely to be extensive as well as unmanageable for data subjects. It makes sense in online environment, especially facing with data-driven controllers. However, in merchandising, parties' commercial

683 *Westphalen and Wendehorst*, BB, 2016, 2179 (2185).

684 *Bix*, in: *Miller and Wertheimer, The Ethics of Consent: Theory and Practice*, 252 (261 and 264 et seq.). It addresses that contract law generally places the burden to read the documents on the party who signs it. However, when faced with standardized forms of contracts, the traditional doctrine of consent is under "distinct challenges".

685 See Part I Section 3.2.2, Part III Section 3.2.

686 *Indenhuck and Britz*, BB, 2019, 1091 (1093f.); Albers/Veit, in *Brink/Wolff*, BeckOK Datenschutzrecht, Art. 6 Rn. 44.

687 See OLG Frankfurt, NJW-RR 2005, 1280 - Skoda-Autokids-Club, Rn. 39; *Indenhuck and Britz*, BB, 2019, 1091 (1094f.); Vgl. *Westphalen and Wendehorst*, BB, 2016, 2179 (2185f.).

purposes overlap. For instance, in the *landlady* case, the data subject would get more consideration if the controller performed more data processing. This was in line with the common desire of both of them. It would also be contrary to the data subject's commercial purpose if she revokes her commission based on the protection of the GDPR when the controller has completed the preliminary work, including optimizing photos, finding partners, and negotiating contracts, etc.

Furthermore, the characteristics of merchandising hardly raise any concern about undermining the protection for data subjects advocated by the GDPR. In merchandising, the data subjects involved are professionals who are usually not in a position with asymmetry of power or information against the controllers. The purposes and methods of data processing are transparent and fair, and the risks are also defined and relatively small.

Last but not least, while the special protection of data subjects (depicted persons) in German law cannot be used as a reason to exclude the application of the GDPR because of the accessoriness of the national law of obligations to the EU data protection law,[688] the overlaps between the two support a reasonable application of the GDPR in merchandising scenarios. The underlined rationale is that the justification for the high-level data protection at the cost of private autonomy is absent or significantly undermined in the B2B context due to the voluntariness and professionality of the data subject as well as the certainty and low risk in data processing and purpose.

(2) The EDPS' resistance towards merchandising in the B2B context?

The explicit and seemingly strongest argument of the EDPS is that "fundamental rights such as the right to the protection of personal data cannot be reduced to simple consumer interests".[689] By warning against "that people can pay with their data the same way as they do with money", the EDPB strongly criticizes the commercialization of personal data as if the

---

688 *Bunnenberg,* Privates Datenschutzrecht: über Privatautonomie im Datenschutzrecht, S. 23; *Peitz and Schweitzer,* NJW, 2018, 275 (275-277).

689 EDPS, Opinion 4/2017 on the Proposal for a Directive on certain aspects concerning contracts for the supply of digital content, 3.

fundamental rights were salable.[690] However, a fundamental right is not necessarily a negative right without positive components.[691]

The fundamental right to protect one's dignity is two-folded. In addition to the protection from devaluation, one shall act as he or she wishes and takes full responsibility for that decision to "be a human and respect the others as human beings" (*Sei eine Person und respektiere die anderen als Personen*)[692] unless an exception prescribed by law, or moral values applies. Thus, the fundamental right to the protection of personal data contains naturally the imperative to prevent the misuse of personal data, but one cannot conclude that enforcing the informational self-determination by disposing of one's data is prohibited in that fundamental right. The BGH has also addressed that the recognition of the pecuniary components of the right of personality is necessary to guarantee protection against commercial use.[693]

A thorough taxonomy that keeps the restrictions within the necessary limits is thus essential. The abundant jurisprudence of the KUG regarding merchandising demonstrates that a general prohibition of commercialization of personal data under all the circumstances is an excessive and unnecessary (and might also be outdated) solution to protect the free development of personality and human dignity. All in all, the nature of fundamental rights is not a reason to prohibit any means of commercializing personal data but merely the translative transfer.

(3) The enforcement of this solution

When the data processing reveals some commercial value and is not auxiliary to the performance of the contract, it is generally excluded from the application of Art. 6 (1) b) GDPR. However, if the contract is about merchandising and the data subject is an entrepreneur who possesses the knowledge of merchandising business and makes a living on it, the data processing can invoke an exception to the teleological reduction of the applicable scope of Art. 6 (1) (b) GDPR.

690 Ibid.3.

691 The fundamental right to protect one's property in Art. 14 of the Charter is two-folded. One shall protect his or her property from intrusion and dispose of it as he or she wishes unless an exception is prescribed by law applies.

692 *Hegel*, Grundlinien der Philosophie des Rechts, § 36, S. 43.

693 Vgl. BGH, GRUR 2000, 709 - Marlene Dietrich, Rn. 35.

In distinguishing the B2C and B2B context, time-for-print contracts would be the borderline case. Admittedly, young models are often suffering from power asymmetry, and the anytime revocable consent is devised to reverse the inequality. However, despite the lack of negotiating power, they are clear about what they are paying for and the risks they are taking. Moreover, German courts are inclined to recognize the knowledge and decisions of young models in merchandising scenarios, i.e., to respect the rationality of the individual in the absence of clear evidence to the contrary. In the *landlady* case, the higher court in Munich did not consider that the permission to publish her nude photos of the person depicted was a youthful mistake; the court further argued that a 24-year-old is capable of making meaningful decisions about her career choice and lifestyle.[694] Even in the borderline case, the objection for the validity of a time-for-print contract revolved around the young model's level of knowledge instead of her weaker position.[695] In this respect, the borderline cases are clearly distinct from the users' merchandising scenario we have pictured. In users' merchandising, data subjects merely have an abstract yet incomplete idea of their rights and obligations – they have obtained "free" services from the controllers. Even if they are aware that their data become accessible for controllers, they do not know what consequences they might face or whether it is a good deal. In a nutshell, power asymmetry and the lack of self-sufficiency of contracting parties are not prominent in time-for-print contracts.[696]

Enlighted by some German scholars, the negotiability of the contract serves as a clear sign for the voluntariness and professionality of the data subject.[697] Merchandising contracts, albeit having models, are scrutinized, and specifically agreed upon by the data subject including the purpose, contents, duration, rights and obligations and sub-licensees or the conditions for selecting sub-licensees. In this wise, users' merchandising is in

694 The court does not consider that the age of 24 when she agreed to publish the nude photos, was too young to make a meaningful decision concerning her career choice and lifestyle. See OLG München, NJW-RR 1990, 999 - Wirtin.

695 The German court has addressed in the "stink fingers" case that the ruling might be different if the case concerns amateur models who lack enough experience. LG Frankfurt/Main, 30.05.2017 - 2-03 O 134/16 - Stinkefingers, para. 70 with further references.

696 Even the GDPR acknowledges this point as the prohibition of coupling tackling with power asymmetry is merely declarative while the duty to inform is absolute and rigorous.

697 Vgl. Albers/Veit, in *Brink/Wolff*, BeckOK Datenschutzrecht, Art. 6 Rn. 30.

general excluded from the exception because, despite it concern merchandising, the contract (the privacy policy) is usually drafted by the controller and the data subject cannot exert any influence on the text.[698] Moreover, it is possible that controllers would grant sub-licenses based on the blanket authorization. Thus, Art. 6 (1) (b) GDPR is only applicable in typical merchandising contracts between professional data subjects such as models, actors/actresses and agencies, advertisers, and manufacturers. It is further supported by the general rule in interpreting exceptions as to understand them narrowly.

(4) Well-balanced protection for both sides

Apart from providing a stable legal relationship for merchandising, well-balanced protection for all contractual parties facilitated by the application of Art. 6 (1) (b) GDPR is also undergirded by the unaffected application of national law in protecting personality interests of the person depicted (the data subject).[699] In other words, the German doctrines including the revocability of consent, the theory of purpose transfer in interpreting the contract, as well as the contractual rights and privileges of the person depicted are all applicable in assessing the validity of that contract.

As demonstrated in Part I Section 3.1.1 (2), the person depicted can revoke consent in a merchandising contract by proving a changed belief of merchandising. In addition, extraordinary opt-out rights of the person depicted, which are always included in merchandising contracts, can also lead to the termination of those contracts when a prescribed violation of the data subject's interests, rights and freedoms emerges. The data subject shall deploy these rights to terminate the legitimacy of data processing by the controller with an *ex nunc* effect. Consequently, the controller must stop data processing by taking down the advertising and delete the stored data.

Admittedly, the data subject does not have as much control over personal data under Art. 6 (1) (b) as consent in Art. 6 (1) (a) GDPR. However, it is in the interest of the data subject to recognize that the data processing is necessary for the performance of the contract. After all, the data subject seeks mainly (more) economic benefits. If he or she retains the right to

698 Such as the invitation emails and links sent by one's friends to invite the person to sign in the platform.

699 Schantz, in *Simitis, et al.*, Datenschutzrecht, Art. 6 Rn. 21.

terminate the contract at any time, very few agencies and advertisers would be willing to cooperate with the data subject. Even if some bold merchandisers exist, they will certainly pay significantly less remuneration to the data subject because of the higher risk they take. Moreover, by placing the integrity of inner beliefs at the heart of personality protection, the prohibition of assignment and the revocability of consent in merchandising scenarios strikes a fair balance between the core interests of one's personality. It is noteworthy that the untouchable human dignity and free development of personality speak for personal autonomy and the inalienability of dignity. Lastly, in case of doubt for the ambit of the data processing, the German doctrine of purpose transfer provides helpful concretization in applying the requirement of necessity. Though this concept should be interpreted autonomously at the EU level, the same origin, namely the principle of purpose limitation, and the same underlined rationale to protecting the interests of data subjects without undermining the effectiveness of their self-determination in concluding the contract both support the indirect application of the abundant German jurisprudence in interpreting and executing the EU provision. Against the merchandising background, if the means of exploitation of personal pictures are not specified in the contract – be they implicitly granted or licensed in gross – the lawful means should be the ones that are indispensable for realizing objectives outlined in the contract.

In this sense, time-for-print contracts can apply Art. 6 (1) (b) GDPR as the lawful ground for data processing as long as it is necessary to achieve the purpose of that contract. The nature of free negotiation of this kind of contracts and the professionality of both parties are strong reasons for invoking the exception for the teleological reduction. Thereby, similar results could be concluded from the application of the GDPR in the "*stink fingers*" case. The commercial exploitation of the personal data by the controller is lawful, but not the processing concerning the disgraceful presentation of the pictures.

A spin-off consequence of the recognition of merchandising contracts under the GDPR is that it paves the way for the recourse for material damages computed on the lost profits can be supported by the GDPR. Hopefully, it can remind people to start paying attention to the commercial value of data and gradually penetrate the users' merchandising.

3.3.2 Disadvantages and objections for this solution

(1) Borderless application of Art. 6 (1) (b) GDPR in sub-licensing situations

The verbatim reading of Art. 6 (1) (b) GDPR might lead to a borderless application, which would render the control of data subjects over personal data factually infeasible.

Common examples often emerge in the context of a data licensing agreement, in which the first data controller, normally a data broker, would transmit the personal data to as many controllers/sub-licensees as possible to get consideration. Thereby, the data subject's control over his or her personal data would be *de facto* deprived if the contract since the data licensing agreement is binding and thus the data subject cannot withdraw the consent; Moreover, by merely asking the first controller to take measures in a proportionate manner according to art. 17 (2) and 19 GDPR, the GDPR does not impose an absolute obligation on the first controller to notify the second and third controllers when the data subject claims rights at it. In this sense, the control of the data subject seems to stop at the first controller.[700] In addition, the obligations for providing information, no matter of the first or the second and third controllers, are limited in effectiveness as the binding nature of the contract would force the data subject to challenge the validity of the contractual obligation at first. Lastly, the omission of these obligations is hardly detrimental to the validity of the contract unless it can be proved that the data subject has exercised the right to informational self-determination in the opposite way because of a serious cognitive error.

Nevertheless, one may argue that Art. 6 (1) (b) GDPR is justified in deliberately not limiting the other party to the contract. Illustrated by the emergence and success of platforms, data subjects can use the one-stop service in platforms to complete numerous matters that previously needed to be done individually. For example, via Amazon, a consumer only signs a contract with the platform instead of signing contracts individually with the provider of the product, the courier company, etc., because the other controllers' legitimacy for processing personal data can be derived from the consumer's contract with the platform. Moreover, this interpretation would not compromise the enforcement of data subject's rights. As the concept of joint controllers has been broadly constructed by the CJEU

700 See *Sattler, in: Pertot, Rechte an Daten*, S. 69f.

since the *Fashion-ID* case, the platform can be held fully responsible according to Art. 82 (4) GDPR.[701] In this wise, it seems non- detrimental if data subjects sign the contract without reading it given some structural and cognitive problems.[702] However, this is the exact situation where data processing is accessory to the performance of the contract. Regardless, Art. 6 (1) (b) GDPR is applicable, and the prevailing opinion is what makes it possible for data subjects to be properly protected.

In summary, the concern about the borderless application of Art. 6 (1) (b) GDPR is well-founded. One can only contend that since the exception of its application is limited in the B2B context like the one in the *landlady* case, the negative consequences could be well maintained coupled with an intensified duty of information of the first controller as well as the second one. Given the self-sufficiency of the data subjects in the B2B context, the clearer the identity of the second controller is in the (context) of the contract, and the clearer the information the data subject has when making the decision, the more justified the second controller is to invoke Art. 6 (1) (b) GDPR. At least, the first controller must at first make some general references of the second and third controllers when it collects the data; when the first controller can identify the others, it should notify the data subject.[703]

(2) Under-protection for data subjects in B2C contexts

By distinguishing the B2C and B2B context and offering Art. 6 (1) (b) GDPR only in the B2C context might result in some under-protection issues for average internet users, i.e., ordinary data subjects. While it is admitted that the applicability of art. 6 (1) (b) GDPR in a B2C scenario may not be a good solution as many academics and EDPB have observed, the commercial value of their data would be acquired by controllers through consent without consideration. As *Langhanke* points out, by qualifying the privacy policy regarding data processing as consumer contracts, a review of the fairness of the content is brought to the fore.[704] For instance, the

---

701 CJEU, Fashion ID, C-40/17, para. 65-85.

702 *Thaler and Sunstein*, Nudge: improving decisions about health, wealth, and happiness, 19 es seq.

703 Schantz, in *Simitis, et al.*, Datenschutzrecht, Art. 6 Rn. 22.

704 Langhanke and Schmidt-Kessel, 4 Journal of European Consumer and Market Law 218 (2015) (220).

China's fastest-growing e-commerce platform, *Pingduoduo*, is embroiled in such a scandal. It encouraged users to keep inviting their friends to join *Pingduoduo* by promising monetary rewards, which could only be withdrawn when the amount reached 500 RMB. However, as the amount gets closer to 500 RMB, the reward for each invitation gets smaller and smaller, which makes it impossible for users to withdraw money *de facto*.[705] Thus, users stop sending invitations to their friends, but the commercial promotion of *Pingduoduo* is not retroactively invalidated. As a result, *Pingduoduo* gets viral in internet and data subjects get nothing.

Therefore, treating the relationship of merchandising as a synallagmatic contract, rather than a mere user's consent, allows the data subject to receive reasonable remuneration and introduces contractual rights common to merchandising contracts to fully protect the personality rights of the data subject. After all, allowing controllers to exploit the commercial value of data without consideration will lead to more exploitation.[706] Taken time-for-print contracts as examples, legal negation of the validity of such contracts due to power asymmetry and paternalistic protection for young models would not only seriously affect the informational self-determination of data subjects but also put the young models in a deadlock situation.[707] Therefore, the rightful solution that the German courts take is to assess the fairness of the reciprocal behavior between photographers and models, and thus draw boundaries for what authorization is necessary.

(3) Art. 6 (1) (b) GDPR as a general clause for fair contracts

This solution is premised on an ideal B2B context where a certain degree of fairness (*qui dit contractuel dit juste*) is presumed.[708] Professional models

705 Sina finance, "在拼多多，一分钱难倒英雄汉"(In *Pingduoduo*, a hero is beaten by a penny), at https://finance.sina.com.cn/tech/2021-06-30/doc-ikqciyzk2719869.shtml. This article articulates the logic under the promoting game set up by *Pingduoduo*. One can at first easily get bonus, but the fission form increases. Since there is always "one penny short of victory (to withdraw deposit)", one has to invite more and more people into this "infinite loop" game.

706 Bietti, 40 Pace law review 310 (2020) (378).

707 Vgl. *Ohly*, "Volenti non fit iniuria": die Einwilligung im Privatrecht, S. 79f, 160. It argues that the anytime revocable consent lay restrictions on both sides of the contract.

708 Cite from *Beale, in: de Elizalde, Uniform Rules for European Contract Law?: A Critical Assessment*, 9 (23); Originally in, *Fouillée*, La science sociale contemporaine, 410.

care about their images and are proactive in asking for information, negotiating the terms and conditions of contract, fighting for benefits, and avoiding risks. Furthermore, models as "professional players" constantly enter into the same type of contracts. They understand and have fully weighed the benefits and risks. However, as a spectrum of the self-sufficiency of data subjects in merchandising scenarios shows (Part III Section 3.2.1), the threshold for professionality of models is elusive. Length of time in practice, income and education are all difficult to use as satisfactory criteria, or they can all be used as criteria. Especially when internet influencers are increasingly coming into the playground, the line between the B2B and B2C contexts is blurring. The BGH considered Cathy Hummels who has more than 600,000 followers as entrepreneur (*Unternehmer*), but how about micro-influencers who have 10,000 followers or less, are they entrepreneurs or average internet users?

Given this, the second condition may be more decisive in enforcing this solution, namely, the negotiability of the contract. In this wise, this solution resembles the minor opinion in literature to some extent as Art. 6 (1) (b) GDPR almost becomes a general clause for fair contracts. Consequently, it suffers similar critics that the negotiability of contract can be easily circumvented by powerful controllers if they possess *de facto* dominant position, such as the scenario between "idol trainees" and powerful agencies.

Establishing a special contract type for merchandising contracts in the B2B context would address this concern. As data subjects who voluntarily and prudently choose merchandising as a career are well respected and protected under the German legal regime, a muster of merchandising contracts under German law taking the contractual right into account is expected to indicate the fairness and necessary protection for data subjects.[709] However, there is hardly a legal basis for this suggestion. Art. 6 (1) (b) GDPR, unlike other lawful grounds, does not offer discretion for the Member States.

709 *Golz and Gössling,* IPRB, 2018, 68 (72); *Beale, in: de Elizalde, Uniform Rules for European Contract Law?: A Critical Assessment,* 9 (31). Instead of focusing on merchandising, the author addresses that harmonization of contract law is more promising in B2B contexts.

3.4 Summary

By applying Art. 6 (1) (b) GDPR as its literal reading to merchandising contracts in the B2B context, merchandisers can rely on valid contracts with professional models to process their personal data and even grant sub-licenses for purposes of merchandising without fearing the anytime revocable consent prescribed in Art. 6 (1) (a) and 7 (3) GDPR. However, there are two detrimental objections to this approach. For one, it can be easily stretched to a general clause for fair contracts as there is hardly a legal basis to limit this approach in merchandising contracts, not to mention this type of contracts is formulated under national law. For two, there is no hard line between the B2B and B2C contexts. As KOL (Key Opinion Leaders) in social media increasingly become a profitable career, the line is more blurring.

Admittedly, the restrictive reading of the ambit of Art. 6 (1) (b) GDPR according to the mainstream opinion would stifle the private autonomy in merchandising. Moreover, even though this solution does not directly address the issue of under-protection for celebrities in unauthorized merchandising cases, the legal recognition of merchandising contracts under the GDPR can support the recourse for the lost profits by celebrities in unlawful data processing scenarios. However, this solution overlooks the users' merchandising in the B2C scenario. If contracts in this scenario are limited to merchandising and does not include direct-marketing, profiling, etc., why should there be reasons to hinder data subjects conclude a binding merchandising contract according to their will? After all, professionalism is a status that acquires by learning. The limitation of the B2B situation would thus be too conservative considering the advent of "digital natives"[710]

---

710 *Prensky*, On the horizon, 2001, 1. The "digital natives" refer to the generation that grew up in the Internet era; correspondingly, "digital immigrants" generally refer to those who gradually learn and use the Internet in their adulthood.

4. *The proposal for a two-tier interpretation of consent*

4.1 The two-tier interpretation of consent

4.1.1 Introduction of this solution

(1) The content of this proposal

Sattler proposes a two-tier interpretation of consent in Art. 6 (1) (a) GDPR.[711] Consent defined in the GDPR has two forms. One is simple and unilateral and can legitimize data processing conducted by the controller according to Art. 6 (1) (a) GDPR. This consent is anytime revocable pursuant to Art. 7 (3) GDPR. The other one is a legal act that is given to establish a legal relationship, which according to Art. 6 (1) (a) shall also provide a lawful ground for data processing. However, the revocability of this consent is not subject to Art. 7 (3) GDPR but to national law regarding legal acts. In this context, the anytime revocability in Art. 7 (3) GDPR is not a mandatory condition for consent anymore.[712] Rather, data subjects can choose between anytime revocable consent and binding consent to dispose of their control over personal data according to their genuine wishes. In doing so, consent given by models in merchandising agreements is allowed to be binding but subject to revocability with due cause according to German law.

Art. 4 (11) GDPR defining consent does not require the anytime revocability. Instead, it defines consent merely as "*any freely given, specific, informed and unambiguous indication of the data subject's wishes*". According to this definition, wiggle room for the two-tier interpretation is presented. All steps in the *ladder of permissions* developed by *Ohly* can be subsumed within the consent since they meet the conditions prescribed in Art. 4 (11) GDPR. In other words, consent, following the definition in the GDPR, could be simple, unliteral consent that is readily revocable, a binding contractual permission, or even an assignment of right if it does not contradict to other provisions of the GDPR.[713] Thus, in *Sattler's* words,

---

711 See *Sattler*, JZ, 2017, 1036 (1043f); *Sattler, in: Lohsse/Schulze/Staudenmayer, Data as Counter-Performance – Contract Law 2.0?*, 225 (243 et seq.); In this direction, see *Sattler*, in: *Bakhoum, Personal Data in Competition, Consumer Protection and IP Law - Towards a Holistic Approach?* , 27 (43 et seq.).

712 *Sattler*, JZ, 2017, 1036 (1044).

713 Ibid., 1043.

Art. 4 (11) GDPR "provides the minimum standard" for consent – the so-called "safety net" (*Sicherheitsnetz*). Consent below the net, which is, for instance, presented in a pre-ticked box, or under huge pressure, is not valid self-determination under the GDPR, whereas consent above this net can have multiple variants.[714]

The dual objectives pursued by the GDPR speak stronger for this interpretation. While the protection of natural persons with regard to the processing of personal data is guaranteed by fundamental rights and freedoms (Art. 1 (2) GDPR), it shall not be the reason to restrict or prohibit the free movement of personal data within the Union (Art. 1 (3) GDPR). Against this backdrop, the freedom of contract as a fundamental freedom in the Union shall not only play a role within the framework of balancing interests regarding the protection, but shall also be considered as an indispensable tool to facilitate the free movement of personal data.[715]

To strike a fair balance of the fundamental rights, namely between the right to the protection of personal data (Art. 8 of the Charter), and private autonomy (Art. 1 of the Charter) and the freedoms to conduct business (Art. 16 of the Charter) in light of the dual objectives of the GDPR, a teleological reduction of the applicable scope of Art. 7 (3) GDPR is argued to facilitate the two-tier interpretation for consent.[716] Anytime revocability is confined within the simple and unilateral consent residing on the lowest layer in the *ladder of permissions*. Thus, it is the least binding disposition for the data subject, which, on the flip side, presents the disposition that best reflects the strong control of the data subject over personal data. In consent above this layer, such as the contractual permission, Art. 7 (3) GDPR is inapplicable. Hence, Art. 7 (3) GDPR is principally optional according to data subjects' wishes.[717]

(2) Its enforcement

According to the two-tier interpretation of consent, Art. 6 (1) (a) GDPR can legitimize data processing of the data controller by following the true will of the data subject, be it a simple consent that reflects a strong will

714 Ibid.
715 Ibid., 1044; CJEU, AGET Iraklis, C-201/15, para. 66 f.; CJEU, Sky Austria, C-283/11, para. 42 ff.
716 *Sattler*, JZ, 2017, 1036 (1046).
717 Ibid., 1044.

to control, or an expression of will that creates an obligation. Art. 6 (1) (b) GDPR is still limited to accessory data processing to the contract, such as delivery and identity verification. While Art. 6 (1) (a) GDPR can be applicable in different situations, in some of which consent is freely revocable and in others not. However, the bottom line is that the consent under the GDPR must be an informed and voluntary indication of a data subject. In this sense, a pre-ticked box or a deceptive privacy policy leads to invalid consent.

Against this backdrop, consent gains flexibility, and the autonomy of data subjects is thus respected. After all, the more stringent the conditions for validity are, the more likely that the legal meaning of the consent deviates from the true will of the data subject.[718] Moreover, it would not undermine the high-level protection for data subjects provided by the GDPR by rendering consent binding in some scenarios. On the one hand, the obligation of information obliges data controllers to inform data subjects about the nature, ambit, and consequences of the consent they are giving. In the absence of clear notification of the binding effect of consent, consent should fall on the "safety net" and be deemed as an anytime revocable consent in the light of the principle of accountability.

On the other hand, the choice of the data subject – to waive Art. 7 (3) GDPR does not lead to his or her permanent subjection to data processing by the data controller. Under the GDPR, the principles of purpose limitation and data minimization confines the content, purpose, means and duration of the processing. Furthermore, the controller must stop processing and delete data when specified purpose(s) are fulfilled. Extraordinary opt-out rights are also not seldom in European contract law in open-ended contracts signed by consumers.[719] At least in Germany, the uneven protection for personality in merchandising contracts disclosed in Part I not only demands the revocability of consent but also regards the extraordinary opt-out right of the person depicted mandatory.

718 *Krönke*, Der Staat, 2016, 319 (326); Cf. *Bix, in: Miller and Wertheimer, The Ethics of Consent: Theory and Practice*, , 252 (252, 256).

719 *Gareth and Peter*, in: *Zweigert and Drobnig, International Encyclopedia of Comparative Law Online*, Vol. VII, § 15 no 30-57.

(3) Argumentation based on the (inter-)systematic interpretation

The Directive on Certain Aspects concerning Contracts for the Supply of Digital Content and Digital Services (DCSD), which had recognized the permission to access to personal data as a counter-performance for the supply of digital content/services in its draft but has deleted that expression in its final version, presents an intensive tension to the GDPR when "the consumer provides or undertakes to provide personal data to the trader" for the supply of digital content/services (Art. 3 (1) DCSD).[720] As the second sentence of Art. 3 (1) DCSD excludes its applicable scope in data processing that is exclusively to supply the digital content/service, Art. 6 (1) (b) GDPR shall not serve as the lawful ground for this situation. Consequently, since the GDPR prevails in any case (Art. 3 (8) and Art. 16 (2) DCSD), consent for data processing given by consumers for receiving the digital content/service is anytime revocable according to Art. 7 (3) GDPR if consent is understood narrowly.[721]

This *status quo* is not beneficial for consumers. Firstly, although the contract between the trader and the consumer who provides personal data subject is concluded and effective but hardly enforceable; though it has been argued that a special opt-out right for consumers is not quite unusual in the EU,[722] a right to withdraw at any time without reason and for an unlimited period of time will dissuade many traders who long for a binding and enforceable legal status.[723] Moreover, the unprotected status for traders who supply digital contents/services would encourage them to exploit to collect and use the data as quickly as possible to recover costs/profit before consumers terminates the contract.[724] Considering the obligations of traders after the termination of such contracts (Art. 16 (3) DSCD), data processing that particularly raises GDPR concerns, such as the inte-

720 Recitals 13, 14, 37, 42, and Art. 3 (1) of the proposal for a directive on certain aspects concerning contracts for the supply of digital content, Brussels, 9.12.2015, COM (2015) 634 final – 2015/0287(COD). Speech of Giovanni Buttarelli (EU-Data Protection Supervisor), available at: https://edps.europa.eu/sites/edp/files/publication/17-01-12_digital_content_directive_sd_en.pdf.; Recital 24 of Directive (EU) 2019/770.

721 *Sattler, in: Lohsse/Schulze/Staudenmayer, Data as Counter-Performance – Contract Law 2.0?*, 225 (232).

722 Langhanke and Schmidt-Kessel, 4 Journal of European Consumer and Market Law 218 (2015) (222).

723 In contrast with natural obligation that often takes places in business regarding lottery and gambling. See *Schulze,* Die Naturalobligation, S. 6.

724 Vgl. *Sattler, in: Pertot, Rechte an Daten,* 49 (80).

gration and analysis of consumers' personal data to generate new data (profiling, personality analysis, etc.) seem to be inevitable.[725] Furthermore, the right to receive a proportionate reduction in the price when the digital content/service is defective is only applicable for consumers who provide money against the supply of the digital content/service according to Art. 14 (4) DCSD. If the "counter-performance" is personal data, the consumer has only the remedy of termination according to Art. 7 (3) GDPR.[726] Lastly, as the consequence of the termination of contracts has been left to national law according to recital 40 of the DCSD, a forum-shopping for traders due to varied judgments in national courts is likely to take place.[727]

Therefore, if the two-tier interpretation for consent is adopted to enable a binding relationship between the trader who supply the digital content/service and the consumer who provide personal data as consideration, the strong consumer protection stipulated in the DCSD can apply indiscriminately in scenarios where "counter-performance" is personal data provided by consumers to solve the discrepancy brought up by the different treatments between the "counter-performance" in manners of money and data.[728]

(4) Questioning the unlimited data paternalism in private sector

Moreover, *Sattler* focuses on the lack of sufficient justification regarding the omnibus approach taken by the GDPR of treating the public and

725 Art. 16 (3) DSCD allow traders to continue their data processing when the condition prescribed in paragraph (a) (b) (c) and (d) is met alternatively. For instance, the trader can still process data that has been aggregated with other data by the trader and cannot be disaggregated or only with disproportionate efforts (Art. 16 (3) (c) DSCD).

726 Admittedly, the threshold for exercising that right appears to be lower than in the case where the consideration is monetary. As Art. 14 (6) DCSD requires that consumers can only terminate the contract "if the lack of conformity is not minor", and Art. 7 (3) GDPR requires the withdrawal to be free, consumers can thus terminate the contract concerning personal data based on minor inconformity. See *Sattler, in: Lohsse/Schulze/Staudenmayer, Data as Counter-Performance – Contract Law 2.0?*, 225 (232).

727 Vgl. Ibid., 237-238.

728 Also addressed by *Sattler*, it is indeed difficult for courts to calculate the amount compensation because the value of personal data is unknown and probably trivial for individual data. See ibid., 232.

private sector alike.[729] For public authorities, all is prohibited unless permitted by law, while for private parties all is permitted unless prohibited by law.[730] The informational self-determination emerged exclusively from the confrontation between individual rights and public power,[731] which needs to be adjusted when it is applied between civil subjects.[732] The justification for data paternalism reflected in the GDPR is more warranted and appreciated when more serious asymmetries of information and power exist between data controllers and data subjects,[733] and it is also acknowledgeable that some private controllers who have massive amounts of data and powerful data processing technologies have already become comparable to public power.[734] This condition is also reflected from the perspective of the EU data protection law. The e-Privacy Directive merely foresaw the possibility to withdraw consent for specific personal data such as location data,[735] as it takes advantages of data subjects due to their bounded recognition to force them to conclude a contract of personal filing when they just want to chat with friends. Moreover, as the BVerfG keenly observed, the more powerful the data controller is and the more control it has that rivals public power, the more justified is the application of the GDPR to it.[736] In the other way round, it is hence questionable whether this direct vertical application of the data paternalism – "the encroachment on the scope of protection of the data subject's general freedom of action" at the cost of "the data controller's freedom of occupation" in private sector – is justified.[737]

---

729 See *Sattler, in: Bakhoum, Personal Data in Competition, Consumer Protection and IP Law - Towards a Holistic Approach?*, 27 (34 et seq.); *Sattler*, JZ, 2017, 1036 (1042).

730 *Sattler, in: Bakhoum, Personal Data in Competition, Consumer Protection and IP Law - Towards a Holistic Approach?*, 27 (36).

731 BVerfG, NJW 1984, 419 - Volkszählung.

732 For instance,BGH, NJW 2009, 2888 - Spickmich, Rn. 31f.; *Di Fabio*, Safeguarding fundamental rights in digital systems, S. 90.

733 *Hermstrüwer*, Informationelle Selbstgefährdung, S. 227 ff.

734 *Bull*, Sinn und Unsinn des Datenschutzes, S. 6; Bundestag, Grundfragen des Datenschutzes, Drs. VI/3826 S. 138

735 See Article 6.3 and 9.3-4 of the Directive 2002/58/EC of the European Parliament and of the Council of 12 July 2002 concerning the processing of personal data and the protection of privacy in the electronic communications sector (Directive on privacy and electronic communications) – the e-Privacy Directive.

736 BVerfG, GRUR 2020, 74 - Recht auf Vergessen I, para. 88; BVerfG, NJW 2011, 1201 - Fraport, para. 60.

737 *Sattler*, JZ, 2017, 1036 (1042).

It questions (*hinterfragt*) the overly extensive application of the paternalistic measures in the GDPR.[738] Without going too deeper and further from the topic of merchandising in this dissertation, the observation revolves around the German experience in regulating the commercialization of personal images. As briefly introduced in Part III Sections 3.1.3 and 3.2.2, one of the main arguments for data paternalism is ill-grounded in merchandising as the models with expertise and equal status voluntarily and deliberately choose a lifestyle that is consistent with their long-term preference. Thus, the financial disadvantages faced by young models are frivolous in warranting a vigorous limitation on the effectiveness of consent. Moreover, the soft-licensing model in Germany also guarantees the inseparability of personal data from the data subject, which reflects the imperative of untouchable human dignity and the principle of freedom. Additionally, protection stemming from German jurisprudence and practice, which also acquires acknowledgment in law, is more suitable and useful for models in merchandising to protect their interests compared to the protective measures in the GDPR. Therefore, the fundamental differences between merchandising and data processing concerned by the GDPR in terms of the knowledge, professionality and power of data subjects, the means and purpose of the processing as well as the overall risks for data subjects speak strongly for cautious application of the paternalistic provisions in the GDPR in merchandising including Art. 7 (3) GDPR.

(5) Universally various connotations of consent

The counterargument that *the ladder of permissions* invoked by *Sattler* is a unique German concept that is inapplicable for interpreting an EU concept, is untenable.

Although *the ladder of permissions* is a doctrinal development under German law, its philosophical and theoretical root is in the Roman maxim *volenti non fit iniuria* (loosely translated as no wrong flows from the harm when the person harmed has consented to[739]). Not only *Kant*, but

---

738 See *Sattler, in: Bakhoum, Personal Data in Competition, Consumer Protection and IP Law - Towards a Holistic Approach?*, 27 (40); *Sattler*, JZ, 2017, 1036 (1045).

739 There are two ways to understand this maxim. One is to regard *volenti non fit iniuria* as a legal fiction that since a person will not harm him- or herself, what that person has consented to is not an actual harm for him- or herself. The other is to negate the unlawfulness flowing from the harm since the person harmed has accepted it. See Feinberg, 1 Canadian Journal of Philosophy 105

also *Mill* have undergirded their philosophy by this universal principle of fairness acclaiming personal autonomy and its associating requirement of self-responsibility.[740] In light of these ethical and legal ideas, consent with multiplicity originated in Greek and Roman culture soon gains wide consensus in the Western world.[741] Very close to the meaning of *the ladder of permissions*, one may use consent to create a right or entitlement or give permission or assume obligation.[742]

Gradually, consent, as a manifestation of voluntary choice, is considered the essence of contract law,[743] and the withdrawal of consent is subject to restrictions given the reasonable reliance of the counterparty triggered by the obtained consent.[744] In other words, the revocability of consent is an exception from the general of *pacta sunt servanda*. Nevertheless, the anytime revocable consent is common in medical and sexual scenarios.[745] There are several strict conditions for a valid consent underlined the principles of autonomy and self-responsibility. Being aware of the content of the consent, free to decide and able to hold independent responsibility for the consequences are the three major conditions.[746] In theory, the violation of any of these conditions would result in invalid consent, but reality is not a black-and-white world. Almost all three conditions are on a spectrum, with an almost unreachable complete satisfaction at one end

---

(1971) (107). The latter is more convincing and has been adopted here because the value judgment of denying illegality of the harm will not affect the legality of other people's justifiable defense behavior.

740 *Ohly*, "Volenti non fit iniuria": die Einwilligung im Privatrecht, 63ff.

741 *Johnston*, in: *Miller and Wertheimer, The Ethics of Consent*, 26 (35 et seq.).

742 *Kleinig*, in: *Miller and Wertheimer, The Ethics of Consent*, 4 (12).

743 Cf. *Bix, in: Miller and Wertheimer, The Ethics of Consent: Theory and Practice*, 252 (252, 257); If a party had "assumed and faithfully promised" (*assumpsit et fideliter promisit)*, then he or she has the obligation to implement order issued by the court to the enforce the contract. See *Ibbetson,* A historical introduction to the law of obligations, 131.

744 *Kleinig, in: Miller and Wertheimer, The Ethics of Consent,* 4 (10); Steyn, 113 The Law Quarterly Review 433 (1997) (433).

745 *Kleinig, in: Miller and Wertheimer, The Ethics of Consent,* 4 (10).

746 See *Beauchamp*, in: *Miller and Wertheimer, The Ethics of Consent*, 56 (66 et seq.). It focuses on the autonomy of consent and dissects it into intentionality, understanding and voluntariness. However, it is considered that intentionality can be reflected by understanding and voluntariness. Moreover, the self-responsibility delineates the boundaries of what can be covered by consent and what cannot. If the given person cannot take responsibility for what he or she consents to, the person shall not be allowed to give that consent. Vgl. *Mill,* On Liberty, 41; *Ohly,* "Volenti non fit iniuria": die Einwilligung im Privatrecht, 77f.

and a complete non-fulfillment at the other.[747] For instance, in medical scenarios, almost all patients do not fully understand the medical approach and accompanying risks despite the physician's lecture.[748] The financial pressure "forces" models who are new to the business to choose between not having the possibility to be photographed at all and letting high-level photographers take pictures for free. A minor shall only be held responsible for things that are at his level of perception.

Against this backdrop, it needs to make necessary concessions to the needs of protection for minors, disadvantaged party due to knowledge and negotiation power by recognizing the (anytime) revocability of consent. Thus, a broad understanding of the nature, type and consequences of consent is a legal fact that is widely accepted in the Western world. The foundation of the interpretation forwarded by German scholars is not objectionable because it is not imposing a German concept on the autonomous legal concept of the EU. In essence, the solution proposed by *Sattler* seeks to restore consent to its original nature upon certain conditions by proposing a teleological reduction of the limitation of consent added by the GDPR.

4.1.2 Counterarguments to this proposal

(1) The opinions of authorities as well as the (intra-)systematic interpretation

Above all, rendering Art. 7 (3) GDPR optional seems to contradict the historical interpretation based on the official documents in drafting the GDPR and the EDPB's understanding of consent.[749] The WP29 has advocated the "possibility to withdraw consent at any time" since the era

747 *Beauchamp, in: Miller and Wertheimer, The Ethics of Consent,* 56 (71-72). The condition of self-responsibility seems not a matter of degree as one can or cannot hold responsible, it is intricated in data processing situation since personal data are entangled and they may also contain some social value. See Part V Section 4.3.

748 *Candilis and Lidz,* in: *Miller and Wertheimer, The Ethics of Consent,* 330.

749 *Funke,* Dogmatik und Voraussetzungen der datenschutzrechtlichen Einwilligung im Zivilrecht, S. 322. It has addressed that the exception for the right of revocation, which in the end always makes the right of revocation a question of balance, was rightly deleted in the Council draft and in return supplemented by more specific exceptions,

of Directive 95/46/EC.[750] Subsequently, the free revocability of consent implied by Directive 95/46/EC has been made clear in the e-Privacy Directive. Reading from the consistent opinions issued by the WP29 and the successor EPDB, the revocability of consent serves two functions.[751] For one, it is used as an indicator for voluntariness as the withdrawal of consent shall not lead to any detrimental effect on the data subject. Moreover, the free revocability is to enhance the control of data subjects by enabling data subjects to call off data processing whenever they wish. In this wise, the limited application of anytime revocable consent in the e-Privacy Directive should be considered as an incubator for the general application of Art. 7 (3) GDPR.[752] Consequently, this unique nature of consent plays a prominent role in the GDPR is par for the course.[753]

Secondly, the anytime revocability in Art. 7 (3) GDPR as one of the rigorous conditions for valid consent is devised to guarantee high-level protection for data subjects by putting the right to determine the legality of data processing in the hands of data subjects. Based on reflections on the opinions and guidelines drafted by the authorities at the EU level, the anytime revocability of consent is indispensable. According to the EDPB, the reason why Art. 21 (1) only mentions Art. 6 (1) (e) and (f) GDPR and does not discuss consent is that withdrawal of consent has the same effect as the right to object.[754] The EDPB further contends that Art. 7 GDPR "sets out these additional conditions for valid consent", and "if the withdrawal right does not meet the GDPR requirements, then the consent mechanism of the controller does not comply with the GDPR".[755] In this wise, it seems that one cannot change the mandatory nature of conditions prescribed in Art. 7 GDPR because the GDPR does not intend to build a higher yet optional standard for consent. Therefore, many scholars also

750 WP29, Opinion 15/2011 on the definition of consent, WP187, 9.

751 Ibid., 9; EDPB, Guidelines 05/2020 on consent under Regulation 2016/679, para. 10 and 46 et seq; WP29, Working Document on the processing of personal data relating to health in electronic health records (EHR), WP 131, 8 and 9; WP29, Opinion 8/2001 on the processing of personal data in the employment context, WP48, 3.

752 The WP 29 has suggested including "an express clause setting up the right of individuals to withdraw their consent". See WP29, Opinion 15/2011 on the definition of consent, WP187, 37.

753 EDPB, Guidelines 05/2020 on consent under Regulation 2016/679, para. 112.

754 Ibid., para. 164.

755 Ibid., para. 103 and 116.

consider Art. 7 (3) GDPR mandatory.[756] While some scholars acknowledge the incompatibility between anytime revocability of one party and the core rule of *pacta sunt servanda* in contract law, they contend for an extremely strict and exceptional exclusion of this mandatory provision.[757] However, since their arguments primary rely on German law instead of a normative start point in the EU data protection law, the advocation for some exceptions for the anytime revocability of consent seems problematic under the GDPR.[758] Against this backdrop, the proposal of *Sattler* is warranted as its starting point is the definition of consent in Art. 4 (11) GDPR instead of national law.[759]

However, this proposal seems to contradict the intra-systematic interpretation for consent due to its conditions for validity in Art. 7 GDPR. Several counterarguments are advanced here as follows.

First, Art. 7 (1) - (4) GDPR imposes different requirements for the validity of consent, paragraph (1) demanding the active duty of proof on the part of the controller, paragraph (2) calling for clarity and independence of the statement of consent, paragraph (3) requiring the revocability of consent, and (4) providing for a prohibition on binding. It lacks sufficient evidence to claim that the paragraphs under the same provision are point-

756 *Voigt*, Die datenschutzrechtliche Einwilligung, S. 156; *Funke*, Dogmatik und Voraussetzungen der datenschutzrechtlichen Einwilligung im Zivilrecht, S. 322-323; *Hacker*, ZfPW, 2019, 148 (170); Stemmer, in *Brink/Wolff*, BeckOK Datenschutzrecht, Art. 7 Rn. 90; Ingold, in *Sydow*, DSGVO: Handkommentar, Art. 7 Rn. 46; Buchner/Kühling, in *Kühling/Buchner*, DSGVO/BDSG, Art. 7 Rn. 39 and 39a; Heckmann/Paschke, in *Ehmann and Selmayr*, DS-GVO, Art. 7 Rn. 93; Schantz, in *Schantz and Wolff*, Das neue Datenschutzrecht: Datenschutz-Grundverordnung und Bundesdatenschutzgesetz in der Praxis, Art. 7 Rn. 532; Langhanke and Schmidt-Kessel, 4 Journal of European Consumer and Market Law 218 (2015) (220 f.); *Metzger*, AcP, 2016, 817 (825); *Spelge*, DuD, 2016, 775 (781); *Laue, et al.*, Das neue Datenschutzrecht in der betrieblichen Praxis, § 2 Rn. 14; Däubler, in *Däubler, Wedde, Weichert and Sommer*, EU-Datenschutz-Grundverordnung und BDSG-neu : Kompaktkommentar, Art. 7 Rn. 50; *Tinnefeld and Conrad*, ZD, 2018, 391 (396).

757 Klement, in *Simitis, et al.*, Datenschutzrecht, Art. 7 Rn. 92; Schulz, in *Gola*, DSGVO, Art. 7 Rn. 57; *Specht*, JZ, 2017, 763 (769); Ronellenfitsch, Siebenundvierzigster Tätigkeitsbericht zum Datenschutz und Erster Bericht zur Informationsfreiheit, 2018, § 4.9.1.

758 For instance, scholars draw the normative grounds on the requirement of good faith (*das Gebot von Treu und Glauben*) in § 242 BGB, while the report of the Hessen Authority relies on the judgment of the German court and probably the balancing of interests according to § 241 (2) BGB.

759 In the direction, see *Funke*, Dogmatik und Voraussetzungen der datenschutzrechtlichen Einwilligung im Zivilrecht, S. 323.

ed to different types of consent (i.e., one for simple consent), and the other three for all types of consent. Secondly, the third sentence of Art. 7 (3) GDPR requires that the right to withdrawal at any time must be informed to the data subject before he or she gives consent. This indicates the revocability of consent is not an active choice of the data subject but an obligation that the controller is required by law to fulfill when it invokes consent as the lawful ground.[760] Thus, it would be a violation of Art. 7 (3) GDPR if the controller informs the data subject that the lawful ground is consent on the one hand and claims that it is irrevocable on the other hand. Thirdly, the teleological reduction of Art. 7 (3) GDPR is inconsistent with the data controller's duty to inform because Art. 13 (2) (c) GDPR requires the controller to inform the right to withdrawal at any time without exceptions. Moreover, from the perspective that the right to withdrawal belongs to the data subject's rights,[761] there are more reasons for its non-waivable nature as all data subject's rights are not optional.

(2) Challenges to its practicability

More importantly, leaving aside whether this two-tier interpretation holds up under the GDPR, it is doubtful that it helps controllers in practice. Considering the higher-tier of consent is a significant deviation from the general understanding of consent under the GDPR (based on the teleological reduction), and presents a binding effect on the data subject him- or herself, the examination of the fulfillment of the controller's duty to inform can become very strict. Taking the *company advertising* case as an example, if the controller unintentionally obscures the revocability of consent, and the data subject has been misguided by the equivocal declaration, the controller must bear the consequence that no invalid consent has been given in any sense (see Part II Section 4.2.2). Whether the controller wants to use the low-tier or high-tier consent, the data subject is likely to be misled into influencing his or her decision. More importantly, as the

760 Taeger, in *Taeger, et al.*, DSGVO - BDSG - TTDSG, Art. 7 Rn. 84.

761 Many scholars consider the revocability of consent in Art. 7 (3) GDPR an embodiment of data subject's rights in light of the right to the protection of personal data anchored in Art. 8 (1) of the Charter. See *Liedke*, Die Einwilligung im Datenschutzrecht, S. 29f.; Frenzel, in *Paal and Pauly*, DS-GVO BDSG, Art. 7 Rn. 16; Heckmann/Paschke, in *Ehmann and Selmayr*, DS-GVO, Art. 7 Rn. 86; Klement, in *Simitis, et al.*, Datenschutzrecht, Art. 7 Rn. 86; Also *Sattler*, JZ, 2017, 1036 (1004).

burden of proof is on the controller, it is difficult for the controller to prove what the data subject had in mind.

Lastly, the applicable scope of the two-tier interpretation of consent seems to be omitted in the scholarly writings. Since the proposal originated as an interrogation of the GDPR's paternalistic protection, it seems fair to assume that it implicitly applies on the premise that data subjects must be fully aware of the implications of the higher-level consent and voluntarily bound by it. However, without a clear sign as the B2B scenario would present, the cost to examine the knowledge of the data subject and to evaluate his or her voluntariness could be unbearably high.[762] Obviously, this cost would be borne by the controller based on the principle of accountability and thus a strong dissuasion for controllers to pursue the higher-level consent.

4.2 Conclusions

It can be distilled that the strongest arguments of the two-tier interpretation of consent under the GDPR are the omission of revocability of consent in its definition and the boundaries of data paternalism, while its weakest position is the intra-systematic interpretation and the opinions of the authorities. Moreover, the cost for compliance and the high possibility of incompliance would seriously discourage controllers from using this method, although this explanation has in their favor. It is conceivable that controllers would still stick to the anytime revocable consent and keep in developing more attractive digital services.

Nevertheless, this proposal offers an innovative perspective to conceptualize consent. In light of *the ladder of permissions*, the anytime revocability of consent is a tool to extend the disposability of rights holders under data paternalism. Otherwise, one could only choose from the two alternatives, one is the absolute maxim of *volenti non fit iniuria* at the cost of not being able to protect the weak, and the other is a complete disregard of the

---

762 According to some scholars, this is one of the economic reasons for adopting paternalistic laws. See Feinberg, 1 Canadian Journal of Philosophy 105 (1971) (119); Kronman, 92 The Yale Law Journal 763 (1983) (766 et seq.). Likely, it is also one of the arguments advanced by the EDPB in excluding the application of Art. 6 (1) (b) GDPR in the business model of "data against services" (see above Section 4.1.2). However, this argument would be problematic when the cost for examination is taken by the counterparty/data controllers instead of courts.

autonomy of data subjects. Thus, the GDPR does not completely deny data subjects the right to dispose of their data, but limits it to a certain extent for the reason of protecting the data subjects themselves. This motivates one to consider whether this restriction is not necessary when the data subject is capable of protecting himself/herself. In this sense, the proposal offers a liberal, ever-changing solution as data subjects mature.

5. *The comparison of the solutions and the result*

5.1 Unsuitable solutions 1 and 2

By continuing the German regulation of merchandising, data subjects can obtain compensation for material damage caused by illegal merchandising and establish relatively stable cooperation with merchandisers under the legal protection catered to their practical needs. In addition, it offers future-oriented protection for data subjects in the increasingly popular users' merchandising scenarios because it is likely that as web users become more familiar with this pure merchandising (which focuses only on user recommendations instead of profiling), data subjects will no longer be disgusted or fearful of this kind of promotion using their likenesses but rather want to receive reasonable remuneration for such exploitation of their likenesses.

However, the legal basis of this solution is under severe objections from both theoretical and practical perspectives. Interpreting Art. 85 (1) GDPR as a mandate for the Member States to legislate national law to reconcile data protection and freedom of expression in purely commercial activities would result in a complete hollowing out of the GDPR's effect as a directly applicable EU Regulation. Moreover, even if Art. 85 (1) GDPR could be interpreted as a stand-alone opening clause, the significantly larger (material and territorial) applicable scope of the GDPR would lead to substantial complexity and uncertainty in legal application in Germany. The production chain of merchandising would be assessed separately. Publication and dissemination would be under the KUG, while other processing including recording, editing, transmitting, transferring, storing, and deleting under the GDPR. It would amount to an unbearable burden for merchandisers, data subjects, and courts.

Apart from the flaws in the legal basis, some advantages of this solution can also be realized without the overly stretched interpretation of Art. 85 (1) GDPR. For instance, models can claim the restitution for fictive license fees based on the law of unjust enrichment in Germany. The binding relationship between models and merchandisers can also be facilitated by interpreting some provisions of the GDPR in a minimal way instead of limiting the applicable scope of the GDPR in general. In a nutshell, the first solution that advocates the direct application of the KUG in merchandising has obvious advantages but is largely unfeasible.

Although the GDPR does not prohibit Art. 6 (1) (f) GDPR to be applied in a contractual relationship, and the balance of interests might be in favor of the controller taking its reasonable reliance deriving from the merchandising contract into account, the solution 2 is unsuitable for unlocking the deadlock between the data subject and the controller in an authorized merchandising scenario in both theoretical and practical terms. It can provide a relatively stable position for the merchandiser premised on a valid merchandising contract, but it is only in theory.

Above all, as the final decision on the weighing of interests is in the hands of courts and not the data controller, and much less the data subject, this solution not only distorts the role of the data subject by mistakenly treating him or her as the person being decided, who is the decider for merchandising, but also ignores the triumph of individual autonomy over the paternalistic law in regulating merchandising. Moreover, the extensive use of Art. 6 (1) (f) GDPR as a "safe harbor" for merchandisers under the GDPR contradicts the function and purpose of general clauses.

In practice, this is not an optimal scenario for data controllers either. Since Art. 6 (1) (f) GDPR does not require the data subject's consent or even his or her knowledge, the compliance requirements for the controller will be relatively high. Moreover, the right to restriction can hold the processing in suspension and force the controller to take down the advertainments at any time as the balancing test puts too much uncertainty in verifying the lawfulness of merchandising. Thus, the controller would have to run its main business in a consistent and great uncertainty. At the same time, merchandising contracts are always essential to prove that the interests pursued by the controller outweigh the rights and freedoms of the data subject due to the commercial nature of merchandising. Therefore, merchandisers have nothing to gain from this solution except for the additional compliance requirements and uncertainty.

In summary, as this solution essentially puts the informational self-determination under a cloak of heteronomy simply for compliance reasons, it is more like a suboptimal solution.

5.2 The comparison between solution 3 and 4

Solutions 3 and 4, despite their different legal bases, share many commonalities. Both expect to find a solution to the incompatibility between the GDPR and merchandising contracts within the framework of private autonomy. More specifically, the two solutions detect the boundaries of data paternalism and find that the high-level data protection would amount to the encroachment of personal autonomy when it exceeds the boundaries. To strike a fair balance between the fundamental rights of individuals in data protection and personal autonomy, they both advocate narrowing the applicable scope of the protective provisions in the GDPR in merchandising. Therefore, both solutions are risky. A little deviation either gives rise to excessive data protection at the cost of the dysfunctionality of contract law or leads to defeating the purpose of data protection. Differentiation is thus essential for both solutions, and merchandising defined in this dissertation serves as the best practice for both solutions.

Moreover, both of them suffer from some legal flaws. Solution 3 runs counter to the (intra-)systematic interpretation of the GDPR and the opinions of the EDPB by rendering the anytime revocability of consent optional. Although the opinions of the EDPB are not decisive, they carry weight with regard to the CJEU's interpretation. Moreover, the two-tier interpretation might constitute a reformative understanding of the GDPR as it would compromise the strong control of data subjects over personal data designed by the EU legislator. On the other hand, solution 3 is also subject to dogmatical objections. Without a clear delineation of merchandising contracts in the B2B context from other contracts, it would easily be stretched to a general clause for contracts if they are fair. Moreover, it cannot answer why an equitable merchandising contract under German law could be used as a typical contract under EU law.

Despite these similarities, comparisons can be made in the following respects.

Solution 3 is limited in the B2B context, whereas the two-tier interpretation of consent is not (though it could be). At this point, solution 4 can tackle the issue of under-protection for data subjects in B2C contexts, while the users' merchandising scenario is excluded from solution 3. According to solution 4, if the controller can prove the exclusion of the anytime revocability of consent anchored in Art. 7 (3) GDPR accords to the genuine wish of the data subject, a binding relationship can be established.

In terms of implementation costs, solution 4 seems more appealing than solution 3 as it has a clear beacon, the B2B scenario whereon both parties to the contract have some degree of self-sufficiency. In the absence of such preconditions, the cost to examine whether the data subject is genuinely willing to enter a contractual relationship is enormous, and the measures remain unknown. For instance, it is worth exploring whether a box waiting to be actively checked by the data subject – to waive the right to withdraw consent at any time – meets the requirement.[763] Even though the GDPR has passed on the cost to the controller according to the principle of accountability, the considerable cost and legal uncertainty would create a strong dissuasive effect. Consequently, instead of pursuing high-level consent, controllers would still settle with the anytime revocable one and attempt to collect as much data as possible and then analyze, exploit, and transmit personal data quickly after collection. On the flip side, the restriction of the B2B situation would be too conservative compared with solution 4. Given the history of the commercialization of portraits over the past hundred years, a similar change in perception might be appreciated in users' merchandising. If data subjects understand the methods, purposes, and risks of merchandising and can make choices after evaluation with the assistance of information and education, the restriction stemming from the boundaries of the justification of data paternalism would also be unjustified. The only justifying reason would be the cost of analysis. However, since controllers take the cost, the choice should be left with them.

However, there are two objections to this consideration. Solution 3 can also presuppose the exact prerequisites to increase clarity and reduce implementation costs as it is a general solution. Besides, as pointed out in Section 4.3.2. (3), it is difficult to delineate the B2B scenario from others. While a muster of merchandising contracts in the B2B context is expected to achieve a certain role of demonstration and instruction, it will no doubt be strained and lacking in legal grounds.

Against this backdrop, the two-tier interpretation of consent might be more future-oriented.

5.3 The result

The overarching applicability of the GDPR stemming from the ambitious and extensive purpose of the EU legislator inevitably permeates those

763 This paper tends to think that this is not enough. Since many people do not understand and do not use the right of withdrawal at any time, it is difficult to assume that people know what the opposite of it means.

places that already have specific legal norms,[764] such as merchandising. Without highlighting the boundaries of the justification of data paternalism within the legal framework of the GDPR, this job that must be done has been left to the CJEU. The lack of attention to those boundaries would not only deviate from the self-determination of data subjects but also lead to the “dysfunctionality” of contract law. Moreover, too much paternalism deprives data subjects of the opportunity to learn from their mistakes, when sometimes it is necessary to make some. In some scenarios, the GDPR is necessary because the price for mistakes made by data subjects is too high to bear, but in cases like the *landlady* or “*stink fingers*”, mistakes are affordable for data subjects.

After the evaluation, while some solutions have more problems worth refuting, every solution is not perfect. Solutions 3 and 4 are preferable compared to solutions 1 and 2. In comparison between solutions 3 and 4, it needs to be admitted that solution 4 is more malleable, while solution 3 is relatively conservative. However, solution 4 is contrary to the interpretation of the data protection authorities at the EU level solution 3 is not. A muster of merchandising contracts in the B2B context at the EU level might alleviate their objections by providing legal certainty and reducing compliance costs. The most important components are the means, content, purpose, and the rights and privileges of the models, including the extraordinary opt-out rights. In this respect, many practice-oriented German commentaries regarding merchandising licensing contracts and contract templates are available for reference.

764 *Bull*, Sinn und Unsinn des Datenschutzes, S. 50; *Lauber-Rönsberg*, AfP, 2019, 373 (375-376).

Part V Conclusions

1. *The traditional German approach*

Thesis 1: Ever since the 1950s, German courts and scholars have established that the right to one's image in § 22 KUG encompasses both commercial and moral interests, and the person depicted has the sole right to decide whether to make the image available as an incentive for the sale of goods regardless of his or her social role if the exploitation serves – exclusively the commercial interests of the merchandiser. In this wise, autonomous commercialization is gradually facilitated to protect against heteronomous commercialization.[765]

Thesis 2: The person depicted is entitled to claim the fictive license fee for his or her persona based on the law of unjust enrichment as unauthorized usually presents "an inadmissible encroachment on the depicted person's economic exclusive right". Alternatively, he or she can claim delictual liability according to § 823 BGB. The injunctive relief and the auxiliary claim for access to information and accounting are seemingly the customary non-monetary reliefs in unauthorized merchandising because they meet the plaintiff's needs best by providing them practical tools to maximize their economic benefits.

Thesis 3: Illustrated by *the ladder of permissions* developed by *Ohly*, consent prescribed in § 22 KUG may lead to a *quid pro quo* contract that creates a legally protected status for the counterparty to enable the commercial exploitation of personal images or an exclusive license to let a third party operate merchandising and sue other infringers in its name. In short, consent in merchandising is legal but revocable with due cause. The theory of purpose transfer is analogous to interpreting the authorization in case of doubt so that it can be limited to the necessary extent concerning the contractual purpose.

765 *Götting* has summarized the legal regime in regualting merchadnsing as "protection from commercialization by commercialization" *(Schutz von Kommerzialisierung durch Kommerzialisierung)*. See, *Götting* in *Götting/Schertz/Seitz,* Handbuch Persönlichkeitsrecht, § 10 Rn. 14. However, a more positive way of understanding is favored here to highlight the autonomy.

Thesis 4: In practice, different merchandising agreements cater to different needs. The triple functions provided by agencies – namely management, sub-licensing, and career planning – make agency agreements for merchandising popular among professionals, while a standard merchandising agreement focusing on one specific authorization is often used in the scenarios of sub-licensing.

Thesis 5: Several contractual rights and privileges for the person depicted are often prescribed in merchandising agreements to secure the licensor's financial and ideal interests, including the right to access information and accounting, the right to reservation for approval, and the right to quality control, and the extraordinary opt-out right. Albeit optional, these rights and privileges are essential benchmarks for measuring the fairness of a merchandising contract. The more extensive, intensive, and lengthier the merchandising contract for the person depicted is, the more reasons there are to encourage the inclusion of these rights in that contract.

Thesis 6: Two messages can be distilled from these legal developments when "transitions that constitute life" have been discovered in social and technological development: Scholars must identify the doctrinal solution that best meets the parties' needs without dismissing the inalienability of personality rights. Moreover, recognizing the active exploitation of the property interest residing on the right to one's image would not objectify the personality and cause the consumption of the personality; instead, it can effectively and actively curb unauthorized merchandising by giving the person depicted economic incentives to take care of his or her images and monitor unlawful exploitation.

2. *Merchandising under the GDPR*

Thesis 7: The GDPR takes precedence over KUG in regulating merchandising that uses personal likenesses, especially celebrities', to encourage consumers to spend on goods/services. Some exceptions exist based on the exceptions to the territorial applicability of the GDPR and the opening clause in Art. 85 (2) GDPR, but they are not the mainstream of merchandising.

Thesis 8: In unauthorized merchandising, data processing is unlawful according to Art. 6 (1) (f) GDPR. The purely commercial interests pursued by the controller, albeit legitimate, still need to yield to the right to informational self-determination and reasonable expectations of the data subject irrespective of his or her social role. The reasonable expectations of the data subject, as prescribed factors for the balance of interests by the GDPR, invite a national and cultural perspective into the overall assessment of the commercial interests pursued by the controller and rights and freedoms of the data subject.

Thesis 9: German courts still rely too heavily on Germany's legal concepts and rules even when they apply the GDPR directly to unauthorized merchandising cases. More than often, they ignore the principle of accountability, the "test grid" of Art. 6 (1) (f) GDPR, and the right to claim compensation granted to data subjects under the GDPR. This is why the current "harmony approach" adopted by some German courts is not supported here.

Thesis 10: Coupled with the detailed and extensive compliance rules in the GDPR, Art. 82 GDPR facilitates a more friendly and robust recourse mechanisms for data subjects. However, the contested judiciary practices in Germany undermines its expected performance.

Thesis 11: While average data subject who suffers moral damages from the data processing would be better off under the GDPR, celebrities who are used to publicity and want to get a fair share from the unlawful data controller would run into difficulties in claiming fictive license fees according to Art. 82 GDPR due to the equivocal attitude of the GDPR towards the commercial interests contained in personal data and the strong resistance of the EDPS towards the commercialization of personal data.

Thesis 12: In light of a reflection on the legislative history and the academic controversy over the protection for sensitive data, the application of Art. 9 GDPR should follow the subjective approach with an emphasis on the reverse burden of proof. Therefore, merchandisers can exclude the application of Art. 9 GDPR by demonstrating that no sensitive information about the data subject's race, ethnic origin, or health status that could be revealed from the stage photos is processed in the sense of the GDPR.

Thesis 13: The high-level data protection in the GDPR is generally very costly and unfriendly to authorized merchandising and likely to make it unsustainable. Since Art. 6 (1) (b) GDPR is not appliable in merchandising as data processing is the primary performance of these contracts, the anytime revocable consent according to Art. 6 (1) (a) in combination with Art. 7 (3) GDPR renders merchandising contracts not binding anymore.

Thesis 14: The rigorous conditions for validity of consent are likely to render consent deviating from the genuine will of the individual, and *vice versa*, controllers are shying away from making a significant and sustained investment in merchandising. Furthermore, although the data subject's rights are applicable and non-negotiable in merchandising contracts, they are neither suitable nor effective.

3. *Divergences and problems*

Thesis 15: While unauthorized merchandising cases are still illegal under the GDPR, compensation for models who suffer no immaterial damages would be significantly less than the previous. An independent recourse system relying on German law would be helpful but may lead to long-term consequences, including the ineffectiveness of civil damages granted by the GDPR and the general insensitivity of data subjects to the commercial value of their data.

Thesis 16: The GDPR almost restricts authorized merchandising to "dysfunctionality", while merchandising contracts have been given considerable respect under German law without prejudice to the untransferable and indispensable parts of the personality.

Thesis 17: Merchandising is forgotten by the GDPR as it differs from the data processing envisioned by the GDPR in contents, means, purposes, and risks. Models in merchandising are also distinct from average internet users in terms of knowledge, attitudes, purposes, and negotiation power.

Thesis 18: While the merchandising law aims to prevent one's images from unexpected/unremunerative exploitation due to publicity, the high-demanding requirements in the GDPR are devised to enhance the control of data subjects over personal data to prevent data subjects from becoming the object of opaque and unfair data processing. The approach of one size fits for all, the reticence for the commercial value of personal data, and data paternalism do not offer a self-explanatory application in merchandising given the differences between merchandising and the data processing envisioned by the EU data protection law.

Thesis 19: The application of the GDPR in merchandising cases is inappropriate and unreasonable

4. Solutions

Thesis 20: The continued application of the KUG based on Art. 85 (1) GDPR as an independent opening clause is advantageous. It would make all the divergences and incompatibilities of the GDPR in merchandising disappear. In addition, it offers future-oriented protection for data subjects in the increasingly popular users' merchandising scenarios. However, the legal basis of this solution is under severe objections from both theoretical and practical perspectives. Interpreting Art. 85 (1) GDPR as an independent opening clause would result in a complete hollowing out of the GDPR's effect as a directly applicable EU Regulation. Moreover, the significantly larger (material and territorial) applicable scope of the GDPR would lead to legal fragmentation in Germany. Moreover, some advantages of this solution can also be realized without the overly stretched interpretation of Art. 85 (1) GDPR.

Thesis 21: Solution 2, namely treating Art. 6 (1) (f) GDPR as the lawful ground for authorized merchandising by taking reliance interests of the controller triggered by the contract into account, does not stand up to close inspection, either. Art. 6 (1) (f) GDPR may unlocking the deadlock between the data subject and the controller in an authorized merchandising scenario by giving the merchandiser a relatively stable position. However, it is more like an illusion because the final decision on the balance test is in the hands of courts not the data controller, and the compliance requirements for the controller are more rigorous. Legal uncertainty and high compliance costs are not welcomed in practice. Moreover, this solution distorts the role of the data subject from the decider to the recipient of merchandising – from individual autonomy to heteronomy. The extensive use of Art. 6 (1) (f) GDPR as a "safe harbor" for merchandisers also contradicts the function and purpose of general clauses.

Thesis 22: The application of Art. 6 (1) (b) GDPR to merchandising contracts in the B2B context allows merchandisers to rely on valid contracts with professional models to process their personal data and even grant sub-licenses for purposes of merchandising without fearing the anytime revocable consent prescribed in Art. 6 (1) (a) and 7 (3) GDPR. However, there are two detrimental objections to this approach. For one, it can be easily stretched to a general clause for fair contracts as there is hardly a legal basis to limit this approach in merchandising contracts, not to mention this type of contracts is formulated under national law. For two, there is no hard line between the B2B and B2C contexts. As micro-influencers in social media increasingly emerge, the line is more blurring.

Thesis 23: A two-tier interpretation of consent can also provide merchandisers a stable legal position by differentiating the anytime revocable consent and the binding consent as a legal act under the GDPR. The strongest arguments of the two-tier interpretation of consent are the omission of revocability of consent in its definition, the boundaries of data paternalism, and its universally acknowledged theoretical ground – multi-meaning consent in light of *the ladder of permissions* stemming from the maxim of *volenti non fit iniuria.* Nevertheless, its weakest position is the intra-systematic interpretation and the opinions of the authorities. Moreover, the cost for compliance and the high possibility of incompliance would seriously discourage controllers from using this method. It is conceivable that controllers would still stick to the anytime revocable consent and keep in developing more attractive digital services.

Thesis 24: The first two solutions are distinctly flawed and impractical. The last two, namely the application of Art. 6 (1) (b) GDPR to merchandising contracts in the B2B context and the two-tier interpretation of consent are comparably reasonable, despite some legal and practical objections. Nevertheless, while the two-tier interpretation of consent is more malleable and future-oriented, the application of Art. 6 (1) (b) GDPR to merchandising contracts in the B2B context is relatively conservative but not contrary to the interpretation of the data protection authorities at the EU level. A muster of merchandising contracts in the B2B context at the EU level might alleviate their objections by providing legal certainty and reducing compliance costs.

Thesis 25: Every solution has an Achilles heel, and they are imperfect. On the road to finding the least imperfect solution, the title of this dissertation is validated that some insoluble conflicts emerge between personality merchandising and the GDPR.

Bibliography

Reports

BT-Drs. 19/4421, Antwort des Parlamentarischen Staatssekretärs Dr. Günter Krings vom 20. September 2018, 2018.

Council of Europe, Convention for the Protection of Individuals with regard to Automatic Processing of Personal Data, European Treaty Series (ETS) No. 108, 1980.

Council of Europe, Explanatory Report to the Convention for the Protection of individuals with regard to automatic processing of personal Data, Nr. 38, 1981.

Council of the EU, Position of the Council at first reading with a view to the adoption of the General Data Protection Regulation, 5419/1/16 REV 1 ADD 1, 2016.

EDPB, Guidelines 5/2020 on consent under Regulation 2016/679, Version 1.1, 2020.

EDPB, Guidelines 3/2018 on the territorial scope of the GDPR (Article 3), Version 2.1, 2019.

EDPB, Guidelines 2/2019 on the processing of personal data under Article 6(1)(b) GDPR in the context of the provision of online services to data subjects, Version 2.0, 2019.

EDPB, Guidelines 4/2019 on Article 25 Data Protection by Design and by Default, 2020.

EDPS, Opinion 4/2017 on the Proposal for a Directive on certain aspects concerning contracts for the supply of digital content, 2017.

EDPS, Meeting the challenges of big data, Opinion 7/2015, 19 November 2015.

EDPS, Assessing the Necessity of Measures that limit the fundamental right to the protection of personal data, 2017.

European Commission, Communication from the Commission to the European Parliament, the Council, the European Economic and Social Committee and the Committee of the Regions, A Digital Single Market Strategy for Europe, COM(2015) 192 final, 2015.

European Commission, Commission staff working document on the free flow of data and emerging issues of the European data economy Accompanying the document Communication Building a European data economy, SWD(2017) 2 final, 2017

European Commission, Proposal for a General Data Protection Regulation, COM(2012) 11 final, 2012.

OECD, Exploring the Economics of Personal Data: A Survey of Methodologies for Measuring Monetary Value, OECD Digital Economy Papers, No. 220, 2013.

OECD, The Explanatory Report The explanatory memorandum of the OECD Guidelines on the Protection of Privacy and Transborder Flows of Personal Data, 2013.

OECD, Guidelines on the Protection of Privacy and Transborder Flows of Personal Data, 1980.

The EU Commission, Communication from the Commission to the European Parliament and the Council, Stronger protection, new opportunities - Commission guidance on the direct application of the General Data Protection Regulation as of 25 May 2018, 2018.

WP29, Working Document on the processing of personal data relating to health in electronic health records (EHR), WP 131, 2007.

WP29, Opinion 15/2011 on the definition of consent, WP187, 2011.

WP29, Opinion 8/2001 on the processing of personal data in the employment context, WP48, Adopted on 13 September 2001, 2001.

WP29, Opinion 6/2014 on the notion of legitimate interests of the data controller under Article 7 of Directive 95/46/EC, WP 217, 844/14/EN, 2014.

WP29, Advice paper on special categories of data ("sensitive data"), Ref. Ares (2011)444105, 2011.

WP29, Opinion 4/2007 on the concept of personal data, WP136, 2007.

WP29, Guidelines on consent under Regulation 2016/679, 17/EN, Adopted on 28 November 2017, 2017.

WP29, Guidelines on the right to "data portability", wp242 rev.01, 2017.

Bureau, the International, Character Merchandising, WIPO, 1994.

Dewenter, Ralf, Rösch, Jürgen and Terschüren, Anna, Abgrenzung zweiseitiger Märkte am Beispiel von Internetsuchmaschinen, Helmut-Schmidt-Universität - Universität der Bundeswehr Hamburg, Fächergruppe Volkswirtschaftslehre, Diskussionspapier, 2014.

Duch-Brown, Nestor, Martens, Bertin and Mueller-Langer, Frank, The economics of ownership, access and trade in digital data, European Commission, JRC Technical Reports, 2017.

Götting, Horst-Peter, Sanktionen bei Verletzung des postmortalen Persönlichkeitsrechts, GRUR 2004, 801.

Körner, Kevin, GDPR – boosting or choking Europe's data economy?, Deutsche Bank, 2018.

Ramirez, Edith, Brill, Julie, Ohlhausen, Maureen K., Wright, Joshua D. and McSweeny, Terrell, Data Brokers: A Call For Transparency and Accountability, Federal Trade Commission, 2014.

Ronellenfitsch, Michael, Siebenundvierzigster Tätigkeitsbericht zum Datenschutz und Erster Bericht zur Informationsfreiheit, Hessischen Beauftragten für Datenschutz und Informationsfreiheit, 2018.

Roßnagel, Alexander, Pfitzmann, Andreas and Garstka, Hansjürgen, Modernisierung des Datenschutzrechts, Bundesministeriums des Innern, 2001.

Simitis, Spiros, Revisiting Sensitive Data, Council of Europe, Reports, studies and opinions, 1999.

Bundestag, Grundfragen des Datenschutzes, Drs. VI/3826, 1971.

Wendehorst, Christiane, Verbraucherrelevante Problemstellungen zu Besitz und Eigentumsverhältnissen beim Internet der Dinge, Rechtgutachten für BMJV, 2016.

Books and Articles

Abidin, Crystal, 2 Social Media + Society 3 (2016).

Abraham, Tony and Oneto, Marguerite, Berkley School of Information W231-1 (2015).

Acquisti, Alessandro and Grossklags, Jens, What can behavioral economics teach us about privacy?, in: *Alessandro Acquisti (ed.)*, Digital Privacy: Theory, Technologies, and Practices, New York: Auerbach 2008.

Albrecht, Jan Philipp, Das neue EU-Datenschutzrecht – von der Richtlinie zur Verordnung, CR 2016, 88.

Albrecht, Jan Philipp and Jotzo, Florian, Das neue Datenschutzrecht der EU, 1. Auflage, Baden-Baden: Nomos 2017.

Alexy, Robert, Theorie der Grundrechte, 1. Auflage, Frankfurt am Main: Suhrkamp 1986.

Andersen, Stella, Gesellschaftspolitische Meinungsäußerungen in der Werbung, 1. Auflage, Baden-Baden: Nomos 2015.

Assmus, Ubbo and Winzer, Florian, Mitarbeiterfotos im Intranet, auf Webseiten und in sozialen Netzwerken, ZD 2018, 508.

Bachmann, Gregor, 4 German Law Jounral 1033 (2003).

Barath, Aljosha, Kommerzialisierung der Sportlerpersönlichkeit, 1. Auflage, Baden-Baden: Nomos 2018.

Barth, Günter, Der Kampf um die Werbung im Internet, Baden-Baden: Nomos 2020.

Beale, Hugh, The Role for European Contract Law: Uniformity or Diversity?, in: *Francisco de Elizalde (ed.)*, Uniform Rules for European Contract Law?: A Critical Assessment, Oxford (et al) Hart 2018.

Beauchamp, Tom, Autonomy and Consent, in: *Franklin G. Miller and Wertheimer, Alan (ed.)*, The Ethics of Consent, Oxford: Oxford University Press 2010.

Benecke, Alexander and Wagner, Julian, Öffnungsklauseln in der Datenschutz-Grundverordnung und das deutsche BDSG - Grenzen und Gestaltungsspielräume für ein nationales Datenschutzrecht, DVBl 2016, 600.

Benedikt, Kristin and Kranig, Thomas, DS-GVO und KUG – ein gespanntes Verhältnis Aufsatz von ZD 2019, 4.

Bergmann, Susanne, 19 Entertainment law journal 479 (1999).

Beuthien, Volker and Schmölz, Anton S., Persönlichkeitsschutz durch Persönlichkeitsgüterrechte, München: C.H.BECK 1999.

Beverley-Smith, Huw, Ohly, Ansgar and Lucas-Schloetter, Agnes, Privacy, Property and Personality, Cambridge: Cambridge University Press 2005.

Bieker, Felix and Bremert, Benjamin, Identifizierung von Risiken für die Grundrechte von Individuen, ZD 2020, 7.

Biene, Daniel, Celebrity Culture, Individuality, and Right of Publicity as a European Legal Issue, IIC 2005, 505.

Bienemann, Linda, Reformbedarf des Kunsturhebergesetzes im digitalen Zeitalter, Baden-Baden: Nomos 2021.

Bietti, Elettra, 40 Pace law review 310 (2020).

Bix, Brian H., Contracts, in: *Franklin Miller and Wertheimer, Alan (ed.),* The Ethics of Consent: Theory and Practice, New York: Oxford University Press 2009.

Bräutigam, Peter, Das Nutzungsverhältnis bei sozialen Netzwerken, MMR 2012, 635.

Brink, Stefan and Eckhardt, Jens, Wann ist ein Datum ein personenbezogenes Datum?, ZD 2015, 1.

Brink/Wolff, BeckOK Datenschutzrecht, 38 Edition, München: C.H. Beck 2021.

Bruni, Barbara, 41 Cardozo Law Review 2203 (2020).

Büchler, Andrea, Die Kommerzialisierung von Personlichkeitsgutern. Zur Dialektik von Ich und Mein, AcP 2006, 300.

Buchner, Benedikt, Die Einwilligung im Datenschutzrecht : vom Rechtfertigungsgrund zum Kommerzialisierungsinstrument, DuD 2010, 39.

Buchner, Benedikt, Informationelle Selbstbestimmung im Privatrecht, Tübingen: Mohr Siebeck 2006.

Bull, Hans Peter, Sinn und Unsinn des Datenschutzes, Tübingen: Mohr Siebeck 2015.

Bunnenberg, Jan Niklas, Privates Datenschutzrecht: über Privatautonomie im Datenschutzrecht, 1. Auflage, Baden-Baden: Nomos 2020.

Burda, Max, Die Zweckbindung im Urhebervertragsrecht, Tübingen: Mohr Siebeck 2020.

Bygrave, L.A., Data Privacy Law: An International Perspective, Oxford: OUP Oxford 2014.

Calabresi, Guido, The Future of Law and Economics: Essays in Reform and Recollection, New Haven: Yale University Press 2016.

Calabresi, Guido and Melamed, A. Douglas, 85 Harvard Law Review 1089 (1972).

Candilis, Philip and Lidz, Charles, Advances in Informed Consent Research, in: *Franklin Miller and Wertheimer, Alan (ed.),* The Ethics of Consent, Oxford: Oxford University Press 2010.

Cooter, Robert, 64 Notre Dame Law Review 817 (1989).

Cowen, Tyler, In praise of commercial culture, Cambridge [u.a.]: Harvard University Press 1998.

Cullagh, Karen Mc, 2 Journal of International Commercial Law and Technology 190 (2007).

Dallmer, Heinz, Das System des Direct Marketing - Entwiddungsfaktoren und Trends, in: *Heinz Dallmer (ed.)*, Das Handbuch Direct Marketing & More, Wiesbaden: Gabler Verlag 2002.

Damm, Renate, Rehbock, Klaus and Smid, Jörg F., Widerruf, Unterlassung und Schadensersatz in den Medien, 3., neubearbeitete Auflage, München: Beck 2008.

Dasch, Norbert, Die Einwilligung zum Eingriff in das Recht am eigenen Bild, München: Beck 1990.

Däubler, Wolfgang, Wedde, Peter, Weichert, Thilo and Sommer, Imke, EU-Datenschutz-Grundverordnung und BDSG-neu : Kompaktkommentar, Frankfurt am Main: Bund-Verlag 2018.

Dausend, Tjorven, Der Auskunftsanspruch in der Unternehmenspraxis, ZD 2019, 103.

Degenhart, Christoph., Das allgemeine Persönlichkeitsrecht, Art. 2 I i. V. mit Art. 1 I GG, JuS 1992, 361.

Dewenter, Ralf and Rösch, Jürgen, Einführung in die neue Ökonomie der Medienmärkte, 1. Auflage, Wiesbaden: Springer 2015.

Di Fabio, Udo, Safeguarding fundamental rights in digital systems, München: C.H. Beck 2016.

Dickmann, Roman, Nach dem Datenabfluss: Schadenersatz nach Art. 82 der Datenschutz-Grundverordnung und die Rechte des Betroffenen an seinen personenbezogenen Daten, r+s 2018, 345.

Dogan, Stacey L. and Lemley, Mark A., 58 Stanford Law Review 1161 (2006).

Dougherty, F. Jay, 27 Colum. J.L. & Arts 1 (2003).

Dregelies, Max, Fotografieren in der Öffentlichkeit und Datenschutz, AfP 2019, 298.

Dreier, Thomas and Spiecker Döhmann, Indra, Die systematische Aufnahme des Straßenbildes, 1. Auflage, Baden-Baden: Nomos 2010.

Dreier/Schulze, Urheberrechtsgesetz, 6. Auflage, München: C.H. Beck 2018.

Drexl, Josef, Legal Challenges of the Changing Role of Personal and Non-Personal Data in the Data Economy, in: *Alberto Di Franceschi and Schulze, Rainer (ed.)*, Digital Revolution - New Challenges for Law: Data Protection, Artificial Intelligence, Smart Products, Blockchain Technology and Virtual Currencies, München, Baden-Baden: C.H. Beck and Nomos 2019.

Dworkin, Gerald, PATERNALISM, The Monist 1 1972, 64.

Ehmann, Eugen, Personenaufnahmen nach der DS-GVO - Mehr Klarheit, als viele befürchtet haben!, ZD 2020, 65.

Ehmann, Eugen and Selmayr, Martin, DS-GVO, 2. Auflage, München: C.H. Beck 2018.

Ehmann, Horst, Das allgemeine Persönlichkeitsrecht - Zur Transformation unmoralischer in unerlaubte Handlungen, in: *Claus-Wilhelm Canaris (ed.)*, Festgabe 50 Jahre Bundesgerichtshof, München: Beck 2000.

Ehmann, Horst, Der Begriff des Allgemeinen Persönlichkeitsrechts als Grundrecht und als absolut-subjektives Recht, in: *Michaël P. Stathopulos (ed.),* Festschrift für Apostolos Georgiades zum 70. Geburtstag, 1. Auflage, München [u.a.]: Beck [u.a.] 2006.

Eidenmüller, Horst, Liberaler Paternalismus, JZ 2011, 814.

Eidenmüller, Horst Effizienz als Rechtsprinzip, 4. Auflage, Tübingen: Mohr Siebeck 2015.

Engeler, Malte, The EDPB's guidelines 02/2019 on Art. 6(1)(b) GDPR, PinG 4 2019, 149.

Engeler, Malte, Das überschätzte Kopplungsverbot, ZD 2018, 55.

Engels, Friedrich, The Origin of the Family, Private Property and the State, Penguin Books 2010.

Erdos, David, 26 International Journal of Law and Information Technology 189 (2018).

Ernst, Stefan, Die Einwilligung nach der Datenschutzgrundverordnung, ZD 2017, 110.

Ernst, Stefan, Die Widerruflichkeit der datenschutzrechtlichen Einwilligung ZD 2020, 383.

Ernst-Moll, Jürgen, Das Recht am eigenen Bildnis - vor und vor allem nach dem Tode, GRUR 1996, 558.

Ettig, Diana, Lizenzansprüche bei Persönlichkeitsrechtsverletzungen, NJW 2021, 1274.

Ettig, Diana, Bereicherungsausgleich und Lizenzanalogie bei Persönlichkeitsrechtsverletzung, Baden-Baden: Nomos 2015.

Evans, A. C., 29 THE AMERICAN JOURNAL OF COMPARATIVE LAW 571 (1981).

Fazlioglu, Muge, 46 Fordham Urban Law Journal 271 (2019).

Feinberg, Joel, 1 Canadian Journal of Philosophy 105 (1971).

Fischer, Annette, Die Entwicklung des postmortalen Persönlichkeitsschutzes: von Bismarck bis Marlene Dietrich, Frankfurt am Main [u.a.]: Lang 2004.

Fisher, William W., Promises to Keep: Technology, Law, and the Future of Entertainment, Stanford, Calif.: Stanford University Press 2004.

Forgó, Nikolaus, Helfrich, Marcus and Schneider, Jochen, Betrieblicher Datenschutz, 3, München: C.H. Beck 2019.

Forkel, Hans, Lizenzen an Persönlichkeitsrechten durch gebundene Rechtsübertragung, GRUR 1988, 491.

Forkel, Hans, Das allgemeine Persönlichkeitsrecht – Betrachtung einer fünfzigjährigen Entwicklung der Persönlichkeitsrechte im deutschen Privatrecht, Würzburg: Ergon 2004.

Forkel, Hans, Gebundene Rechtsübertragungen: ein Beitrag zu den Verfügungsgeschäften über Patent-, Muster-, Urheber- und Persönlichkeitsrechte, Köln; München [u.a.]: Heymann 1977.

Fouillée, Alfred, La science sociale contemporaine, 2, Paris: Librairie Hachette 1885.

Franck, Georg, Ökonomie der Aufmerksamkeit, München: Hanser 1998.

Franck, Lorenz, Schadensersatz nach Art. 82 DS-GVO wegen Auskunftsfehlern, ZD 2021, 680.

Freitag, Andreas, Die Kommerzialisierung von Darbietung und Persönlichkeit des ausübenden Künstlers, 1. Auflage, Baden-Baden: Nomos 1993.

Frömming, Jens and Peters, Butz, Die Einwilligung im Medienrecht, NJW 1996, 958.

Funke, Michael, Dogmatik und Voraussetzungen der datenschutzrechtlichen Einwilligung im Zivilrecht, 1. Auflage, Baden-Baden: Nomos 2017.

Fuster, Gloria Gonzalez, The Emergence of Personal Data Protection as a Fundamental Right of the EU, Brussel: Springer International Publishing 2014.

Gareth, H. Jones and Peter, Schlechtriem, Contracts in General, in: *K. Zweigert and Drobnig, Ulrich (ed.),* International Encyclopedia of Comparative Law Online, Brill 2019.

Geissler, Dennis and Ströbel, Lukas, Datenschutzrechtliche Schadensersatzansprüche im Musterfeststellungsverfahren, NJW 2019, 3414.

Gierschmann, Sibylle, Was "bringt" deutschen Unternehmen die DS-GVO? - Mehr Pflichten, aber die Rechtsunsicherheit bleibt, ZD 2016, 51.

Gierschmann, Sibylle, Schlender, Katharina and al., et, Kommentar Datenschutz-Grundverordnung, Köln: Bundesanzeiger Verlag 2018.

Gola, Peter, DSGVO, 2. Auflage, München: C.H. Beck 2018.

Gola, Peter and Schulz, Sebastian, Der Entwurf für eine EU-Datenschutz-Grundverordnung – eine Zwischenbilanz, RDV 2013, 1.

Golla, Nina and Herbort, Elisabeth, Zivilrechtlicher Bildnisschutz im Vorfeld von Weitergabe und Veröffentlichung, GRUR 2015, 648.

Golz, Robert and Gössling, Patrick, DSGVO und Recht am Bildnis, IPRB 2018, 68.

Gordon, Harold R., 55 Northwestern University law review 553 (1960).

Götting, Horst-Peter, Persönlichkeitsrechte als Vermögensrechte, Tübingen: Mohr Siebeck 1995.

Götting, Horst-Peter, Reflections on the commercialisation of Personality Rights in the U.S. and Germany, in: *Horst-Peter Götting and Schlüter, Claudia (ed.),* Nourriture de l'esprit: Festschrift für Dieter Stauder zum 70. Geburtstag, Baden-Baden: Nomos 2011.

Götting, Horst-Peter, Satirische Meinungsäußerungen über Prominente in der Werbung, GRUR Int 2015, 657.

Götting, Horst-Peter and Lauber-Rönsberg, Anne, Aktuelle Entwicklungen im Persönlichkeitsrecht, Baden-Baden: Nomos 2010.

Götting/Schertz/Seitz, Handbuch Persönlichkeitsrecht, 2. Auflage, München: C.H. Beck 2019.

Gounalakis, Georgios, Bildberichte über Prominente und private Prägung der Aufnahmesituation, NJW 2020, 3692.

Gramlich, Ludwig and Lütke, Hans-Josef, Besserer Persönlichkeitsschutz bei Bildaufnahmen durch StGB-Novellierung?, MMR 2020, 662.

Gregoritza, Anna, Die Kommerzialisierung von Persönlichkeitsrechten Verstorbener, Berlin: Duncker & Humblot 2003.

Gsell, Beate, Weller, Marc-Philippe and Geibel, Stefan, GROSSKOMMENTAR zum Zivilrecht: BeckOGK, München: C.H. Beck 2019.

Gusy, Christoph, Einseitige oder allseitige Transparenz? Das Informationsverwaltungsrecht und die post-privacy-Debatt, in: *Lothar Knopp and Wolff, Heinrich Amadeus (ed.),* Umwelt - Hochschule - Staat : Festschrift für Franz-Joseph Peine zum 70. Geburtstag, Berlin: Duncker & Humblot 2016.

Hacker, Philipp, Daten als Gegenleistung: Rechtsgeschäfte im Spannungsfeld von DS-GVO und allgemeinem Vertragsrecht, ZfPW 2019, 148.

Hahn, Das Recht am eigenen Bild – anders betrachtet, NJW 1997, 1348.

Hansen, Hauke and Brechtel, Sandra, KUG vs. DS-GVO: Kann das KUG anwendbar bleiben? , GRUR-Prax 2018, 369.

Harris, D. J., O'Boyle, Michael and Warbrick, Colin, Law of the European Convention on Human Rights, 2. edition, Oxford: Oxford University Press 2009.

Härting, Niko, Was ist eigentlich eine "Kopie"?, CR 2019, 219.

Hegel, Georg Wilhelm Friedrich Grundlinien der Philosophie des Rechts, Hamburg: Felix Meiner 2017.

Heinzke, Philippe and Engel, Lennart, Datenverarbeitung zur Vertragserfüllung – Anforderungen und Grenzen, ZD 2020, 189.

Helle, Jürgen, Besondere Persönlichkeitsrechte im Privatrecht, Tübingen: Mohr Siebeck 1991.

Henry, Michael (ed), International Privacy, Publicity and Personality Laws, London [u.a.]: Butterworths 2001.

Herberger, Marie, Veröffentlichung von Kinderfotos zu kommerziellen Zwecken gegen den Willen eines Elternteils, NZFam 2021, 1088.

Herfurth, Constantin, Interessenabwägung nach Art. 6 Abs. 1 lit. f DS-GVO, ZD 2018, 514.

Hermann, Tobias, Der Werbewert der Prominenz, Baden-Baden: Nomos 2011.

Hermstrüwer, Yoan, Informationelle Selbstgefährdung, Tübingen: Mohr Siebeck 2016.

Hert, Paul, Papakonstantinou, Vagelis, Malgieri, Gianclaudio, Beslay, Laurent and Sanchez, Ignacio, 34 Computer Law & Security Review 193 (2018).

Hildebrand, Angela, Künstlerische Straßenfotografie ohne Einwilligung der abgebildeten Person, ZUM 2018, 585.

Hoeren, Thomas, Anm. in LG Frankfurt am Main - 2-03 O 283/18, ZD 2018, 587.

Hornung, Gerrit, Eine Datenschutz-Grundverordnung für Europa? - Licht und Schatten im Kommissionsentwurf vom 25.1.2012., ZD 2012, 99.

Hubmann, Heinrich, Das Persönlichkeitsrecht, 2. Auflage, Köln: Böhlau 1967.

Hubmann, Heinrich, Der Bereicherungsanspruch im Persönlichkeitsrecht, in: *Georg Roeber (ed.),* Der Urheber und seine Rechte: Ehrengabe für Eugen Ulmer, Baden-Baden: Verl. für Angew. Wiss. 1965.

Ibbetson, David J., A historical introduction to the law of obligations, Oxford [u.a.]: Oxford Univ. Press 2001.

Indenhuck, Moritz and Britz, Thomas, Vom Datenschutzrecht zum Datenschuldrecht – Neue Leitlinien zur Verarbeitung personenbezogener Daten bei Online-Dienstleistungen, BB 2019, 1091.

Ingman, Terence, 26 Jurid. Rev. 1 (1981).

Janger, Edward J. and Schwartz, Paul M., 86 Minnesota Law Review 1219 (2002).

Jangl, Jana, Berichten ja, Bebildern nein? Presseberichterstattung über das nicht öffentliche Scheidungsverfahren einer prominenten deutschen Schauspielerin mit Blick auf das Verhältnis von KUG und DSGVO, ZUM 2021, 103.

Jarrett, Kylie, Through the Reproductive Lens: Labour and Struggle at the Intersection of Culture and Economy, in: *Chandler David and Christian, Fuchs (ed.)*, Digital Objects, Digital Subjects: Interdisciplinary Perspectives on Capitalism, Labour and Politics in the Age of Big Data, London: University of Westminster Press, 2019.

Jentzsch, Nicola, Datenhandel und Datenmonetarisierung: Ein Überblick, in: *Stiftung Datenschutz (ed.)*, Dateneigentum und Datenhandel, Berlin: Erich Schmidt 2019.

Johnston, David, A History of Consent in Western Thought, in: *Franklin Miller and Wertheimer, Alan (ed.)*, The Ethics of Consent, Oxford: Oxford University Press 2010.

Kahl, Jonas and Piltz, Carlo, Wer hat Vorfahrt: Datenschutz oder Meinungs- und Pressefreiheit? , K&R 2018, 289.

Klein, Florian, Personenbilder im Spannungsfeld von Datenschutzgrundverordnung und Kunsturhebergesetz, Frankfurt am Main: Peter Lang GmbH 2017.

Klein, Susanne, Immaterieller Schadensersatz nach der DS-GVO, GRUR-Prax 2020, 433.

Kleinheyer, Gerd, Rechtsgutsverwendung und Bereicherungsausgleich, JZ 15/16 1970, 471.

Kleinig, John, The Nature of Consent, in: *Franklin Miller and Wertheimer, Alan (ed.)*, The Ethics of Consent, Oxford: Oxford University Press 2010.

Klippel, Diethelm, Der zivilrechtliche Schutz des Namens, Paderborn u.a: Schöningh 1985.

Korch, Stefan, Schadensersatz für Datenschutzverstöße, NJW 2021, 978.

Koreng, Ansgar and Lachenmann, Matthias, Formularhandbuch Datenschutzrecht, München: Beck 2021.

Kraßer, Rudolf, Schadensersatz für Verletzungen von gewerblichen Schutzrechten und Urheberrechten nach deutschem Recht, GRUR Int 1980, 259.

Kremer, Michael J. R., Conrady, Jan and Penners, Anja, Data Privacy Litigation, ZD 2021, 128.

Kremer, Sascha, Das Auskunftsrecht der betroffenen Person in der DSGVO, CR 2018, 560.

Krönke, Christoph, Datenpaternalismus: Staatliche Interventionen im Online-Datenverkehr zwischen Privaten, dargestellt am Beispiel der Datenschutz-Grundverordnung, Der Staat 3 2016, 319.

Kronman, Anthony T., 92 The Yale Law Journal 763 (1983).

Krüger, Stefan and Wiencke, Julia, Bitte recht freundlich – Verhältnis zwischen KUG und DS-GVO, MMR 2019, 76.

Krusche, Jan, Kumulation von Rechtsgrundlagen zur Datenverarbeitung, ZD 2020, 232.

Kühling, Jürgen, Das „Recht auf Vergessenwerden" vor dem BVerfG – November(r)evolution für die Grundrechtsarchitektur im Mehrebenensystem, NJW 2020, 275.

Kühling, Jürgen and Martini, Mario, Die Datenschutz-Grundverordnung: Revolution oder Evolution im europäischen und deutschen Datenschutzrecht?, EuZW 2016, 448.

Kühling, Jürgen, Martini, Mario and al., et, Die DSGVO und das nationale Recht, 2016, Münster: Monsenstein und Vannerdat 2016.

Kühling/Buchner, DSGVO/BDSG, 3. Auflage, München: C.H. Beck 2020.

Kuner, Christopher, 18 German Law Journal 881 (2017).

Ladeur, Karl-Heinz, Fiktive Lizenzentgelte für Politiker?, ZUM 2007, 111.

Langhanke, Carmen and Schmidt-Kessel, Martin, 4 Journal of European Consumer and Market Law 218 (2015).

Lanier, Jaron, Weyl, Glen and McQuaid, Michael J., A Blueprint for a Better Digital Society, Harvard Business Review 2018, 2.

Lauber-Rönsberg, Anne, Zum Verhältnis von Datenschutzrecht und zivilrechtlichem Äußerungsrecht, AfP 5 2019, 373.

Lauber-Rönsberg, Anne, Verletzung von Bildnisrechten durch künstlerische Fotografie: Anspruch auf fiktive Lizenzgebühr?, GRUR-Prax 2015, 495.

Lauber-Rönsberg, Anne and Hartlaub, Anneliese, Personenbildnisse im Spannungsfeld zwischen Äußerungs- und Datenschutzrecht, NJW 2017, 1057.

Laue, Philip, Nink, Judith and Kremer, Sascha, Das neue Datenschutzrecht in der betrieblichen Praxis, 1. Auflage, Baden-Baden: Nomos 2016.

Lausen, Matthias, Der Schauspieler und sein Replikant, ZUM 1997, 86.

Leibold, Kevin, Gerichtliche Entscheidungem zum Schadensersatz nach Art. 82 Abs. 1 DS-GVO, ZD-Akutell 2021, VI.

Lenk, Klaus, Der Staat am Draht, 1. Auflage, Berlin: Edition Sigma 2004.

Lettl, Tobias, Allgemeines Persönlichkeitsrecht und Medienberichterstattung, WRP 2005, 1045.

Lettmaier, Saskia, Prominente in der Werbung für Presseerzeugnisse - Ende des Presseprivilegs?, WRP 2010, 695.

Lettmaier, Saskia, Das allgemeine Persönlichkeitsrecht in der zivilrechtlichen Fallbearbeitung – zugleich ein Spiegel der neueren Rechtsprechung, JA 2008, 566.

Lewinski, Kai v., Wert von personenbezogenen Daten, in: *Stiftung Datenschutz (ed.)*, Dateneigentum und Datenhandel, Berlin: Erich Schmidt 2018.

Liedke, Bernd, Die Einwilligung im Datenschutzrecht, Edewecht: OlWIR Verl. für Wirtschaft, Informatik und Recht 2012.

Loef, Robert, Medien und Prominenz, 1, Baden-Baden: Nomos Verlagsgesellschaft mbH & Co. KG 2009.

Loewenheim, Ulrich (ed), Handbuch des Urheberrechts, 2. Aufl., München: Beck 2010.

Lupton, Deborah and Williamson, Ben, 19 New Media & Society 780 (2017).

Magold, Hanns Arno, Personenmerchandising, Frankfurt am Main [u.a.]: Lang 1994.

Mahmoud-Davis, Sara A., 19 Wash. U. GLOBAL Stud. L. REV. 1 (2020).

Matejek, Michael and Mäusezahl, Steffen, Gewöhnliche vs. sensible personenbezogene Daten, ZD 2019, 551.

McCarthy, J. Thomas and Schechter, Roger E., The rights of publicity and privacy, St. Paul, Minn.: West Group 2021.

McDonald, Aleecia M. and Cranor, Lorrie Faith, 4 A Journal of Law and Policy for the Information Society 543 (2008).

Melville, B. Nimmer, 19 Law and contemporary problems 203 (1954).

Metzger, Axel, 8 JIPITEC 2 (2017).

Metzger, Axel, Dienst gegen Daten: Ein synallagmatischer Vertrag, AcP 6 2016, 817.

Mill, John Stuart, On Liberty, The Project Gutenberg EBook 2011.

Miscenic, Emilia and Hoffmann, Anna-Lena, The Role of Opening Clauses in Harmonization of EU Law: Example of the EU's General Data Protection Regulation (GDPR), EU and comparative law issues and challenges series (ECLIC) 2020, 44.

Nettesheim, Martin, Datenschutz und Meinungsäußerungsfreiheit – Zur Reichweite der Freistellung allgemeiner Meinungsäußerungen nach Art. 85 Abs. 1 DSGVO, AfP 2019, 473.

Neun, Andreas and Lubitzsch, Katharina, Die neue EU-Datenschutz-Grundverordnung – Rechtsschutz und Schadensersatz, BB 2017, 2563.

Ohly, Ansgar, Verändert das Internet unsere Vorstellung von Persönlichkeit und Persönlichkeitsrecht?, AfP 2011, 428.

Ohly, Ansgar, Harmonisierung des Persönlichkeitsrechts durch den Europäischen Gerichtshof für Menschenrechte? Rechtsvergleichende Anmerkungen zum Urteil in der Sache von Hannover/Deutschland, GRUR Int 2004, 902.

Ohly, Ansgar, "Volenti non fit iniuria": die Einwilligung im Privatrecht, Tübingen: Mohr Siebeck 2002.

Ohly, Ansgar, Generalklausel und Richterrecht, AcP 1 2001, 1.

Ohm, Paul, 88 Southern California law review 1125 (2015).

Oostveen, Manon and Irion, Kristina, The Golden Age of Personal Data: How to Regulate an Enabling Fundamental Right?, in: *et al Bakhoum (ed.),* Personal Data in Competition, Consumer Protection and IP Law - Towards a Holistic Approach? , Berlin: Springer 2017.

Oster, Jan, Media Freedom as a Fundamental Right, Cambridge: Cambridge Univ. Press 2015.

Paal, Boris P., Schadensersatzansprüche bei Datenschutzverstößen, MMR 2020, 14.

Paal, Boris and Pauly, Daniel, DS-GVO BDSG, 3. Auflage, München: C.H. Beck 2021.

Passman, Donald S., All You Need to Know About the Music Business, 9, New York: Simon & Schuster 2015.

Peers, Steve, Hervey, Tamara, Kenner, Jeff and Ward, Angela, The EU Charter of Fundamental Rights: A Commentary, 1. Auflage, Baden-Baden: Nomos 2014.

Peifer, Karl-Nikolaus, Persönlichkeitsrechte im 21. Jahrhundert – Systematik und Herausforderungen, JZ 2013, 853.

Peitz, Martin and Schweitzer, Heike, Ein neuer europäischer Ordnungsrahmen für Datenmärkte?, NJW 2018, 275.

Pertot, Tereza, Die Auslegung des datenschutzrechtlichen Koppelungsverbots – Lockerung durch den Corte di Cassazione, Zeitschrift für das Privatrecht der Europäischen Union 2019, 54.

Peukert, Helmut, Persönlichkeitsbezogene Immaterialgüterrechte?, ZUM 2000, 710.

Pfaff/Osterrieth (ed), Lizenzverträge: Formularkommentar, 4. Auflage, München: C.H. Beck 2018.

Pietzko, Joachim, Die Werbung mit dem Doppelgänger eines Prominenten, AfP 1988, 209.

Piltz, Carlo, Die Datenschutz-Grundverordnung – Teil 1, K&R 2016, 557.

Plath, Kai-Uwe, DSGVO/BDSG, 3. Auflage, Köln: Otto Schmidt 2018.

Posner, Eric and Weyl, E. Glen, Radical Markets: Uprooting Capitalism and Democracy for a Just Society, Princeton, Oxford: Princeton University Press 2018.

Posner, Richard, An Economic Theory of Privacy, Regulation: the Cato review of business and government 1978, 19.

Pötters, Stephan, Primärrechtliche Vorgaben für eine. Reform des Datenschutzrechts, RDV 2015, 10.

Preibusch, Sören, Kübler, Dorothea and Beresford, Alastair, Price versus privacy: An experiment into the competitive advantage of collecting less personal information, Electronic Commerce Research 2013, 423.

Prensky, Marc, Digital Natives, Digital Immigrants Part 2: Do They Really Think Differently?, On the horizon 2001, 1.

Radin, Margaret, 15 Journal of Law and Commerce 509 (1996).

Raji, Auswirkungen der GD-GVO auf nationales Fotorecht, ZD 2019, 61.

Rehbinder, Manfred, Schweizerisches Urheberrecht, 3.Auflage, Bern: Stämpfli 2000.

Rehbinder, Manfred and Peukert, Alexander, Urheberrecht: ein Studienbuch, 17. Auflage, München: Beck 2015.

Reidenberg, Joel R., 52 STAN. L. REV. 1315 (2000).

Remmertz, Frank R., Aktuelle Entwicklungen im Social Media-Recht Überblick der relevanten Themen aus Unternehmenssicht, MMR 2018, 507.

Renz, Hartmut T and Frankenberger, Melanie, Compliance und Datenschutz, ZD 2015, 158.

Reuter, Wiebke, Umgang mit sensiblen Daten bei allgemeiner Videoüberwachung, ZD 2018, 564.

Reuter, Wiebke and Schwarz, Johanna, Der Umgang mit Personenbildnissen nach Inkrafttreten der DSGVO, ZUM 2020, 31.

Riemensperger, Frank and Falk, Svernja, Digitale Geschäftsmodelle: Die Bedeutung von Daten für die Wettbewerbsfähigkeit der Industrie, in: *StiftungDatenschutz (ed.)*, Dateneigentum und Datenhandel, Berlin: Erich Schmidt 2018.

Riemer, LG Köln: Der Datenauskunftsanspruch als „discovery“ im deutschen Zivilprozess Urteil vom 19.06.2019 - 26 S 13/18 mAnm Riemer, ZD 2019, 413.

Riesenhuber, Karl, Die Einwilligung des Arbeitnehmers im Datenschutzrecht, RdA 2011, 257.

Robrahn, Rasmus and Bremert, Benjamin, Interessenskonflikte im Datenschutzrecht, ZD 2018, 291.

Rogers, D.L., The Digital Transformation Playbook: Rethink Your Business for the Digital Age, New York Chichester, West Sussex: Columbia University Press 2016.

Rogosch, Patricia and Hohl, Erik, Data Protection and Facebook: An Empirical Analysis of the Role of Consent in Social Networks, Münster: LIT Verlag 2012.

Rombey, Sebastian, Über die Geltung des Medienprivilegs für YouTuber - Impulse aus Luxemburg als Chance für das neue Datenschutzrecht, ZD 2019, 301.

Roßnagel, Alexander, Datenschutzgrundsätze – unverbindliches Programm oder verbindliches Recht?, ZD 2018, 339.

Roßnagel, Alexander, Regulierung – was leistet unser Datenschutzrecht (nicht)?, in: *Hermann Hill (ed.)*, E-Transformation. Veränderung der Verwaltung durch digitale Medien, Baden-Baden: Nomos 2014.

Rott, Peter, Bündelverträge aus verbraucherrechtlicher Perspektive, GRUR Int. 2018, 1010.

Ruijsenaars, Heijo, Character Merchandising, München: VVF 1997.

Ruijsenaars, Heijo E., WIPO-Studie über Character Merchandising, GRUR Int 1994, 309.

Rüpke, Giselher, Lewinski, Kai v. and Eckhardt, Jens, Datenschutzrecht, 1. Auflage, 2018.

Sack, Rolf, Die Lizenzanalogie im System des Immaterialgüterrechts, in: *Hans Forkel and Kraft, Alfons (ed.)*, Beiträge zum Schutz der Persönlichkeit und ihrer schöpferischen Leistungen: Festschrift für Heinrich Hubmann zum 70. Geburtstag, Frankfurt am Main: Metzner 1985.

Sattler, Andreas, Personenbezogene Daten als Leistungsgegenstand, JZ 2017, 1036.

Sattler, Andreas, Personenbezug als Hindernis des Datenhandels, in: *Tereza Pertot (ed.)*, Rechte an Daten, Tübingen: Mohr Siebeck 2020.

Sattler, Andreas, Autonomy or Heteronomy – Proposal for a two-tier interpretation of Art. 6 GDPR, in: *Lohsse/Schulze/Staudenmayer (ed.)*, Data as Counter-Performance – Contract Law 2.0?, Baden-Baden: Nomos/Hart 2020.

Sattler, Andreas, From Personality to Property, in: *et al Bakhoum (ed.)*, Personal Data in Competition, Consumer Protection and IP Law - Towards a Holistic Approach? , Berlin: Springer 2017.

Schantz, Peter, Die Datenschutz-Grundverordnung – Beginn einer neuen Zeitrechnung im Datenschutzrecht NJW 2016, 1841.

Schantz, Peter and Wolff, Heinrich Amadeus, Das neue Datenschutzrecht: Datenschutz-Grundverordnung und Bundesdatenschutzgesetz in der Praxis, München: C.H. Beck 2017.

Schefzig, Jens, Wem gehört das neue ÖL? - Die Sicherung der Rechte an Daten, K&R Beihefter 2015, 3.

Schertz, Christian, Merchandising, München: Beck 1997.

Schertz, Christian and Bergmann, Susanne, Chapter 7 Germany, in: *H.E. Ruijsenaars (ed.)*, Character Merchandising in Europe, Springer Netherlands 2003.

Schertz, Christian and Bergmann, Susanne, Character Merchandising in Germany, in: *Heijo E. Ruijsenaars (ed.)*, Character Merchandising, München: VVF 1997.

Schippan, Martin, Prüfungspflichten einer Bildagentur bei der Weitergabe von Fotos, ZUM 2011, 795.

Schlechtriem, Peter, Bereicherung aus fremdem Persönlichkeitsrecht, in: *Robert Fischer, Ulmer, Peter and u.a. (ed.)*, Strukturen und Entwicklungen im Handels-, Gesellschafts- und Wirtschaftsrecht : Festschrift für Wolfgang Hefermehl zum 70. Geburtstag am 18. September 1976, München: Beck 1976.

Schlechtriem, Peter, Bereicherung aus fremdem Persönlichkeitsrecht, in: *Robert Fischer and Ulmer, Peter (ed.)*, Strukturen und Entwicklungen im Handels-, Gesellschafts- und Wirtschaftsrecht, München: Beck 1976.

Schmidt, Kirsten Johanna, Datenschutz als Vermögensrecht: Datenschutzrecht als Instrument des Datenhandels, Wiesbaden: Springer 2020.

Schnabel, Christoph, Das Recht am eigenen Bild und der Datenschutz, ZUM 2008, 657.

Schneider, Jochen, Schließt Art. 9 DS-GVO die Zulässigkeit der Verarbeitung bei Big Data aus?, ZD 2017, 303.

Schneider, Jochen, Datenschutzthemen - Rückschau 2020 und Ausblick auf 2021, ZD 2021, 1.

Schneider/Schindler, Videoüberwachung als Verarbeitung besonderer Kategorien personenbezogener Daten, ZD 2018, 463.

Schricker/Loewenheim, Urheberrecht, 6. Auflage, München: C.H. Beck 2020.

Schröder, Markus, Der risikobasierte Ansatz in der DSGVO, ZD 2019, 503.

Schulze, Götz, Die Naturalobligation, Tübingen: Mohr Siebeck 2008.

Schulze, Reiner and Zoll, Fryderyk, European Contract Law, Oxford, München, Baden-Baden: Hart, C.H. Beck, Nomos 2018.

Schwartmann, Rolf, Jaspers, Andreas, Thüsing, Gregor, Kugelmann, Dieter and Leutheusser-Schnarrenberger, Sabine, DS-GVO/BDSG, 2., neu bearbeitete Auflage, Heidelberg: C.F. Müller 2020.

Schwartz, Paul M., 52 Vanderbilt Law Review 1609 (1999).

Seitz, W. and Schmidt, G., Der Gegendarstellungsanspruch, München: Beck C. H. 2017.

Simitis, Spiros, Hornung, Gerrit and Döhmann, Indra Spiecker gen., Datenschutzrecht, Baden-Baden: Nomos 2019.

Simonite, Tom, MIT Technology Review (2014).

Solove, Daniel, 126 Harvard Law Review 1880 (2013).

Solove, Daniel, The digital person, New York: New York University Press 2004.

Specht, Louisa, Daten als Gegenleistung – Verlangt die Digitalisierung nach einem neuen Vertragstypus?, JZ 2017, 763.

Specht, Louisa, Reformbedarf des Kunsturheberrechts im digitalen Zeitalter, MMR 2017, 577.

Specht-Riemenschneider, Louisa, Konsequenzen der Ökonomisierung informationeller Selbstbestimmung, Köln: Heymanns 2012.

Spelge, Karin, Der Beschäftigtendatenschutz nach Wirksamwerden der Datenschutz- Grundverordnung (DS-GVO) –Viel Lärm um Nichts?, DuD 2016, 775.

Spies, Axel, Sind manche Datensätze schützenswerter als andere?, ZD 2020, 117.

Spindler, Gerald, Die neue EU-Datenschutz-Grundverordnung, DB 2016, 937.

Spindler/Schuster, Recht der elektronischen Medien, München: C.H. Beck 2019.

Steyn, Johan, 113 The Law Quarterly Review 433 (1997).

Strittmatter, Treiterer and Harnos, Schadensbemessung bei Datenschutzrechtsverstößen am Beispiel von data leakage-Fällen, CR 2019, 789.

Strube, Michael, Anwendungsbereich des Rechts auf Datenübertragbarkeit, ZD 2017, 355.

Sundermann, Steffen, Fotografien von Menschenansammlungen nach der DSGVO, K&R 2018, 438.

Sydow, Gernot, DSGVO: Handkommentar, 2. Auflage, Baden-Baden: Nomos 2018.

Taeger, Jürgen, Gabel, Detlev and Arning, Marian, DSGVO - BDSG - TTDSG, 4, Frankfurt am Main: Fachmedien Recht und Wirtschaft 2022.

Tavanti, Pascal, Datenverarbeitung zu Werbezwecken nach der Datenschutzgrundverordnung (Teil 2), RDV 2016, 295.

Tavanti, Pascal, Datenverarbeitung zu Werbezwecken nach der Datenschutz-Grundverordnung (Teil 1), RDV 2016, 295.

Thaler, Richard H. and Sunstein, Cass R., Nudge: improving decisions about health, wealth, and happiness, New Haven, Conn. [u.a.]: Yale Univ. Press 2008.

Thalmann, Dominik, Nutzung der Abbilder von Personen des öffentlichen Interesses zu Werbezwecken, 1, Baden-Baden: Nomos Verlagsgesellschaft mbH & Co. KG 2016.

Thüsing, Gregor and Forst, Gerrit, Beschäftigtendatenschutz und Compliance, 3, München: C.H. Beck 2021.

Tinnefeld, Marie-Theres and Conrad, Isabell, Die selbstbestimmte Einwilligung im europäischen Recht, ZD 2018, 391.

Ullmann, Eike, Persönlichkeitsrechte in Lizenz?, AfP 1999, 209.

v. Gamm, Otto-Friedrich, Wettbewerbsrecht, 5, Köln: Carl Heymanns 1987.

Vacca, Thomas, Das vermögenswerte Persönlichkeitsbild, Baden-Baden: Tectum 2017.

Veil, Winfried, The GDPR: The Emperor's New Clothes, Neue Zeitschrift für Verwaltungsrecht 10 2018, 686.

Veil, Winfried, DS-GVO: Risikobasierter Ansatz statt rigides Verbotsprinzip - Eine erste Bestandsaufnahme ZD 2015, 347.

Veil, Winfried, Einwilligung oder berechtigtes Interesse? – Datenverarbeitung zwischen Skylla und Charybdis, NJW 2018, 3337.

Vogler, Ralf, Ausgewählte rechtliche Probleme bei "Time for Print"-Verträgen, AfP 2011, 139.

Voigt, Marlene, Die datenschutzrechtliche Einwilligung, 1. Auflage, Baden-Baden: Nomos 2020.

Voigt, Paul and Bussche, Axel von dem, The EU General Data Protection Regulation (GDPR): A Practical Guide, Cham: Springer International Publishing 2017.

Wandtke, Artur, Doppelte Lizenzgebühr im Urheberrecht als Modell für den Vermögensschaden von Persönlichkeitsrechtsverletzungen im Internet?, GRUR 2000, 942.

Weberling, Johannes and Bergann, Johanna, Aktuelle Fragen der Umsetzung des Medienprivilegs der DSGVO, AfP 2019, 293.

Weichert, Thilo, „Sensitive Daten" revisited, DuD 9 2017, 538.

Wendehorst, Christiane and Graf v. Westphalen, Friedrich, Das Verhältnis zwischen Daten- schutz-Grundverordnung und AGB-Recht, NJW 2016, 3745.

Wenzel, Karl Egbert, Burkhardt, Emanuel , Gamer, Waldemar, Peifer, Karl-Nikolaus and Strobl-Albeg, Joachim von, Das Recht der Wort- und Bildberichterstattung, 6. Auflage, Köln: Otto Schmidt 2018.

Westphalen, Friedrich Graf von and Wendehorst, Christiane, Hergabe personenbezogener Daten für digitale Inhalte - Gegenleistung, bereitzustellendes Material oder Zwangsbeitrag zum Datenbinnenmarkt?, BB 2016, 2179.

Wiedemann, Gerhard, Handbuch des Kartellrechts, 3. Auflage, München: C.H. Beck 2016.

William, L. Prosser, 48 California law review 383 (1960).

Williamson, Oliver E., The mechanisms of governance, New York [u.a.]: Oxford Univ. Press 1996.

Worms, Christoph and Gusy, Christoph, Verfassung und Datenschutz, DuD 2012, 92.

Wybitul, Tim and Brams, Isabelle, Welche Reichweite hat das Recht auf Auskunft und auf eine Kopie nach Art. 15 I DS-GVO? , NZA 2019, 672.

Wybitul, Tim, Haß, Detlef and Albrecht, Jan Philipp, Abwehr von Schadensersatzansprüchen nach der Datenschutz- Grundverordnung, NJW 2018, 113.

Wybitul, Tim, Neu, Leonie and Strauch, Martin, Schadensersatzrisiken für Unternehmen bei Datenschutzverstößen ZD 2018, 202.

Zagouras, Georgios, Commercial Exploitation of the Personality and Licence Requirements for Satiric Advertisements Under German Law, IIC 2011, 74.

Zech, Herbert, 11 Journal of Intellectual Property Law & Practice 460 (2016).

Ziebarth, Lennart and Elsaß, Lennart, Neue Maßstäbe für die Rechtmäßigkeit der Nutzung von Personenbildnissen in der Unternehmenskommunikation?, ZUM 2018, 578.

Web pages

„Notifizierungspflichtige Vorschriften Deutschlands gemäß der Verordnung (EU) 2016/679 des Europäischen Parlaments und des Rates vom 27. April 2016 zum Schutz natürlicher Personen bei der Verarbeitung personenbezogener Daten, zum freien Datenverkehr und zur Aufhebung der Richtlinie 95/46/EG (Datenschutz-Grundverordnung) Gesetze des Bundes“, at https://ec.europa.eu/info/sites/default/files/de_notification_articles_49.5_51.4_83.9_84.2_85.3_88.3_90.2_publish.pdf, 2018.09.27, last accessed on 2022.06.22.

Facial recognition in school renders Sweden's first GDPR fine, EDPB, at https://edpb.europa.eu/news/national-news/2019/facial-recognition-school-renders-swedens-first-gdpr-fine_sv, 2019.08.22, last accessed on 2022.06.22.

Adequacy decisions, EU Commission, at https://ec.europa.eu/info/law/law-topic/data-protection/international-dimension-data-protection/adequacy-decisions_en, last accessed on 2022.02.22.

FAQs zur Datenschutz-Grundverordnung, “Unter welchen Voraussetzungen ist das Anfertigen und Verbreiten personenbezogener Fotografien künftig zulässig?” (Under what conditions is the taking and dissemination of personal photographs permissible in the future?), The Federal Ministry of the Interior, at https://www.bmi.bund.de/SharedDocs/kurzmeldungen/DE/2018/04/faqs-datenschutz-grundverordnung.html, last accessed on 2022.06.22.

Badshah, Nadeem, Facebook to contact 87 million users affected by data breach, The Guardian, at https://www.theguardian.com/technology/2018/apr/08/facebook-to-contact-the-87-million-users-affected-by-data-breach. , 2018.04.08, last accessed on 2022.06.22.

Brandt, Mathias, Merchandising ist ein Milliardengeschäft, at https://de.statista.com/infografik/11520/die-zehn-groessten-merchandising-lizenzgeber/. last accessed on 2022.06.22.

Datenschutzbehörde, Strafverfahren gegen Österreichische Post AG, OTS0095, at https://www.ots.at/presseaussendung/OTS_20191029_OTS0095/strafverfahren-gegen-oesterreichische-post-ag, 2019.10.29, last accessed on 2022.06.22.

Edwards, Lilian and Abel, Wiebke, The Use of Privacy Icons and Standard Contract Terms for Generating Consumer Trust and Confidence in Digital Services, CREATe Working Paper 2014/15, at https://www.create.ac.uk/publications/the-use-of-privacy-icons-and-standard-contract-terms-for-generating-consumer-trust-and-confidence-in-digital-services/, last accessed on 2022.06.22.

Edwards, Lilian, Finck, Michèle, Veale, Michael and Zingales, Nicolo, Data subjects as data controllers: a Fashion(able) concept?, Internet Policy Review, at https://policyreview.info/articles/news/data-subjects-data-controllers-fashionable-concept/1400, 2019.06.13, last accessed on 2022.06.22.